# CENTRAL LOANS TO STATES AND FINANCE COMMISSION

# CENTRAL LOANS TO STATES AND FINANCE COMMISSION

**TAPAN KUMAR SHANDILYA**
M.A. (Gold Medalist), Ph.D.
Pro-Vice-Chancellor, Veer Kunwar Singh University,
Ara (Bihar)

*and*

**ABHISHEK KUMAR**
Tata AIG, Muzaffarpur, Bihar

**DEEP & DEEP PUBLICATIONS PVT. LTD.**
F-159, Rajouri Garden, New Delhi-110027

CENTRAL LOANS TO STATES AND FINANCE COMMISSION

ISBN 978-81-8450-370-8



Typeset by S.S. COMPOSERS
3190, Mohindra Park, Shakur Basti, Delhi-110034.

Printed in India at MAYUR ENTERPRISES
WZ Plot No. 3, Gujjar Market, Tihar Village, New Delhi-110018.

Published by DEEP & DEEP PUBLICATIONS PVT. LTD.
F-159, Rajouri Garden, New Delhi-110027.
Phones: 25435369, 25440916
E-mail: ddpbooks@yahoo.co.in • ddpubs@gmail.com
*Showroom:*
2/13, Ansari Road, Daryaganj, New Delhi-110002 • Telefax: 23245122

# Contents

# Preface

Loan financing is a vital issue because it is an important instrument in the hands of the Government for regulating the economy. We mean loan financing has occupied very important place as method of resource mobilization to finance economic development in a modern state. It is now used as a means to stimulate economic development and achieve the wider objectives of economic planning. The Eighth Finance Commission took the view that "there is nothing basically wrong in the growth of public debt. With the expanding public functions, no Government particularly in a developing economy can undertake large scale programmes of development without recourse to borrowing." The Sarkaria Commission in its Report on Centre State Relations has agreed to the above observation. Basically, it is because of the limited availability of financial resources on the one hand, the need for increasing state investment for development of welfare expenditure, on the other, the volume of public debt has been rising and thus the debt policies have come to occupy a significant role in the fiscal policy of the state.

The impact of public debt and loans may be analysed under two heads, firstly, these effects are related with the raising of the loans and their spending, and secondly, these effects are due to the existence of the debt. The first may be called the 'process or preliminary effects' and the second may be termed as 'asset effects' and 'transfer effect.' The bad fiscal health of the economy of Bihar has affected its economic and social development very badly and consequently, the financial position of Bihar State is completely upset. Bihar is affected with the loans in two ways—positive and negative. The loan financing has strengthened the financial capacity of Bihar on one side while it has increased financial burden in terms of liability to pay the loans on the other. The impact of financing loan has undoubtedly fulfilled the need for expenditure for various projects that were pertinent to be completed for the welfare of the state but suggestion may be forwarded that loan beyond the limit may have inverse impact on the fiscal health of the State.

We feel highly privileged to express my profound regard and heartfelt indebtedness to Dr. S.D. Sharma, Rtd. Professor of Economics, R.D. and D.J. College, Munger, T.M. Bhagalpur University, Bhagalpur for his help and encouragement in my academic pursuits. We also express our sincere regards to Dr. R.D. Sharma, Retd. Professor and Head, P.G. Department of Economics, T.M. Bhagalpur University, Bhagalpur and Dr. R.P. Sharma, Vice-Chancellor, J.P. University, Chapra for valuable comments and suggestions to complete this academic work.

We also record deep sense of gratitude to Dr. Subash Prasad Sinha, Hon'ble Vice-Chancellor, Veer Kunwar Singh University, Ara, Bihar for his constant guidance, helpful discussions and valuable suggestions. Due to his valuable guidance and regular encouragement could we able to complete this hard and tedious work and fulfilment of our dream. We shall remain highly indebted to him throughout our life.

We express our sincere regards to them who encouraged us throughout the academic work. We are thankful to Dr. Anil Kumar Thakur, PG Department of Commerce, College of Commerce, Patna and Secretary and Treasurer, Indian Economic Association, Dr. Bipin Kumar, Head, Department of Economics, R.R.S. College, Mokama (Patna), Dr. Umesh Prasad, Department of Economics, College of Commerce, Patna, Dr. K.B. Padmadeo, Department of Commerce, College of Commerce, Patna, Sri Samir Kumar Administrative Head, SAMS Institute for Hotel and Business Management, Shivpur, Airport Road, Varanasi (U.P.), Dr. Shambhu Kumar, Principal, P.N. College, Parsa (Saran) and Sri Ashutosh Kumar, Civil Judge (Patna City) for their help and suggestions in finalizing the book. We are also thankful to our colleagues, friends and relatives who have helped us directly or indirectly in completing the book in time.

We are thankful to Dr. Binod Choudhary, Department of Rural Economics, D.N. College, Masaurhi, Patna and Shambhu Kumar, Research Scholar, Department of Economics, Magadh University, Bodh Gaya, for their co-operation and support.

We owe our gratitude to the composer Shashi Bhushan Kumar for the painstaking efforts in getting the manuscript typed.

Lastly, we are very much thankful to Mr. G.S. Bhatia, Deep & Deep Publications Pvt. Ltd., New Delhi, who deserves special mention and gratitude for publication of the book within the stipulated time frame.

TAPAN KUMAR SHANDILYA
ABHISHEK KUMAR

# 1

# Background of Central Loans to States

Loan financing has occupied a very important place as a method of resource mobilization to finance economic development in a modern state. It is now used as a means to stimulate economic development and achieve the wider objectives of economic planning. The Eighth Finance Commission took the view that "there is nothing basically wrong in the growth of public debt. With the expanding public functions, no Government particularly in a developing economy, can undertake large scale programmes of development without recourse to borrowing." The Sarkaria Commission in its "Report on Centre-State Relation" has agreed with the above observation of the Commission. The Eighth Finance Commission took the stand, "the Centre has to view States' requirements in perspective of total national needs." "The development of the country as a whole is a collective responsibility of the Centre and State Governments. For the purpose of development, the Central Government territory includes all the States." The Eighth Finance Commission also views, "The growing volume of central assistance for the plan is an indication of the partnership between the union and states in the common endeavour for future economic development. Thus, loan financing has become 'an important instrument in the hands of the

Government for regulating the economy'. Loans are "raised by the Governments in order to pursue their economic growth-oriented policy and also to promote the social welfare of the society." No doubt, till the recent times it was not conceived of as playing a significant role. The classical economists believed in the policy of balanced budgets. So they viewed loan with high eyebrows and uneasiness, loan had a place of contempt in their analysis. Loan financing for public projects was accepted on the ground that the projects were of a productive character, so that the debt would be ultimately liquidated and the projects would be of a self-financing character. The general belief still was that the debt, if inevitable, should be repaid as soon as possible and a country should have a clean state as in case of the private individuals. The reasons were to be found in their adverse attitude towards public expenditure which was considered wasteful and therefore, unnecessary. They assumed full employment, inelastic money supply and unproductiveness of public expenditure. But those were unrealistic assumptions, which could not be justified under actual conditions. The depression of 1930's was an eye-opener and it exposed the hallowness of the classical principles and practices. The Keynesian revolution challenged the classical doctrines and gave public debt a place of pride the gamut of the fiscal of the Government. No doubt, the Keynesian theory was applicable in the short period and his main concern was the problem of depression in a developed economy. He supported the increase in public debt even for unproductive purposes. Harris observes, "Once the economists, in more realistic mood, allowed for unemployment, assumed elasticity in money supplies, and agreed that government expenditure could be productive and need not necessarily be wasteful, the case for public borrowing was strengthened. The post-Keynesians economists had assigned the government a more positive role to play in the development of an underdeveloped economy. It is so because, as Kurihara observes, in the underdeveloped economy "private initiative and risk-taking are obviously too deficient to bring about productive investment in sufficient quantities. He observes further, "the Harrod-Domar-Robinson models of *laissez-faire* growth have the negative virtue of demonstrating how precarious and unfruitful it is to leave the secular growth of an economy to the vagaries of private saving and investment to the accident of profit, motivated inventions and innovations, and to the working of unguided market forces. All these growth models have this positive lesson for underdeveloped economies that the state should be allowed to play not only a stabilizing role but also a developmental role. If these economies are to industrialize more effectively and rapidly that the new industrialized economies did in conditions of *laissez-faire*. While Keynes emphasized the stabilizing role of the state, the post-Keynesian economists stressed the developmental role. But this new task presupposes huge government expenditure, which generally exceeds their revenues leading to deficit budget, which can be financed by raising revenues from taxation, i.e., by increasing the existing rates or imposing new taxes. But there are certain limits beyond which rates of taxation cannot be increased without creating adverse effects on the investment level and production and so on the rate of economic growth. There are also certain administrative and political difficulties in adopting a policy of continuous rise in tax-rates. Basically, it is because of the limited availability of financial resources on the one hand the need for increasing state investment for development of welfare expenditure, on the other that the volume of public debt has been rising and thus the debt policies have come to occupy a significant role in the fiscal policy of the state.

In our country the case for public debt was strengthened after 1951 when planning was adopted. The State of Bihar, like other states of the country, has relied increasingly on loan during all her plans. The Central loans to the State Governments constitute a overwhelming part of the states' total public debts. The trends in the pattern of indebtedness of Bihar. The position of the state of Bihar is not different.

The fiscal situation of states has deteriorated drastically since 1997-98, and state finances held in total disarray. The combined revenue deficit of all states zoomed from Rs. 5309 crores in 1991-91 to Rs. 5,00,000 crores in 2003-04. Their fiscal deficit increased from Rs. 18,787 crores to Rs. 116000 crores during the same period. The outstanding liabilities of states increased relatively from Rs. 1,60,077 crores in 1993-94 to Rs. 8,00,000 crores in 2003-04. The debt GSDP ratio increased from 18.6 percent to 29.1 percent over the same period. The growth of debt and deficit of states has been a matter of concern. The persistence of states fiscal deficit in the past two decades and the sharp rise in the deficits after 1998 requires careful analysis.

The normative rules of fiscal deficit and public debt management have been provided in the optimal debt management models of Barro (1979). But they are not sufficient to explain the actual path of public sector deficit and debt. The positive theory of fiscal deficits and debt is in its early stages of development. Buchanan and Wagner (1977) and Brennan and Buchanan (1980) attempted to explain the accumulation of debt in terms of physical illusion and voters' irrationality. Nordhaus (1975) and Lindbeck (1976) tried to explain high deficit at the end of the term of any political party in office, and the deficits should go down after the election. Alesina (1987) and Tabellinbi (1990) viewed that when a government perceives a lower probability of getting reelected, tend to go for more debt-financed expenditure, and they likely to issue more public debt, what is optimum from social point of view. The post-independence period in India saw same party coming back to power through elections for the first twenty years in the states. Electoral uncertainty further increased from mid-1970s, and a rapid growth of debt and deficits and which is consistent with Alesina and Tabellinbi's hypothesis (1990). Thus, it is difficult to assert anything more about the positive theory of fiscal deficit. Until mid-1970s fiscal discipline in India for both centre and states was associated with prevalent political power configuration, when the same party was in power.

State loans are classified as follows:

(1) *Internal debt*: It has five components, namely: (a) Market loans, (b) Compensation and other bonds, (c) Ways and Means Advances from RBI, (d) Loans from banks and other institutions and (e) Special securities issued to NSSF.

(2) Loans and Advances from Centre.
(3) *Total provident funds*: (a) State Provident Funds, and (b) Insurance and Pension Fund Trust and Endowments.

## OUTSTANDING LIABILITIES OF THE CENTRAL GOVERNMENT

The outstanding liabilities of the Central Government, after reaching 63.33 per cent of GDP in 2004-05, started declining consistently (Table 1). This is because an economy can maintain a stable debt-GDP ratio and incur a primary deficit as long as the average nominal interest rate on debt is lower than the nominal GDP growth rate. This decline occurred even though a new component had been added to internal debt in 2004-05, which is not reflected in the fiscal deficit. The Government of India introduced the Market Stabilisation Scheme (MSS) in consultation with the RBI in April 2004. Under the scheme, the Government of India raises money through the issue of dated securities/treasury bills to absorb excess liquidity in the market on account of foreign inflows. The amount so raised was to be kept in a separate account with the RBI and was not meant to meet the expenditure needs of the government. Despite a sharp increase in the fiscal deficit in the years 2008-09 and 2009-10, a marginal decline in the ratio of outstanding debt to GDP is projected even in these two years.

Among the components of outstanding debt, there is an increase in the share of internal debt. Because of the developments unfolding since the global crisis, the Centre increased its net market borrowings sharply, from Rs. 1,31,768 crore in 2007-08 to Rs. 2,61,972 crore in 2008-09 and further to Rs. 3,97,957 crore in the budget estimates for 2009-10. Following the global downturn, the Memorandum of Understanding (MoU) signed with the RBI was amended in February 2009 to allow a part of the amount in the MSS account to be transferred to the Consolidated Fund of India as part of the government's normal market borrowing programme. Following this, an amount of Rs.12,000 crore was transferred from the MSS account to the Consolidated Fund of the Centre in March 2009. A further amount of Rs. 28,000 crore raised through MSS was de-sequestered in May 2009. (FC-XIII)

TABLE I

**Outstanding Liabilities of the Central Government**

*(per cent of GDP)*

| | 1999-00 | 2000-01 | 2001-02 | 2002-03 | 2003-04 | 2004-05 | 2005-06 | 2006-07 | 2007-08 | 2008-09 (RE) | 2009-10 (BE) |
|---|---|---|---|---|---|---|---|---|---|---|---|
| I. Public Debt | 39.58 | 41.37 | 43.20 | 44.01 | 43.12 | 42.45 | 41.45 | 39.74 | 40.66 | 40.14 | 42.60 |
| *Of which:* | | | | | | | | | | | |
| *a) Internal Debt* | 36.59 | 38.23 | 40.06 | 41.58 | 41.45 | 40.51 | 38.82 | 37.27 | 38.29 | 37.85 | 40.24 |
| *b) External Debt* | 2.99 | 3.14 | 3.14 | 2.43 | 1.67 | 1.93 | 2.63 | 2.48 | 2.37 | 2.29 | 2.35 |
| II. Other Liabilities | 12.72 | 14.22 | 16.75 | 19.51 | 19.92 | 20.88 | 21.68 | 21.49 | 19.41 | 18.79 | 17.00 |
| *Of which:* | | | | | | | | | | | |
| *Reserve Funds and Deposits* | 2.43 | 2.78 | 3.21 | 3.26 | 3.35 | 2.95 | 3.06 | 3.17 | 2.69 | 2.31 | 2.11 |
| **Total Liabilities (I+II)** | **52.31** | **55.58** | **59.96** | **63.52** | **63.05** | **63.33** | **63.13** | **61.23** | **60.07** | **58.93** | **59.68** |

Notes: 1. Balances of external debt are according to book value.
2. Other Liabilities include National Small Savings Funds, State Provident Funds, other accounts such as Special Deposits of Non-Government Provident Funds and Reserve Funds and Deposits.

Source: Basic data from Central Budget documents

## OUTSTANDING DEBT RELATIVE TO GSDP: STATE-WISE POSITION

The debt-GSDP ratio represents the final outcome of all the budgetary transactions, particularly the borrowings contracted to finance fiscal deficits over the years, and is an important indicator of fiscal correction. In consonance with the reduction in fiscal deficits there was reduction in the debt-GSDP ratio of the general category states by over 5 percentage points of GSDP in 2007-08 over 2004-05 (Table 2). In seven out of the 17 general category states, debt-GSDP ratio exceeded 40 per cent in 2004-05 as compared to the group average of 39.18 per cent. By 2007-08, the number of such states had come down to four, viz., Bihar, Rajasthan, Uttar Pradesh and West Bengal. Among these, Uttar Pradesh, and West Bengal have fiscal deficits exceeding 3 per cent of GSDP. Bihar, though a revenue surplus state, had the highest debt-GSDP ratio in 2004-05. All the states except Goa and Jharkhand managed to bring about reduction in their debt-GSDP ratio. FC-XII recommended that the debt-GSDP ratio be brought down to 28 per cent over a period of time so as to be consistent with the fiscal deficit target.

Though the aggregate debt-GSDP ratio of the special category states in 2007-08 was lower as compared to the 2004-05 level, the debt position of six of the 11 states, which had registered a revenue surplus in all three years since 2005-06, worsened by 2007-08. The debt-GSDP ratio of special category states continues to remain at a much higher level than that of the general category states. Low levels and fluctuating nature of GSDP growth partly explains the high debt-GSDP ratios in some of these states.

TABLE 2

**Outstanding Debt Relative to GSDP: State-wise Position**

*(per cent of GSDP)*

| States | 2004-05 | 2005-06 | 2006-07 | 2007-08 | Difference (5-2) |
|---|---|---|---|---|---|
| 1 | 2 | 3 | 4 | 5 | 6 |
| Andhra Pradesh | 35.30 | 33.70 | 32.18 | 31.16 | -4.14 |
| Bihar | 58.02 | 58.01 | 49.61 | 48.49 | -9.53 |
| Chhattisgarh | 27.31 | 24.11 | 22.00 | 18.95 | -8.37 |
| Goa | 37.89 | 37.58 | 39.21 | 38.27 | 0.38 |
| Gujarat | 37.59 | 37.02 | 34.56 | 31.44 | -6.15 |
| Haryana | 25.91 | 25.40 | 22.63 | 19.73 | -6.18 |
| Jharkhand | 26.33 | 31.55 | 30.98 | 31.10 | 4.77 |
| Karnataka | 31.32 | 31.10 | 30.64 | 27.94 | -3.39 |
| Kerala | 39.63 | 38.45 | 36.61 | 35.78 | -3.85 |
| Madhya Pradesh | 41.23 | 42.27 | 41.56 | 38.81 | -2.42 |
| Maharashtra | 30.91 | 32.11 | 30.34 | 26.70 | -4.21 |
| Orissa | 50.53 | 48.98 | 43.30 | 37.29 | -13.24 |
| Punjab | 46.89 | 45.25 | 39.97 | 39.47 | -7.41 |
| Rajasthan | 51.28 | 51.28 | 47.93 | 46.29 | -4.98 |
| Tamil Nadu | 27.25 | 27.15 | 25.25 | 22.14 | -5.11 |
| Uttar Pradesh | 53.28 | 53.21 | 51.96 | 50.60 | -2.68 |
| West Bengal | 50.01 | 47.88 | 44.35 | 42.82 | -7.19 |
| **Total: GCS** | **39.18** | **38.82** | **36.44** | **34.01** | **-5.17** |
| Arunachal Pradesh | 62.29 | 80.09 | 69.73 | 68.13 | 5.84 |
| Assam | 33.40 | 32.22 | 31.13 | 29.87 | -3.53 |
| Himachal Pradesh | 71.68 | 68.44 | 63.73 | 60.73 | -10.94 |
| Jammu and Kashmir | 58.47 | 63.27 | 64.04 | 67.17 | 8.70 |
| Manipur | 67.48 | 77.09 | 78.37 | 79.40 | 11.92 |
| Meghalaya | 37.43 | 40.61 | 39.68 | 41.30 | 3.87 |
| Mizoram | 110.44 | 109.48 | 103.70 | 102.74 | -7.69 |
| Nagaland | 52.62 | 56.30 | 55.71 | 54.00 | 1.38 |
| Sikkim | 69.10 | 73.82 | 71.70 | 76.33 | 7.24 |
| Tripura | 50.40 | 47.06 | 44.79 | 42.08 | -8.31 |
| Uttarakhand | 115.79 | 112.11 | 103.21 | 94.13 | -21.66 |
| **Total: SCS** | **60.56** | **60.58** | **58.02** | **56.30** | **-4.26** |
| **All States** | **40.49** | **40.12** | **37.69** | **35.28** | **-5.21** |

Note: GCS: General Category States; SCS: Special Category States.

Source: Basic data from State Finance Accounts

## Debt Position of Government of Bihar

In our country the case for public debt was strengthened after 1951 when planning was adopted. The state of Bihar, like other states of the country, has relied increasingly on loan during all her plans, The Central loans to the State Governments constitute a overwhelming part of the states' total public debts. The trends of out standing debt of Bihar are given in Table 3.

The case of public debt of Bihar is worse. There is rapid increase since independence. Table 3 present a picture of outstanding debt of the Government of Bihar from 1951 to 2000 and the loans from the centre constitute the greatest share.

TABLE 3

**Outstanding Debt of the Government of Bihar**

*(In Lakhs)*

| *Years* | *Amount of outstanding debt* |
|---|---|
| 1951-52 | 450 |
| 1951-55 | 6109 |
| 1960-61 | 14524 |
| 1965-66 | 32960 |
| 1968-69 | 66186 |
| 1973-74 | 82047 |
| 1977-80 | 119905 |
| *Years* | *Amount of outstanding debt* |
| 1982-83 | 159664 |
| 1983-84 | 254003 |
| 1984-85 | 296670 |
| 1987-88 | 325404 |
| 1988-89 | 698402 |
| 1994-95 | 1553352 |
| 1995-96 | 1638490 |
| 1999-00 | 2682644 |
| 2000-01 | 3205585 |

*Source*: Report of Different Finance Commissions, Government of India. New Delhi.

Table 3 shows that outstanding debt of the Government of Bihar has although been rising and rising very rapidly. In 1951-52 the debt was Rs. 450 lakhs only, which increased very rapidly and by the end of 2000-01 the debt among, was unbelievable figure of Rs. 32,055,851 lakhs. This was stupendous increase in outstanding debt of the government.

**Central Loans to Bihar**

The loans operations of the State have led to the centralization an deinstitutionalization of the public debt in the state. Consequently, the management of public debt has become easier. It was made clear in course of the discussion with an important office of the Finance Department, Government of Bihar, that even in public borrowing the individuals and the other non-bank institutions contributions is almost nil these days. The commercial banks also do not contribute much after the nationalization of the Banks. Now the public borrowing is made mainly from the nationalized banks. The Life Insurance Corporation is the greatest non-bank source and its contribution is very negligible.

The States receive central assistance in three forms-share in taxes and duties, grants and loans; and there are three institutional processes through which states are receiving funds from the centre, namely, (1) on the basis of recommendation of the Finance Commission, (2) on the basis of suggestions of Planning Commission, and (3) at the discretion of the Central Ministries. It is plant as well as discretionary transfer by which central loans are given to the State Governments. The plan assistance comprises of both conditional grants and conditional loans. It is significant to note that grant-loan proportion of the plan assistance was not uniform before 1969 and also the loan component varied from programme to programme and from state to state.

Central loans of Bihar has increased in present time, we can see the Table 4 the central loan position of Bihar State is clear. In 1991 the total central loan of Bihar was Rs. 5792.35 crores which increased to Rs. 15691.20 crores by 2006. Thus, the central loan almost tripled in reform period. We have studied about the read picture of central loan in Chapter 5 in the research work.

**Borrowing by States:**

Under the constitution, the State Governments can borrow only within the territory of India. The constitution empowers the central government under Article 293 to provide loans to the States. Article 293 states like this:

TABLE 4

**Central Loan to Bihar**

*(Rs. in Crores)*

| *Year* | *Loans* |
|---|---|
| 1991 | 5,792.35 |
| 1992 | 6401.30 |
| 1993 | 6858.82 |
| 1994 | 7368.00 |
| 1995 | 7957.25 |
| 1996 | 8772.32 |
| 1997 | 9735.72 |
| 1998 | 11,061.48 |
| 1999 | 13,374.90 |
| 2000 | 15862.02 |
| 2001 | 13009.59 |
| 2002 | 13,759.73 |
| 2003 | 14,217.66 |
| 2004 | 5,091.78 |
| 2005 (RE) | 16263.60 |
| 2006 (BE) | 15691.20 |

*Source*: State Finances: A Study of Budgets of 2005, R.B.9. 2005

(1) Subject to the provisions of this article the executive powers of a state extend to borrowing within the territory of India upon the security of the Consolidated Fund of the state within such limits, if any, as made from time to time be fixed by the legislature of such state by law and to the giving of guarantees within such limits, if any, as may be so fixed.

(2) The Government of India may, subject to such conditions as may be laid down by or under any law made by Parliament, make loans to any state or, so long as any limits fixed under Article 292 of the Constitution are not exceeded, give guarantees in respect to loans raised by any state, and any sums required for the purpose of making such loans shall be changed not without the Consolidated Fund of India.

(3) A state may not without the consent of the Government of India raise any loan if there is still outstanding any part of a loan which has been made to the Sate by the Government of India or by its predecessor government, or in respect of which a guarantee has been given by the Government of India or by its predecessor government.

(4) A consent under clause 3 may be granted, subject to such conditions, if any, as the Government of India may think fit to impose.

Clearly, the Government of India has been providing short-term loans in form of ways and means advances and some medium and long-term loans from the Consolidated Fund of India to the State Government.

No doubt, the Constitution empowers the Central Government to make loans to state. But it was thought that the capital needs of a state would be normally met by its own borrowing. But this assumption has now broken down because of the policy of planned development and so also the centre-states fiscal relations are strained. It is, sometimes, complained that the states have been financially assisted by means that appears to be a doubtful use of Articles 293. of the constitution of India. This Article 293 is a unique provision in our Constitution, which has no parallel in other federal constitutions. But from the text of the article, it seems that only open borrowing is intended. As the article has been used to advance loans to the states on a large scale, the centre hardly keeps watch over the use of fund. The huge sums are used imprudently. No doubt, the borrowing powers of state have been unduly restricted by the Constitution. The Constitution does not permit states to borrow outside India. Even internally the borrowing is subject to limitations:

(a) as many be imposed by the state legislature under Article 293(i); and

(b) if the Union Government has guaranteed an outstanding loan of the state without the consent of the Union Government as per Article 293(3). It

> is argued that such restrictions do not obtain in a federation like the U.S.A. If it is felt that in a planned economy like India there is need for some such restriction, it should apply only to long and medium-term borrowing from the open market and not to borrowing from financial institutions or to short-term loans for less than one year. In this context, we would like to quote the observations of the Sarkaria Commission. The commission feels "a solution lies in making a distinction between short-term loans under one year and Medium and long-term loans." According to the Commission, "The Union Government should give its consent freely to states for borrowing from banks and financial institutions for periods less than one year under clause (4) of Article 293 of the Constitution. Since most of these are now nationalized, no irremediable risk could be involved".

Loans are also given to the states against the net collection of small savings. Share in small savings collections constitutes an important source of finance for non-plan schemes. Under the arrangement, two-thirds share of the net receipts collected in a stage was allowed to be retained by that state loan. Very recently, the Union Government has decided to raise the state's share in the net small savings collection from two-thirds to three-fourths, effective from 1987-88. These loans carry an initial moratorium of five years and are repayable in 25 years. In 1984, about Rs. 7,000 crores small savings loans were outstanding against which repayment obligation of Rs. 960 crores was estimated by the Eighth Finance Commission for the period 1984-89. The other non-plan loans given to the states are mainly fertilizer loans, ways and means advances and loans to clear overdrafts. The State Government in general, argue that the small savings loans may be treated as loans in 'perpetuity' as they are given in net to them after taking into consideration fresh mobilization. The Seventh Finance Commission had agreed to this demand but Union Government did not accept its recommendation in this regard. However, the Union

Government did not insist on collection of payment of those loans during the Sixth Plan Period. In the Eighth Finance Commission, there was a difference of opinion among the members but the majority view supported continuation of repayment of these loans as it thought that sufficient moratorium on them was granted.

The Sarkaria Commission in its report has observed, "Treatment of small saving loan is a matter of judgment by the Finance Commission in relation to the overall debt burden of the states. As long as small savings keep increasing and there is a surplus every year after repayment of due loans, the Union is not called upon to repay any loan not already covered by the net transfer principle. If and when the option changes in any year, when the outgo is greater than the inflow, the States would be responsible for their share of the net small savings collections. If formula is adopted for such recumbent of revenue from the states, the recommendations of the Finance Commission will be workable. This aspect will have to be examined by the National Economic and Development Council".

The collection under the National Savings Scheme is going up year by year. This is a healthy sign. But since the Government of India do not have to repay the amounts invested in National Savings from their own resources, there is no justification, what ever to treat the states share of saving as disbursable loans from the centre. Whatever withdrawals are effected or whatever may be the size of the discounting of various certificates issued under the scheme, they are debited against the total collection of that year in the state and as, only the collection net of withdrawals is divided between the centre and the states; it is not fair to treat the state's share of thc savings which in any case are mobilized, mainly through their efforts, as loans and to make them repay the same with interest. The Finance Commission should go into this question and since withdrawals and discounting under the scheme, if any, do not have any financial impact on the resources of the centre, there is no justification whatever to pass on the state's share as long and to recover the same with interest.

It was thought desirable to evolve some objective

principles for allocation of central assistance during discussions on the memorandum relating to the Fourth Five Year Plan in June, 1965. The Chief Ministers of some states discussed this problem. Their views were not unanimous. Therefore, the Planning Commission was requested for this work. Consequently the Planning Commission finalized the guidelines. The finalization of the Fourth Plan was postponed because of the out-break of War with Pakistan. Then annual plan for 1966-67 was finalized before the conclusion of discussion on the Fourth Five Year Plan. So *ad hoc* principle was formulated for the central assistance for the concerned years. The ad hoc principle was adopted for 1967-68 also. Some states were not satisfied with their shares in central assistance granted on ad hoc basis. They claimed for making up the shortfall in 1968-69. The Planning Commission agreed to make up the shortfall. The commission adjusted one-third of difference between the assistance, which was claimed by a state and the amount actually received by it during the two years, i.e., 1966-67, and 1967-68. The new Fourth Five Year Plan was formulated and a new formula, known as Gadgil formula was evolved which formed the basis for distribution of central assistance for Fourth Five Year Plan. Under the formula the loan component was fixed uniformly as 70 per cent of the plan assistance for the states other than J & K, Sikkim, Tripura, Nagaland, Meghalaya and Assam.

After meeting the needs, the remaining balance should be distributed among the remaining 14 states on the basis of the criteria which follow below:

(a) 60 per cent of the basis of population.
(b) 10 per cent on the basis of per capita state income to be given to those states whose per capita income is below the national average.
(c) 10 per cent on the basis of tax efforts of the states.
(d) 10 per cent for the major continuing irrigation and power projects.
(e) 10 per cent for special problems of individual states.

The Gadgil formula introduced the system of block

loans and grants. It reduced the area of discretion of the Planning Commission and brought about objectivity into the process. Central assistance was distributed on the basis of Gadgil formula during the Fourth Five Year Plan and it was continued for 1974-75, 1975-76 and 1976-77 also. The formula was reviewed in 1976 and the National Development Council revised it accordingly. The Planning Commission set apart an amount of Rs. 100 crores for providing extra assistance to states for schemes financed by I.D.A. assistance. This amount of Rs. 100 crores was in addition to the amount set apart for special problems of individual states. The balance amount was to be distributed as under the original Gadgil formula. The National Development Council resolved in March 1979 to form a committee to discuss fiscal arrangement and review the Gadgil formula. The committee made a slight modification in 10 per cent to be given under special problems. This modified formula was to be applicable for four years 1979-83. The National Development Council resolved in August 1980 to distribute central assistance to the states on the basis of a modified Gadgil formula. The formula is as under:

(1) A lump-sum amount was to be set apart for meeting the needs of eight states, viz., Jammu and Kashmir, Assam, Himachal Pradesh, Sikkim, Nagaland, Meghalaya, Manipur and Tripura.
(2) The balance of central assistance is to be allocated to the remaining 14 states on the following grounds:
    (a) 60 per cent on the basis of population.
    (b) 10 per cent on the basis of tax-efforts.
    (c) 20 per cent on the basis of average per capita income to be given to those states only whose per capita income is below the national average.
    (d) 10 per cent for special problems of individual states.

The modified Gadgil formula is being followed for the Seventh Plan also. It was stated in the Gadgil formula for central plan assistance that the total amount of assistance will be 30 per cent in form of grants and 70 per cent in form of loans.

The concerned authorities did not strictly follow the Gadgil formula. Further even under the Present Gadgil formula, the loan component of the plan assistance for the different programmes is not specified. The proportion of economically remunerative sectors in the state plan outlays could not justify the present normal pattern of 70 percent loan and 30 per cent grant in central assistance. In the Sixth Five Year Plan outlays sectors like forest, irrigation, power, large and medium industries and road transport constituted about 54 per cent of the total state plan outlays. Even among these sectors commercial returns are very small.

It is so secret that the bulk of the plan investments by the states have been on roads, health and educational facilities, water supply, power generation and transmission lines and on building up of other infrastructures. Obviously, such investments do not generate enough new resources to meet the repayment obligation of the loan component of the plan assistance, which commences from the year following the one in which the assistance is received. Frankly, it is the Government of India's policy of giving plan assistance with a heavy dose of loan that is largely responsible for the present crushing burden of the state's liability. The loan component of such assistance ought to be substantially scaled down. Under the arrangement in force during the Fourth Plan period, the central plan assistance has a loan component of 70 per cent and a grant component of 30 per cent. The Sarkaria Commission also recommends for a review of the Gadgil formula. The Commission observes that the two-fold pattern of central assistance of 30 : 70 and 90 : 10 grant and loans needs to be reviewed by the Planning Commission in view of the latest developments. If the new formula leads to a need for greater revenue transfers to the poorer, average and special category states, this amount can be deducted from the transfer to the advanced and medium states, on the principle that these states having substantial revenue surpluses must be able to look after their revenue requirements by suitable adjustments. Our advice would be not to do away with the present methodology. There are correctives in the system, which seems to work. If, on the other hand, the states want to experiment with the new idea, it is for them to rise the issues when the plan is under consideration. It will be for the Planning Commission and the National Economic and Development Council to take decision on any revision of methodology that they may think wise and proper.

The position has, of course, been further aggravated by the centre's policy of treating 25 per cent of its assistance of relief expenditure as loan. Relief operations are admittedly not in the nature of development programmes and they do not yield and new wealth or resources to enable the state to repay the loan component with interest. Besides, central assistance for flood damage repairs is generally received 100 per cent in the share of loan-bearing normal rates of interest. Repairs are pure revenue expenditure and no new assets are created thereby clearly loans for flood repairs or for that matter those relating to relief operations have to be serviced by making inroads on other resources which could, otherwise, have been utilized for economic development of state.

We have seen that the Union Government provides assistance/loans to the states with a new to correct the vertical and the horizontal imbalances. These imbalances are inherent in our constitution, which will be clear if an attempt is made to study the existing Centre-State relations. We know that ours is a federal country, which comprises the Central at the top and the State and local Government at the lower level. The constitution has divided the function and resources between the centre and the states in such a way that the centre is more fortunate than the states because the former has elastic sources of revenue to meet the inelastic functions, whereas the states have inelastic revenue and elastic functions—functions which are gradually growing. This gives rise to the problem of non-correspondence between functions and resources of the Centre and The State Governments, situation called vertical fiscal imbalance. It is because of this situation that Mrs. Ursula Hicks has remarked, "The National Government will tend to have more than it needs, while the states will not be able to perform their duties without a considerable amount of help. This imbalance is in fact typical of almost all federation; it is naturally more serious for the poorer states who have less opportunity of raising revenue, and for this reason it tends to be a more acute problem in a development federation than in an advanced one".

Horizontal fiscal balance has been defined as a situation where each state in a federation has the capacity to provide services at a standard, comparable to that of others, provided that it imposes taxes and charges at a comparable standard. It is an unusual thing that separation of revenue resources between the Central and the State Governments lead to more elastic and productive sources of revenue for the Central Government. State Governments are left with less elastic and unproductive sources of revenue along with a large number of functions and responsibilities. Thus, the states are in a oligopolistic situation as contrasted to the Federal Government which enjoys a monopoly. Michael D. Reagon remarks, "In less colourful language the proposition is that we suffer from a fiscal mismatch. That is to say, it is relatively much easier for the national government to increase its tax revenue each year... and expenses for public services rests primarily at the doors of the lower jurisdictions". Thus, there is possibility of emergence of financial imbalance, generally faced by the units forming the Union. The fiscal imbalance presents some irritants, some disquieting features leading to centre-state conflicts. The conflict is unfortunately inherent in our federation itself. The Indian Federation has not evolved in the same way as in the case of certain other federations where independent states through their own mutual consent have come together to form a federation. In such a case, at the time of joining the union or federation, each state takes every care to secure its financial independence and self-sufficiency. Consequently, the area of conflict is reduced and the donor-receiver equation is rectified. But in our country the federal structure has come from above as the states were already functioning as provinces of unified India. At no stage, it was the intention of the British Government to introduce a parliamentary system in India. Thus, the definitions and demarcations, especially fiscal were slurred over. The reality is that the whole attitude to federal fiscal transfers was originally developed and used by Sir Otto Nemeyer for a colonial country. Different Finance Commissions simply modified the approach here and there but they did not bring any fundamental change in it. They have not formulated any new approach keeping in view the progressive policies of a socialist welfare state. Even the distribution of financial powers under the new constitution has been very much influenced by the Government of India Act of 1935. Hence, the basis of the sharing of taxes in India has been out of date and out of time with the changed objectives of public policy and fiscal needs of the country. No doubt, the Indian Constitution is federal in character. But it is, however, often missed that, unlike older federations such as the United States of America or Australia, the Union of India came into being not by aggregation of independents or sovereign units agreeing to establish federation but by a devolution, that is, by decentralization of powers and functions of what was unitary state. This historical burden of strong central bias seems, as it were, to have loomed large on the founding fathers of the Indian Constitution, so that, while making elaborate provisions outlining division of functions between the union and the states, they chose to reserve the residuary powers for the union.

Thus, there is the problem of non-correspondence between the needs and resources of the states. There is the problem of vertical and horizontal fiscal imbalance and this imbalance was not unexpected. This was very much expected by the framers of the constitution. "These imbalances are imbued in the very structure of the federal financial system as the centre possesses the most elastic and productive sources of revenue and relatively in expansive functions while states are left with inflexible sources or revenue with expenditure and expensive functions and the need for which has been growing steadily. In the words of the Fifth Finance Commission, "The imbalance between the functional responsibilities assigned to the states and the financial resources allocated to them, which is a general feature of many full-fledged federations, also exists in India". Lakdawala pointed out, "Imbalance arises in a federal system either as a result of overlapping tax powers or the imbalance between the allocation of functions and distribution of tax powers among the two layer of government". As there is no such overlapping of tax powers between the centre and the states, the imbalance in India is mostly due to the second factor. The framers of the constitution made provisions for the eradication of the problem. Provisions were made for the Finance Commission in the constitution under Article 280. Later on, Planning Commission was established. It is non-statutory body providing for assistance for plans. Besides, discretionary transfers are also made to states. The need for transfer of resources from the centre to the states arose because of the imbalance between resources and responsibilities. While the states are saddled with more responsibilities, their financial powers are very limited. In recognition of this, the constitution provides enabling provisions for transfer of resources from the centre to the state in accordance with the awards of the Finance Commission to be appointed every five years. The constitution also provides for transfer of resources to the states in the form of grants and loans for any public purpose. Over the years, other channels though not specifically provided for in the constitution have become important in the transfer of resources to the states. With inauguration of planning in India Planning Commission has become an important channel regulating the flow of central assistance for states' plans. Besides the Finance Commission and Planning Commission, sizeable transfers are being affected by the Central Ministries. In addition to these budgetary transfers, there are a number of non-budgetary flows of resources affected by institutions, which are directly under the control of the Central Government. These flows are in the shape of assistance made by term-lending financial institutions like commercial banks and Central Government investments in the states. The problem of the imbalance between the centre and the states relating to needs and means, has aggravated with the lapse of time; especially following the advent of planning in India.

The age-old principle applied in the field of federal finance in our country has come in for a close scrutiny in recent years. The more pertinent among them are those, which govern the devolution of resources from the centre to the state on the recommendations of the Finance Commission and the plan assistance according to the Gadgil formula. The Union States Financial relation is not smooth. It has all along been strained. Every Finance Commission from the Second Finance Commission onwards has called for a review of the constitutional provisions. The states are not satisfied either with the quantum of revenue transferred to their distribution inter-se. Here we would like to quote K.V.S. Shastri. He has remarked, "In any federation it has proved impossible to effect a clean separation of the finances of the several layers of Governments; and India is no exception to this. As a matter of fact, it would seem that the federal state fiscal relations in India are much more complex than in any of the three older major federations in the World, the USA, Canada and Australia". Similar view has been expressed by Sri Venkataraman when remarks, "It is true that is no federation have the Central and State Governments seen eye to eye". In this connection Mrs. U.K. Hicks has also the same things to say when she remarks, "As things have developed, financial relations are more complicated in India than in almost any other federation, certainly more than they are in the U.S.A., Canada, Australia or Nigeria. A formidable problem of co-ordination is implied." The Fifth Finance Commission in its final report has also expressed similar experience. "The imbalance between the functional responsibilities assigned to the states and the financial resources allocated to them which is a general feature of many full-fledged federations, also exists in India".

The financial responsibilities of the states have increased. The Economic Social and Development Service like agriculture, co-operation, small and cottage industries, public health; education, etc. require local supervision. Naturally, they are the responsibility of the states, which are in direct contact of the people. Patna is decidedly nearer than New Delhi. The services mentioned above are such that they will grow rapidly. In a country like ours, which is vast in area and diverse in character, administration cannot function and planning cannot reach the people in the remote corner of the rural area without the help and co-operation of the regional governments. Therefore, the State Governments have increasing responsibilities in a developing country like ours, especially in view of the adoption of Democratic Planning in the country. The effective implementation of plan objectives the correction of the regional imbalances, the removal of the economic in equality and concentration, wealth and power, ushering in an area of decentralization and dispersal of economic and political powers promotion of people's participation in the economic programmes of planning, formation of village leadership, etc. fall under the domain of the State Government. These functions are costly affairs and the states have to bear the entire responsibilities.

The nation's socialistic and revolutionary policies are throwing on the states new financial responsibilities, which were not, clearly visualized when the constitution was framed. The national policy of "Garibi Hatao" and evolving of an "Equalitarian Society" is also having an impact on the finances of the states. In persuasion of such policy, the Government of Bihar exempted small tenancy holdings from land rent resulting in a recurring annual loss to the exchequer. The general law and order problem is also the concern of the states. In Bihar, this problem has, over a number of years, been rather difficult but this has been further aggravated by extensive Naxalite activities in the State. To tackle this problem, the Bihar Government has had to augment and strengthen the police force.

The few odds mentioned above, perhaps, illustrate the severe strain on the meager and limited resources, of the state of Bihar. The mounting cost of administration, successive years of famines, drought, and flood, and the heavy burden resulting from ever-increasing debt serving liability are all making it still poorer.

The power of the State to levy taxes is, indeed, very much limited. Even so the tax potentiality in Bihar has been exploited almost to the point of saturation. The rural sector being afflicted by one calamity after another is unable to contribute its mite to the extent desired. Indeed resources, otherwise husbanded, have had to be frequently diverted to provide relief and scour to the people in the countryside. In the years of famine, drought or floods, there is not only a heavy drain on the meager resources of the state but even the normal recovery of land rent, loans and other dues is suspended which depletes the state's normal receipt. This creates a vicious circle and this creates ways and means difficult and introduces an element of financial instability.

There is chronic gap between the states' own revenues and their expenditure commitments and consequently the states find it difficult to discharge their responsibilities adequately without financial assistance from the centre. There has been a persistent and growing need for larger transfers of revenues to the states.

It is clear from what have been discussed above that there is excess concentration of resources at the hands of the centre, but this is not a special feature of the Indian Federation. The states in U.S.A. and Canada make the same type of grievances against the federal government. Prof. Colin Clark has accurately remarked, "the State Governments which rely on grants from the Central Government rather than their own resources rapidly become completely irresponsible in their demand". Such a development also leads to the concentration of political and financial power, which is always dangerous in a democracy.

The framers of the Constitution were fully conscious of the eventuality of imbalance between the resources available to the states and the functions and the responsibilities enjoined on them. They realized that the delimitation of revenues and functions between the union and the state called for appropriate corrective measures to achieve better correspondence between the resources and responsibilities of the two layers of the federal structure. The Constitution-makers, therefore, sought to correct this inherent imbalance between the functions and resources of the union and states by embodying in the constitution both mandatory and enabling provisions for wide ranging transfer of resources from the centre to the states. In devising aforesaid system of fiscal transfers, the framers of the constitution also seem to have taken note of the then prevailing situation in which there was considerable disparity in the growth and development of different states. Their intention was not merely to provide for periodic transfer of resources to the states but also at the same time to remove inter-state disparities in regard to resource availability through equitable fiscal transfers. It is in the background that the provision has been made in the constitution for appointment of a Finance Commission by the President to make a quinquennium review of union-state financial relations generally, and to evolve a framework or system of fiscal transfer as would achieve a better correlation between the resources and responsibilities of the states on the one hand and those of the union on the other. We are constrained to observe that these objectives have not so far been fulfilled in spite of the labours of the Eighth Finance Commission. The Backward stated in particular continue to be practically at the same distance from the advanced states as they were fifty-seven years ago. The situation, therefore calls for not only a bold approach on the part of the Ninth Finance Commission but also a basic change in the perspective towards regional imbalances in all their manifestations.

It may not be out of place to mention here that the conventionally accepted principles like, equity, elasticity and adequacy, have not lost their relevance, even though, in practice, the over-riding consideration in evolving a pattern of fiscal relations within a federal structure, more so in the case of our country, has been one of experience and expediency. While the principle of adequacy implies that in working out a pattern of revenue sharing arrangement, the functions and responsibilities of the states assigned to them under the constitution, and how those functions are discharged in practice should be taken into consideration, elasticity requires that allocation of resources both in nature and quantum, should be such as to be consistent with growing needs in future. The criteria of equity means that, not only both the centre and the states should be free in their respective fields, in utilizing their means of revenue and ordering expenditure there form, but also they should together contribute their right in sharing common burdens on equitable basis. It is not that these principles are unknown, or they had not been urged before the earlier commissions, but they seems to have preferred not to deviate, very much in substance, from the well-trodden grounds covered by their predecessors and thus they have largely formulated their views on grounds of expediency, or in other words, previous experience. The resultant situation has been that (i) the states still continue to be heavily dependent on receipts from shared taxes and loans from the centre, (ii) a large quantum of resource-transfer to the states has been not from assured channels, but from channels other than those under the recommendations of the Finance Commission, and (iii) large surpluses have been created for the centre and deficits in the states and more so, developed states have turned out to be batter-off, while the backward states still remain far behind the more fortunate states in this regard. To remedy this situation, the commission should set in motion a process to alter this picture, for it will argue well for the future of happier union-state financial relations.

Before proceeding with a discussion of the principles evolved by successive commissions, it is necessary to allude to the emergence of Planning Commission as a dominant arbiter of transfer of resources from the centre to the states. The constitution had only made provision for appointment of an independent body like the Finance Commission, which afforded a measure of assurance to the states that, the entire problem of financial relations between the union and the states would be dealt with in accordance with rationally evolved principles. Planning Commission does not have the sanction of constitutional provisions behind it, as it was set-up executive order. But by the high powered status, which was give to it, the Planning Commission has emerged, over the years, as the supreme economic authority and its area of operation has come to embrace both physical and financial planning. In fact, future development in all fields of administration except defense has come under the overall scrutiny and control of the Planning Commission. Consequently, a significant part of the financial arrangements between the union and the state has gone out of the purview of the Finance Commission and a state of quality and overlapping of functions between the two commissions has come to stay.

**Debt Restructuring**

The Sarkaria Commission Report (1988) observed,

"Some State Governments as well experts have complained and the borrowing powers of the States have been unduly restricted by the Constitution. The Constitution does not permit States to borrow outside India. Even internally the States are not free to borrow, i.e., if the Union Government has guaranteed an outstanding loans of the State, without the consent of the Union Government. It is argued that restrictions do not obtain in a federation like USA. If it is felt that in a planned economy like India there is need for some such restrictions, it should apply only on long and medium-term borrowing from the open market and not to the borrowing from financial institution or to short-term loans for less than one year. In fact, the State Governments or states enterprises should be encouraged to access markets on the basis of their financial strengths and viability rather through tax incentives which distort the allocation of resources."

It may be mentioned that the 12th Finance Commission has suggested a fundamental change in the borrowing pattern, which absolve the Union Government from any such responsibility and expose the poor States to higher interest cost. The practice of Centre giving loans, (including plan loans) to the State has been stopped, which requires that all plan assistance now onwards will flow as grants. Thus, under the new scheme of market borrowings, the State will have to compete with the Centre and other corporate bodies to raise resources from the market. This may make the financing of plan difficult and enforce the State Governments to cut the size of their plans.

Then, of course, in order to give some relief to the State, the 12th Finance Commission has suggested consolidation the State public debt, rescheduling the repayment for 20 years at 7.5 percent rate of interest. The second part consists of debt write-off, which is linked to reduction in revenue deficit. But to get these relieves the State will have to enact Fiscal Responsibility and Budget Management legislation, which further entails many preconditions like phasing out the revenue deficit by 2008-09, keeping the fiscal deficit at 3 percent, etc. Then State will have to create sinking funds outside their Consolidated Funds to ensure a smooth redemption of public liability.

It must be mentioned that in view of the precarious resource positions of the State these are only temporary aberrations, which do not go deep into the problem of States' indebtedness. Loans are not always bad infused productively and lead to fall in debt-income ratio, therefore, in order to monitor the related issues there is a need to create Union-State Loans Council and have its regular sittings.

Then there is a chronic problem of imbalance in the resource position of the Centre *vis-à-vis* the State. Another chronic controversy deals with the working of the Finance Commission and the Planning Commission. Since the grant component in the transfer for resources through the Planning Commission has surpassed that of the Finance Commission, which is a constitutional body, the issue has to be looked into and needs a serious debate.

### DEBT Relief Scheme

The Twelfth Finance commission has recommended a Debt Relief Facility (DRF) in place of Fiscal Reform Facility (FRF). There are two components of the scheme. One relates to consolidation and rescheduling of the loan and passage of FRBM. Act. The second relates to reduction of revenue deficit and maintaining GDF at 2000-05 level.

The Commission has recommended that the central loans to the State contracted till 31.03.2004 and outstanding on 31.03.2005 may be consolidated and re-scheduled for fresh term of twenty years; and interest rate of 7.5 percent be charged on this amount with certain conditionality. The first condition to be fulfilled to attain eligibility for relief is that each State should enact the Fiscal Responsibility Legislation. The total relief, which can be availed of by all the States, can go upto Rs. 33,000 crores in five years of the award period. The interest saving will be about Rs. 21,300 crores and principal repayment saving of Rs. 11,900 crores.

### Special Scheme of DEBT Relief

A special scheme of debt write-off linked to reduction of revenue deficit of the State has also been introduced. The salient features of this scheme are:

The three years average (2001-02, 2002-03 and 2003-

2004) amount of Revenue Surplus/Deficit will be taken as the base year figure for 2003-04.

For Revenue Surplus States, which continue to remain in revenue surplus during the award period, the repayment of loans will be written-off if they do not go below base year figure. If the surplus figure goes below the base year figure, no write-off will be given.

In case of revenue deficit States, the write-off will be given if the revenue deficit goes below the base year figure. For the purpose of determining the scale at which the relief will be provided, the repayment due by the State during the period 2005-10 to the base year figure of revenue deficit has been worked out. This determines the amount of write-off of repayment that will be allowed to each State for the reduction of each rupee of revenue deficit. In case of U.P. this ratio is 0.44.

The write-off amount will be restricted to the repayment due on the consolidated loan for the year.

Further, each State will be required to achieve in each year of award period a reduction in the revenue deficit, which compared to base year figure is cumulatively higher than the cumulative reduction attributable to interest relief.

If the revenue deficit level deteriorates, then the performance in the subsequent year will be measured for not that particular year figure is cumulatively higher than the cumulative reduction attributable to interest relief.

The benefit of write-off would be available only if the fiscal deficit of the State is contained to the level of 2004-05.

The enactment of FRBM Act is a necessary pre-condition. The savings, which the State will have if the conditions are fulfilled, have not been quantified. However, these can be up to the principal repayment amount subject to a ceiling fixed for each State in terms of formula.

**New Policy of Central Loans**

The Twelfth Finance Commission has recommended a new policy of Central loans to States. According to this scheme, the Centre should release only the grant portion (30%) of Central Assistance for State plan and leave it to the State to raise loan portion (70%) from other sources. The

Central Government should not act as an intermediary for future lending and allow the States to approach he market directly. If some fiscally weak States are unable to raise funds from the market, the Centre could borrow for the purpose of on lending to such States, but the interest rates should remain aligned to marginal cost of borrowing for the Centre. Government of India has accepted this new approach in principle, to be implemented in phases, in consultation with RBI. The Action Taken Report (ATR), presented by the Twelfth Finance Commission, further states that from 2005-06 the States would be allowed at their discretion not to draw the loan portion of CPA.

The new loan policy and ceiling on borrowings suggested by the Twelfth Finance Commission and implemented by the Govt. of India in full and not gradually as given ATR clearly favours the Central Government and not the States, With no provision of block loans, the Centre has reduced its capital disbursement and thereby its gross fiscal deficit. This is the second device of notionally reducing the GFD. Earlier, the Govt. of India had taken out the loans against small savings from the consolidated account and had created a separate National Small Saving Funds (NSSF) and thereby reduced the GFD. This fiscal engineering not fiscal restructuring has been done by Govt. of India to fulfil the FRBM Act. targets.

Further the Finance Minister in his budget speech for 2005-06 said that because of the Twelfth Finance Commission recommendations, "I was left with no option but to press the pause button *vis-à-vis* the FRBM Act". But the close examination of the impact of the Twelfth Finance Commission recommendations on budget (*EPW*, April 23, 2005, pp. 1675-1679) shows the Govt. of India will have a saving of Rs. 12,248 crores because of non-disbursement of plan Rs. 29,003 crores even with an incremental burden of Rs. 19,755 crores in the shape of high tax shares and grants-in-aid. Thus as a result of the Twelfth Finance Commission recommendations the Govt. of India has gained without affecting any fiscal restructuring.

For the first time, the Twelfth Finance Commission has recommended annual borrowing limits for the State

Government. While discussing dimensions of restructuring, the Twelfth Finance Commission has suggested the need to specify annual ceiling of borrowing for each State and implement a hard budget constraint. This is one of the most important and far reaching recommendations of the Twelfth Finance Commission. The Commission has recommended both the limit and its institutionalization. For this purpose the 2004-05 has been taken as a base year and this has been made a pre-condition for debt relief also.

For institutionalizing this limit the Twelfth Finance Commission talks of Loans Council. The Government of India has not responded to the recommendation. The government of India will try to enforce this condition while giving permission to States for borrowing under Article 293(3) of the constitution of India. But there are certain borrowings where permission of Central Government is not required like Provident Fund and Small Savings. Sometime the State may overshoot the limit of borrowings and it is not clear how the Government of India will then enforce the ceiling.

### Back to Back Transfer of External Aid

External assistance may be transferred to States on the same term and conditions as attached to such assistance by external funding agencies, thereby making Government of India a financial intermediary without any gain or loss. The external assistance passed on to the State should be managed through a separate fund in the public account. Though Govt. of India has accepted the recommendation but has put a condition that the service cost and exchange rate fluctuations would also be passed on to the states.

In the earlier regime, the EAP Central Assistance used to come as part of block loan and block grant and the repayment clearly laid down. Now with many donor agencies funding the project with different conditions of loans, it will be very difficult for the States to project the receipt and the liability of payment hence difficult to make adequate provisions in the budget. There is a need to discuss this issue in greater detail and the Ministry of Finance has to come out with a detailed procedure of release of the amount and its repayment and accounting.

**Sinking Fund**

All State should set-up Sinking Fund (SF) for amortization of all loans including loans from banks, liabilities on account of NSSF, etc. The Fund should be maintained outside the Consolidated Fund of the State and the Public Account and should not be used for any other purpose, except for redemption of loans.

**Guarantee Redemption Fund**

State should set-up Guarantee Redemption Fund (GRF) through earmarked guarantee fees. This should be preceded by risk weighing of guarantees. The quantum of contribution to the fund should be decided accordingly. On the above line a Sinking Fund and Guarantee Redemption Fund will have to be set-up in the State.

Though the creation of these funds is a welcome step and recommended earlier by RBI also but it has not been made mandatory for the States. With the condition of reduction of revenue deficit already there for restructuring and debt relief, will it be prudent for a revenue deficit State to set apart a substantial part of revenue outside public account and thereby raise its revenue deficit further and thus loose the chance getting some debt relief under the special relief scheme.

**Accounting Procedures**

As per ATR, presented by the Twelfth Finance Commission, the Govt. of India has accepted this recommendation in principle. The Government Accounting Standard Board (GASB) in the office of C&A.G. of India would be asked to draw a detailed road map and operational framework for its implementation.

To conclude we can say that because of certain developments in the post-reform period, there is an urgent need to examine afresh the working of Union-State relations. The various committees and commissions, which have so far been appointed, appear to expect too much from the State Governments. Finance Commission is always bound by their terms of reference. Therefore, too much cannot be expected from them insofar as the working of federal financial relations is concerned. Since in a developing federation like India some dynamism in the working of financial relations between different tiers of the government is an ongoing process, therefore, there is an urgent need to keep a constant vigil. The meetings of the Inter-State Council and other similar bodies should be regular and more frequent and some new such institutions as Loan Council can be created to deal with the chronic problem of indebtedness.

The Twelfth Finance Commission has paid special attention on the improvement of fiscal health of the state by constitutional amendments. As we are aware, in accordance with Article 280(3)(a) of the constitution and Para (4) 1 of terms of reference (TOR), the 12th Finance Commission was, asked to make recommendation for the distribution of net proceeds of from financial resources between the union and the states. Prior to the enactment of the Eightieth Amendment Constitution Act, 2000 the sharing of the union tax revenues with the states was in accordance with the provision of Article 272, of the Constitution while Article 270 of the Constitution provided for the compulsory, sharing of the net proceeds of income tax (excluding corporation tax), Article 272 of the Constitution permitted for sharing of the net proceeds of union duties of excise (excluding Excise Duties on medicine and toilet preparation). Consequently, the principles adopted for sharing the revenue differed between the two taxes significantly.

The Eightieth amendment of the Constitution altered the pattern of sharing the union taxes in a fundamental way. Under amendment Article 272 was dropped and Article 270 was substantially changed. The new Article 270 provides for sharing of all taxes and duties referred to in the union list except the taxes and duties referred to in Articles 268 and 269 respectively, surcharges on taxes and duties referred to in Article 271 and any cess levied for specific purposes. Twelfth Finance Commission approved the proposals of Tenth Finance Commission, which suggested in its alternative scheme of tax devolution that instead of sharing of individual taxes, the states might have a share in total net proceeds of all central taxes excluding surcharges and cases.

The trend of vertical sharing and transfers from centre

to state reveal that transfers have accounted for about 60 and 70 percent of total central transfers to states and have also shown variation over time. State have almost unanimously, sought an increase in total share of central taxes. Many states asked for increasing the share of states in the shareable pool from 29.5 percent some states have even suggested figures of 50 percent. The Twelfth Finance Commission has used grants to a larger extent as an instrument of transfers. It has also recommended that the share of the state in the not proceeds of shareable central taxes be raised from 29.5 percent to 30.5 percent. Further, the indicative amount of overall transfers to state in central gross revenue receipts, which was fixed at 37.5 percent by the Eleventh Finance Commission, may be raised at 38 percent. As regards the horizontal sharing determination as interest share of the states, the basic aim of the Finance Commission transfers in the part has been to: (a) correct the differentiates in revenue capacity and cost disability factors inherent in the economic of states, and (b) to foster fiscal efficiency among the states.

Like the Eleventh Finance Commission, the Twelfth Finance Commission has also recommended for fiscal discipline. The Twelfth Finance Commission has tried to evolve a formula that balances equity with fiscal efficiency. The plan of the Twelfth Finance Commission of debt restructuring involves consolidation of the debt of the states to the centre to be repaid in a specified number of years. It is suggested by the Twelfth Finance Commission that Central government should progressively reduce its intermediation in the state borrowing. Where it is essential in the case of extent assistance, it should be done through public accounts. If 'on-lending' to states remains part of center's fiscal deficit, the 3 percent fiscal deficit target should prove to be too narrow. As Centre stops 'on-lending' to States, the repayments made by the State become available to the Centre to meet its capital expenditure targets. States should be allowed to borrow the repayment amount from the market in addition to its borrowing requirement according to the stipulated path of fiscal deficit in the plan for restructuring state finances. It has suggested restructuring in revenue, pension, tax revenue, non-tax revenue, expenditure, subsidies, and salaries to government employees, system of fiscal transfers public debt, etc. for improving the fiscal health of the States.

**Centre-State Conflict on Finance**

In the last few decades, there has always been growing conflict and tension between the Indian Union and the States in the matter of finance. This conflict has often been aggravated by political and ideological differences between the different parties governing the Centre and the States.

The framers of the Indian Constitution provided for grants and loans so that the Centre might come to the help of those States which were in difficulty and also to bring about balanced development of the different regions. The use of grants and loans in the last 40 years or so, however, has resulted in the complete domination and control of the States by the Centre and to a certain extent, even financial irresponsibility and indiscipline on the part of the States. The enormous increase in transferred resources from the Centre to the States, the phenomenal growth in loan assistance to the states and the political pressure amounting to blackmail by the Centre through the instrument of grants have frightened the States. Hence, there has been an insistent demand for a comprehensive review of Centre State relations in general and Centre-State financial relations in particular. The J.K. Thavaraj Committee (Report of the Taxation Enquiry Committee, Kerala Government), the Rajamannar Committee on Centre-State relations appointed by the DMK Government of Tamil Nadu and the document on Centre-State relations (1978) adopted by the West Bengal cabinet led by the CPI-M United Front all these have the same theme viz., political and financial autonomy for the States and drastic restriction of the power and financial resources of the centre.

According to the Constitution, the Centre has to concern itself with the most generalised features of the Indian economy such as the creation and maintenance of the banking system, railways and ports as well as facilities for national economic planning with the regulation and development of large-scale industries, exploitation of mineral resources, regulation of foreign trade, etc., besides, of course, the defense of the nation from foreign aggression. On the other hand, the States are concerned with important aspects of the life of the people, such as the maintenance of law and order, the construction and maintenance of irrigation, power, road transport, etc. the development of educational and health facilities, the promotion of primary sector such as agriculture, fisheries, forests and secondary sector viz., tiny, small and medium industries.

In order to carry out these responsibilities the Constitution provided for different types of financial resources. The Union is entrusted with taxes on personal incomes and profits of companies, excise duties and customs duties. In a rapidly developing economy, these are precisely the most productive taxes in the country. In the case of the States, land constitutes an important base of taxation. In a densely populated country like India, the volume of land coming under tax remains almost stationary.

Therefore, land, as a source of revenue has been responsible for the inelastic nature of State revenues to a considerable extent. On the other hand, the various taxes on commodities and services like sales tax, State excise duties, duties in electricity rates, motor vehicles tax, etc. can be quite productive.

Taxation of industrial and commercial properties has been the preserve of the Centre, and tremendous expansion in the base of industrial and commercial property, income and wealth as a result of economic development has been responsible for raising the financial resources of the Centre. At the same time while rapid industrial development boosted Central excise duty collection, expansion of imports pushed up customs duty collections. This seems to have given a buoyancy to the Central revenues which is not available to any tax head assigned to the States except sales tax.

The period since 1951 has witnessed an enormous expansion of financial powers of the Central Government whose dimensions have progressively increased in relation to the combined resources of all State Governments put together. For instance, the current tax revenues of the Centre have risen from Rs. 360 crores in 1950-51 to Rs. 65,000 crores in 1994-95 and to Rs. 4,42,410 crores in 2006-07 (budget) On the other hand, current tax revenues of the States (excluding transfers from the Centre) have risen from Rs. 280 crores in 1951-52 to Rs. 53,400 crores in 1994-95. and Rs. 2,15,250 crores in 2004-05 (budget). The rate of growth of revenues of the Centre is much faster as compared to that of the States. But then, the Centre has only limited functions to perform while the functions of the States are almost unlimited.

In a way, the Indian Constitution it self is responsible for the existence of a financially strong-Centre and weak States. Until partition, there was a growing consensus in favour of the corporation tax and export duties to be included in the divisible pool. This was the case made out before the Sircar Committee known as the Expert Committee on Financial Provisions. It was partition which alerted the Constituent Assembly against possible dangers to the unity of India arising from the divisive forces. Its effect is reflected in the strong-Centre theme which runs through the Constitution. The financial provisions of the Constitution clearly reflect this strong-Centre bias.

West Bengal, Jammu and Kashmir, Punjab, Maharashtra and Southern states have generally been very agitated over the question of state's autonomy. The Centre-State conflict on financial relations is only a part of the overall Centre-State relations and the demand for political and fiscal autonomy. The sources of conflict as listed by the states, at different times, are as follows:

(i) The basic assumption of the Constitution in favour of a strong Centre and weak and dependent states is no longer acceptable and States like West Bengal insist that a strong Centre requires equally strong and autonomous States.

(ii) The nature of functions to be performed by the States and the necessity to promote cultural, linguistic and the special conditions of each State require that States should be autonomous.

(iii) Since Independence, the Centre has been gradually extending its functions in such a way as to keep the States completely dependent on it. This process has been encouraged in the first two decades after Independence by the Congress Party which was iu power both, at the Centre, and at the States. The process was further strengthened during the period of Emergency, 1975-77.

(iv) The Centre has been duplicating unnecessarily a number of departments which have no real functions to perform, i.e., education, public health, etc., which are all State subjects. There is even a move that these subjects should be put on the concurrent list.

(v) The Centre has been interfering in the affairs of the State even in the field of law and order which is purely a State subject by setting up the Central Reserve Police, the Border Security Force, the Industrial Security Force, etc.

(vi) The Centre, with too little to do, is entrusted with too much financial resources while the State Governments with so many vital functions to perform are starved of financial resources.

(vii) The financial resources of the Centre are highly elastic, while those of the States are relatively inelastic. Accordingly, the States have been forced to depend upon the Centre to a large extent for their financial requirements.

As the share of taxes and duties was inadequate to meet the growing revenue and capital expenditure (specially before the Seventh Plan award) the States had to resort more and more to grants-in-aid and loans from the Centre. There was a growing feeling of uncertainty and indecision, loss of initiative and irritation on the part of the States. The States had become further suspicious of the behaviour and motives of the Centre on the question of raising and sharing of tax revenues with the States.

(i) The Centre had not taken sufficient initiative to impose all the taxes under Article 269 whose proceeds would go to the States.

(ii) The corporation tax was excluded from the scope of sharing with the States from the very beginning. The States felt sore because their contribution to the development of the corporate sector was quite large. For example, they incurred considerable expenditure in providing the direct infrastructural facilities like power, water, raw materials, roads, lands, etc. Besides they provide considerable financial incentives for the setting up of industries. It was therefore, fair and appropriate that the States should have a share in the proceeds of the corporation tax as well.

(iii) The Central excise duties were continuously expanded by including under them a growing number of items previously taxed by the States.

(iv) The divisible pool of excise duties was limited to basic duties and additional excise duties; the special and auxiliary duties were kept out of the divisible pool. The rates of additional excise duties which had to be shared with the States were kept low, while raising steadily the rates of excise duties and of special and auxiliary duties which were not to be shared with the States or to be shared only in smaller proportions.

(v) The railway passenger tax whose proceeds were to go to the States was abolished and the Centre fixed arbitrarily a grant in lieu of railway passenger tax. This grant was much less than what the railway passenger tax would have brought to the States.

(vi) The surcharges on income tax were imposed by the Central Government but the proceeds were not shared with the States. The Central Government raised the exemption limit of income periodically and reduced the divisible pool of income tax. The Central Government, however, did not suffer much loss, as the loss was more than offset by the increase in the surcharge.

(vii) The main source of revenue of the States has been the sales tax which accounts for 60 per cent of the States' own tax revenue. The Centre has wanted to abolish the sales tax by introducing value added tax (VAT). There were also proposals to abolish octori duties and state excises.

Further, the Planning Commission had asked the States to raise resources by enhancing electricity charges. But in the 1978-79 budget, the Centre decided to tap this source also by imposing excise duties on electricity, thus removing the scope for raising electricity tariff by the States (this was given up later). The States were thus left with no proper resources to raise their revenues. By depending upon the Centre, the States were running the risk of losing their economic independence.

While the revenues of the States are increasing only gradually, the expenses of the States are increasing at a fast rate. For instance, state plan outlays are increasing with every five year plan. Besides, the various policies of the Central Government (monetary, fiscal and general economic policies) affect the price situation in the country. Whenever there is a rise in price level; there is naturally a demand for increased D.A. from the Government and semi-government employees. Again, the Central Government appoints Central Pay Commission to revise salaries and dearness allowances of the Central Staff. The state Governments employees too demand rise in salaries and DA parallel to Central Government staff. The Central Government has vast financial resources to meet such demands, but the State Governments fund it difficult to meet such periodical demands from their staff. It is important, therefore, that the Centre consults the States before agreeing to the grant of additional D.A. and also provide resources to the States for this purpose.

Too much dependence of the States on the Centre in the form of grants-in-aid and loans has had four serious adverse consequences:

(i) The Centre could be generous or mean to the different States. Some of the States have felt it humiliating to make frequent visits to New Delhi for funds.

(ii) A second difficulty is the uncertainty in the budgeting of the States. For instance, in the absence of firm commitments of the Central Government in the matter of grants-in-aid, it is difficult for the States to decide about the various projects of development they have to undertake.

(iii) That the States are notable to fulfil the various electoral promises because of inadequacy of financial resources.

(iv) Finally, most States have resorted to unauthorized overdrafts to finance plan projects.

A serious complaint of some of the States like Kerala is about the regional imbalance in industrial development. The complaint is that the Centre has not used its fiscal dominance over States to correct regional imbalances. Nor has the Centre used other instruments at its disposal to narrow down the unevenness in regional development. In the absence of integrated approach to the development of the backward regions, location of the Central sector projects and even the location of private industries through licensing policy have not created much of an impression on the problem of regional imbalances. In fact, regional disparities have worsened during the plans. It was thought that the Planning Commission would bring about a closer economic integration of the country through rapid increase in national income, higher standards of living of the masses, reduction of inequalities between regions, expansion of agriculture, industry, power arid transport. While some degree of economic development has been achieved in every direction, yet from the point of view of balanced regional development, planning may be said to be a dismal failure. Now, with the acceleration of the planning process the responsibilities and commitments of States, have increased much more than their financial resources. The result was a kind of centralisation at the federal level bringing the economic functioning of the State Governments under Central directive and control through the mechanism of grants and loans. Correspondingly, the financial powers of the States are far too meagre in relation to their clearly defined responsibilities. It was really unfortunate that the framers of the Indian Constitution could not visualise the financial implications of large-scale programmes of planned development.

The Rajamannar Committee on Centre-State relations (it submitted its report in May 1971) and the West Bengal Memorandum came out with a string of suggestions and recommendations aiming at autonomy of the states, consistent with the integrity of the country. The suggestions of the West Bengal Memorandum, which revived the controversy on the question, were as follows:

(i) The powers and functions of the Centre and the States should be clearly marked and specified, and if necessary, the Constitution should be amended suitably.

(ii) The Centre's jurisdiction should be restricted to defence, foreign affairs and foreign trade. communications, currency and economic coordination. All other powers should be exclusively reserved for the States. There should be no interference or control by the Centre in the exercise of its powers by the States.

(iii) The present instrument of Centre's control and interference in the affairs of the States viz., the Indian Administrative and Police Services, the Central Reserve Police, the Border Security Force, the Industrial Security Force, etc., should be removed forthwith.

(iv) The Planning Commission and the National Development Council which have an important role in planning and economic co-ordination should be specifically referred to in the Constitution.

(v) 75 per cent of the central revenues should be automatically transferred by the Centre to the divisible pool of the States and the Finance Commission should have power only to recommend the principles for the distribution of this divisible pool among the States.

Other important suggestions made by the West Bengal Memorandum and the Rajamannar Committee on Centre-State relations included equal representation for all States in the Rajya Sabha, the maintenance of the special status of Kashmir in the Indian Union, the retention of English as the link language between the Centre and the States, the right to use mother tongue at all levels, industrial licensing to be vested with the States, except for large companies of national importance, inter-state water disputes to be settled by the Supreme Court, etc.

The problem of Centre-State financial relations has thus been a part of the general and more important problem of Centre-State relations. The West Bengal Memorandum would allow the Centre to perform only three or four functions and leave the rest of the functions to the States. The States would like to have a say, at least indirectly, even in the limited powers and functions of the Centre. For example, the States would like to influence the location and distribution of defence industries, the use of foreign exchange reserves, allocation for the projects of communication and also monetary and fiscal policies, etc. At the same time, the Centre should be left with only 25 per cent of the revenue raised while 75 per cent of the revenue should go to the States automatically. All these things clearly indicate that the ultimate intention was to have strong states and a weak and emaciated Centre.

There is also the fear that some of the States ideologically different from others might like to break away from the federation on some pretext or the other. The DMK ideology at one time, the Khalistan movement in Punjab and Assam agitation-all these had separatist tendencies. The supporters of strong states cite the example of United Soviet Socialist Republic (USSR). It was the presence of a common political ideology and supreme Central authority which held together the culturally diverse autonomous States in the U.S.S.R. When the common political ideology and the strong Central authority disappeared, USSR disintegrated. State autonomy can thus be dangerous to the national integrity and India cannot be allowed to go the USSR way.

The argument that 'State autonomy' would liberate creative energies at present inhibited by constant central interference and domination and that state autonomy would promote rapid economic growth is high: questionable in the Indian context. It is the Centre's case that except for communist parties who are wedded to economic ideology, other regional political parties are very parochial in their outlook. Most of them are financed by big business in industry, trade, transport, films, etc. They: are corrupt to the core and destinies of these states are controlled by men, among whom some have very close links with smugglers and anti-social elements. The politicians cannot see beyond their noses and want to state autonomy to further their selfish ends so as to remain in power. In any case there is no positive correlation, between state autonomy and the rapid development of different states.

In this connection it should be emphasized that the States do already enjoy considerable autonomy. They have exclusive control over such key sectors as agriculture. irrigation and power, administration, social welfare, law and order, etc. But not all States have performed these functions properly in any appreciable degree. The advanced states have continued to march ahead and the backward states have remained backward.

The States' complaint about inadequate financial resources and their demand for large taxation powers would sound more reasonable if the States had fully exploited the resources they command. They are not only reluctant to tax agricultural incomes but have been abolishing land levies despite the gaping deficits in their budgets. The financial difficulties thus arise in part from their own lack of political courage. It is also an accepted fact that State tax administration is hopelessly corrupt and inefficient. Still the Centre has been sympathetic to their pleas for assistance and their share of the divisible pool of Central taxes has progressively increased over the years.

States generally resort to alternative methods for overcoming their budgetary gaps and this was mostly done through grants-in-aid and loans from the Centre before 1967. After 1967, the non-Congress dominated States and even the Congress-controlled States were in a rebellious mood and they resorted to unauthorised overdrafts on the Reserve Bank, which they insisted should be converted into regular loans. In spite of pressure from the Reserve Bank, these over-drafts continued to create inflationary pressure in the economy and constituted serious financial indiscipline.

The inadequacy of financial resources was sought to be

made up by the use of Central grants-in-aid. The grants-in-aid were also meant to help backward States to come up to the level of others. Besides grants, the State. approach the Centre for loans and advances. The resource: transferred from the Centre have accounted for over 45 per cent of the total expenditure of the States.

It is thus clear that the States have become increasingly dependent on the Centre for their expenditure. Such dependence is the natural consequence of the enormous command enjoyed by the Centre over relatively larger and expanding revenue resources. The massive indebtedness of the States had led to a kind of creditor-debtor relationship between the Centre and the States breeding a sense of irresponsibility among the borrowing States. In a sense, the position of dependence on the Centre has suited the States well. It has enabled them to avoid taking unpopular tax measures and to attribute their inefficiency and failure to the Centre.

By 1983, the Centre-State relations were almost at a breaking point with Khalistan demand for a separate Sikh state, and the Southern States forming a regional council, and so on. It was to settle this problem once and for all that the Central Government appointed the Sarkaria Commission, with comprehensive terms of reference covering constitutional, legislative, financial and administrative aspects of Centre-State relations.

The Sarkaria Commission submitted its report to the Government in January 1988. According to the Commission, it was necessary to preserve the unity and integrity of the country and, accordingly, the Commission rejected the various suggestions made before it either to reduce the functions of the Centre or modify them. The Commission rejected the suggestion of transfer of subjects like preventive detention, education, labour and electricity to the state list or concurrent list on the ground that it would disturb the basic scheme of the Constitution. The Commission called for a process of consultation by the Centre of all concurrent subjects. It also made a strong case for inter-state councils, for the retention of National Development Council (NDC) and for activisation of zonal councils.

In the financial sphere, the Sarkaria Commission favoured the amendment of the Constitution to provide for sharing of corporation tax between the Centre and the States but rejected all other suggestions for enlarging the divisible pool. The Commission also rejected the suggestion that the devolution of funds from the Centre to the States should be automatic. The Commission recommended the setting up of expert committees to examine taxation reforms and resource mobilisation, to study in depth the agricultural income tax and to review the loan-grant pattern. The Commission accepted that the present division of functions between the Finance Commissions and the Planning Commission as reasonable and that it should continue. However, it suggested that the terms of reference of the Finance Commission should be drawn up in consultation with the State Governments. Finally, the Commission recommended legislation to levy consignment tax and constitutional amendment to enable levy of tax on advertisements in broadcasting.

The Central Government did not accept all the recommendations of the Sarkaria Commission. In any case, the Sarkaria Commission's recommendations are not the last word on the question of Centre-State relations. The question is still wide-open. However, on the question of Centre-States financial relations, the States welcomed one recommendation of the Sarkaria Commission-viz., the inclusion of corporation tax in the divisible pool. This was a longstanding demand of the States before every Finance Commission till now. The Central Government did not accept this important recommendation because of its own heavy revenue deficits in the last few years. However the Tenth Finance Commission (1995) suggested a vertical devolution of all Central taxes. This suggestion was accepted and 80th Amendment (2000) to the Constitution was passed. The 11th and 12th Finance Commissions have given awards under which the states share a percentage of all the tax proceeds of the Centre. As a consequence, to a large extent, the conflict between the Centre and the States on the sharing of Central taxes has almost disappeared. However, many serious problems still exist such as sharing of river waters. The UPA Government has proposed the setting up of a new commission on the lines of Sarkaria Commission.

**Thirteenth Finance Commission (2010-15)**

The TFC was constituted in terms of the Presidential Order November 13, 2007 to make recommendations relating to tax devolution between the Centre and States; grants-in-aid to States; and measures needed to augment the Consolidated Fund of a State to supplement the resources of the Panchayats and Municipalities. In addition to the above, the Commission has also been mandated to review the state of finances of the Union and States, keeping in view, in particular, the operation of the States' Debt Consolidation and Relief Facility 2005-10 introduced by the Central Government on the basis of the recommendations of the Twelfth Finance Commission, and suggest measures for maintaining a stable and sustainable fiscal environment consistent with equitable growth. Subsequently, the Commission was given additional terms of reference including the mandate to review the roadmap for fiscal adjustments and suggest a suitably revised one with a view to maintaining the gains of fiscal consolidation through 2010 to 2015 particularly considering the need to bring the liabilities of the Central Government on account of oil, food and fertilizer bonds into the fiscal accounting, and the impact of various other obligations of the Central Government on the deficit targets. The TFC has since submitted its Report.

Despite the commendable correction achieved by the Centre and states through implementation of the Fiscal Responsibility and Budget Management (FRBM) legislation across the 2005-10 period, the closing debt-GDP ratio for 2009-10 is estimated at 82 per cent, well above the FC-XII target of 75 per cent. Our starting point was to determine the feasible target for the debt-GDP ratio, consolidated across the Centre and the states, by 2014-15. A major task, then, before this Commission was to determine the extent to which fiscal consolidation could reduce the medium-term combined debt-GDP ratio over the time horizon 2010-15, based on our projection of the medium-term macro-economic situation. We are proposing a target of 68 per cent for a combined Centre and state debt to GDP ratio to be achieved by the year 2014-15 and 45 per cent for the Central Government debt-GDP ratio. We then specified a time path, whereby the Centre and specify would be able to return to the process of fiscal adjustment, in the aftermath of the deviation necessitated by the events of 2008-09. These developments also signalled the need to specify more closely the circumstances under which such deviations were to be triggered and a more desirable distribution of he burden of incidence of stabilisation and counter-recessionary measures.

The fiscal roadmap for 2010-15 needs to take account of the combined macro-fiscal position of the Central and State Governments and to set macrofiscal targets with reference to the overall position. The two key indicators in this context are the combined fiscal deficit and the combined debt to GDP ratio. The latter is not a simple aggregation of the outstanding liabilities of the Central and State Governments. Inter-governmental transactions such as loans to states from the Centre need to be netted out. Table 5 provides a picture of the combined liabilities and combined fiscal deficit of the Central and State Governments from 2004-05 to 2008-09 (BE). Combined liabilities1 have fallen consistently from 91.7 per cent of Gross Domestic Product (GDP) in 2004-05 to 81.9 per cent by the budget estimates for 2008-09. The combined fiscal deficit also fell from 7.3 per cent in 2004-05 to 5.0 per cent in 2008-09 (BE). Subsequent to the budget for 2008-09, there was a global slowdown which continued in the year 2009-10.

TABLE 5

**Aggregate Position of Centre and States**

*(per cent of GDP)*

| | 2004-05 | 2005-06 | 2006-07 | 2007-08 (RE) | 2008-09 (BE) |
|---|---|---|---|---|---|
| RD | 3.6 | 2.6 | 1.2 | 0.6 | 0.4 |
| FD | 7.3 | 6.6 | 5.3 | 5.3 | 5.0 |
| Debt | 91.7 | 91.2 | 88.2 | 86.5 | 81.9 |

Source: Indian Public Finance Statistics 2008-09

The macro-fiscal correction prescribed by the Twelfth Finance Commission targeted the combined fiscal deficit of the Centre and states, in line with the assumed availability of household savings at 10 per cent of GDP and an acceptable level for the current account deficit at 1.5 per cent of GDP. After allowing for absorption by the private sector at 4 per cent of GDP and by non-departmental public sector enterprises at 1.5 per cent of GDP, this yielded a feasible, sustainable, combined fiscal deficit of 6 per cent of GDP. However, it should be noted that this fiscal deficit was the target for the last year of FC-XII projections (2009-10) and that the combined deficit figures projected for the years leading up to the final year were higher. A constant fiscal deficit of 6 per cent with nominal GDP growth rate of 12 per cent for the economy, as assumed in the FC-XII projection exercise, would stabilise debt in the long-term at 56 per cent. However, the economy approaches such a long-term resting point, asymptotically, only at infinity. After factoring in the fiscal deficit progression assumed for the projection period of FC-XII, to the final targeted fiscal deficit of 6 per cent of GDP, their targeted debt for 2009-10 worked out to 75 per cent of GDP.

Despite the commendable fiscal correction achieved by the Centre and states, the closing debt to GDP ratio for 2009-10 is estimated to reach 82 per cent, well above the FC-XII target of 75 per cent, owing largely to the adverse macroeconomic circumstances in 2008-09. Given the imperative of creating an environment favourable to private investment in the Indian economy, it is necessary that the ratio of consolidated liabilities to GDP be reduced, not merely below the level presently estimated for the close of 2009-10, but also that targeted by the previous Finance Commission.

In our view, it should be possible to reduce the combined debt of Centre and states to around 68 per cent of GDP by 2014-15. This target has been arrived at as the feasible and desirable correction, based on our projections of the medium-term macroeconomic situation during the award period and our assessment of the resource position of the Centre and states over this horizon. Accordingly, the fiscal deficit targets prescribed for the Centre and states are such as to secure the targeted correction in the combined debt to GDP ratio to around 68 per cent. In the sections that follow, we obtain the individual components of the Centre and states within this overall target.

The Fiscal Responsibility and Budget Management Act (FRBMA), 2003 is, in essence, a target-based framework to ensure that government finances are managed with a view to achieving equitable, long-term macroeconomic stability consistent with attainment of the medium-term growth target of the Indian economy. It requires the government to maintain a medium-term fiscal strategy that can be monitored over a multi-year period.

It is clear that in spite of improved performance in the first three years of the FC-XII award period, the Centre will not be able to achieve the FRBM targets by the end of 2009-10. Looking ahead, the government has not set a firm time limit for fiscal performance to be brought back on its FRBM envisaged path. This, then, becomes a central task for this Commission. In addition, the impact of the recent counter-recessionary measures on the fiscal stance indicate two important priorities for the present Commission: (i) to ensure that the fiscal sustainability of the Centre is protected and improved through measures to reduce the debt to GDP ratio, which rose as a consequence of not meeting the FRBM targets, and (ii) to be mindful of the need for the FRBM Act targets to be adjusted when exogenous unanticipated shocks occur.

The Commission has considered the targets prescribed in the FRBMA and has taken into account the views of the Central Government and Reserve Bank of India (RBI) on the value and utility of these targets. Our discussions and a perusal of their memoranda reinforce our belief that a targetbased framework needs to be maintained for the award period of this Commission.

The enactment of Fiscal Responsibility Legislation (FRL) in 26 states has resulted in significant fiscal correction. In aggregate, these states have reached their expenditure and debt targets ahead of schedule. Revenue buoyancy, both due to improved own tax revenues of the states and due to the derived benefit of high central tax buoyancies (through share in central taxes) has mainly been responsible for the fiscal correction. Another encouraging feature is that, in the aggregate, the states have been able to reduce their debt to Gross State Domestic Product (GSDP) ratio to less than 30 per cent. An equally, noteworthy outcome of the implementation of FRL has been the welcome exit of all general category and three special category states from a post-devolution non-plan revenue deficit. However, there is wide variation in performance among the states. The Commission's objectives are, therefore, to maintain the virtuous improvements in state finances, to protect state finances against exogenous shocks to the extent feasible and to incentives those states that continue to face fiscal stress towards undertaking urgent fiscal correction.

## REFERENCES

The Report of Eight Finance Commission, (1984), Government of India, New Delhi.

Thimmaiah, G. (1988), "Burning Issues in Centre-State Financial Relations", Ashish Publishing House, 8/81, Punjabi Bagh, New Delhi.

Gaur, Achal Kumar (1988), "Federal Finance in India: Emerging Trends", Deep & Deep Publications, F-159, Rajouri Garden, New Delhi.

Harris, S.E. (1947), "National Debt and the New Economics", McGrow Hill Book Company, New York and London.

Kurihara, K.K. (1959), "The Keynesian Theory of Economic Development George Allen & Unwin Ltd., 40, Museum Street, London, W.C.I.

The Constitution of India, Article 293.

The Sarkaria Commission (1988), "Report on Centre-State Relation", Government of India, New Delhi.

The Report of the Fifth Finance Commission (1969), Government of India New Delhi.

Sinha, R.K. (1986), (Edt.), "Centre-State Financial Relations in India", Deep & Deep Publications, New Delhi.

*The Reserve Bank of India Bulletin*, September 1978, Mumbai.

*The Reserve Bank of India Bulletin*, July 1985, Mumbai.

*The Economic Times*, New Delhi Edition, July 5, 1985, Vol. XII.

Dr. P.R. Brahmanand's Article, *The Times of India*, Patna Edition, Feb. 25, 1989.

*The Times of India*, Patna Edition, Feb. 23

Hicks, U.K. (1965), "Development Finance—Planning and Control",

Regan, Michael D. (1972), "The New Federation", Oxford University Press, New York.

Chandrashekhar, S. (1983), "Andhra Pardesh Finances", School of Economics, Andhra University, Waltair.

Lakdawala, D.T. (1967), "Union-State Financial Relations in India", Lalwani Publications.

Sastri, K.V.S. (1966), "Federal State Fiscal Relations in India". Oxford University Press, Bombay.

Venkataraman, K.V.S. (1968), "States Financial Relations in India", George Allien and Unwin Ltd., Ruskin House, Museum Street, London.

Hicks, U.K. (1965), "Some Fundamental Problems of Federal Finance", Supplement to Capital.

Govt. of India (2002), Report of the National Commission to Review the Working of the Constitution, Vol. I.

Gupta, Janak Raj (2003), "Emerging Scenario of Federal Financial Relations in India", *The Indian Journal of Economics*, Prof. K. Mehta Centenary Vol. LXXIV, Number 332.

*India Today* (August 15, 2005), "The State of the States", New Delhi.

Reddy, Y.V. (2002), "Restructuring of Public Finances and Macro-Economic Stability".

Raj Kapila and Uma Kapila (Eds.), "Decade of Economic Reforms in India, The Past, The Present and The Future", Academic Foundation, New Delhi.

Singh, Ajit Kumar (2005), "Vertical Transfers and TFC: How the States Really Gained", (Paper present at the National Seminar on Recommendations of the Twelfth Finance Commission and Their Implications for the States), Giri Institute of Development Studies, Lucknow, 6-7 May.

Govt. of India (July 2004), Report of the Task Force on Implementation of the Fiscal Responsibility and Budget Management Act, 2003, p. 57.

Govt. of India (1995), Ministry of Finance, Report of the Tenth Finance Commission, New Delhi.

Report of the Eleventh Finance Commission (2000), Government of India, New Delhi.

Report of the Twelfth Finance Commission (2004), Government of India, New Delhi.

Commission on Çentre-Sate Relations, Report, Part I, Govt. of India, New Delhi.

Bhargava, R.N. (1967), The Theory and Working of Union Finance in India, George Allen & Unwing (London).

Indian Constitution, Article 270.

Indian Constitution, Article 272.

Indian Constitution, Article 280.

Shrivastava, M..P. (2004), Union State Financial Relations in India, Anmol Publications, New Delhi.

Union Budget, 2005-06, Govt. of India, Ministry of Finance.

Union Budget, 2003-04, Govt. of India, Ministry of Finance.

Planning Commission: Tenth Five-Year Plan, 2002-07.

Government of India, Economic Survey, 2003-04 and 2004-05.

Chelliah, R.J. (1979), Reports of the Finance Commissions, *Indian Economic Review*, April, Vol. XIV, No. 1.

Government of India (2003), Fiscal Responsibility and Budget Management Act, 2003, Ministry of Finance.

Shandilya, Tapan Kumar (2005), "Emerging Issues in Centre-State Financial Relations: Approach of Twelfth Finance Commission, *Indian Economic Journal* (Conference Vol.), Vishakhapattanam (Andhra Pradesh), p. 903.

Shandilya, Tapan Kumar (1991), "Central Loans to States Under Five Year Plans", Deep and Deep Publications, New Delhi.

Shandilya Tapan Kumar (1994) (Edt.), Centre State Financial Relation in India. Deep & Deep Publications, New Delhi.

RBI, Hand Book of Statistic of the Indian Economy, 2002-03.

Gorge, K.K. and Gulati, I.S., Centre State Revenue Transfers 1951-84.

Budget at a Glance, Govt. of India, New Delhi.

Thirteenth Finance Commission (2010-15), Govt. of India.

# 2

# Finance Commission and Planning Commission

The allocation of financial resources between the centre and the state in any federal set-up is the most vital and at the same time the most difficult problem. Perhaps no federation in the world has fully solved this problem. Every federation has tried to reduce the intensity of the problem in its own way. In this sphere, the Indian Constitution provides for a financially strong Centre. Following the precedent set in the Government of India Act, 1935; the Constitution has sought to make a more or less clear division of the financial resources between the Centre and the States. In principle, each tax has been assigned exclusively to that layer of Government, which is in the best position to levy and collect it by and large; overlapping of taxes has been totally avoided. All growth-responsive taxes have been under the domain of the Central Government and the power of borrowing in the domestic as well as in the foreign markets.

Since the major elastic sources of revenue were allocated to the Central Government, the Constitution of India did acknowledge that the resources of the State Government would provide inadequate for the discharge of their functions. Accordingly, it provided for the obligatory sharing of income tax receipts (Article 270) and permissive sharing of Union excise duties (Article 272) between the Centre and the

States and grants-in-aid of the revenue to the state (Article 275). Articles 268 and 269 deal with taxes to the states whether collected by the Centre or the States.

The Constitution, however, did not indicate either the total share of the states or its distribution inter-se except the appointment of a Finance Commission for this purpose. Such a provision was made just to obviate the frequent political pressures to which the Parliament and the Cabinet and likely to be subjected in revising the system of Union-State transfers.

So far Twelve Finance Commissions have submitted their reports. Details of different Finance Commissions have been presented in Table 1.

TABLE I

**Details of Different Finance Commissions**

| *Finance Commission* | *Year of Establishment* | *Chairman* | *Operational Duration* | *Year of Submitting Report* |
|---|---|---|---|---|
| First | 1951 | K.C. Niyogi | 1952-57 | 1952 |
| Second | 1956 | K. Santhanam | 1957-62 | 1957 |
| Third | 1960 | A.K. Chanda | 1962-66 | 1961 |
| Fourth | 1964 | P.V. Rajamannar | 1966-69 | 1965 |
| Fifth | 1968 | Mahaveer Tyagi | 1969-74 | 1969 |
| Sixth | 1972 | Brahmanand Reddy | 1974-79 | 1973 |
| Seventh | 1977 | J.M. Shellet | 1979-84 | 1978 |
| Eighth | 1983 | Y.B. Chawan | 1984-89 | 1984 |
| Ninth | 1987 | N.K.P. Salve | 1989-95 | 1989 |
| Tenth | 1992 | K.C. Pant | 1995-00 | 1994 |
| Eleventh | 1998 | A.M. Khusro | 2000-05 | 2000 |
| Twelfth | 2003 | C. Rangarajan | 2005-10 | 2004 |
| Thirteenth | 2007 | Dr. Vijay Kelkar | 2010-15 | 2010 |

*Source*: *The Indian Economic Association Journal*, Conference Vol. 2005. Thirteenth Finance Commission (2010-15), Vol. 1, Govt. of India.

It is clear from the Table 1 that the First Finance Commission was established in 1951 and submitted its report in 1952. Like wise the Second Finance Commission was set-up in 1956 and submitted its reports in 1957. The Third

Finance Commission was established in 1960 and its report was submitted in 1961. The Fourth Finance Commission was set-up in 1964 and submitted its report in 1965. The Fifth Finance Commission was constituted 1968 and its report was submitted in 1969. The Sixth Finance Commission was came in to existence in 1972 and submitted its report in 1973. The period of establishment of Seventh Finance Commission was 1977 and its report was submitted in 1978. The Eighth Finance Commission came into operation in 1983 and it has submitted its report in 1984. The Ninth Finance Commission was established in 1987 and submitted its report in 1989. In 1992 the Tenth Finance Commission was set-up and its report was submitted in 1994. The Eleventh Finance Commission was established in 1998 and its report was submitted in 2000. The Twelfth Finance Commission was established in 2003 and submitted its report in 2004. The Thirteenth Finance Commission (FC-XIII) was constituted by the President under Article 280 of the Constitution on 13 November 2007 to make recommendations for the period 2010-15. Dr. Vijay Kelkar was appointed the Chairman of the Commission.

In the Six decades of Plans, the nation has laid the foundations of a modern self-reliant economy and has strengthened it further by achieving self-sufficiency in food, diversifying industrial structure and making significant progress in science and technology. The progress so far achieved has been slower than envisaged but steady and substantial. To quote our former Prime Minister Mrs. Gandhi (1980-85), "We can now speak of an Indian in which the fruits of growth will reach to the last".

How the fruits of growth should reach to the last should become the starting point for a New Finance Commission, as its recommendations will greatly influence the states' finances for the coming five years. The past performances of the State Governments do not throw any light that things would change in near future and the fruits of growth will reach to the last. The backward states still remain at the same distance from the advanced states, as they were in the beginning of the Plan and in some cases the situation has further worsened. The objective of equity in the form of adequate flow of funds to the poor states to compensate for their deficiencies in fiscal capacity has yet to be achieved.

The salient feature of Indian Constitution is that it has provided for setting up a periodic award of Finance Commission in order to regulate the inter-governmental fiscal relations in the country. Since the inauguration of the Constitution, Twelfth Finance Commissions have submitted their reports to the President of India, covering a span of more than 60 years. Definitely, one of the major tasks before these periodic awards was to evolve a set of sound principles of transfer of financial resources to the states such that a healthier relation between the Centre and the State would be established. Moreover, a set of issues has emerged in the sphere of Centre-State fiscal relations within the period covered by these successive awards and therefore the Finance Commissions were expected to deal with them efficiently.

In the present section an attempt has been made to evaluate the approach as well as methodology of the successive Finance Commissions in the broader spectrum of sound federal-state relations in India. At the same time, it will be significant to observe the limitations and constraints that are attached with the periodic award of the Finance Commission. For example, besides the task of distribution between the Centre and the State of the net proceeds of taxes which are to be, and may be, divided between them along with recommending the principles that would govern grants-in-aid, Finance Commission cannot consider any other problem of Indian fiscal federalism if they are not referred to them by the President of India. Therefore, the terms of references affect significantly to the working as well as functioning of the Finance Commissions. Secondly, emergence of the Planning Commission as an influential channel of Central resource transfer to the states has no doubt reduced the role and importance of the Finance Commission. Thirdly, the jurisdiction of the Finance Commission is confined, by and large, to the revenue account of the budget, which is mainly due to the Constitutional structure of the Finance Commission as well as the guidelines issued to it by the President of India. Finally, almost all the Finance Commissions have realized the lack of requisite information and data material, especially within the reasonable awards.

## TERMS OF REFERENCE

The constitution has laid down the following board terms of reference, under Article 280(3), for the Finance Commissions, which are as follows.

"The President within two years from the commencement of this Constitution and thereafter at the expiry of every fifth year or at such earlier time as the President considers necessary, by order constitute a Finance Commission which shall consist of a Chairman and four other members to be appointed by the President.

Parliament may by law determine the qualifications, which shall be requisite for appointment as members of the Commission and the manner in which they shall be selected.

It distribution between the Union and the states of the net proceeds of taxes which are to, or may be, divided between them the allocation between the states of the respective share of such proceeds.

The principles, which should govern the grants-in-aid of the revenues of the states of Consolidated Fund of India.

Any other matter referred to the Commission by the president in the interest of sound finance.

The Commission shall determine their procedure and shall have such powers in the performance of their function as parliament may by law confer on them."

The above narration clearly reveals that coverage as well as approach of the Finance Commission will be influenced significantly through the terms of reference and other matters referred to it by the President of India. The past Eleven Finance Commissions have been issued broad guidelines by the President of India with a view to ensure, perhaps, the healthier Centre-State financial relationship.

The First Finance Commission was asked to discharge its constitutional duties, i.e., to recommend a share in the proceeds of Income tax along with the principles on the basis of which these shares would be distributed among the states. In addition, the Commission was asked to make recommendations regarding two issues, namely, grants-in-aid to some states in lieu of their share of the export duty on jute and jute products and the sums payable to the states that were in need of assistance as grants-in-aid under the substantive portion of clause (i) of Article 275 of the Constitution.

The Second Finance Commission was assigned a detailed chart of terms of reference than the First Finance Commission. For example, in addition to determine the share in Income tax and Union Excise duties, the Commission was asked to recommend principles that would govern the distribution of proceeds from certain taxes levied under Article 269 such as estate duty and tax on railway fares, which were levied and collected by the Centre but the proceeds of which had to made to the States. Further, the commission was asked in deciding the amount of assistance by way of grants-in-aid under Article 275, to consider, (i) the requirement of the Second Five Year Plan, and (ii) the effort made by those States to raise additional revenue from sources available to them. Moreover, the commission was assigned to recommend the modifications, if any, in the rates of interest and the terms of repayment of the loans given to various States by the Central Government between the 15th August 1947 and 31st March 1956.

The Third Finance Commission was assigned, by and large, the same guidelines, which were issued to the Second Finance Commission

The guidelines issued to the Fourth Finance Commission were rather much comprehensive than its predecessors. The Commission was asked, in deciding the volume of assistance to the states by way of grants-in-aid, to consider:

1. The revenue resources of those states for the five years ending with the financial year 1970-71 on the basis of the level of taxation likely to be reached in the financial year 1956-66;
2. The requirements of those states to meet the committed expenditure on maintenance and upkeep of Plan schemes completed during the Third Plan;
3. Any further expenditure likely to devolve upon those states for the serving of their debt;

4. Creation of a fund out of the excess, if any, over a limit to be specified by the Commission of the net proceeds of Estate Duty on property other than agricultural land according to a state in any financial year, for the repayment of the state's debt to the Central Government; and
5. The scope for economy consistent with efficiency, which may be effected by states in their administrative expenditure.

In addition to above, the Fourth Finance Commission was asked to consider the effect of the combined incidence of a state's sales tax and Union Duties of Excise on the production, consumption or export of commodities or products, the Duties on which are sharable with the states, and the adjustments, if any, to be made in the state's share of Union Excise Duties if there is any increase in the state's sales tax on such products over a limit to be specified by the Commission.

Here it is worth-mentioning that the dimension as well as direction of guidelines issued to the Fourth Finance Commission was completely different than its predecessors. For instance, the Second and the Third Finance Commission were asked to consider the efforts to be made by states to raise additional resources available to them while the Fourth Finance Commission was asked to consider merely the resources that would be available to the states at the levels of taxation existing in the base year. Next, the Fourth Finance Commission had to consider "the scope for economy consistent with efficiency expenditure" while the earlier Commissions were not asked to recommend in this context.

For the first time, the Fifth Finance Commission was asked to consider the principles that would govern grants-in-aid to the states under Article 275 of the Constitution of India while the terms of reference issued to the earlier Commissions mentioned only the determination of the quantum of grants to be paid to the needy state. The terms of references issued to the Fifth Finance Commission clearly stated that the requirements of the Five Year Plans should not be considered while fixing grants to the states under Article

275 of Constitution of India. The consideration, which has to be kept in mind by the Commission while making recommendations pertaining to grant-in-aid were as follows:

1. The revenue resources of those states for the five years ending with the financial year 1973-74 on the basis of the levels of taxation likely to reached at the end of the financial year 1968-69;
2. The requirements on revenue account of those states to meet the expenditure on administration, interest charges in respect of their debt, maintenance and upkeep of plan schemes completed by the end of 1968-69, transfer of funds to local bodies and aided institutions and other committed expenditure; and
3. The scope for better fiscal management as also for economy consistent with efficiency which may be effected by the States in their administrative, maintenance, development and other expenditure.

Here it is significant to note that while the Second as well as the Third Finance Commissions were asked to consider the efforts made by the states to raise resources, the Fourth and the Fifth Finance Commissions were asked to take into account only the scope for economy on the expenditure side. Besides, the Fifth Finance Commission was asked to consider the scope for raising revenue from the taxes/duties, mentioned in Article 269 of the Constitution but not levied at present.

The Sixth Finance Commission was asked to consider a set of comprehensive issues. For assessing the needs on revenue account of the states to meet the expenditure on administration, the Commission was asked to take into account such provisions for the emoluments of government employees, teachers and local body employees, as obtaining on a specified date as the Commission deem it proper in the light of the state's capacity and needs. Further, the Commission was asked to have regard to the existing practice in regard to determination and distribution of Central assistance for financing state plans, the need for adequate maintenance and upkeep of capital assets and maintenance of Plan schemes completed by the end of 1973-74. Moreover, the Commission had to consider the requirements of the states, which were backward in standards of general administration for upgrading the administration with a view to bringing it to the levels obtaining in the more advance states over a period of ten years.

Here, it should be noted that the Fifth Finance Commission was not asked to consider the Plan requirements in determining grants-in-aid while the Sixth Finance Commission had to bear in mind the existing practice in the determination and distribution of Central assistance for the states plans.

The highlights of terms of reference issued to the Seventh Finance Commission were, by and large, same at those issued to the Sixth Finance Commission was asked while recommending the share of the state in divisible pool of taxes and grants, to consider, among other like.

The resources of the Central Government and the demands thereon on account of the expenditure of civil administration, defense and border security, debt servicing and other committed expenditure or liabilities.

The need for ensuring reasonable returns on investments in irrigation and power projects, transport undertakings industrial and commercial enterprises and the like.

In addition to above, the Seventh Finance Commission had to make an assessment of the non-plan capital gap of the states on an uniform and comparable basis for the five years ending with 1983-84. In the light of such an assessment, the Commission was expected to undertake a general review of the State's debt position with particular reference to the Central loans advanced to them and likely to be outstanding as at the end of 1978-79 and suggest appropriate measures to deal with non-plan capital gap, having regard *inter alia* to the overall non-plan gap, of the states, their relative position and the purpose for which the loans have been utilized, and the requirement of the Centre.

The terms of reference issued to the Eighth Finance Commission were also more or less same as those issued to the Seventh. The salient feature of the terms of reference issued to the Eighth Finance Commission was asked to examine the scope for raising revenue from the taxes and duties mentioned in Article 269 of the Constitution but not levied at present and for scope enhancing revenue from the duties mentioned in Article 268. Besides, the Commission had to review the policy and arrangements pertaining to the financing of relief expenditure by the natural calamities and suggested such modifications, as it considers appropriate such that the wasteful expenditure can be avoided.

The broad features that emerges through the outgoing review of terms of reference issued to the successive Finance Commissions may be summarized as follows:

The terms of reference issued for the successive Finance Commissions have been increasing continuously and such a process has, virtually, become a regular feature of the periodic awards; and

The successive Finance Commissions were asked to consider the problem of state's indebtedness to the Central Government.

It is significant to observe that there were frequent changes in the terms of reference issued to the successive Finance Commission and in fact there was lack of symmetry among them. For example, the Second and the Third Finance Commission were asked to consider tax performance of the States that were in need of assistance while the next Commission were advised to take into amount the scope for fiscal management and economy in expenditure. Even in case of expenditure, the issue that had to be considered by the Finance Commission had gone changed from time to time. For instance, the Fourth Finance Commission was asked to consider "the requirements of those states to meet the committed expenditure on maintenance and upkeep of Plan schemes completed during the Third Plan", while the Fifth Finance Commission was asked to have regard to "the requirements on revenue account of those states to meet the expenditure on administration, interest changes in respect of their debt, maintenance and upkeep of Plan schemes completed by the end of 1968-69, transfer of funds to local bodies and aided institutions and other committed expenditure." The list was further enhanced in case of the Sixth Finance Commission, which included "Provision for emoluments of government employees, teachers and local body employees as obtaining on a specified date as the Commission deem it proper in the light of the State's capacity and needs." Apparently, capacity in this context had to be taken as taxable capacity.

Next, the manner in which the terms of reference were formulated has introduced a dichotomy between devolution of tax-share and grants-in-aid. Indeed, tax-share and grants-in-aid are media of assistance. But it is not clear that why the successive Finance Commissions have assigned grants-in-aid to only those states that were in need of assistance after devolution of taxes of them.

Lastly, in India grants-in-aid under Article 275 of Constitution are provided on the basis of recommendations of the Finance Commission while those under Article 282 of Constitution are provided on the basis of recommendations of the Planning Commission. The terms of reference issued to the successive Finance Commissions have risen on controversy pertaining to the bifurcation of grants under Article 275 of Constitution as revenue grants and those under Article 282 of Constitution as capital grants (conditional grants). The grants-in-aid under Article 275 of Constitution, which is governed by the Finance Commissions, have been confined to current budget of the States only. It is, therefore, the grants under Article 275 of the Constitution have been provided mostly for meeting the non-plan budgetary gaps of the states on their current account whereas the grants under Article 282 of Constitution have been made mostly for meeting the plan needs of the State Governments on their capital account.

Thus, the increasing number of terms of reference issued by the Central Government has adversely affected the working and functioning past Finance Commissions. Here the significant question is that whether it is appropriate for the Central Government to issue any guidelines to an independent Constitutional body like the Finance Commission? The most appropriate method would have if the Centre had presented its views and suggestions to the

Finance Commissions through a separate memorandum and thus leaving the Finance Commissions free to determine their scope of recommendations.

## RECOMMENDATIONS OF THE NINTH FINANCE COMMISSION

The Ninth Finance Commission was appointed in June 1987 under the Chairmanship of Sri. N.K.P. Salve to make recommendations for the Six Year Period 1989-90 to 1990-95. The other Members of the Commission are Sri Justice Abdus Sattar Qureshi, Dr. Raja J. Chelliah and Sri Lal Thanhawala. The Ninth Finance Commission was required to submit to the first report covering the period of one year 1989-90 and the second report for the period 1990-95 making its recommendations on the terms of reference as set by the Presidential Order. Accordingly it gave its first award that its recommendations are in continuation to that of the last Commission.

### The Terms of Reference (TOR)

The terms of reference of the Ninth Finance Commission has aroused lot of apprehensions and criticism among the States men administrators and academics. Apart from the traditional terms of reference of tax sharing of Income Tax, and Union Excise Duties as well as the Article 275 Grants-in-Aid, the Ninth Finance Commission has been asked to suggest changes, if any, to the criteria of distribution among the states of the net proceeds of the additional Duties of Excise leviable under the Additional Duties of Excise Act, 1957 and the grants in lieu of the tax under the repealed Railway Passenger Fares Tax Act, 1957. The Ninth Finance Commission has also been asked to examine the feasibility of the merger of additional Duties of Excise in lieu of sales tax with basic Duties of Excise. This has been opposed by almost all the states that such a merger would amount to the encroachment of the Centre upon the States subjects. The Terms of Reference also asks the Ninth Finance Commission to make an assessment of the debt position of the States and to suggest such corrective measures as deemed necessary. The corrective measures would be with particular reference to investments made in infrastructure projects and to have linkage with improvement in financial and managerial efficiency. Another important terms of references was that the Ninth Finance Commission might review the policy and arrangements in regard to the financing of relief expenditure by the States affected by natural calamities and suggest modifications in the existing arrangements with a view of avoid wasteful expenditure. The Ninth Finance Commission was also asked to examine, *inter alia,* the feasibility of establishing a National Insurance fund to which the State Governments may contribute a percentage of their receipts. Several State Government have expressed their resentment for the establishment of such a Fund for which only State Governments have to contribute from their revenues. The President Order, for the first time, has asked the Ninth Finance Commission, while making its recommendations, (i) to adopt a normative approach in assessing the receipts and expenditures on the revenue account of the State and Centre and, in doing so, keep in view of the special problems of each state, if any, and the special requirements of the Centre such as defense, security, debt servicing and other committed expenditures or liabilities, (ii) to have due regard to the need for providing adequate incentives for better resource mobilization and financial discipline as well as closer linking of expenditure and revenue raising decisions; (iii) to take into account the need for speed, efficiency and effectiveness of Government functioning and of delivery systems for government programmes; and (iv) to keep in view the objective of not only balancing the receipts and expenditure on revenue account of both of the State and the Centre, but also generating surpluses for capital investment.

The terms of reference of the Ninth Finance Commission had made a departure from the earlier commission and contained certain novel features. For the first time, the Ninth Finance Commission has been asked to consider the total revenue account without making distinction between plan and non-plan, which has been appreciated by almost all the States. However, the States have stoutly objected the use of the world 'shall' in paragraph (4) of the

Presidential Order, which was construed almost as a directive from the Centre. The normative approach to be followed by the Ninth Finance Commission also led to criticism among the States as such an explicit reference was not made in the Terms of Reference earlier. Especially the States ruled by the non-Congress (I) party have taken serious objection to the normative approach and demanded the Centre to change the Terms of Reference in order to allay the apprehensions of the States. However, the controversy has been set aside by the Chairman who wrote to all the Chief Ministers dispelling their fears about the application of the normative approach and other sensitive items of the Terms of Reference.

**Approach of the Commission**

The terms of reference that requires the Ninth Finance Commission to adopt a normative approach has, not been, considered by the Ninth Finance Commission as a directive from the Centre. Moreover, the Ninth Finance Commission has regarded it as a statutory measure to induce fiscal management both at the Centre and the States. Therefore, the Ninth Finance Commission has adopted the normative approach. In this regard, the Ninth Finance Commission has rightly chosen to observe two principles: (a) maintenance of fiscal responsibility and uncompromising commitment to economy and efficiency, and (b) inter state equity. As a first step in the process of normative approach, the Commission has opted for a selective adoption for norms in the assessment of revenues and expenditure for the year 1989-90 because the adoption of a normative approach marks of radical departure and involves several conceptual and methodological issues. Moreover, the Ninth Finance Commission would not like to dislocate the planning process already initiated by the States in the last year of the Seventh Five Year Plan by following the normative approach strictly for the year 1989-90 itself. The Ninth Finance Commission used a Co-variance model with the help of pooled data in order to assess the tax of low income States. Though the Ninth Finance Commission has applied the regression method by using per capita SDP, proportion of non-agricultural SDP to total SDP and the Lorenz ratio of consumer expenditure as explanatory variables to estimate the tax potential of the States but depended on the traditional approach of the trend growth rate method in assessing the tax revenue to the Centre.

The Ninth Finance Commission simply adjusted the trend growth rate upward form 14.5 percent to 15 percent while assessing its revenue potential. Moreover, it has maintained the *status quo* for assessing the non-tax revenue of the States.

The selective adoption of the normative approach followed by the Ninth Finance Commission between the Centre and the State and also with references to tax and non-tax revenue of the State does not look to be rational. The Ninth Finance Commission followed the procedure adopted by the Eighth Finance Commission regarding the assessment of the revenue expenditure for the States allowing a very unrealistic amount of the revenue expenditure of the State, i.e., 6 percent for adjustment of inflation. The Ninth Finance Commission made some downward adjustments in regard to the re-assessment of the Central Government's expenditure. It estimated a revenue deficit of Rs. 7994 crores during 1989-90 after transferring Rs. 13,662.42 crores and Rs. 11,774 crores on non-plan and plan accounts respectively.

The Ninth Finance Commission has estimated the revenue component of the Plan expenditure. Accordingly it awarded plan grants 95 percent of the 30 percent grant component of the Central assistance. The expansion of the scope of Article 275(1) of Constitution made by the Ninth Finance Commission grants to the State recommended on this account is quite discouraging. However, this recommendation has, not been, accepted by the Government. The Ninth Finance Commission has also not taken into account the increased expenditure incurred already by the States on account of revision of pay scales and other allowances of the employees. The methodological flows and the arbitrariness in the moderation applied to the normative estimates of tax revenue of the States have put some states in an undue advantageous position. The trend estimates and the normative estimates of the year 1989-90 shows that states like Haryana, Punjab and Tamil Nadu, etc. got undue advantage in the assessment of tax potential.

**The First Award-Devolution**

As a measure to reduce imbalance, the Ninth Finance Commission recommended an estimated amount of Rs. 13,662.41 crores by way of shared taxes, additional Excise Duties, tax on railway passenger fares and non-plan grants, etc. In addition to this an amount of Rs. 2475.52 crores has been recommended as grants-in-aid for revenue plan of the States. But the increase in the proportion of the estimated transfers on the non-plan revenue account in the Central revenues is not much when compares with that of the previous year. Not much improvement could be found in the proportion even if the plans are added. But it is also necessary to look at the problem from the point of view of the possible larger budgetary deficits at the Centre.

Moreover, the fiscal transference recommended by the Ninth Finance Commission left several States with huge surpluses after adjusting the devolution. This stands as a testimony of the Commission's efforts in reducing the vertical fiscal imbalance.

The Ninth Finance Commission has not recommended any major changes in the schemes of devolution recommended by the Eight Finance Commission. Even though it made a tall claim that it has not followed the traditional 'gap filling' approach, but it also filled the revenue gaps by awarding grants-in-aid after adjusting the devolution. It retained the states' share in the yet yield from Income Tax at 85 per cent and Union Excise Duties at 45 per cent as recommended by the earlier Commissions. Of the 45 per cent from the Union Excise Duties, 40 per cent is to be distributed among all the States and the remaining 5 per cent is to be distributed among the deficit States. The Commission introduced by the poverty ratio criterion for *inter se* distribution of the net proceeds from Income Tax and Union Excise Duties set apart for States' purpose. The Ninth Finance Commission recommended that out of the 90 per cent and 40 per cent States' share fo:m Income Tax and Union Excise Duties respectively 12½ per cent be distributed on the basis of proportion of poor people in the State to the total number of poor people according to the estimates for 1983-84 made by the Planning Commission. After *inter se* distribution of the devolution, grants have been recommended to the Thirteen States, which have deficits. In addition to the revenue gap grants, an amount of Rs. 171.67 crores has been recommended to for up gradation of standards of administration in 1989-90. A novel feature of grants-in-aid recommended by the Ninth Finance Commission recommended an amount of Rs. 537 crores for special problems like slum improvement, the law and order situation, elementary education, etc. The Ninth Finance Commission has continued the scheme of financing of relief expenditure and the amount of grant in lieu of Tax on Railway Passenger Fares, Additional Duties of Excise, debt relief as recommended by the Eighth Finance Commission with a view that whatever changes they would like to bring either in the amount of its *inter se* distribution could be brought in the final Report of the Commission.

Though it is not the first time that a Finance Commission addressed itself to the special purposes or problems faced by the States while using Article 275(1) of the Constitution in awarding grants-in-aid, the grants-in-aid recommended by the Ninth Finance Commission has been subjected to vehement criticism. The good intention of the Ninth Finance Commission was to assist some States, which find a resource crunch in tackling certain important problems in understandable. But unfortunately, it has awarded considerable amount of grants-in-aid to some of the richer States. For instance, the commission recommended Rs. 50 crores each by way of one time special grant-in-aid to the Government of Maharashtra and West Bengal for slum clearance, iron mental improvement of slums and provision of basic amenities in the cities of Bombay and Calcutta. Similarly, grants have been given to State like Punjab, Haryana, Himachlal Pradesh and West Bengal to control the terrorist and separatist activities. It is afraid that it may become a bad precedent in the fiscal federalism in future. Moreover, heavy amount of grants-in-aid have been given to some States with reference to some special though the basic philosophy of awarding such grants cannot be objected the choice of the special problems as well as the selection of the grantee states may be questionable. For instance, Jammu and

Kashmir has been awarded grant-in-aid under this head for restoration of Dal Lake. This generally gives an impression that the Commission could not find a better purpose and a serious problem than this.

Under the Ninth Finance Commission award the richer states of Maharashtra, Gujarat, Haryana and West Bengal bagged the lion's share resulting in a high degree of inequity. This is evident from the fact that relatively backward States like Orissa, Kerela and Karnataka fared better under the Eight Finance Commission than under the Ninth Finance Commission's award period. This fact is further confirmed when an analysis of the budgetary surpluses after devolution of the States is made. The increase in the coefficient of variation between the Eight Finance Commission and Ninth Finance Commission would suggest a worsening of the inequalities in the distribution of the after devolution surpluses. However, it cannot be concluded that the devolution does not have any equalizing impact, but the progressiveness, which has been achieved under the Eighth Finance Commission, has not been continued under the Ninth Finance Commission's first award.

One of the important reasons for the less progressively in the total transfers as well as in the devolution may be attributed to the distribution formula of the shared taxes. Because of the poverty ratio criterion, the share in the devolution of several advanced states like Maharashtra and West Bengal has increased while that of the backward State like Bihar, Utter Pradesh, Kerala and Assam has decreased. The Ninth Finance Commission is also not unaware about the limitations and the serious implications of the use backwardness but they cannot be used as a factor in any criteria of distribution of federal funds as long as reliable and comparable data for all the States are available. Therefore, serious objections were raised regarding the use of this factor in the formula.

Another important factor that led to less progressively in the total devolution may be the award of grants for special problems. The proportion of grants-in-aid in the total devolution has gone up from 6.7 percent under the Eighth Finance Commission to 10.1 percent by the Ninth Finance

Commission. But the huge amount of grants for special problems given to certain advanced States seems to have upset the efforts of the Ninth Finance Commission in applying the much "enunciated principles" of grants-in-aid. The new dimension given to Article 275(1) of the Constitution by the Ninth Finance Commission needs to be upheld but care should be taken to see that the grants-in-aid reach the most needy and deserving States. It would be appreciated that the Commission recommended social and administrative services by making an assessment of need without making the distinction between grants for administration and grants for special problem.

### The Final Award

The second, i.e., the Final report of the Ninth Finance Commission were submitted to the President of India on December 18, 1989. The Report was placed in the Lok Sabha along with memorandum of action of the Commission have not caused, any flutter among the academics administrators politicians, etc. as it was the case with the Terms of Reference (TOR) of the Commission. However, the Commission itself has claimed that it has made several departures in its approach as well as in its recommendations. Therefore, an attempt is made to analyze the recommendations critically and to examine whether or not, the cherished objectives of vertical and horizontal equity has been achieved by the Ninth Finance Commission.

### Approach of the Ninth Finance Commission

The Ninth Finance Commission in its approach for the award for the period 1990-95 has kept mainly two things in view, firstly, a fair appointment of revenue resources between the Centre and the States. Secondly, the fiscal transference should serve the fiscal autonomy of the states and promote such things as fiscal prudence, tax effort, growth impulses and interstate equity, etc. The Ninth Finance Commission has made a normative assessment of the States determining the volume of federal transfers. On the basis of an approach which the Ninth Finance Commission itself has preferred to call as a modified representative tax system. Tax capacity of different States has been estimated for a base year and then projected to the year 1989-90. For estimating non-tax revenues, actual have been used in the case of fees and user charges while normative rates of return have been used in the case of dividends and interest received by the Government. The Ninth Finance Commission adopted a different procedure for different kinds of expenditure needs, for instance, the expenditure needs of the general services have been defined ad the justifiable costs of providing an average standard of services. With regard to the social and economic services, expenditure needs are calculated on the basis of an average justifiable costs with due allowance to the cost disability factors. Engineering norms have been applied in the case of maintenance of assets while estimated costs are the basis for expenditure needs such as elections. The Ninth Finance Commission has fixed the expenditures needs at a uniform level in the case of certain expenditures such as Social Welfare Schemes. On the basis of its partial normative assessment the Ninth Finance Commission as estimated the tax revenues of the states, as a whole would increase at the rate of 11.5 percent per annum in nominal terms while that of the Centre at 12.8 percent per annum on the basic assumption that the price rise would be 5 percent per annum. With a view to phasing out the revenue deficits during the period of recommendations the Ninth Finance Commission has postulated and annual average increase of 7 percent in non-plan revenue surplus/deficit of the 14 major States, it has made some adjustments in the normative estimates of tax revenue and non-plan expenditure comparing with that of the conventional or trend estimates. The Ninth Finance Commission has recommended non-plan deficit grants under Article 275 of the Constitution of India to the full extent of the deficit of the states, which have a net non-plan revenue deficit after the adjustment of the proceeds from devolution of taxes and duties.

The Ninth Finance Commission has assumed that the minimum total plan revenue expenditure of the 14 non-specials Category State would be Rs. 40,000 crores during the period 1990-95. Then the minimum per capita plan revenue expenditure has been estimated for each of the 14 major

TABLE 2

**Net Non-Plan Revenue Surplus (+)/Deficit (-) and Grants-in-aid of States: 1990-95**

(Rs. Crores)

| Sl. No. | States | Net Non-Plan Revenue Position without Devolution of Taxes and Duties | Net Non-Plan Revenue Surplus After Devolution of Taxes and Duties | Net Non-Plan Revenue Deficit After Devolution of Taxes and Duties | Plan Deficit | Total Grants-in-Aid* |
|---|---|---|---|---|---|---|
| | | 1 | 2 | 3 | 4 | 5 |
| 1. | Andhra Pradesh | (-)22886.25 | 4289.22 | - | 341.25 | 341.25 |
| 2. | Arunachal Pradesh | (-) 827.38 | - | 302.79 | - | 302.79 |
| 3. | Assam | (-) 35.29 | - | 560.32 | 313.91 | 874.23 |
| 4. | Bihar | (-)7095.38 | 2575.15 | - | 1374.27 | 1374.27 |
| 5. | Goa | (-) 505.12 | - | 166.58 | - | 166.58 |
| 6. | Gujarat | (+)563.26 | 3957.94 | - | - | - |
| 7. | Haryana | (+)1374.00 | 2505.06 | - | - | - |
| 8. | Himachal Pradesh | (-)1792.52 | - | 523.09 | - | 523.09 |
| 9. | Jammu and Kashmir | (-)3300.44 | - | 1083.12 | 13.30 | 1096.42 |
| 10. | Karnataka | (+)708.77 | 4670.79 | - | - | - |
| 11. | Kerala | (-)2916.81 | 2.29 | - | 412.54 | 412.54 |
| 12. | Madhya Pradesh | (-)5306.50 | 1227.98 | - | 1047.18 | 1047.18 |
| 13. | Maharashtra | (+)5489.20 | 11525.56 | - | - | - |

(Contd.)

TABLE 2 (*Contd.*)

| | 1 | 2 | 3 | 4 | 5 |
|---|---|---|---|---|---|
| 14. Manipur | (-)1081.72 | - | 371.65 | - | 371.65 |
| 15. Meghalaya | (-)814.39 | - | 256.18 | - | 256.18 |
| 16. Mizoram | (-)1070.26 | - | 379.79 | - | 379.79 |
| 17. Nagaland | (-)1240.55 | - | 458.67 | - | 458.67 |
| 18. Orissa | (-)4792.29 | - | 528.48 | 554.50 | 1082.98 |
| 19. Punjab | (-)114.77 | 1400.45 | - | 53.91 | 53.91 |
| 20. Rajasthan | (-)5100.22 | - | 486.39 | 960.40 | 1446.79 |
| 21. Sikkim | (-)240.93 | - | 84.68 | - | 84.68 |
| 22. Tamil Nadu | (-)1712.12 | 4296.04 | - | 43.79 | 43.79 |
| 23. Tripura | (-)1422.67 | - | 466.01 | - | 466.01 |
| 24. Uttar Pradesh | (-)14225.14 | - | 348.60 | 2886.50 | 3235.10 |
| 25. West Bengal | (-)4678.98 | 1581.77 | - | 998.65 | 998.65 |
| Total | (-)64001.33<br>(+)8135.23 | 38032.25 | 6016.35 | 9000.83 | 15017.18 |

*Note*: Surplus/Deficit of each year has been netted to arrive at the five-year position.
" Excluding grant for relief expenditure.

*Source*: Report of the Ninth Finance Commission (1989), Govt. of India, New Delhi..

TABLE 3

**Total Transfers to State: 1990-95**

(Rs. Crores)

| Sl. No. | States | Income Tax | Basic Excise Duties | Additional Duties of Excise | Tax on Railway Passenger Fares | Total |
|---|---|---|---|---|---|---|
| | | 1 | 2 | 3 | 4 | 5 |
| 1. | Andhra Pradesh | 1717.52 | 3976.81 | 824.99 | 53.15 | 6575.47 |
| 2. | Arunachal Pradesh | 15.28 | 497.67 | 11.50 | 0.05 | 524.59 |
| 3. | Assam | 550.54 | 2113.07 | 294.66 | 11.30 | 2969.57 |
| 4. | Bihar | 2598.47 | 6116.65 | 893.41 | 62.00 | 9670.53 |
| 5. | Goa | 23.02 | 290.01 | 24.51 | 1.00 | 338.54 |
| 6. | Gujarat | 552.09 | 1765.43 | 634.31 | 42.85 | 3394.68 |
| 7. | Haryana | 260.31 | 609.56 | 248.89 | 12.30 | 1131.06 |
| 8. | Himachal Pradesh | 124.50 | 1077.48 | 66.70 | 0.75 | 1269.43 |
| 9. | Jammu and Kashmir | 145.43 | 1968.20 | 99.79 | 3.90 | 2217.32 |
| 10. | Karnataka | 1031.18 | 2276.27 | 330.02 | 24.55 | 3962.02 |
| 11. | Kerala | 780.29 | 1712.19 | 399.92 | 26.56 | 2919.10 |
| 12. | Madhya Pradesh | 1712.71 | 4006.76 | 769.56 | 48.45 | 6534.48 |
| 13. | Maharashtra | 1713.79 | 2875.85 | 1276.79 | 169.75 | 6036.36 |

(Contd.)

TABLE 3 *(Contd.)*

| | *1* | 2 | 3 | *4* | 5 |
|---|---|---|---|---|---|
| 14. Manipur | 35.78 | 651.31 | 22.88 | 0.10 | 710.07 |
| 15. Meghalaya | 43.52 | 493.98 | 20.41 | 0.30 | 558.21 |
| 16. Mizoram | 15.28 | 614.88 | 7031 | - | 337.47 |
| 17. Nagaland | 20.09 | 747.65 | 12.89 | 1.25 | 781.88 |
| 18. Orissa | 905.21 | 2972.03 | 374.47 | 12.10 | 4263.81 |
| 19. Punjab | 356.98 | 755.43 | 379.51 | 23.30 | 1515.22 |
| 20. Rajasthan | 1011.93 | 3063.87 | 503.68 | 34.35 | 4613.83 |
| 21. Sikkim | 6.28 | 144.34 | 5.58 | 0.05 | 156.25 |
| 22. Tamil Nadu | 1659.56 | 3538.09 | 758.81 | 51.70 | 6008.16 |
| 23. Tripura | 63.40 | 863.09 | 29.87 | 0.30 | 956.66 |
| 24. Uttar Pradesh | 3512.68 | 8673.61 | 1574.45 | 155.80 | 13876.54 |
| 25. West Bengal | 1688.98 | 3660.68 | 877.09 | 54.00 | 6260.75 |
| Total | 20925.00 | 5565.00 | 10742.00 | 750.00 | 87882.00 |

*Source*: Report of the Ninth Finance Commission (1989), Govt. of India, New Delhi..

| Sl. No. | States | GRANT-IN-AID Non-Plan Deficit | Plan Deficit | Total | Total (Col. 5+8) | Grants Towards Meeting Relief Expenditure | Total Transfer (Col. 9+10) |
|---|---|---|---|---|---|---|---|
| | | 6 | 7 | 8 | 9 | 10 | 11 |
| 1. | Andhra Pradesh | - | 341.25 | 341.25 | 6916.72 | 322.05 | 7239.22 |
| 2. | Arunachal Pradesh | 302.79 | - | 302.79 | 827.38 | 7.50 | 834.88 |
| 3. | Assam | 650.32 | 313.91 | 874.23 | 3834.80 | 112.50 | 2956.30 |
| 4. | Bihar | - | 1374.27 | 1374.27 | 11044.80 | 131.25 | 11176.50 |
| 5. | Goa | 166.58 | - | 166.58 | 505.12 | 3.75 | 508.87 |
| 6. | Gujarat | - | - | - | 3394.68 | 318.75 | 3713.47 |
| 7. | Haryana | - | - | - | 1131.06 | 63.75 | 1194.81 |
| 8. | Himachal Pradesh | 523.09 | - | 523.09 | 1792.52 | 67.50 | 186.02 |
| 9. | Jammu and Kashmir | 1083.12 | 13.30 | 1096.42 | 3313.74 | 45.00 | 3358.74 |
| 10. | Karnataka | - | - | - | 2962.02 | 101.25 | 4063.27 |
| 11. | Kerala | - | 412.54 | 412.54 | 3331.64 | 116.25 | 3447.89 |
| 12. | Madhya Pradesh | - | 1047.81 | 1047.81 | 7582.29 | 261.00** | 7843.29 |
| 13. | Maharashtra | - | - | - | 6036.36 | 165.00 | 6201.36 |
| 14. | Manipur | 371.65 | - | 371.65 | 1081.72 | 3.75 | 285.47 |
| 15. | Meghalaya | 256.18 | - | 256.18 | 814.39 | 7.50 | 821.89 |

*(Contd.)*

TABLE 3 *(Contd.)*

| | 6 | 7 | 8 | 9 | 10 | 11 |
|---|---|---|---|---|---|---|
| 16. Mizoram | 379.79 | - | 379.79 | 1017.26 | 3.75 | 1021.01 |
| 17. Nagaland | 458.67 | - | 458.67 | 1240.55 | 3.75 | 1021.01 |
| 18. Orissa | 528.48 | 554.50 | 1082.98 | 5346.49 | 776.25 | 5523.04 |
| 19. Punjab | - | 53.91 | 53.91 | 1569.13 | 105.00 | 1674.13 |
| 20. Rajasthan | 486.39 | 960.40 | 1446.79 | 6060.62 | 465.00 | 6525.62 |
| 21. Sikkim | 84.68 | - | 84.68 | 240.93 | 11.25 | 252.18 |
| 22. Tamil Nadu | - | 43.79 | 43.79 | 6051.95 | 146.25 | 6198.20 |
| 23. Tripura | 466.01 | - | 466.01 | 1422.67 | 11.25 | 1433.92 |
| 24. Uttar Pradesh | 348.60 | 2886.50 | 3235.10 | 17111.64 | 337.50 | 17449.14 |
| 25. West Bengal | - | 998.65 | 998.65 | 7259.40 | 150.00 | 7407.40 |
| Total | | | | | | |

*Includes Rs. 122.25 crores for Bhopal Gas Leak . Tragedy.

*Soruce*: Report of the Ninth Finance Commission, 1989. Govt. of India, New Delhi.

States of the total. Minimum Plan Expenditure of Rs. 40,000 crores. According to the Commission States are required to mobilize resources for their minimum plan needs (a) 40 percent (not more than) of their non-plan revenue surpluses, if they are having surpluses, (b) their respective share of plan grant under the Gadgil formula as applicable during the Seventh Plan period. The Ninth Finance Commission again assumed that the total amount of such plan grant for all the non-special category States would be Rs. 10,000 crores during 1990-95. Then the Commission has determined the plan deficit grant as 50 percent of the deficit that still remains after adjusting the amounts under (a) and (b) as stated above State's not non-plan surplus/deficit before and after tax devolution, net plan deficit and total amount of grants (excluding grants towards meeting relief expenditure).

**Scheme for Debt Relief**

Unlike the earlier Finance Commissions, the Ninth Finance Commission has been asked to assess the debt position of the States and to suggest corrective measures with particular reference to investment in infrastructure projects and improvements in their performance. After knowing the States' views the Ninth Finance Commission was on the view that rescheduling and write-off of the loans must be avoided in future. It felt that the terms of which the Centre lends funds to the State must be reasonable and equitable. The Ninth Finance Commission has given more thrust to make some changes in the terms and conditions of the Central loans rather than to provide short-term relief by way of writing-off and rescheduling of loans. The Ninth Finance Commission has recommended, a long-term measure to reduce states' indebtedness that the sates should be allowed to raise a greater portion of plan loans as additional market borrowings. Though this arrangement sounds good theoretically, but is not without problems that arise due to the differences in the loan raising capacity of the states. It has also recommended to change the maturity period of 20 years of the central loans to state plans loans advanced to States during the 5 years 1984-89 and outstanding as on 31 March 1990, on the basis of their financial and managerial efficiency of their investment in infrastructure projects. Regarding the external assistance to externally aided projects of the States, it has recommended that the entire assistance should be passed on to the State implementing those projects. It has sympathetically recommended that an amount of Rs. 91.62 crores be given to Madhya Pradesh in connection with the Bhopal Gas Leak Tragedy and some amount of Plan loans given to the newly constituted States of Arunachal Pradesh, Goa and Mizoram should be written-off. In all, the Ninth Finance Commission has recommended a total debt relief of Rs. 975.62 crores to different States during 1990-95 in respect of loans outstanding at the end of 1989-90. The Ninth Finance Commission estimated the debt relief during the period 1990-95 to be Rs. 2000 crores as a result of its recommendations including moratorium given to Punjab, revision of maturity periods, interest rates and other measures.

**Evaluations of the Recommendations**

As stated earlier, the fiscal imbalances are imbued in the constitutional division of powers and functions between the Centre and the States. The Ninth Finance Commission is supposed to aim its recommendations and also addresses itself to reduce the vertical fiscal imbalance by fiscal transference. Though there appears a substantial increase in the total fiscal transfers, no significant improvement could be found in the total transfers as a proportion of the Central Governments' revenue. The proportion of total transfers in the Centre's revenue during the period 1990-95 is estimated to be 22.74 per cent compared to 22.65 percent during 1985-90. The marginal increase in the proportion explains that the Ninth Finance Commissions' recommendations have not reduced the vertical fiscal imbalance substantially.

Horizontal equity assumes greater importance in the Indian federal fiscal structure. Any reduction of vertical fiscal imbalance without being followed by suitable a criterion of distribution of the fiscal resources among the states is likely to accentuate the existing inter-state inequalities. The Ninth Finance Commission made considerable efforts in evolving different criteria for equitable distribution of resources set apart for the States' purpose. As a result, the differences in the per capita non-Plan revenue surpluses of the non-special category States are comparatively less than that of the earlier Finance Commissions. In order to evaluate the equity aspect of the Ninth Finance Commission recommendations, regression analysis of the linear model is employed. Per Capita SDP of 1982-85 average is taken as the independent variable and total per capita transfers and tax share as dependent variables separately for the period covered by the Ninth Finance Commission. Per capita income has been taken as a sole indicator of the level of development of the States. The results of the regression analysis are presented in Table 4.

TABLE 4

**Regression Result of Per Capita Tax Shares and Total Devolution—Ninth Finance Commission**

| *Eq. No.* | *Dependent Variable* | *Constant a* | *B* | $R^2$ | *F-Value* |
|---|---|---|---|---|---|
| 1 | Per Capita Tax Share | 10.5991 | -0.48587* (5.16477) | 0.66386* | 26.6749 |
| 2 | Per Capita Total Devolution | 12.0595 | -0.65824* (4.74953) | 0.62382* | 22.5580 |

*Notes*: 1. Figures in parenthesis show T-value.
2. *Significant at 1% level.

*Source*: The ninth Finance Commission Report (1989) Govt. of India, New Delhi.

As may be seen from the Table above coefficients of pre capita income are statistically significant at 1 percent level and have negative sings. It indicates that the resource transfer recommended by the Ninth Finance Commission is equitable. However, it may de due to the criteria followed by the Ninth Finance Commission for the *inter se* distribution of the net proceeds through shares taxes. This calls for a positive change in the criteria of distribution of shared taxes by the Tenth Finance Commission. Award of Plan grants for revenue purposes is an important and remarkable step in the history of the Indian Finance Commission, but the Ninth Finance Commission had to work out the total and each State's share of the Plan grants subject to a number of constraints and with only under certain assumptions. A further improvement in this direction is to be made by the Tenth Finance Commission.

Another important and appreciable effort of the Ninth Finance Commission is its aim of phasing out the revenue deficit of the Centre. But in no single year so far during the period 1990-95, the revenue deficit of the Centre was confined to the limits as fixed by the Ninth Finance Commission. This explains that the Ninth Finance Commission's assessment of revenue and expenditure is base on unrealistic assumptions and projections. For instance, while assessing the revenue expenditure of the States, it has assumed unrealistically a 5 percent growth in prices. The Ninth Finance Commission's recommendations regarding the calamity relief expenditure has enhanced the fiscal autonomy and freedom of action of the States while the recommendations with regard to debt relief have been made in the right direction and with a long-term perspective to reduce States' indebtedness. Even though the Ninth Finance Commission has avoided conveniently putting its fingers into certain issues that have become irritants in the Centre-State financial relations like the inclusion of Corporation Tax in the divisible pool, abolition of surcharge on Income Tax, a higher percentage of Market Borrowings, treating the Small Savings Loans as loans in perpetuity and overdrafts, etc., it has carved out a place for itself by making several innovative efforts in its assessment and recommendations.

## TENTH FINANCE COMMISSION'S RECOMMENDATIONS

The Tenth Finance Commission was constituted in 1992 by the President of India under the chairmanship of Sri K.C. Pant. The other members of the commission are Sri B.P.R. Vithal and Sri M.C. Gupta and Sri. Arun Sinha as member-secretary the commission has submitted its report in 1994 of financial resource sharing between centre and state for the five year period 1995-2000.

In addition to the major recommendation regarding devolution of resources, the Tenth Finance Commission has also made some general observations regarding the resource positions of the Central and State Governments. In what follows, the Twelfth Finance Commission examines some of these observations without expressing any critical comments thereon. Needless to say, these observations have a special significance, as they have been made by a constitutionally appointed authority on the subject.

The Tenth Finance Commission Report observes that the change in the fiscal regime in 1982-83 from revenue surplus to revenue deficit has meant that it was earlier a non-debt creating source of financing has become a source of rising internal indebtedness. Earlier, while the revenue receipts used to cover a part of the capital expenditure, now an increasing part of the capital receipts are used to finance revenue expenditure. The consequent build up of public debt and the interest burden, which is now the largest and fastest growing item of expenditure, further fuelled the growth of revenue expenditure. This led to a spiral of growing deficits, rising debt, escalating interest costs and further expansion of deficit.

The Report points out that it is a matter of serious concern that investments in irrigation, power and road transport, which constitute the bulk to State Government's investment do not yield enough returns. A shortsighted perception of political necessity has persuaded States, to fix user charges in irrigation and power at levels, which do not cover, even the operation and maintenance expenditure in irrigation and generate meager surpluses, if at all in power. Several State Electricity Boards are over-staffed and run at substantial losses. The artificially depressed under charges result in criminal waste of water and electricity—both very scare resources. In this connection, it is observed that no society can move forward if its citizens are encouraged to believe that costs of services do not have to be borne by those who benefit from them especially when capacity to pay is not a constraint. Other general subsidies need to be phased out as quickly as possible, and those on food better targeted.

Expenditure control should involved questioning every

item of expenditure every year, rather than giving automatic approvals on the basis of continuity if schemes or projects. Over the years, employment in government has grown manifold. There is scope for Central and State Governments to shed many activities and absorb the Staff rendered surplus in other activities and to encourage them to avail of retirement with attractive benefits. Viable methods of reducing the strength of government employment must be explored, otherwise economic reforms may lose its way, in bureaucratic maze, observes the Commission.

The Report is critical of the continued persistence of a large number of Centrally Sponsored Schemes. Although, a Committee set-up by the National Development Council has closed a number of them down following a review, these were relatively small, representing an annual provision of only about Rs. 200 crores, as against a total for all Centrally Sponsored Schemes of about Rs. 14,000 crores. Central interaction through such schemes is presumably acceptable to the States because they carry with them additional resources. The continuance of these schemes makes for large and sprawling bureaucracies at the Centre, dealing with, are primarily States subjects, e.g. agriculture, rural development, education and public health.

The Twelfth Finance Commission Report also makes observations on the changing role of the Planning Commission in the wake of the economic reforms underway. It says that the greater market orientation of the economy and the enhanced role for private and foreign investment will put additional responsibility on the public sector to strength the economic and social infrastructure and reinforce the legislative, legal and judicial process which make for good governance.

In particular, public outlays on education and health will need to be increased substantially. This means a greater responsibility for State Governments whose resource base will have to be correspondingly augmented. In this connection, it is recommended that the present artificial distinction between plan and non-plan expenditures, which runs across revenue and capital.

The Report also recommends that a full-fledged Finance

Commission Division appropriately staffed and with adequate technical expertise, be created at the earlier under a senior officer and made to function with the Ministry of Finance. The Division should be actively associated with the annual plan exercises of the Planning Commission so that the maintenance of assets already created does not suffer from either lack of attention or lack of resource allocation because of the anxiety of the States to have progressively larger plan.

**Result of Statistical Analysis**

1. The coefficient of correlation between per capita transfers to Stats as laid down by the Ninth and Tenth Finance Commission was 0.978 thus indicating that the pattern of resource devolution evolved by the Tenth Finance Commission is not significantly different from that evolved by the Ninth Finance Commission. This fact is further confirmed by the total transfers as per the Ninth and Tenth Finance Commissions' recommendation which was as high as 0.992.
2. The total transfer of resources to the States is highly correlated with the States SDP during both the periods. This was 0.819 as per the Ninth Finance Commission's recommendations.
3. The rank correlation coefficient between economic backwardness of States (as given by lower levels of per capita SDP) and per capita transfers was low in both periods. This was only 0.150 during the Ninth Finance Commission period. The low correlations between economic backwardness of States and per capita, which have comparatively high per capita SDP, also enjoy comparatively higher levels of per capita transfers.

## ELEVENTH FINANCE COMMISSION'S RECOMMENDATIONS

The President K.R. Narayanan constituted the Eleventh Finance Commission on 3rd July 1998, under the

TABLE 5

**Ninth Finance Commission's Transfers**

| *State* | *Total Transfer (1990-95) (Rs. Crores)* | *Per Capita Transfers (Rupees)* | *% of Share of States in Total Transfers* |
|---|---|---|---|
| Andhra Pradesh | 7239.22 | 1088 | 6.827 |
| Arunachal Pradesh | 834.88 | 9663 | 0.787 |
| Assam | 3956.6 | 1765 | 3.731 |
| Bihar | 11176.05 | 1294 | 10.540 |
| Goa | 508.87 | 4349 | 0.480 |
| Gujarat | 3713.43 | 899 | 3.502 |
| Haryana | 1194.81 | 726 | 1.127 |
| Himachal Pradesh | 1860.20 | 3597 | 1.754 |
| Jammu and Kashmir | 3358.74 | 4351 | 3.168 |
| Karnataka | 4063.27 | 903 | 3.832 |
| Kerala | 3347.89 | 1151 | 3.157 |
| Madhya Pradesh | 7843.29 | 1185 | 7.397 |
| Maharashtra | 6201.36 | 786 | 5.848 |
| Manipur | 1085.47 | 5909 | 1.024 |
| Meghalaya | 821.89 | 4630 | 0.775 |
| Mizoram | 1021.01 | 14797 | 0.963 |
| Nagaland | 1244.30 | 10283 | 1.173 |
| Orissa | 5523.04 | 1744 | 5.209 |
| Punjab | 1674.13 | 825 | 1.579 |
| Rajasthan | 6525.62 | 1481 | 6.154 |
| Sikkim | 252.18 | 6196 | 0.238 |
| Tamil Nadu | 6198.20 | 1110 | 5.845 |
| Tripura | 1433.92 | 5201 | 1.352 |
| Uttar Pradesh | 17449.14 | 1254 | 16.456 |
| West Bengal | 7409.40 | 1088 | 6.988 |

*Source:* The Twelfth Finance Commission Report, 2004, Govt. of India, New Delhi.

Chairmanship of Shri A.M. Khusro. The other members of the Commission are N.C. Jain, J.C. Jatil, Amarish Bagchi and T.N. Shrivastava as secretary. The Commission has submitted its report on financial resource sharing between the Centre and State in 2000 for the Five year period 2000-05.

TABLE 6

**Tenth Finance Commission's Transfers**

| *State* | *Total Transfer (1990-95) (Rs. Crores)* | *Per Capita Transfers (Rupees)* | *% of Share of States in Total Transfers* |
|---|---|---|---|
| Andhra Pradesh | 18081.54 | 2719 | 7.978 |
| Arunachal Pradesh | 1768.36 | 20467 | 0.780 |
| Assam | 8328.05 | 3716 | 3.675 |
| Bihar | 24665.56 | 2856 | 10833 |
| Goa | 622.25 | 5318 | 0.271 |
| Gujarat | 8875.59 | 2149 | 3.916 |
| Haryana | 2793.11 | 1696 | 1.232 |
| Himachal Pradesh | 4761.66 | 9208 | 2.101 |
| Jammu and Kashmir | 7322.08 | 9486 | 3.231 |
| Karnataka | 10520.83 | 2339 | 4.642 |
| Kerala | 7721.81 | 2654 | 3.404 |
| Madhya Pradesh | 16093.97 | 2432 | 7.101 |
| Maharashtra | 13709.08 | 1737 | 6.049 |
| Manipur | 2136.62 | 11631 | 0.943 |
| Meghalaya | 1888.85 | 10641 | 0.833 |
| Mizoram | 1802.01 | 26116 | 0.795 |
| Nagaland | 2993.04 | 23083 | 1.232 |
| Orissa | 9706.55 | 3066 | 4.283 |
| Punjab | 3589.47 | 1777 | 1.584 |
| Rajasthan | 11400.87 | 2587 | 5.030 |
| Sikkim | 698.89 | 17172 | 0.308 |
| Tamil Nadu | 13360.57 | 2392 | 5.895 |
| Tripura | 2873.21 | 10422 | 1.268 |
| Uttar Pradesh | 36158.91 | 2599 | 15.954 |
| West Bengal | 14980.42 | 2200 | 6.610 |

*Source*: The Twelfth Finance Commission Report, 2004, Govt. of India, New Delhi.

**Major Recommendations of EFC (2000-2005)**

1. In the overall scheme of the transfer, 37.5 percent of the gross revenue receipts of the Centre is suggested to be transferred to the States.
2. In assessing the revenue gaps of the States a normative approach has been followed as far as possible.

3. The tax base of the States and the local bodies needs to be wide read by better administration of property taxes and other taxes.
4. The total share of the States in net proceeds of shareable Union taxes and duties would be 29.5 percent.
5. The Commission has recommended grants totaling Rs. 4,972.93 crores towards upgradation of standards of administration and special problem grants to States.
6. The criteria and relative weight for determining inter-se share of States are population (10%), distance (62.5%), area (7.5%), index of infrastructure and fiscal discipline (7.5%).
7. The Commission has recommended a total grant of Rs. 1,600 crores for the Panchayats and Rs. 400 crores for the municipalities for each of five years starting from the financial year 2000-01.

**Twelth Finance Commission and Recommendations**

The president of India Dr. A.P.J. Abul Kalam has set-up the Twelfth Finance Commission under the chairmanship of Dr. C. Rangrajan in 2003. The other members of the commission are Sri. T.R. Prasad and Prof. D.K. Srivastava. Sri Som Pal has become part time member upto 15/5/2004 and other part time member Dr. Shankar N. Acharya w.e.f. 1/7/2004. Dr. G.C. Srivastava was secretary was upto 30/6/2003 and there after he became member secretary. The commission has submitted its report in Nov. 2004 on financial resources searing between centre and states for the period 2005-10 along with Action Taken Report (ATR).

The Twelfth Finance Commission has observed that the report of the Eleventh Finance Commission has been welcomed in almost all circles. The Twelfth Finance Commission hopes that the Centre and the States would be able to plan their revenue and expenditure programmes in a better way under the new arrangement.

This section deals with recommendation of Twelfth Finance Commission (TFC) in relation to improve the indebtedness of states. The major tasks of the finance commission are to recommend:

(i) The distribution of proceeds from central taxes between the centre and states and among the states *inter se;*

(ii) Grants-in-aid to be given to the states out of the Consolidated Fund of India for the states, in need of assistance under Article 275; of the Constitution of India.

(iii) Measures needed to augment the consolidated fund of the states to supplement the resources of urban and rural local bodies on the basis of recommendations made by the State Finance Commissions.

(iv) Any other matter referred to the Commission in the interest of sound finance. Under (iv) a number of directives have been given to every Commission, which have often raised controversies.

The Terms of Reference (TOR) of the Eleventh Finance Commission (EFC) went a step further and specified that the Commission should review the state finances of the centre and states and recommend measures for restructuring public finances so as to "restore budgetary balance and maintain macroeconomic stability". The TOR of the Twelfth Finance Commission stipulates that the Commission should review the finances of the centre and states and suggest a plan by which the governments collectively and severally, may bring about restructuring of public finances restoring budgetary balance, achieving macroeconomic stability and debt reduction along with equitable growth.

There was some improvement in fiscal balance until mid 1990s in terms of revenue, primary and fiscal deficits but the subsequent period has seen worsening fiscal imbalance in terms of quantity and even more in quality.

The Fiscal Responsibility and Budget Management Act (FRBM Act) set the targets for the revenue deficit. GDP ratio to be reduced to zero and fiscal deficit to be brought down to 3 percent to GDP by 2008-09. The TFC has reiterated the core strategy indicated in FRBM Act. of reducing public disserving and increasing public investment in infrastructure. According to the Twelfth Finance Commission's plan for restructuring the overall saving rate should be increased from 24 percent of GDP in 2004-05 to 26 percent by 2009-10 and investment rate should be increased from 24.5 percent to 27.5 percent during the same period.

The aggregate fiscal deficit as a ratio of GDP should be brought down from 8.9 percent to 6 percent by 2009-10 and revenue deficit should be eliminated completely from the level of 4.5 percent. During the period, capital expenditure should be increased from 5.6 percent of GDP to 6.6 percent.

The TFC recommends a number of general suggestions: tax administration should be improved, user charges should be levied on a variety of services and this should be determined by an autonomous regulatory body, subsidies should be contained, salary expenditures as a percentage of GDP should be rolled back to the level that prevailed in 1996-97. The management of public expenditures should be guided by economy, efficiency and effectiveness of expenditures so as to focus on outcomes rather than expenditures, indeed such statements can be found in all the Finance Commission Reports, since the Ninth. The Twelfth Finance Commission also recommends that the States should implement Value Added Tax (VAT) in place of their sales tax systems.

There are two separate sets of conditionality for the interest concessions and the debt write-off. The interest rate reduction to 7.5 percent requires the enacted of FRBMA Act.

### The Debt Writes-offs

A very high interest on compulsory borrowings from centre as a component of plan assistance had grossly distorted the fiscal situation of states. The share of debt owed to the centre in the total debt stock for the major states was 13.64 percent as on March 31, 2005. It was 10.17 percent for the special category states; because of the lower stipulated share of compulsory borrowing in total plan assistance from the centre for special category states.

Although the write-off constitute only 4.3 percent of the

total estimated transfer recommended by the TFC for the five-year period and given that this is a small proportion, it is not clear whether the states will respond to the inventive. It can be seen that:

(i) The relatively better-off states receive larger benefits from the debt write-off scheme,
(ii) These states have relatively lower revenue deficits.

It means that the states with larger deficits will gain less in terms of debt write-off in relation to the overall transfers they receive. The states have to show lower revenue deficits in the next five years while preparing the budgets. Therefore many states would not be in a position to provide adequate power sector subsidies and losses of the public enterprise to show lower revenue deficits.

It can be said that the structure of incentives implicit in the debt write-off plan is appropriate and the scheme is designed in a better manner than the EFC. The Finance Commissions have two instruments of transfers, i.e. tax devolution and grants. The successive Finance Commissions have tried to contain the proportion of resources transferred to state by limiting the tax devolution and increasing the grant proportion of the transfers, because the fiscal imbalances at the centre increased. The Eleventh Finance Commission increased the grant proportion form 8.96 percent to 13.47 percent and the Twelfth Finance Commission recommended that the states be expected to receive 18.27 percent by way of grants.

The states prefer tax devolution to grants because of its responsiveness to increases in prices and incomes. As per the Twelfth Finance Commission almost 20 percent of transfers will be in absolute amounts and will not respond to changes in prices, this is likely to put greater pressure on state finances.

Another important suggestion made by the Twelfth Finance Commission is that the central government should stop giving loans to the states and ask them to borrow from the market. The states should be treated as autonomous units and be asked to determine for themselves the levels of revenues and expenditure. The Twelfth Finance Commission has made significant recommendations on debt relief for states.

On an average, the cost of funds for the states was about 8 per cent in the late 1980s. This has increased to 12 per cent by the mid-1990's. Even with this high interest rates, the states did not experience any deterioration in their finances until 1996-97. The fiscal situation of the states deteriorated from 1997-98. This was due to the following reasons:

(i) Implementation of the Fifth Pay Commission report by the States for their employees. As a result, salary expenditure per employee shot up from Rs. 47,398 in 1995-96 to Rs. 75,364 in 1999-2000 or, i.e. by 60 percent (TFC Report, p. 486).

(ii) In the case of more developed or fast growing states such as Maharashtra, Gujarat, Karnataka and Tamil Nadu, the tax revenue losses on account of sales tax exemptions or concessions offered to new industries have been substantial. The total losses to all states together on account of such tax concessions could be of Rs. 20,000 crores per annum.

(iii) State finances have been affected by the deceleration in the growth of central tax revenues since 1997-98 via devolution. The negative impact was on poorer states whose dependence on devolution was heavier.

(iv) The states by and large, tried to overcome their deteriorating fiscal situation by resorting to increased borrowings and diverting a large share of their borrow funds for meeting current expenditure rather than capital expenditure. As a result, revenue of 1990's to over 60 percent by the end of the decade.

(v) When all states are taken together, the share of salaries has been declining during the last few years; the shares of interest and pension have been steadily increasing. The pension liability is likely to increase in the near future. The employees who have joined their services in 1970's will retire during the next five to ten years.

The combined outstanding direct debt of the states has crossed Rs. 9,00,000 crores at the end of March 2005. In addition to this, the combined outstanding contingent liabilities of the states is about Rs. 2,00,000 crores. These are mostly borrowings by the State Public Enterprises (SPE) with state guarantees.

**Composition of Outstanding Debt**

The total outstanding long-term debt of the State Governments doubled in each of the five-year periods, i.e. between 1995 to 2000, and 2000-05. The composition of the outstanding state debt has undergone significant changes over the past decades. Loans from the centre accounted for 63 percent of the outstandings in 1995. The share of market loans from banks, etc. was 17.1 percent and 1.9 percent respectively as internal debt. The remaining 18 percent were on account of provident funds, etc.

The share of central loans came down from 63 per cent to 52.4 per cent by the end of March 2000. The main reason for the reduction in the share of central loans was the creation of National Small Savings Funds on April 1, 1999. Small savings collections were treated as a part of the consolidated funds of the centre till March 1999 and the loans given to the states from these collections were treated as central loans to the states. The entire net collections of small savings from April 1, 1999 were deposited in the newly created public account of NSSF. Loans form NSSF to states accounted for 6.6 percent of the total outstanding at the end of March 2000.

Again the composition of the outstanding states debt has undergone significant structural changes between March 2000 and March 2005. The main reason for this has been the phenomenal growth in loans form NSSF. Earlier these collections were shared between the centre and states in the ratio of 20:80. From 2002-03 the entire net collections have been made available to the states. At the end of March 2005 loans from NSSF has become the single most important component of outstanding loans of the states, accounting for about 31 percent of total.

The centre has introduced the debt swap scheme from September 2002 for the state to enable to substitute their high cost loans by fresh low cost loans. Until March 2005, around Rs. 1,03,000 crores of State Governments debt was swapped under this scheme. However, the limited nature of the swap has limited the beneficial effects for the states. It has brought down the annual interest payments by around Rs. 4000 crores.

(i) A consolidation of all outstanding debt to the centre at the end of 2004-05 at an interest rate of 7.5 percent to be repaid in 20 years, and
(ii) A debt relief scheme linked to the achievement in reducing revenue deficits.

The benefits to states arising from consolidation, rescheduledment and internal rate reduction of central loans as recommended by the Twelfth Finance Commission are considerable. The pre consolidation repayment liability was of Rs. 44,128 crores and the post-consolidation repayment liability is of Rs. 32,200 crores of the states. In this, benefit of the states is of Rs. 12,000 crores. The pre-condition to avail this benefit is passage of fiscal responsibility legislation. By the time the Twelfth Finance Commission submitted its report, five states, namely, Karnataka, Kerala, Punjab, Tamil Nadu and Uttar Pradesh has passed the legislation. Later on five more states viz. Assam, Haryana, Maharashtra, Orissa and Rajasthan have also done so. It is expected that the other states will also pass the legislation by the end of the financial year so that they will benefit from this scheme.

The centre has indicated that the states are expected to comply with the obligations regarding reduction of fiscal and revenue deficits imposed by the legislature. It is stated that the centre would request the Next Finance Commission to make appropriate adjustment in case the state availing the benefit is not able to comply with the Fiscal Responsibility Legislation (FRL). There is no doubt that the state will get the benefit of consolidation, rescheduledment and reduction of interest rates irrespective of the compliance.

The benefits of debt write-off scheme are conditional. The quantum of write-off would be linked to the absolute amount by which the revenue deficit is reduced in each successive year. The benefit of this scheme would be available only if the fiscal deficits of the states are reduced to the level of 2004-05. If any year, the fiscal deficit exceeds this level, the benefit or write-off would not be given. It means that the passing of Fiscal Responsibility Legislation is not sufficient to get the benefit of a debt write-off.

The total write-off benefits to all states over the five years together could be Rs. 32,200 crores. To get this benefit, all states together should wipe their revenue deficit of the order of Rs. 63,900 crores by 2008-09. It means that, on an average, for every one rupee write-off the state will have to reduce their revenue deficit by two rupees. It implies that all the states will not get equal benefits from this scheme. The states with relatively smaller average revenue deficits in relation to the repayment dues will find it easy to benefit. On the other hand states with large revenue deficits in relation to repayment dues will not find it easy to benefit from the scheme. For example, Andhara Pradesh with a relatively small revenue deficit in relation to repayment dues will get the benefit of write-off of Rs. 1.30 for every one-rupee reduction in the revenue deficit. On the contrary West Bengal with a relatively large revenue deficit in relation to repayment dues will get the benefit of a write-off of only 27 paise for every one rupee reduction in the revenue deficit.

The special category states have revenue surpluses. They will quote to maintain the base year level of revenue surplus in each year to get benefits from the write-off scheme. If in any particular year the revenue deficit is less than the base year, the state will not get the benefit of a write-off that year. All the revenue surplus states are highly dependent on central transfers for their revenues; the maintenance of revenue surplus depends on such transfers.

Altogether, the write-off constitutes just about 4.3 percent of the total estimated transfer recommended by the Twelfth Finance Commission. It is not clear that the states

TABLE 7

**Proposed Debt Write-off and Revenue Deficits of States**

| *States according to descending order of average per capita GSDP (1992-2002)* | *Potential debt write off from 2005-10 (Rs. Crores)* | *Estimated Total Transfers (Rs. Crores)* | *Write-off as Percentage of Transfers (Rs, Crores)* | *Revenue Deficit-GSDP (percentage)* |
|---|---|---|---|---|
| Goa | 132.13 | 1425 | 9.27 | -2.44 |
| Punjab | 763.42 | 12885 | 5.92 | -4.53 |
| Maharashtra | 1953.22 | 36194 | 5.40 | -3.09 |
| Haryana | 581.43 | 8042 | 7.23 | -1.32 |
| Kerala | 1063.05 | 19608 | 5.42 | -4.17 |
| Gujarat | 2615.98 | 25608 | 10.22 | -4.66 |
| Tamil Nadu | 1718.17 | 36688 | 4.68 | -2.5 |
| Karnataka | 2079.54 | 31416 | 6.62 | -2.21 |
| Andhra Pradesh | 3834.29 | 50353 | 7.61 | -2.03 |
| West Bengal | 2425.07 | 50877 | 4.77 | -5.47 |
| High Income States (Above Rs. 17,000) | 17166.30 | 273096 | 6.29 | NA |
| Rajasthan | 708.38 | 39062 | 4.37 | -3.87 |
| Chhattisgarh | 570.31 | 18274 | 3.12 | Na |
| Madhya Pradesh | 1875.10 | 46322 | 4.05 | -2.05 |
| Jharkhand | 659.49 | 23657 | 2.79 | Na |
| Orissa | 1751.29 | 36943 | 4.74 | -4.91 |
| Uttar Pradesh | 4585.12 | 133471 | 3.44 | -2.98 |
| Bihar | 1926.02 | 75646 | 2.55 | -1.87 |
| Low Income States (Below Rs. 17,000) | 13075.71 | 373375 | 3.50 | NA |
| Arunachal Pradesh | 97.39 | 3526 | 2.76 | 1.76 |
| Assam | 524.95 | 24329 | 2.16 | -1.9 |
| Himachal Pradesh | 206.06 | 14450 | 1.43 | -7.3 |
| Jammu and Kashmir | 473.84 | 20880 | 2.27 | -1.8 |
| Manipur | 188.54 | 6870 | 2.74 | -2.5 |
| Meghalaya | 80.27 | 4368 | 1.84 | 0.84 |
| Mizoram | 67.85 | 4661 | 1.46 | -9.07 |
| Nagaland | 80.15 | 7453 | 1.08 | -2.12 |
| Sikkim | 48.07 | 1829 | 2.63 | 11.3 |
| Tripura | 117.53 | 8417 | 1.40 | -0.61 |
| Uttaranchal | 72.02 | 12194 | 0.59 | Na |
| Special category states | 1956.67 | 108977 | 1.80 | -3.19 |
| Total | 32198.70 | 755448 | 4.26 | -3.15 |

*Note*: Na—Not Available/Not Estimated.

*Source*: *The Economic and Political Weekly*, p. 3432, July 30-August 5, 2005, p. 3409.

would respond to this incentive. It would be seen that the relatively better off states receive larger benefits from the debt write-off scheme. These states have relatively lower revenue deficits. This can be seen in Table 7.

### Debt-GSDP Ratio

There has been a massive increase in the debt-GSDP ratio across the states during 1998-99 to 2002-03. The overall debt-GSDP ratio for all states increased from 19.6 percent to 27.8 per cent. Sikkim was the only state in which debt-GSDP ratio exceeded 60 percent in 1998-99. There were 4 states of this category in 2002-03. On the other hand, there were 5 states with the ratio of more than 20 percent in 1998-99, but there was not a single state having less than 20 percent debt-GSDP ratio in 2002-03.

The growth in debt burden in states like Orissa (from 37.8 to 62.9%), Bihar (from 33.1 to 55.3%), Rajasthan (from 28.9 to 45.4%), Uttar Pradesh (from 28.0 to 37.1%), Assam (from 23.2 to 33.9), Gujarat (from 18.1 to 33.9%) and Tamil Nadu (from 16.4 to 26.8%).

Most of the states with high debt GSDP ratio were relatively smaller states in 1998-99. This did not affect the overall debt burden of the states and the consolidated debt of the states in a significant manner. The situation has completely changed in 2002-03. Several major states have debt levels in relation to their GSDP that are very high. This has serious implications for their own fiscal sustainability and also for the overall fiscal sustainability.

### The States on the Basis of Interest Burden in Relation to Total Revenue Receipt

The interest is burden in relation to revenue receipts is a more serious problem to the major states as a compared to smaller states. The smaller states belong to the special category receive 90 percent of plan assistance as grants and a number of them have revenue surpluses instead to revenue deficits.

During 1998-99 the interest payments did not exceed 35 percent of the revenue receipts in any states. The highest level was in Punjab is 33.3%. There were seven states where the level was below 10 percent has increased to 44.3% in West Bengal. (Table 8)

TABLE 8

**Debt-GSDP Ratio and Interest Payment—Total Receipt Ratio**

| States | Debt-GSDP Ratio | | Interest-Total Receipt | |
|---|---|---|---|---|
| | 1998-99 | 2002-03 | 1996-1999 | 2000-03 |
| Andhra Pradesh | 20.3 | 28.9 | 16.8 | 22.4 |
| Arunachal Pradesh | 40.2 | 55.5 | 7.2 | 11.3 |
| Assam | 23.2 | 33.9 | 13.6 | 17.2 |
| Bihar | 33.1 | 55.3 | 23.6 | 27.5 |
| Goa | 34.2 | 28.2 | 15.9 | 19.5 |
| Gujarat | 18.1 | 33.9 | 17.1 | 24.6 |
| Haryana | 21.1 | 27.9 | 19.8 | 23.4 |
| Himachal Pradesh | 55.9 | 63.3 | 18.2 | 28.8 |
| Jammu and Kashmir | 48.0 | 53.8 | 13.0 | 14.8 |
| Karnataka | 17.5 | 25.1 | 13.4 | 18.1 |
| Kerala | 27.1 | 36.3 | 19.0 | 27.3 |
| Madhya Pradesh | 18.6 | 32.3 | 14.9 | 19.2 |
| Maharashtra | 13.1 | 21.6 | 14.7 | 20.8 |
| Manipur | 44.7 | 43.11 | 9.2 | 17.5 |
| Meghalaya | 23.4 | 32.2 | 8.3 | 11.1 |
| Mizoram | 58.4 | 81.6 | 9.0 | 14.0 |
| Nagaland | 50.9 | 52.1 | 12.5 | 15.1 |
| Orissa | 37.8 | 62.9 | 28.6 | 35.9 |
| Punjab | 34.6 | 48.5 | 33.3 | 38.5 |
| Rajasthan | 28.9 | 45.4 | 23.2 | 30.6 |
| Sikkim | 64.4 | 60.3 | 10.4 | 11.1 |
| Tamil Nadu | 16.4 | 26.8 | 13.4 | 18.6 |
| Tripura | 37.2 | 37.8 | 11.0 | 14.3 |
| Uttar Pradesh | 28.0 | 39.1 | 27.9 | 29.2 |
| West Bengal | 26.2 | 41.2 | 27.3 | 44.3 |
| Total | 19.6 | 27.8 | - | - |

Source: *The Economic and Political Weekly*, p. 3432, July 30-August 5, 2005.

### Composition of Outstanding Loans

The impact of the debt relief recommended by the Twelfth Finance Commission for each state depends on the

TABLE 9

**Percentage Share of Different Components of Outstanding Loans—States-wise**

*(31.03.2005)*

| *States* | *NSSF* | *Central Loans* | *Provident Fund* | *Other Internal Relief Including Market Loans* |
|---|---|---|---|---|
| Andhra Pradesh | 21.0 | 30.3 | 7.6 | 41.1 |
| Arunachal Pradesh | 0.6 | 61.9 | 27.7 | 9.8 |
| Assam | 25.0 | 14.6 | 17.0 | 43.4 |
| Bihar | 28.1 | 32.5 | 14.4 | 25.2 |
| Goa | 33.8 | 25.5 | 14.2 | 26.3 |
| Gujarat | 43.8 | 24.7 | 6.5 | 25.0 |
| Haryana | 32.5 | 13.7 | 25.4 | 28.4 |
| Himachal Pradesh | 9.4 | 17.2 | 19.5 | 53.9 |
| Jammu and Kashmir | 7.6 | 37.0 | 28.2 | 27.2 |
| Karnataka | 24.8 | 29.7 | 16.1 | 29.4 |
| Kerala | 13.6 | 16.4 | 36.9 | 33.1 |
| Madhya Pradesh | 22.3 | 22.7 | 17.2 | 37.8 |
| Maharashtra | 38.3 | 22.6 | 11.7 | 27.4 |
| Manipur | 0.7 | 35.4 | 20.6 | 43.3 |
| Meghalaya | 5.6 | 24.1 | 20.3 | 50.0 |
| Mizoram | 0.5 | 18.0 | 33.3 | 48.2 |
| Nagaland | 1.4 | 32.7 | 17.9 | 48.0 |
| Orissa | 9.8 | 27.6 | 24.1 | 38.5 |
| Punjab | 33.8 | 15.1 | 18.4 | 32.7 |
| Rajasthan | 32.3 | 14.6 | 21.0 | 32.1 |
| Sikkim | 4.8 | 25.4 | 27.2 | 42.6 |
| Tamil Nadu | 24.4 | 23.5 | 14.1 | 38.0 |
| Tripura | - | 20.8 | 47.5 | 31.7 |
| Uttar Pradesh | 26.6 | 25.6 | 13.9 | 33.9 |
| West Bengal | 44.1 | 15.8 | 4.9 | 35.2 |
| Total | 30.8 | 23.3 | 15.5 | 30.4 |

*Source*: *The Economic and Political Weekly*, p. 3433, July 30-August 5, 2005.

composition of the outstanding loans. If the share of central loans is substantial for a state the debt relief benefits to it will be substantial. If the central loans constitute only a smaller share of the total debt of state, then the total relief from the Twelfth Finance Commission recommendations will be relatively small (Table 9).

**Causes for the States Indebtedness**

The origin of states indebtedness could be traced back to the pattern of plan expenditure followed by them over the last 54 years. With the advent of planning, grants from the centre for their annual plan assumed a major role. However, the plan grants were never meant to meet the entire revenue component of the states. With the introduction of Gadgil Formula in 1969, the plan assistance were given to non-special category states in the form of 30 percent grants and 70 transfers. The plan assistance has been passed on the states without any assessment of the ability of the states to repay the loan component. As plan grants did not match revenue expenditure, a large segment of plan revenue expenditure was met out of borrowing in most of the states.

The non-plan revenue budget of states has to bear the burden of running assets during the earlier plans. The practice of mingling revenue and capital parts in plan outlay and financing a large part of plan revenue expenditure by borrowing seems to be a common practice. States usually try to secure approval for larger plan outlays from Planning Commission every year. Despite their adverse impact on the fiscal imbalances on the revenue account. The Planning Commission, morally responsible for the growing fiscal deficit and the resulting debt burden on it, approves larger plan outlay without the match resources.

The overall fiscal situation of the states has undergone substantial deterioration over the last seven years. Substantial upward revision of salaries of the employees in the states has been the principal cause. There has been a deceleration of the growth of revenue. The tax-GSDP ratio of all states combined has been stagnation around 6 percent for the past several years. Resorting to massive borrowing has filled the resultant revenue and consequently the debt burden of the states has reached unsustainable levels.

**Restructuring of State Debt**

The Twelfth Finance commission has introduced several measures in order to reduce the burden of debt. The Twelfth Finance Commission has introduced a package for debt reduction with two main components:

(i) The consolidation of all state debt outstanding to the Centre on March 31, 2004 at an interest rate of 7 percent to be repaid over 20 years.
(ii) New debt relief of 7 percent to be repaid over 20 years.

The issue of social return appears to be completely ignored by the Twelfth Finance commission. The Twelfth Finance commission is ignoring the social role that can be played to public employees and even loss making public enterprises that fulfil some social functions. The states should be take loan directly from the market. The Centre should not work as mediator. Such a practice will bring the required fiscal disciple.

**Debt Relief Recommended by Finance Commissions**

The growth of debt of states was a serious concern and earlier Finance Commissions provided various forms of debt related relief, viz., write-offs, rescheduling of loans with a view to shifting the timing of repayments, consolidation of past loans on common terms, and reducing of interest rate.

The Second Finance Commission was asked to make recommendation to reduce the states debt problem, and the Commission, iner alia, suggested the postponement of repayments but did not help to tackle the problem. The Fourth Finance Commission expressed its in ability to suggest a lasting solution in a short period of time as its disposal. The Fifth Finance Commission recommended that the centre should pay the amount of state unauthorized over drafts to RBI by adjusting that amount against the grants. The Sixth Finance Commission recommended moratorium on the repayment of central loans and write-offs a few old loans of small amount. The Eighth and Ninth Finance Commission recommended debt reliefs of Rs. 2285 crores (for the period

1984-89) and Rs. 494 crores (1990-95) respectively. The debt relief scheme of the Tenth Finance Commission has two parts: (a) a scheme for general debt relief for all states linked to fiscal performance, and (b) specific relief for states with high fiscal stress.

The Eleventh Finance Commission (EFC) was required to make an assessment of the debt position of the states as on March 31, 1999 and suggested such corrective measures as are deemed necessary keeping in view of the long-term sustainability of the debt of the centre and states. However, the recommendations of the Eleventh Finance Commission did not address the question of long-term sustainability of debt of either the centre or the states. The debt relief package recommended by the Eleventh Finance Commission worked out to around Rs. 700 crores for 2000-05.

**Debt Reliefs under Twelfth Finance Commission**

The state finances were under deep stress on account of the high interest payment obligation of the States. One of the major attempts to reduce the pressure, the centre introduced the debt swap scheme in September 2002. Under this scheme high cost debts., i.e. debts carrying an interest rate of 13 percent or above, on state plans or small savings, could be exchanged for market borrowing and small savings securities, which at that point carried interest of around 7 percent. This scheme helped to reduce the average interest rate paid by states and also changed the maturity profile and composition of the state debts. Under this scheme Rs. 1,03,000 crores of state debt was swapped till the end of 2004-05.

The Twelfth Finance Commission was asked to make an assessment of the debt position of the states as on March 31, 2004, and suggested such corrective measures as are deemed necessary, consistent with macroeconomic stability and debt sustainability. The states have to qualify by bringing such legislation. Despite this incentive many states may sacrifice fiscal virtue at the altar of populist pressure for expenditure.

The Twelfth Finance Commission recommended that the centre should not act as an intermediary in the borrowing programme of the states. States are asked to rely on market rather than the centre for their borrowing. As the states are increasingly exposed to the market for borrowing, the markets would increasingly assess their fiscal position. Therefore, the Twelfth Finance Commission relied on two mechanisms for fiscal correction: self-evaluation under the Fiscal Responsibility Act (FRA) and exposure to the market.

The major recommendation of the Twelfth Finance Commission, which has been accepted by the union cabinet, related to the stipulation that any transfer from centre to the state would henceforth (including the plan assistance) not take the form of loans. While recommending the doing away of the loan component of central assistance, the Twelfth Finance Commission had asked to states to mobilize the same amount directly from the market. It should be noted that market borrowings have their own limitations. The increased borrowing by states is likely to increase the interest rates. This has actually happened. Further, the repayment of market borrowings would cause problems in the long-run, as huge repayment would be required to be made in the coming years and at that time the economy may not be able to bear the quantum of market borrowings required to be raised then. Therefore, an appropriate mix of various aspects introduced, a package for debt reduction with two main components.

The first is the consolidation of all state debts outstanding. Under scheme as soon as a state passes a Fiscal Responsibility Act, (FRA) the entire loan owed by it to the centre as on March 31, 2004 gets consolidated into a single loan with a fresh term of 20 years and at an interest rate 7.5 percent. This debt consolidation is expected to provide a relief to the states to the extent of Rs. 33,000 crores spread over five years (2005-10). One drawback of the scheme is that the Twelfth Finance Commission recommendation for providing such large debt relief to states for doing no more than passing a law. A front-loaded debt consolidation is necessary to give the states a fighting chance to get out of the debt trap.

The second, and much problematic proposal of the Twelfth Finance Commission is a new debt relief scheme linked to the reduction in the revenue deficits of states. Under this scheme, the repayment, due on central loan from

2005-06 to 2009-10, will be eligible for write-off. But the amount of write-off a repayment will be linked to the absolute amount by which the revenue deficit is reduced in each successive year over the entire period. The enactment of the Fiscal Responsibility Act is precondition for the eligibility of this scheme. Accordingly this scheme will available to the states only from the year they forms of borrowing, including institutional borrowing should be worked out.

## THIRTEENTH FINANCE COMMISSION

The Thirteenth Finance Commission (FC-XIII) was constituted by the President under Article 280 of the Constitution on 13 November 2007 to make recommendations for the period 2010-15. Dr. Vijay Kelkar was appointed the Chairman of the Commission.

The Presidential orders that provide the Terms of Reference (ToR) for the Thirteenth Finance Commission can be viewed as setting the Commission three different types of tasks. The first or 'core' task of the Commission is to recommend distribution, between the Union and the states, of the net proceeds of taxes to be divided between them under Chapter I, Part XII of the Constitution of India, commonly termed as the 'divisible pool'. Second, the Commission has also to recommend the allocation between the states of such proceeds. Under Article 275 of the Constitution the Commission may provide general purpose grants to states which are 'in need of assistance' and other specific purpose grants. Third, the Commission has been asked to recommend measures to supplement the resources of the panchayats and municipalities in different states by augmenting the consolidated funds of individual states, taking into account the recommendations of the respective State Finance Commissions (SFCs).

Every Commission is required by its Terms of Reference to keep specific policy considerations in mind while undertaking its core task. Thus, the Thirteenth Finance Commission has to take account of:

(i) The need to balance the receipts and expenditure

on revenue account of all the states and the Union and generating surpluses for capital investment.

(ii) The impact of the proposed implementation of the Goods and Services Tax (GST) from 1 April 2010, including its impact on the country's foreign trade.

(iii) The need to improve the quality of public expenditure.

(iv) The need to manage ecology, environment and climate change consistent with sustainable development.

(v) The need to ensure commercial viability of public sector and departmental undertakings, as also of irrigation and power projects.

(vi) The taxation efforts of the Central Government and each State Government and the potential for additional resource mobilisation to improve the tax—Gross State Domestic Product/Gross Domestic Product Ratio.

These specific considerations are taken account of by the Commission in the assessment of the financial needs of the Centre and the states and in the design of specific purpose grants.

The ToR assign FC-XIII a specific 'macro-policy task', which is to review the state of the finances of the Union and the states and the operation of the states' Debt Consolidation and Relief Facility (DCRF) 2005-10 and suggest measures to maintain a stable fiscal environment, consonant with equitable growth. A subsequent addition to our ToR mandates us to review the roadmap for fiscal adjustment and suggest a suitably revised roadmap that would maintain the gains of fiscal consolidation through 2010-15.

The issues that we have to consider, therefore, directly emanate from the ToR of this Commission. In this chapter we will outline the broad considerations that inform the Commission's approach to its core and policy tasks. We also discuss the main issues and our proposed approach.

The overall approach of the Commission is to foster 'inclusive and green growth promoting fiscal federalism'. This is the vision underlying the Commission's recommendations on inter-governmental fiscal arrangements and on the roadmap for fiscal adjustment. This vision has to be given effect within the overall structure of inter-governmental fiscal arrangements, whose contours are Constitutionally specified.

The federalist development State is a domain for evolutionary policy-making, responsive to internal and external policy imperatives such as political integration and globalisation, with sovereign powers to fulfil its mandate. These powers are, however, not absolute. The development project of the state is enabled by evolutionary policy-making, while circumscribed by the laws that mandate the exercise of its sovereignty in the formulation and implementation of policy.

Kautilya argued for a social contract defined by laws, principles and doctrines in Dharmasastra and Arthasastra, delimiting the Constitutional metes and bounds of Monarch and State. The Indian Constitution can, thus, be seen from a variety of perspectives, as providing a regulatory framework within which the developmental federalist State undertakes its project. The structure of the inter-governmental fiscal framework has to serve the purposes of the contemporary development project, while at the same time, ensuring that it functions within the regulatory framework defined, in our time, by the Constitution of India.

Inclusive growth is the cornerstone of India's development project. India's recent economic growth performance has, indeed, been creditable. However, such growth must make a demonstrable difference to the lives of the poorest and most vulnerable citizens. On this, as reflected in the Millennium Development Goals (MDGs) there is global consensus, of which our nation is a part. India has the potential and the means to secure such a future for its citizens. The stress laid on inclusive growth in the Eleventh Plan has meant that such growth has been accompanied by a concerted effort, by all levels of government, to invest in the delivery of public services, particularly those which promote progress in achievement of the MDGs. But, to achieve this potential, it is necessary that resources be mobilised and deployed in such a manner that the recent high rates of growth are maintained and even increased. Thus, sustainable and inclusive growth are prerequisites for achieving the MDGs.

Inclusively informs our recommendations in every sphere. In our formula for horizontal devolution, the highest weightage amongst all the variables is for correcting the fiscal disability of a state *vis-a-vis* those of the top-ranked states. Further, we also recognise the fiscal disability of the special category states by computing their fiscal distance from the top-ranked states after setting their tax effort at the average for the special category alone, in place of an all-state average. Inclusivity is justified, not merely to ensure equal treatment of citizens by governments, but also for long-term economic efficiency reasons, so as to minimise the burden of fiscally-induced migration on high-income states. It also underlies our attempt to prescribe a fiscal roadmap targeting elimination of the revenue deficit so that net new borrowing is directed towards creation of public infrastructure which would benefit all. It also underlies many of our grant provisions, for instance, maintenance for the new village connectivity roads financed under Pradhan Mantri Gram Sadak Yojana (PMGSY). And finally, inclusivity underlies our substantially enhanced grant for local bodies, including those of the Schedule V and VI areas, so as to enable provision of sanitation and other public goods.

Fiscal consolidation promotes growth. By fiscal consolidation we do not mean a reduction in the role of the State. In a complex and developing economy like India, the government will continue to mobilise and deploy a significant proportion of resources to promote public welfare. Rather, fiscal consolidation refers to measures to improve the quality and effectiveness of the processes of public expenditure and resource mobilisation. We are of the view that there are feasible pathways for fiscal consolidation with high growth, as a study by the NIPFP for this Commission shows analytically. In the present context, this also means providing the fiscal space to promote both public and private investment, so as to secure the highest possible sustainable, green and inclusive rate of growth for the Indian economy. For the Commission, this involves proposing ways to incentivise such consolidation within the mandate and instruments at our disposal. We have been particularly mindful of this challenge in our recommendations with respect to the future fiscal roadmap.

For achieving a greener and more inclusive growth path we need a fiscally strong Centre, fiscally strong states and fiscally strong local bodies, or the third tier of government. Therefore, we are proposing the strategy of 'expansionary fiscal consolidation' with no compression of development expenditures. Such a fiscal strategy will provide a more propitious environment for increasing both public and private investments, as well as for better handling of adverse economic shocks that we may face due to external developments. In other words, the proposed fiscal strategy will also improve our country's economic security.

A high growth economy minimises the risk of 'crowding out' of the private sector, by allowing the government to increase fiscal space for public investment consistent with fiscal prudence. In fact, in such an environment, the private sector becomes a valuable actor. Better targeted public good delivery systems can be used to engage the private sector in the provision of key public goods, particularly infrastructure. Effective fiscal consolidation ensures that the government gets the best value for money from such engagement. In assessing the resources available for overall transfers the Commission has also taken into account the total resources available, including potential inflows from disinvestment.

Green growth involves rethinking growth strategies with regard to their impact on environmental sustainability and the environmental resources available to poor and vulnerable groups. It is significant to note that many stimulus packages announced globally to combat recession incorporated a green component. International experience is that green growth promotes inclusivity. Further, the renewable energy sector is relatively labour intensive, with the potential for generating more jobs than the oil and gas industries.

Securing the environment is critical for India's future generations and not just a matter of international commitment. A degraded environment reduces the quality of life for all citizens, but the impact is particularly pronounced on the poor and vulnerable groups, as it is they who suffer the most from degraded access to clean water, air and sanitation, as well as from climate shocks. It is for this reason that, despite the fact that India's per capita greenhouse gas emissions are much below the world average and far lower than the average of developed countries, we have pursued policies which complement efforts towards mitigation of climate change. It is, therefore, important to incentivise fiscal policies that promote measures for energy conservation, renewable energy, soil conservation, afforestation and more effective and affordable access to clean water at different levels of government. This would impact all levels of government, including local bodies, which face mounting challenges in delivering better access to clean water, better solid waste management and enhanced, but green local infrastructure. Our grant proposals are supportive of such an approach.

In India, Finance Commissions have had to face three important challenges. First, there has been a historically high degree of vertical imbalance between the Centre and the states. Recently, there has also been an increase in the size of the non-shareable portion of central revenue receipts. Second, there is spatial inequality in the fiscal capacity and fiscal needs of different states. The reasons underlying this spatial inequality vary considerably, depending on the state in question. Further, different states are at different stages of the development transformation, so their fiscal needs also vary over time. The Constitution provides general guidance on addressing the needs of the states and the Centre as well as taking account of state-specific needs, but does not provide the prescriptive framework for Finance Commissions. Third, it is a fact that recent decentralisation initiatives and the increasing pace of urbanisation have considerably increased the fiscal obligations of the third tier of government, but not the devolution of human and financial resources to discharge these obligations. This has increasingly become an important dimension of the work of every Finance Commission. Thus, the work of every Commission is multi-dimensional in nature.

Added to this are the new domestic challenges that

have emerged. The imperatives of urbanisation, empowerment of India's villages and improved information flows have collectively increased the expectation and demand for public and merit goods. In meeting this demand the challenge of sustainable development has to be kept firmly in mind, so that present generations do not diminish the lives and capabilities of future generations. Further, India has one of the world's youngest populations. This is a one-time demographic dividend which needs to be harnessed through appropriate investments in human development, particularly in education and public health, so that the country, having undertaken its long-term development transformation, is then able to cater to the long-term challenge that this dividend poses—that of an ageing population. In making its awards the Commission has to be mindful of the short and long-term implications that these challenges pose for the public finances of India and the need to foster the appropriate fiscal incentives to address these challenges.

An important challenge faced by our Commission was that the assessment of the resource position of the Centre and the states has had to be made in the face of more than normal uncertainties, given the developments in the global economy and the consequent need for resources to be devoted to stabilisation and countercyclical measures by the Centre as well as the states. The Commission's recommendations for vertical and horizontal devolution have to be consistent with the requirement that the Commission '.... Suggest a suitably revised roadmap with a view to maintaining the gains of fiscal consolidation through 2010 to 2015'. The impact of countercyclical measures on the absolute and relative finances of Central and State Governments will affect the future fiscal roadmap. This, in turn, has to be taken into account in preparing the forecasts necessary to calculate consistent and appropriate vertical and horizontal devolutions.

All Commissions have to approach their tasks, recognising that the data base for many important economic variables (e.g., taxable capacity) is less than perfect and may require approximations and normative corrections. We are well aware that it is desirable to make the fiscal awards more incentive-compatible and better targeted to securing the different objectives enjoined on the Commission in its terms of reference. This requires the Commission to identify and use reliable and widely acceptable data which is regularly available, easily understood and does not require interpretation or normative assessment by any agency during the Commissions' award period. Data limitations, thus, act as a reality check on our aspirations in this direction, as does the fact that Finance Commissions have to take account of the limits and constraints of political economy that any country faces in working out inter-governmental/jurisdictional fiscal transfers.

## FISCAL CONSOLIDATION AND DEBT RELIEF (FC-XIII)

The states, in their individual memoranda, have raised various issues regarding the roadmap for fiscal consolidation and debt relief. On the issue of elimination of revenue deficit, the states have agreed with the approach of FC-XII and accept that, as a prudent fiscal policy, borrowings should not be used for government consumption expenditure. They have suggested that this 'golden rule' should be made an integral part of the roadmap for 2010-15. On the issue of fiscal transparency the states have criticised the practice of off-budget borrowings. Some states have represented that this should not be used as an excuse for relaxation in the fiscal targets for the Centre. In their collective memorandum the states have pointed out that all grants to local bodies and to other aided institutions are classified as revenue expenditure.

Hence, a mechanical application of the revenue deficit conditionality detracts from the efforts of State Governments to decentralise development expenditure.

On the subject of fiscal targets, the states have suggested that targets should not be mechanically set, but should depend on the states' capacity to service debt. Some states have suggested that the targets should allow them to take up their development spending. A few states have pointed out that the path to fiscal correction should allow counter-cyclicality and in years of high revenues, restrict excessive spending. They have also suggested the setting up of a National Fiscal Stabilisation Fund. It has further been represented that GSDP is not a very reliable denominator for fixing the targets and the roadmap. Instead, they suggest that targets be set for both interest payments and debt stock in terms of total revenue receipts.

With regard to debt relief, the states have asserted that interest rates on loans from the National Small Savings Fund (NSSF) are high and sought an intervention on this front. While some states have sought reduction of interest rates to 9.5 per cent on the pre-2003-04 loans, some have sought its inclusion in the Debt Consolidation and Relief Facility (DCRF) at an interest rate of 7.5 per cent. Some states have sought a reduction in the difference between the interest rates on open market loans and NSSF loans. It has also been suggested that the interest rate should not be more than 50 basic points higher than the average cost of funds. Some states have suggested that it should be linked to the Central Government Securities (G-Sec) rate to eliminate the anomalies in interest rates for all time. The joint memorandum of the states urges us to take into account the total loan burden of the states, including NSSF loans and loans of ministries other than Finance in recommending effective debt relief measures.

**Adjusted the Outstanding Debt**

For the purpose of our analysis we have adjusted the outstanding debt figures of the Central Government for the year 2009-10. We have netted out certain liabilities that have been double counted, in particular the NSSF liabilities of State Governments. We have also adopted the Ministry of Finance revaluation of external debt at current exchange rates.

Since the National Small Savings Fund is maintained in the public account of the Central Government, the total amount invested by the Fund in special securities of the Central and State Governments is accounted under 'other liabilities' within the 'total outstanding liabilities' of the Central Government. However, the amount invested in State Government securities are loans to the states from the Fund, primarily financing the fiscal deficit of the State Governments. It is shown within the outstanding liabilities of the Central Government merely for accounting purposes, but should be treated as outstanding debt of the states alone. While arriving at the outstanding debt of the Central Government, this amount has been deducted from the reported debt stock. Finally, an adjustment has been made to account for external debt at the current exchange rate. This is presently accounted at book value in 'outstanding debt' as reported in the Union Budget. The adjustments made to arrive at the outstanding debt at the end of 2009-10 are as shown in Table 10.

TABLE 10

**Adjusted Delhi Stock of Central Government**

| Component | As on 31 March 2010 (Rs. crore) |
|---|---|
| 1. Outstanding Liabilities (Budget Documents 2009-10) | 3495152 |
| 2. Investment in Special State Government Securities | 463337 |
| 3. Outstanding Liabilities of GoI Net of Amounts Invested in State Securities [1-2] | 3031815 |
| 4. Off-Budget Liabilities *Of which* | 201236 |
| *(a) Securities Issued to Oil Companies* | *157536* |
| *(b) Securities Issued to FCI* | *16200* |
| *(c) Securities Issued to Fertiliser Companies* | *27500* |
| 5. Adjustment on Account of Valuation of External Debt on Current Exchange Rate | 142441 |
| 6. Adjusted Debt [3+5] | 3174256 |
| *(as per cent of GDP)* | *(54.2%)* |

*Source*: Thirteenth Finance Commission, Vol. 1 (2010-15), Govt. of India.

In line with the above adjustments, Central Government debt is projected at 54.2 per cent of GDP at the conclusion of 2009-10. Taking into account the expected reduction in fuel and fertilizer prices, along with the expected return to the trend growth rate of over 13 per cent from

2011-12, in conjunction with other reforms including reduction of subsidies along a prescribed path, we project a feasible level for outstanding liabilities of the Centre at 45 per cent of GDP by 2014-15, while at the same time maintaining adequate resources for public investment.

### Consolidated Fiscal Reform Path of Centre and States

Based on the fiscal reform path prescribed for the Centre and states, the consolidated position during the award period will be as per Table 11. Average lending from the Centre to states on account of external aid for the period 2006-09 has been Rs. 6050 crore. The stock of central loans consolidated as per the recommendation of FC-XII and loans of those states whose loans have not yet been consolidated, put together, amount to Rs. 1.23 lakh crore. Assuming that these have to be paid in twenty equal instalments, the recovery from these loans would be Rs. 6175 crore, which is almost equal to the average disbursement of loans. Thus, we have assumed that there would be no net disbursement of loans from the Centre to states during the projection period.

TABLE 11

**Consolidated Fiscal Reform Path of Centre and States**

(per cent of GDP)

| | 2009-10 | 2010-11 | 2011-12 | 2012-13 | 2013-14 | 2014-15 |
|---|---|---|---|---|---|---|
| Fiscal Deficit - States | 2.8 | 2.6 | 2.5 | 2.5 | 2.4 | 2.4 |
| Fiscal Deficit - Centre | 6.8 | 5.7 | 4.8 | 4.2 | 3.0 | 3.0 |
| Net Central Loans to States | 0.1 | 0.0 | 0.0 | 0.0 | 0.0 | 0.0 |
| Fiscal Deficit - Consolidated | 9.5 | 8.3 | 7.3 | 6.7 | 5.4 | 5.4 |
| Debt Stock - States | 27.1 | 26.6 | 26.1 | 25.5 | 24.8 | 24.3 |
| Debt Stock - Centre | 54.2 | 53.9 | 52.5 | 50.5 | 47.5 | 44.8 |
| Outstanding Central Loans to States | 2.5 | 2.2 | 2.0 | 1.7 | 1.5 | 1.3 |
| Consolidated Debt | 78.8 | 78.3 | 76.6 | 74.3 | 70.8 | 67.8 |

*Source*: Thirteenth Finance Commission, Vol. 1 (2010-15), Govt. of India.

It is important to recognise that for successful fiscal consolidation, the key lies in maintaining the growth dynamism of our economy. There is a two-way relationship between growth and fiscal consolidation; or what is called the 'strategy of expansionary fiscal consolidation', where fiscal consolidation leads to higher growth due to higher levels of public and private investments, which in turn, further facilitates maintenance of fiscal stability.

However, in order to sustain such a virtuous circle, the proposed fiscal strategy will need to be augmented by reform measures or structural measures in areas such as widening and deepening of markets—particularly factor markets, improving productivity of public expenditure, implementation of competition policy covering both private and public sector enterprises and above all, better governance at all levels of government through increased transparency and accountability.

**Debt Relief for States**

Our Terms of Reference require us to: '... review the state of the finances of the Union and the States, keeping in view, in particular, the operation of the States' Debt Consolidation and Relief Facility 2005-10 introduced by the Central Government on the basis of the recommendations of the Twelfth Finance Commission and suggest measures for maintaining a stable and sustainable fiscal environment consistent with equitable growth.'

With regard to the broad approach to the issue of debt sustainability, FC-XII was of the view that debt relief measures were required as a pre-requisite for achievement of revenue balance. FC-XII observed that, apart from providing for specific debt relief, qualitative and quantitative measures were also to be prescribed to restrict the future growth of debt stock of states beyond sustainable levels. FC-XII was of the view that the debt relief measures recommended with regard to central loans to states needed to be substantial so as to encourage better fiscal performance on the part of states. FC-XII also recommended disintermediation and accordingly, central lending to states was discontinued, except in the case of fiscally weak states that are not able to raise loans from the market, or in case of external loans. In case of such states, FC-XII recommended that computation of interest rates for future loans to the states be placed on a rational footing. In addition, future repayments, particularly on open market borrowings, needed to be catered to in a manner that would preclude undue fiscal stress in the event of bunching or bullet payments.

FC-XII also observed that states should make efforts to eliminate their revenue deficits so that borrowings are utilised for generating capital assets, rather than for financing revenue expenditure. It recommended that in the first instance, as a measure of fiscal discipline, all states should enact fiscal responsibility legislation prescribing specific annual targets for reduction of revenue and fiscal deficits as well as providing a ceiling for borrowings. It unambiguously recommended that the fiscal responsibility legislation should provide for revenue deficits of states being brought down to zero by 2008-09.

FC-XII examined the debt position of the states and recommended debt relief (referred to as DCRF), which had two separate components of relief in the form of debt consolidation and debt write-off. The debt consolidation component provided for consolidation of central loans to states amounting to Rs. 1,28,795 crore, contracted till 31 March 2004 and outstanding on 31 March 2005, along with rescheduling for a fresh term of 20 years, to be repaid in 20 equal instalments. Interest at the rate of 7.5 per cent was to be charged on the consolidated rescheduled central loans and the repayments due from states during the period 2005-06 to 2009-10 on these were eligible for write-off. The quantum of write-off was linked to the absolute amount by which the revenue deficit was reduced in each successive year during the award period. The DCRF envisaged that if a state was able to bring down its revenue deficit down to zero by the targeted year 2008-09, the entire repayments due from the state during the FC-XII award period would be written-off. Enacting the fiscal responsibility legislation, as stated above, was to be a necessary pre-condition for availing of debt relief. For debt write-off, there was an additional pre-condition stipulating that the fiscal deficit of the states should be contained at the level of 2004-05.

The performance of states in aggregate under DCRF is given in Table 12. Twenty-six states have availed of debt consolidation till October 2009. This has resulted in interest relief amounting to Rs. 15,689 crore to these states as against

Rs. 21,276 crore estimated by FC-XII. Sikkim and West Bengal have failed to receive the benefit of debt consolidation, not having met the conditionality of enacting fiscal responsibility legislation. Cumulatively, central loans amounting to Rs. 1,13,601 crore have been consolidated, which is lower than the FC-XII estimates by Rs. 15,194 crore. Out of the said differential, Rs. 9893 crore is accounted for by West Bengal (Rs. 9700 crore) and Sikkim (Rs. 192 crore). The balance is attributable to disparity in the actual base year stock of debt and delays in enactment of FRLs by some states. As regards the debt waiver component, waiver benefit of Rs. 8,717 crore has accrued to the states by the end of 2008-09, as against the estimate of Rs. 32,199 crore by FC-XII for the five year award period.

TABLE 12

**Summary of Performance Under DCRF**

*(Rs. crore)*

| | Estimated by FC-XII for 2005-10 | Availed of by States till 2008-09 |
|---|---|---|
| Debt Consolidation | 1,28,795 | 1,13,601 |
| Interest Relief | 21,276 | 15,689 |
| Debt Waiver | 32,199 | 18,717 |

*Source*: Thirteenth Finance Commission, Vol. 1 (2010-15), Govt. of India.

The scope of FC-XII recommendations excluded two categories of loans, viz. loans given to the states from NSSF and central loans given to State Governments for centrally sponsored schemes/central plan schemes through central ministries/departments other than Ministry of Finance. NSSF loans were excluded from the scope of debt relief on the grounds that NSSF is maintained in the public account of the Government of India and central loans not administered by MoF were excluded on the grounds that data for the same were not available.

**Planning Commission**

As has been described in the earlier, the right to levy certain taxes by the federal government and the unit governments as well as the right to share the proceeds of certain federal taxes has been governed by the constitutional provisions of the respective federations. Even in the older federations like USA many inter-governmental financial problems are still live problems and are not resolved satisfactory for all. More serious problems arise in federations, which have adopted the model of planning for economic development. Such problems rise with regard to the right of different unit governments to raise loans and the rights and duties in respect of planning and economic development. These problems did not arise when the older federations like USA and Canada were formed, as economic development was not then a national objective. However, for new federations like India, the problem of planned economic development is vital and fiscal equalization has assumed added significance in the light of the objectives of the planned process of development.

The democratic set-up of India contains federal form of government. The Constitution of Indian maintains a clear-cut provision of devolution of tax proceeds and grants to the states on the basis of recommendation of Finance Commission. Categorically, the emergence of Planning Commission, which was set-up by a resolution of the Government of India, added a new dimension in the Centre-State financial relationship. The 'Economics and Social Planning' is a concurrent subject, which means, the Central as well as the State Governments are equally responsible for formulating, financing and executing the plans for the development of the economy. In order to avoid any confliction between the Centre and the States in the affairs of formulation, finance as well as execution of the development plans, the Central Government has been equipped with ample powers through the Constitution. The powers retained by the Centre in this connection have been used by the Centre in order to evolve some conventions. For example, the Central Government has evolved the organizational administration of planning in such a way that there has been no major conflict arising either between the Central Government and the State Governments or between the Central Government and the agencies, which have been responsible of the formulation and implementation of development plans. According to this convention, the Prime Minister has been the Chairman and the Finance Minister and the Planning Minister have been members, in addition to some non-official expert members. The National Development Council (N.D.C.), which was established by the Government of India resolution of August 6, 1952 is virtually responsible for co-ordination the plans of the Centre and the States. Since, NDC consists of the Prime Minister as the Chairman along with the Chief Ministers of all the states and all the members of the Planning Commission as its members, the possibility of any kind of conflict happens to be least.

Next, the Central Government has been endowed with comparatively more elastic and lucrative sources of revenue while major responsibility pertaining to execution of the plans remains with the State Governments. This necessitates Central Plan assistance to the states for implementing and carrying out the development plans. These development plans are divided mainly in two parts form viewpoint of finance. The first part is concerned with the development plans of the individual State Governments formulated by them and the other part includes the plans sponsored by the Central Government.

The State Governments receive funds from the Centre for financing the development plans, by way of grants and loans. Article 282 of the Indian Constitution empowers the Government of India or a state to make grants for any public purpose notwithstanding the fact that the purpose is not one with respect to which Parliament of legislature of a state, as the case may be make law. However, since the inception of planning, plan grant are being given to the states under this Article. Moreover, certain non-plan grants are given to the states happens to be insignificant and, therefore, it is not discussed here. Loans are given by the Centre to the states or given guarantees for loans raised by the states. Further, Article 293 of the Constitution provided for loan assistance by the centre to the states. Although this is permissive provision and not an obligation on the part of the centre, however, considerable loan assistance is being provided under this article by the Planning Commission. Both the grants and loans provided, under articles 282 and 293, of the Constitution are determined, by the Planning Commission.

The Planning Commission was established by a resolution of the Central Cabinet on 15th March, 1950. The comprehensive terms of reference required the Planning Commission.

1. To make an assessment of the material, capital and human resources of the country, and to investigate the possibilities of augmenting such of these resources as might be found to be deficient in nation's requirements.
2. To formulate a plan for the most effective and balanced utilization of the country's resources.
3. On a determination of priorities to define the stage in which the Plan should be carried out and to propose the allocation of resources for the due completion of each stage.
4. To indicate the factors which tend to retard economic development and to determine the conditions, which in view of the current social and political situation, should be established for the successful execution of the Plan.
5. To determine the nature and machinery which will be necessary for securing the successful implementation of each stage of the Plan in all its aspects.
6. To appraise from time to time the progress achieved in the execution of each stage of the Plan and to recommend the appraisals policy and measures that such appraisals might show to be necessary.
7. To make such interim or ancillary recommendations as might be appropriate on a consideration to the prevailing economic conditions, current policies, measures and development programmes, or an examination of

such specific problems as might be referred to it for advice for Central or State Governments for facilitating the discharge of duties assigned to it.

In fact, these terms of reference alone were sufficient to make the Planning Commission a very influential and prestigious institution. However, the membership of the Commission further added to its strength.

The Planning Commission is not just advising on plan policy, in fact, it is making it. "When presented to the Cabinet and the National Development Council, its recommendations already have the support of the Prime Minister and several leading members of the Cabinet," observed Professor Hanson, "hence their acceptance is more or less a foregone conclusion". By and large, the emergence of the Planning Commission as an institution regulating the partial flow of financial transfers has narrowed the scope of the Finance Commission. The range of fiscal equalization is wider for the Planning Commission than that of the Finance Commission. The Planning Commission proceeds from where the Finance Commission concludes. It draws heavily on the Finance Commission's calculations regarding states fiscal capacity and needs but altogether follows a different procedure for the hearing the devolution of finances. While the Finance Commission after hearing the Central and State Governments, submits its recommendations in the nature of an award, the Plan financing is the result of a consensus at the National Development Council meeting.

### The National Development Council

Like the Planning Commission, the National Development Council also came into existence through a resolution of the Central Cabinet in August 1952. The Resolution defined its functions as under:

1. Review the working of the National Plan from time to time.
2. Consider important questions of social and economic policy affecting national development.
3. Recommend measures for the achievement of the

aims and targets set out in the National Plan, including measure to secure the active participation and cooperation of the people, improve the efficiency of the administrative services, ensure the fullest development of less advanced regions and factions of the community and, through sacrifices borne equally by all citizens, build up resources for national development.

The National Development Council is consulted at various stages of the formulation and review of the Plan and also formulates the principles determining the allocation of Central assistance for plan purposes. The principles, which regulate the inter-state allocation of Central plan assistance was formally approved by the Council in 1968 and again modified in February 1979. The NDC is a very powerful body, which makes decisions, has a direct bearing on inter-state equalization in terms of economic development.

**Central Plan Assistance to State**

The process of Central assistance for financing developmental schemes of the states was continued even before advent of the Five Year Plans. During the year 1947-48 to 1951-51, i.e., after the Second World War, state governments received some funds for certain developmental projects like "Post-War Developmental Projects" and "Grow More Food Campaign", etc.

In the First Five Year Plan, along with some post-War reconstruction and development schemes, some new schemes like social education, local works and others were included in the state sector.

Accordingly, the magnitude of Central Plan assistance to the states amounted to Rs. 1087 crores during this period. Facts reveal that the major programmes that were provided in the Central sector but were being implemented by the states outside the states plans were transferred to the state sector and included in the State Plans during the Second Five Year Plan. It is revealed by Table 13 that Rs. 2200 crores were given to the states during the Second Plan in form of Central Plan assistance.

TABLE 13

**Central Plan Assistance to States**

*(Rs. Crores)*

| *Period* | *Grants* | *Loans* | *Total* |
|---|---|---|---|
| First Plan (1951-56) | 288 | 799 | 1087 |
| Second Plan (1956-61) | 789 | 1411 | 2200 |
| Third Plan (1961-66) | 1304 | 3100 | 4404 |
| Annual Plans (1966-69) | 1389 | 2776 | 4165 |
| Fourth Plan (1969-74) | 3831 | 6708 | 10539 |
| Fifth Plan (1974-79) | 8998 | 8978 | 17976 |
| Sixth Plan (1979-80) | 2288 | 2697 | 4985 |
| Sixth Plan (1980-85) | 17741 | 23722 | 41663 |
| Seventh Plan (1985-90) | 42005 | 48945 | 90950 |
| Annual Plan (1990-91) | 13202 | 14476 | 27678 |
| Annual Plan (1991-92) | 16079 | 12285 | 28364 |
| Eighth Plan (1992-97) | 06467 | 88430 | 194897 |
| 1997-98 (RE) | 23380 | 29112 | 52492 |
| 1998-99 (RE) | 28223 | 29117 | 57340 |
| | 266184 | 272556 | 538740 |

*Sources*: K.K. George and I.S. Gulati, Central-State Revenue Transfers, 1951-84 *op. cit.* and Budget at a Glance.

As a result of market progress attained during the first decade of India's planned economic development, optimistic environment for accelerated economic development had been laid. The general approach of development adopted by the Planning Commission during the Third Plan was broadly based on the basic pattern and experience of the Second Plan, though in some respects, the Third Plan showed a wider view of the problems of development and recognized the need for more intensive efforts in this context. The Third Plan envisaged strengthening of the agriculture sector, basic industries, power and transport, attaining marked progress towards equality of opportunity and socialist pattern of society and providing employment for the entire addition to the labour force. Especially, the plan size of individual states during the Third Plan was determined after considering the needs, problems, state's own resource, potential for growth and past progress, etc. Facts show that the Government of India to the states for plan purposes gave Rs. 4404 crores during the Third Plan. Similarly, the states received Rs. 4165 crores from the Central Government as plan assistance during the three Annual Plans.

At the beginning of the Fourth Plan, it was realized by the Government of India that the then prevailing tempo of economic activity in the country was insufficient to provide gainful employment to all and bring about significant improvement in living standards of the people. The Fourth Plan proposed strengthening of both agriculture and industrial sectors along with to ensure further technological advancement and void with to ensure further technological advancement and avoid dispersal in the level of economic development. In the light of these objectives, the states received Rs. 10,539 crores as Central plan assistance during the Fourth Plan Period. Similarly, it is obvious from Table 14 that respective volume of funds attained by the states as Central Plan assistance were Rs. 17,976 crores and Rs. 41,663 crores during the Fifth Plan and the Sixth Plan respectively. In the Seventh Plan the Plan assistance provided by the Centre to the States was Rs. 90,950 crores. For the period 1990-91 and 1991-92 the Central plan assistance received by the states was Rs. 27,678 crores and Rs. 28,364 crores respectively. In the Eighth Plan the volume of Central Plan assistance received by the states was Rs. 1,94,897 crores. In 1997-98 and 1998-99 the revised estimate of Plan assistance provided by the centre to the states were Rs. 52,492 crores and Rs. 57,340 crores respectively.

It is obvious that the Central Plan assistance to the states has increased continuously since advent of the First Plan but the significant question is that what considerations and principles have been taken into account while distributing the amount among the states. Categorically, the removal of 'glaring regional economic disparities' and realization of 'Balanced Regional Development' have been the most cherished objective of our planned economic development. In this context, the Second Plan, for the first time, stated that—

> "There is another type of disparities which should be mentioned in this context, namely, disparities in levels of development as between different regions in the country. In a comprehensive Plan of development, the special needs of the less developed areas have to be kept in view, so that the entire pattern of investment is adopted to the securing of balanced regional development in the country. This question has been recently considered by the National Development Council and it has been agreed in principle that within the resources available for development in different parts of the country ... The National Development Council recommended that there should be continuous study of the problem of diminishing regional disparities and a suitable set of indicators should be evolved."

The Third plan document contained a full chapter on "Balanced Regional Development" where the prime objective was "to secure the fullest possible utilization of resources of each region so that it can contribute its best to the national pool and take its due share from the benefits accruing from national development.

At another place, it was opinion of the Commission that.

> "In a country with a large rural population, extremely low-living standards and widespread regional and cultural differences, the social aspects of development are not less important that the economic, ... as it proceeds, economic development may widen disparities between rural and urban areas, increase differences in levels of development in different parts of the country, and accentuate the problem of economic inequality ... In any scheme of long-term development, these aspects must receive special attention so that the social objectives outlined earlier are speedily realized."

The objective of reduction in the level of regional economic disparities has been, by and large, stressed by the planners during the successive Five Year Plans. Recently, it is recognized by the Seventh Five Year Plan that the two critical determinants of a region's economic status are agricultural productivity and human resource potential and reduction in interregional disparities in these two elements will help greatly in the task of reducing regional imbalances.

So far as distribution of Central Plan assistance among the states is concerned, there was no any definite approach in this contest before the beginning of the Fourth Five Year Plan. This reality was admitted by the Planning Commission in one of the meetings of the NDC that—

> "The State's First Five Year Plan include projects/ programmes which were in progress before the commencement of planned economic development. A broad view was taken about the development efforts that were envisaged in the different states and after assessing the resources to be raised by individuals states, the quantum of Central assistance was fixed for each for the entire Plan period. During the Second Plan, the quantum of central assistance was not pre-determined. It continued to change from year to year in the light of financial position of states and the Centre and the requirements of projects taken up in both the states as well as the central sector... The National Development Council, it may be mentioned, did not specifically consider the principles for allocation of central assistance to states either in the Second or the Third Five Year Plans."

For the first time, in the meeting of the National Development Council (NDC) during July 1965, it was realized that there should be some principles on the basis of which, the distribution pattern of Central Plan would be determined. As a result, a formula was evolved by the Planning Commission according to which about seventy percent of the central assistance was first to be distributed on the basis of population strength of the states. The balance was to be distributed after taking into account (i) the special needs of J&K, Assam and Nagaland to enable them to have a reasonable plan, (ii) the special needs of some states which are required to contribute huge amounts of expenditure on ensuing schemes of irrigation and power of national importance, and (iii) the need for accelerated development of certain backward areas of the country. Since the formula was not clear, the states again demanded for the distribution of Central Plan assistance on the basis of some acceptable objective formula. Therefore, the Planning Commission prepared a five-factor formula, which was finally accepted by NDC in September 1968 and the approach is popularity known as Gadgil formula, under the adopted criteria.

It was decided that after providing for the requirements of the states of Assam, Nagaland and J & K, the central assistance to the remaining states the Fourth Plan be distributed on the basis of population, per capita income if below the national average, tax-effort in relation to the per capita income, commitments in respect of major continuing irrigation and power projects and for special problems like those relating to metropolitan areas, floods, chronically drought affected areas and tribunal areas in the ratio of 60 percent and 10 percent for the remaining each, respectively.

In the case of plan assistance, the proportion between grants and loans at 30:70 for the general category states and 10:90 for the special category states has counterpart in the interest rate charged by the central government on the plan loans to the states. In other words, plan grants are not really interest-free grants. Over the time, these are recovered back in the form of higher interest receipts. Plan grants should be given as genuine grants and states may be encouraged to borrow from the market directly. Such a change would require delinking of grants from loans in plan assistance. This would facilitate determination of grants according to needs and loans according to capacities. The plan size of each state needs to take into account the sustainable level of debt and the capacity to borrow from the market.

A restructuring plan must include reforms relating to the planning process. Part of the distortion in the structure of expenditure derives from the distinction between plan and non-plan expenditures. It is inefficient to show preference for creating new assets or undertaking new schemes being part of the plan, while sacrificing maintenance of already created assets. As a result, there remain many incomplete projects/ schemes not yielding services on one side and ill-maintained and fast depreciating assets, on the other. Over the time, plans have become more scheme-oriented rather than projects returns to service the debt that was used to finance plan expenditures are neither being created nor maintained.

In the case of centrally sponsored schemes also, there should be grant element and no loans linked to grant. A state should be given its total entitlement of grants and allowed to select its own mix of centrally sponsored (CS) schemes floated by different ministries within the limit of the total grant. The CS schemes would then start competing among themselves and pressure would come on the ministries to design schemes that are in demand. This would do away with the present supply-driven approach where schemes are characterized by large numbers, duplication, and lack of monitoring. The CS schemes have been the subject of study by many committees. The general consensus has been towards reducing their number, but the flow-up action has been weak.

## Fiscal Frameworks for Reforms

In the nineties, many countries around the world able to achieve fiscal consolidation, attaining primary surpluses. Widespread reforms including debt ceilings and deficit targets have strengthened fiscal framework. Expenditure rules and transparency in the fiscal management has also been emphasized in these fiscal frameworks. Evaluations of these fiscal consolidation efforts have identified certain factors that account for reliable and durable adjustments. Accordingly, fiscal consolidation is more likely to be successful when based on cuts in expenditure, particularly when undertaken by countries with high levels of debt. Widespread reforms in fiscal frameworks require institutional reforms aimed at achieving and maintaining fiscal consolidation, while leaving room for fiscal policy to respond to business cycles through automatic stabilizers and policy actions.

Recent institutional reforms can be classified into three broad groups: formal deficit and debt rules, expenditure limits and transparency. The main examples of this approach are European countries bound by the Maastricht Treaty as supplemented by the Stability and Growth Pact. The UK since 1997 has operated a Golden Rule whereby borrowing is done only to finance capital spending and the limit on net debt is 40 per cent of GDP over a cycle. Several countries have deficit and debt rules at the sub-national level. In the US, all but two, states have laws requiring balanced budgets and limiting the states to raise debt. Nine provinces and territories of Canada have fiscal rules with balanced budgets requiring them to take on debt only for the purpose of financing investment projects. Canada has also focused on instituting a rigorous expenditure review process. Debt-ceilings have been driven not by calculations based on theory, but run by the concern about reducing high debt levels and are thus generally chosen on the basis of the experience of the individual countries. The main criticism of the deficit rules in general, and balanced budget rules in particular, is that they are invariant and, therefore, tends to be pro-cyclical. This is a more important consideration for national governments as compared to sub-national government. For this reason, the deficit rules in the national government have increasingly been defined in terms of a cyclically adjusted deficit measures or as an average over the economic cycle. Thus, these rules allow the operation of domestic stabilizers and to some extent also provide room for discretionary policy within the cycle.

Countries like New Zealand, Australia and UK have emphasized transparency in fiscal management. The key elements in this approach are an explicit legal basis, elaboration of guiding principles of fiscal policy, requirement that objectives are clearly stated, emphasis on the need for a long-term focus to fiscal policy and fiscal reporting to the public. The UK, US and New Zealand have enacted legislations for transparency, which require statements providing the objectives for deficits and debt. The US places relatively greater emphasis on expenditure and deficit rules. Expenditure rules typically emphasize ceilings on specific areas of expenditure like discretionary expenditure and in some cases with respect to particular progarammes. Thus, three structural changes can help restore the fiscal health in India, namely; (i) legislative enactments that can restrict fiscal imprudence and set targets such as those relating to fiscal and revenue deficits, debt, and rules for expenditure cuts contingent on specified conditions, (ii) transparency requirements in fiscal management, which help a better understanding of the fiscal health of government by its citizens and their representatives, and (iii) exposure to market discipline, particularly in raising debt.

## TO SUM UP

The outgoing discussion depicts a clear-cut scenario about the working as well as functioning of the Finance Commission and the Planning Commission. The Finance Commission, a statutory body, was excepted to develop set of sound principles on the basis of which the states would get resources from the Centre according to their needs. Removal of regional economic disparities was to be attained through the scheme of resource transfer as recommended by the Finance Commissions. Equally it is true that the successive Finance Commissions have asserted frequently pertaining to realization of the said objectives. On the other hand, a careful analysis of the recommendations of the successive Finance Commissions reveals that the statutory approach has not been much conducive in this context. For example, the successive Finance Commissions, by and large, have endorsed population factor in their scheme of resource transfer to the states. Further, resource has been given to the state on the basis of recommendation of successive Finance Commissions in order to cover the budgetary deficits of the State Governments. Almost, the Finance Commissions have estimated the gap between revenue resources and expenditure of the states and this gap, has been attempted to be covered through the tax-share and grants-in-aid. In fact, in comparison to population factor, there is much substance in the other factors like inverse of per capita income, Tax-efforts as well as economy in expenditure performance of the states, which have been ignored by the successive Finance Commissions in their scheme of resource transfer. Moreover, the accent on budgetary need of the states has not been much congenial in realizing the well-desired objective of reduction in the regional economic disparities.

The Planning Commission has emerged as an important channel of resource transfer to the states. Since, inception of planned economic development in India, realization of economic growth with social justice has been the supreme target. Reckoning of the facts indicate that Plan transfers were not much conducive towards realization of the said been designed in such a manner that it has resulted in reverse flow of resources from the states to the Centre in form of repayment of interest as well as principal. Such a trend has created major financial problems before the State Governments, especially the economically backward states and thus the gap between backward states and economically developed states has widened over the period. Here, it should be noted that while assigning Plan grants to the states, the Planning Commission has assigned higher weightage to the population, which is rather less satisfactory in the Indian context. At the same time, the factors like 'Tax-efforts of the states,' 'Inverse of per capita income of the states,', etc. have not been given due weightage and relatively backward states have been assigned smaller quantum of resources in per capita terms. It is, therefore, the entire approach of the Planning Commission towards Central resource regarding realization of reduction in the regional economic disparities not it has established a healthy Centre-State fiscal relationship in India.

Thus, the Finance Commission as well as the Planning Commission has failed to evolve a set of sound principles for central resource transfer to the states and, therefore, they have not succeeded in order to establish an amicable relationship between the Centre and the Sates in the field of finance. It is virtually the policies of the Finance Commission and the Planning Commission due to which several anomalies have emerged like mounting Central loan to the states, problem of state's overdrafts, the questions of fiscal autonomy of the states.

## References

Article 280 of the Indian Constitution, Government of India.

Gaur, Achal Kumar (1985), Centre-States Financial Relations and Finance Commission, Allahabad: Chugh Publications.

Report of the Seventh Finance Commission (1978), Government of India, New Delhi.

Sastri, K.V.S. (1966), Federal-States Fiscal Relations in India, Oxford University Press, London.

Cabinet Secretariat Resolution (1950), Setting up the Planning Commission, dated March 15.

Thimmaiah, G. (1981), A Critique of The Finance Commission, Allahabad: Kheeler Publications.

Budget of Indian Government, New Delhi, (1974-51).

Draft Third Five Year Plan (1961), Planning Commission: Government of India, New Delhi.

Draft Fourth Five Year Plan (1966), Planning Commission: Government of India, New Delhi.

Second Five Year Plan, A Draft Outline (February 1956), Planning Commission: Government of India, New Delhi.

Draft Seventh Five Year Plan, Planning Commission, Government of India, New Delhi.

Government of India, Planning Commission, Summary Record of the 24th Meeting of the NDC, December 1 and 2, 1967.

Chapter V, Central Loan to the States.

George, K.K. and Gulati, I.S. (February 16, 1985), "Centre-State Resource Transfers, 1951-84: An Appraisal", *Economic and Political Weekly*, Vol. XX, No. 7.

Mohare, R.Y. (2005), Twelfth Finance Commission and Indebtedness of States, *Indian Economic Journal* (Conference Vol.), Vishakhapattanam, (Andhra Pradesh), p. 951.

Pillai, G. Karunakaram (2005), On sustainability of the debts of state and Twelfth Finance Commission's Proposed Debt Reduction Package, *Indian Economic Journal* (Conference Vol.). Vishakhapattanam, (Andhra Pradesh), p. 959.

Shandilya, Tapan Kumar (2005), "Emerging Issues in Centre-State Financial Relations: Approach of Twelfth Finance Commission, *Indian Economic Journal* (Conference Vol.), Vishakhapattanam (Andhra Pradesh), p. 903.

Rangrajan, C. (2005), "Twelfth Finance Commission: Approach and Recommendation, *Economic and Political Weekly*, Vol. XL, No. 31, July 30, 2005.

Report of the Twelfth Finance Commission (2005), Government of India, New Delhi.

Report of the Eleventh Finance Commission: (2000), Government of India, New Delhi.

Gupta, M.K. and Singh, Asha (2005), "Restructuring Public Finance: An Approach of Twelfth Finance Commission, *Indian Economic Journal* (Conference Volume), Vishakhapattnam.

Haller Walter, W. (1966), New Dimensions of Political Economy, Harvard University Press.

Hicks Ursula, K. (1965), Development Finance, Oxford University Press, London.

Hanson, A.H. (1966), The Process of Planning, Oxford University Press, London.

Lakdawala, D.T. (1979), Plan Finance in a Federal Economy. Dr. V.S. Krishna Memorial Lecturer.

*Indian Economic Journal* (2005), Conference Vol., Vishakhapattnam, Amdhra Pradesh.

*Bihar Economic Journal,* Conference Vol. (19_).

Thirteenth Finance Commission (2010-15), Govt. of India.

# 3

# Magnitude of Central Loan to States

The Development programmes envisaged in successive plans required capital outlay on a massive scale. The assumption of greater responsibility by the States on this account made such a heavy demand by way of huge expenditure that the State resources alone could not meet the same. Hence, the State Governments have had to depend more and more on large-scale borrowings, particularly from the Central Government. Since the effort of planned development necessarily involved in a substantial volume of capital outlay, it is not surprising that the indebtedness of the State has increased considerably during the era of planned development. The States, particularly, the backward States do not have sufficient surpluses on the revenue account for investments and development. They have; therefore, depended on barrowing in order to finance their development plans. The Union Government gives plan assistance to the States in the form of loans and grants mainly according to the Gadgil formulae: 70 percent of the total assistance in form of loans and 30 percent in form of grant. The manner of development and measurement of capital resources have resulted in increasing indebtedness of the States. The debt liability of the Sates to the Centre has been growing space. No doubt, in Bihar, the problem of repayment of the principal and interest was not acute during the first, second and third plan periods as the total plan assistance (both loan and grant) received during these periods exceeded the amount of loan instalment and the interest thereon payable to the centre. But from 1967-68, this trend was reversed and in that year the total repayment liability (including interest) exceeded the total plan assistance by Rs. 5.99 crores. This disparity has continuously been showing an upward trend in Fourth Five Year Plan.

The States' indebtedness in India, particularly Central loans to States have been growing rapidly since the advent of planning. Therefore, the mounting debt-burden of the States *vis-à-vis* the Centre is the most abrasive and irrigating element in the Centre-state financial relation. In Federal type of Government the State Governments burdened with expensive social and development functions whereas the sources of tax revenues assigned to them are rigid. The problem is more difficult in India where the State Governments have not fully exploited their tax resources due to the fear of losing votes. On the other hand, their fiscal needs have increased on account of expansion of social and development services.

The states have had very little surpluses after meeting their non-development expenditure. The surplus over non-development expenditure has not grown. Markedly, in spite of the buoyancy of states revenues whatsoever and the efforts of additional taxation, the increase in revenues having been absorbed particularly by the mounting interest charged on debts. This is a very strange situation indeed. This shows how much the growing predominance of the capital account has affected the state finances adversely leading to deficit budgets and borrowing. Added to these things, the capital outlay of the states does not go to commercially viable investments. The states provide major portion of infrastructural facilities for social and economic development but the irony of the situation is this that the developmental outlay on this account is not income yielding. Unfortunately, even those projects, which are expected to be income yielding are not showing sufficient returns. Loans and advances given to the Electricity Board, Road Transport Corporation,

Irrigation Projects, etc., are not giving sufficient returns. Moreover, the pattern of plan assistance according to Gadgil formula is also responsible to a great extent, for the prevailing debt burden. Even the assistance for relief against natural calamities is often in the form of loans. Curiously enough the phenomenon of inadequacy starts with the policy of the Finance Commission. The budgetary projections of the states are scrutinized with utmost care, as if states are financially imprudent. In this process, many legitimate parts of projections are cancelled. The expenditure of states is also under-estimated. The net result is that many states appear to have surplus or non-plan revenue account for the projected period while in reality they may face even heavy deficits. We may also add the policy of the central government to the total picture of inadequacy. There are examples when central government has ignored the interests of the states and taken measures to irritate them. Firstly, the centre has not taken adequate steps to levy all the taxes under article 269 of the constitution, the proceeds of which go to States. Secondly, in case additional Excise Duties the central government has not cared to impose the duties on those items whose proceeds would go to the States. Thirdly, change in tax-laws to convert a part of income tax into corporation tax has also reduced states' share in the proceeds of income tax. Moreover, it is Central Government's responsibility to keep prices stable because currency and mint, money and Banking and many other relevant financial powers are with it. But its failure to check the price rise has made the situation of states even worse. It may be emphasized that the blames for the existing difficulties of the states do not lie entirely with the Centre, states should exploit their tax and revenue and partly because of the growing fiscal needs of the State Governments, there has been an enormous growth in their public debt.

The public debt today constitutes an important part of the total assets (Public and Private) created in the economy. In USA the Public Debt is almost half of the total debt existing the country. It forms an important part of the assets of all major financial and institutional investors in that country. A similar condition prevails in other developed countries. In the developing countries the state borrows mainly for the purpose of financing the investment under the plans, which require generally large amounts of financial outlays. Thus, the development of the economy brings about simultaneous increase in the private and public debts and public assets form a significant part of the total assets, which are constantly being created in the economy.

The History of Public Debt in India is characterized by a continuous increase in the volume of the pubic debt. In the post-independence period, the needs of the government increased enormously at it have adopted an ambitious programme of development. This happened not only in the case of the Central Government but also with State Governments. Their expenditure also increased enormously due to the development programmes undertaken particularly after planning was launched for the economic development. Thus, the requirements of both the Central and State Governments increased enormously. In this situation if the entire requirements were met through taxes, the burden on the community would be too heavy. It would also adversely affect incentives and thereby retard development. It is desirable to finance a development programme, especially one that results in the creation of remunerative capital assets, partly through loans. This would achieve equity overtime and the burden on the present generation would not be too heavy. Thus the role of public borrowing was recognized and its importance was gradually emphasized.

The quantum of state debt is an important factor in Macroeconomic management. In India, till recently unplanned borrowing by the State Governments through the extensive overdraft from the Reserve Bank of India (RBI) was constantly a source of fiscal instability for more than two decades. In a fiscal federalism it is important to look at the institutional arrangements for borrowing by State Governments. We generally note two types of arrangement, namely total freedom and coordinated and centrally controlled programmes.

In the USA, states are debarred from borrowing to meet operating expenses but can do so for capital expenditures. This facility was exploited by them more than the federal government. In India, the states are technically empowered to borrow from the market but the amount of borrowing and the timing of issues have to be determined in consultation with the Central Government or the RBI. If, for example, both the Central and the State Governments are allowed to enter the market for raising loans, care would have to be taken that the timings, amounts, terms and other conditions of loans are not working at cross purposes. Normally, the Central Government is able to borrow at lower rates than the State Governments. Therefore, the rates of interest offered on Central and State Governments, loans should vary to accommodate this fact. Again different governments should avoid entering the market at the same time, or in quick succession if the availability of funds in the market is limited compared with the combined requirements of the governments.

If the State Governments are permitted independent borrowing powers, it may have both positive and negative effects. On the positive side, this power will encourage the state to cultivate the market and develop them. Experience shows that on the negative side, it may encourage sometimes-financial indiscipline. There has been excessive reliance on borrowing because it was preferred to taxation as a political alternative and as an expedient method. This results in undesirable competition for loanable funds in the market with a consequent rise in interest rates. It is likely to work against the stabilization objectives of the government. Further, less developed states with no capital markets may find it difficult to have their loans contributed. So there is need of co-ordination of debt issues.

One way to achieve co-ordination is centralized borrowing. It is appropriate for the stabilization purpose as it enables the Central Government to keep a firm hand on the issue of debt. But here the distribution of borrowed amount becomes a source of friction, which may weaken the federalism. This becomes the case specially when in the economy, political issues dominate our economic considerations. Different State Governments receive loans from the Central Government itself. This practice is followed in U.K. Australia and Canada but not in France and USA. In India too this practice is followed but is different from the

British Practice. It reflects common financial resources organized by the Central Government for financing the development plans and resources are transferred through both loans and grants. The growing burden of the central loans on states has now become a cause of concern.

Another problem has also emerged in recent past in the form of unauthorized overdrafts by states from the RBI. While the centre can borrow any amount from the RBI. and the latter cannot refuse to oblige, a state is authorized to overdraw only within agreed limits and that too only for a stipulated duration. The states have consistently resorted to violation of this provision of their agreements with the RBI and this has created problems in debt management. The Fifth Finance Commission condemned the system of unauthorized overdrafts on the ground that no country with a unified currency system could offered to have more than one independent authority taking measures which result in increase in money supply. In other words, unauthorized overdrafts run counter to the principle of sound monetary management.

In India, the task of coordinating different issue of debt management of both the Central and the State Governments lies with the Reserve Bank of India, and co-ordination is achieved through this agency. The RBI is the agent of both the Central and the State Governments in all debt operations. It also advises them regarding the timing, terms and the amounts of loans that car, be raised in the market undue difficulty.

Public debt has increased in the post-independence period largely because of the rising needs of planned economic development. Foreign assistance has also to be resorted to because of foreign exchange requirement of the five-year plans. Foreign assistance has been available to India in various forms but a large part of it has been in the form of interest loans.

## NEW CLASSIFICATION OF PUBLIC DEBT OF GOVERNMENT OF INDIA

The public debt of the Government of India has now been classified into the following three major groups:

**1. Internal Debt**

Internal debts comprise market borrowing or market loans raised in the open market through sale of securities and otherwise. They were formerly known as funded debt or permanent debt. They also include compensation and other bonds, 15 years annuity certificates. Besides, it also includes borrowing of temporary nature. Such borrowings include treasury bills issued by Government of India, State Governments, Commercial Banks, etc.

**2. External Debt**

External debt comprises loans taken by the Government of India against the non-negotiable, non-interest bearing securities issued to international financial institutions, such as IMF, IBRD, IDA, etc. Besides, the government of India has also raised loans from friendly countries outside India.

**3. Other Outstanding Liabilities**

Other outstanding liabilities comprise loans taken against the various small savings schemes, Public Provident Fund, of Central Government Departments (such as railways, post and telegraph, etc.) and certain other deposits like deposits of Income tax, super-tax, etc. All these are outstanding liabilities, which the Government of India is liable to repay on maturity. They formerly knew as unfounded debt.

The Table 1 indicates the rising trend of all the above loans as taken by the Government of India. The rising trend is mainly due to loans taken by the Government of India for financing the development plans during five-year plans.

## COMPOSITION OF PUBLIC DEBT IN INDIA

The composition of public dent in India may be classified into following three categories.

**I. Composition of Internal Public Debt**

The composition of internal public debt comprises loans raised by the Government of India in open market through

TABLE I

**Public Debt of Government of India**

(Rs. In Crores)

| Year | Internal Debt | External Debt |
|---|---|---|
| 1950-51 | 2022.00 | 32.00 |
| 1955-56 | 2329.00 | 114.00 |
| 1960-61 | 3975.00 | 761.00 |
| 1965-66 | 5415.00 | 2611.00 |
| 1970-71 | 7663.00 | 6485.00 |
| 1974-75 | 12371.00 | 6419.00 |
| 1980-81 | 36864.00 | 11298.00 |
| 1985-86 | 71039.00 | 18153.00 |
| 1990-91 | 154004.00 | 31525.00 |
| 1991-92 | 172750.00 | 36948.00 |
| 1992-93 | 199100.00 | 42269.00 |
| 1993-94 | 245712.00 | 47345.00 |
| 1994-95 | 266467.00 | 50929.00 |
| 1995-96 | 307869.00 | 51249.00 |
| 1996-97 | 344776.00 | 54239.00 |
| 1997-98 | 388997.78 | 55331.70 |
| 1998-99 | 458842.40 | 55960.10 |
| 1999-2000 (B.E.) | 709301.79 | 56134.34 |

*Sources*: (i) Reserve Bank of India, Reports on Currency and Finance, 1999-2000.
(ii) Economy Survey, 1999-2000).
(iii) Public Finance, Theory and Practice, R.C. Agarwal, L.N. Agarwal, Agra-3.

**Chart: Public Debt of Government of India**

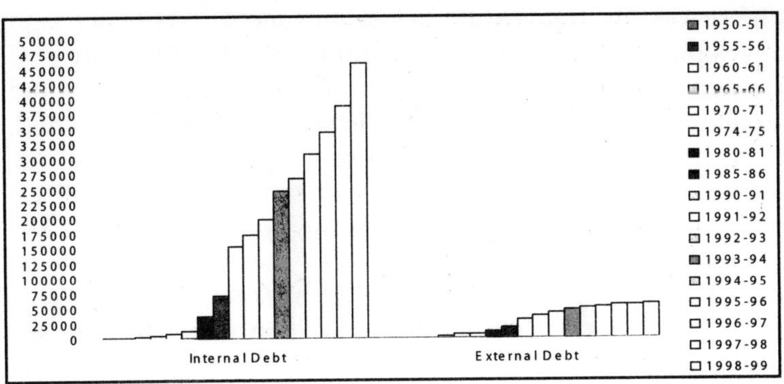

sale and purchase of securities and otherwise. These borrowings are of permanent as well as temporary in nature. The permanent includes compensation bonds and other bonds and 15 year Annuity Certificates while temporary includes market borrowings, treasury bills, issued by the Government of India to the Reserve Bank, State Governments, Commercial Banks and other parties.

Further, there are certain outstanding liabilities for which the government is liable to make repayments. Though these outstanding liabilities impose a burden of repayment on the Government of India, still they are considered as debt upon the government. They consists of liabilities against the deposits of:

(i) Various small saving schemes.
(ii) Public Provident Fund Contributions, State Provident Fund Contributions and Non-government Provident Fund Contributions.
(iii) Reserve Funds and Deposits of Various government departments.

A view of the internal public debt of Government of India is evident from the Tables 2 and 3.

## GOVERNMENT DEBT

Typically, the fiscal responsibility rules world over are anchored in balanced budget and debt targets with clear differences in framework across advanced economies and developing countries. In India, under the FRBMA, the rule focused on incremental assumption of liabilities. By and largethis rule was adhered to in the post-FRBMA period; since 2008-09, there has been a rise in the assumption of net incremental liabilities as a result of the expansionary fiscal policy stance. As a result, with the revised GDP series (2004-05) released by the CSO, the ratio of outstanding liabilities to the GDP after falling from a level of 61.6 per cent in 2004-05 to 56.3 per cent in 2008-09 (RE), has risen marginally to 56.7 per cent in 2009-10(BE).

TABLE 2

**Internal Public Debt of Government of India (2000-2005)**

(Rs. In Crores)

| State | State Plan | Brought Loans | Others | Central Sector | Centrally Sponsored Schemes | Total Plan | Small Savings Loans | Moderni-zation of Police | Housing of IAS Officers | Others | Total Non-Plan | Total Non-Plan |
|---|---|---|---|---|---|---|---|---|---|---|---|---|
| 1 | 2 | 3 | 4 | 5 | 6 | 7 | 8 | 9 | 10 | 11 | 12 | 13 |
| Andhra Pradesh | 280166 | 173 | 0 | 0 | 9506 | 289845 | 91923 | 178420 | 420 | 26 | 92547 | 382392 |
| Arunachal Pradesh | 14854 | 0 | 0 | 473 | 124 | 15451 | 979 | 298 | 0 | 0 | 1277 | 16728 |
| Assam | 84631 | 0 | 0 | 5661 | 850 | 91142 | 49037 | 120 | 33 | 414 | 49604 | 140746 |
| Bihar | 224327 | 0 | 0 | 630 | 1102 | 226059 | 114481 | 245 | 155 | 68 | 114949 | 341008 |
| Goa | 16493 | 0 | 0 | 17 | 118 | 16628 | 5083 | 31 | 0 | 0 | 5114 | 170 |
| Gujarat | 131395 | 0 | 13 | 2490 | 1917 | 135815 | 199788 | 122 | 154 | 170 | 200234 | 336049 |
| Haryana | 57321 | 0 | 0 | 432 | 8766 | 58619 | 58592 | 70 | 70 | 0 | 58732 | 117351 |
| Himachal Pradesh | 14935 | 1 | 0 | 23 | 2157 | 17116 | 40063 | 57 | 92 | 0 | 40212 | 57328 |
| Jammu and Kashmir | 91410 | 0 | 0 | 297 | 335 | 920272 | 21305 | 127 | 28 | 0 | 21460 | 113532 |
| Karnataka | 133201 | 0 | 942 | 260 | 4221 | 138624 | 103140 | 164 | 40 | 601 | 103945 | 242569 |
| Kerala | 109814 | 125 | 0 | 542 | 4262 | 114743 | 51229 | 121 | 40 | 47 | 51437 | 166180 |
| Madhya Pradesh | 173370 | 378 | 0 | 1755 | 4422 | 182925 | 69231 | 284 | 112 | 7 | 69634 | 252559 |
| Maharashtra | 2167202 | 0 | 0 | 402 | 3569 | 220673 | 290767 | 211 | 115 | 0 | 291093 | 511766 |
| Manipur | 7468 | 0 | 192 | 107 | 221 | 7988 | 1478 | 290 | 49 | 0 | 1817 | 9805 |

(Contd.)

TABLE 2 *(Contd.)*

| *1* | *2* | *3* | *4* | *5* | *6* | *7* | *8* | *9* | *10* | *11* | *12* | *13* |
|---|---|---|---|---|---|---|---|---|---|---|---|---|
| Meghalaya | 6027 | 0 | 208 | 9 | 445 | 6689 | 2700 | 37 | 45 | 233 | 3015 | 9704 |
| Mizoram | 4685 | 0 | 0 | 291 | 232 | 5208 | 965 | 69 | 35 | 1 | 1070 | 6278 |
| Nagaland | 8070 | 0 | 82 | 223 | 199 | 8574 | 1447 | 105 | 82 | 0 | 1634 | 10208 |
| Orissa | 143672 | 0 | 0 | 2634 | 5191 | 151497 | 40643 | 129 | 63 | 0 | 40835 | 192331 |
| Punjab | 254616 | 0 | 0 | 2634 | 5191 | 151497 | 40643 | 129 | 63 | 0 | 40835 | 192332 |
| Rajasthan | 150013 | 308 | 0 | 216 | 4566 | 155100 | 91598 | 689 | 57 | 1359 | 93703 | 248812 |
| Sikkim | 4376 | 0 | 0 | 0 | 614 | 4884 | 995 | 16 | 28 | 0 | 1039 | 5928 |
| Tamil Nadu | 2253920 | 525 | 0 | 528 | 2373 | 227146 | 83920 | 281 | 285 | 0 | 84486 | 311632 |
| Tripura | 7827 | 0 | 0 | 12 | 398 | 8237 | 5186 | 383 | 31 | 481 | 6081 | 14318 |
| Uttar Pradesh | 476667 | 0 | 0 | 443 | 13112 | 490222 | 282051 | 298 | 331 | 31 | 282711 | 772933 |
| West Bengal | 1695338 | 0 | 0 | 153 | 2266 | 171952 | 284628 | 190 | 2481 | 3510 | 290809 | 462761 |
| Total | 3008522 | 1310 | 1443 | 17702 | 65728 | 3094705 | 1991498 | 4635 | 5026 | 41064 | 2042223 | 5136928 |

*Source*: Public Finance Theory and Practice, A.C. Agarwal, p. 334.

TABLE 3

## Internal Public Debt of Government of India (2000-2005)

*(Rs. In Crores)*

| *Internal Debt* | *2022.30* | *3978.00* | *86313* | *154004* | *245712* | *266467* | *307869* | *344476* | *388998* | *458842* | *709302* |
|---|---|---|---|---|---|---|---|---|---|---|---|
| *1* | *2* | *3* | *4* | *5* | *6* | *7* | *8* | *9* | *10* | *11* | *12* |
| 1. Market Loan | 1438.4 | 2555.72 | 40832 | 70520 | 110611 | 130908 | 163986 | 183976 | 216464 | 281375 | 348593 |
| 2. Market Loans in Course of Repayment | 6.49 | 22.27 | 48 | 46 | 70 | 99 | 108 | 125 | 134 | 134 | 134 |
| 3. Compensation and other bonds, etc. | 6.73 | - | 1359 | 1739 | 1639 | 2556 | 3292 | 4006 | 4594 | 6648 | 9136 |
| 4. Treasury Bills | 364.77 | 1106.29 | 198776 | 8031 | 40981 | 40492 | 45665 | 64759 | 27842 | 27842 | 27842 |
| 5. Securities Issued to International Financial Institutions | 212.60 | 274:18 | 4350 | 6566 | 20365 | 20365 | 22771 | 19562 | 17100 | 19980 | 20526 |
| 6. Treasury Bill Funded into Special Securities | - | - | 18500 | 66000 | 71000 | 71000 | 71000 | 101818 | 101818 | 101818 | 101818 |

*(Contd.)*

TABLE 3 *(Contd.)*

| *1* | *2* | *3* | *4* | *5* | *6* | *7* | *8* | *9* | *10* | *11* | *12* |
|---|---|---|---|---|---|---|---|---|---|---|---|
| 7. Other Special Securities Issued to RBI | - | - | 1367 | 1101 | 1046 | 1046 | 1046 | 1046 | 1046 | 1046 | 1046 |
| 8. Special Securities Converted into Marketable Securities | - | - | - | - | - | - | - | - | 20000 | 20000 | 20000 |
| 9. Securities against small savings | - | - | - | - | - | - | - | - | - | - | 180207 |

*Source*: Public Finance Theory and Practice, A.C. Agarwal, p. 334.

## TABLE 4

# Outstanding liabilities of the Central Government

**Table 3.6 : Outstanding liabilities of the Central Government**

(end-March)

| | 2004-05 | 2005-06 | 2006-07 | 2007-08 | 2008-09 (RE) | 2009-10 (BE) |
|---|---|---|---|---|---|---|
| | | | (Rs. crore) | | | |
| 1. **Internal Liabilities #** | **19,33,544** | **21,65,902** | **24,35,880** | **27,25,394** | **30,14,441** | **33,57,772** |
| (a) Internal Debt | 12,75,971 | 13,89,758 | 15,44,975 | 18,08,359 | 20,14,451 | 23,56,940 |
| (i) Market Borrowings | 7,58,995 | 8,62,370 | 9,72,801 | 10,92,468 | 13,58,940 | 17,66,897 |
| (ii) Others | 5,16,976 | 5,27,388 | 5,72,174 | 7,15,891 | 6,55,511 | 5,90,043 |
| (b) Other Internal Liabilities | 6,57,573 | 7,76,144 | 8,90,905 | 9,17,035 | 9,99,990 | 10,00,832 |
| 2. **External Debt (Outstanding)*** | **60,878** | **94,243** | **1,02,716** | **1,12,031** | **1,21,634** | **1,37,680** |
| 3. **Total Outstanding Liabilities (1+2)** | **19,94,422** | **22,60,145** | **25,38,596** | **28,37,425** | **31,36,075** | **34,95,452** |
| 4. Amount due from Pakistan on Account of Share of Pre-partition Debt | 300 | 300 | 300 | 300 | 300 | 300 |
| 5. Net Liabilities (3-4) | 19,94,122 | 22,59,845 | 25,38,296 | 28,37,125 | 31,35,775 | 34,95,152 |
| | | | (As per cent of GDP) | | | |
| 1. **Internal Liabilities** | **59.7** | **58.4** | **56.9** | **55.1** | **54.1** | **54.5** |
| (a) Internal Debt | 39.4 | 37.5 | 36.1 | 36.5 | 36.1 | 38.2 |
| (i) Market Borrowings | 23.4 | 23.3 | 22.7 | 22.1 | 24.4 | 28.7 |
| (ii) Others | 16.0 | 14.2 | 13.4 | 14.5 | 11.8 | 9.6 |
| (b) Other Internal Liabilities | 20.3 | 20.9 | 20.8 | 18.5 | 17.9 | 16.2 |
| 2. **External Debt (Outstanding)*** | **1.9** | **2.5** | **2.4** | **2.3** | **2.2** | **2.2** |
| 3. **Total Outstanding Liabilities** | **61.6** | **61.0** | **59.3** | **57.3** | **56.3** | **56.7** |
| **Memorandum Items** | | | | | | |
| (a) External Debt (Rs crore)@ | 1,91,182 | 1,94,078 | 2,01,204 | 2,10,083 | 2,64,076 | 2,80,122 |
| (as Per Cent of GDP) | 5.9 | 5.2 | 4.7 | 4.2 | 4.7 | 4.5 |
| (b) Total outstanding Liabilities (adjusted) (Rs crore) | 21,24,726 | 23,59,980 | 26,37,084 | 29,35,477 | 32,78,517 | 36,37,894 |
| (as Per Cent of GDP) | 65.6 | 63.7 | 61.6 | 59.3 | 58.8 | 59.0 |
| (c) Internal Liabilities (Non-RBI)## | 17,71,117 | 19,69,106 | 22,17,671 | 24,71,396 | 27,07,443 | 30,60,774 |
| (as Per Cent of GDP) | 54.7 | 53.1 | 51.8 | 49.9 | 48.6 | 49.7 |
| (d) Outstanding Liabilities (Non-RBI) ## (Rs crore) | 19,62,299 | 21,63,184 | 24,18,875 | 26,81,479 | 29,71,519 | 33,40,896 |
| Outstanding Liabilities (Non-RBI) (as Per Cent of GDP) | 60.6 | 58.4 | 56.5 | 54.2 | 53.3 | 54.2 |
| (e) Contingent Liabilities of Central Government (Rs crore) | 1,07,957 | 1,10,626 | 1,09,826 | 1,04,872 | n.a. | n.a. |
| Contingent Liabilities of Central Government (as Per Cent of GDP) | 3.3 | 3.0 | 2.6 | 2.1 | n.a. | n.a. |
| (f) Total Assets (Rs crore) | 10,83,422 | 11,94,446 | 13,39,119 | 15,71,668 | 15,80,300 | 16,71,532 |
| Total Assets (as Per Cent of GDP) | 33.4 | 32.2 | 31.3 | 31.8 | 28.3 | 27.1 |

Source: 1. Union Budget documents. 2. Controller of Aid Accounts and Audit. 3. Reserve Bank of India.

n.a. : not available.

* External debt figures represent borrowings by Central Government from external sources and are based upon historical rates of exchange.

@ Converted at year-end exchange rates. For 2004-05, the rates prevailing at the end of March 2005 and so on.

# Internal debt includes net borrowing of Rs 64,211crore for 2004-05, Rs 29,062 crore for 2005-06, Rs 62,974 crore for 2006-07 Rs 1,70554 crore for 2007-08, Rs 88,773 crore for 2008-09(RE) and Rs 40,737 crore for 2009-10(BE) under the Market Stabilisation Scheme.

## This includes marketable dated securities held by the RBI.

Note : The ratios to GDP at current market prices are based on the CSO's National Accounts 2004-05 series.

Internal debt, mainly market borrowings, continued o be the main component of outstanding liabilities Figure.

**Figure: Debt GDP Ratios**

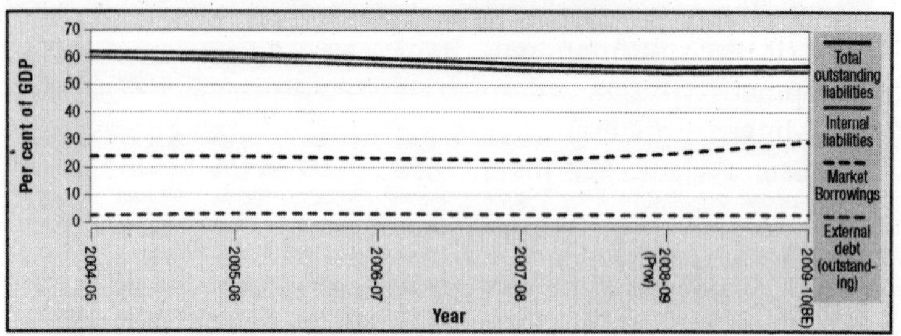


## II. Composition of External Debt

Since internal public debts fall short of the requirements, the Government of India is compelled to raise

TABLE 5

**External Public Debt**

| *Year* | *Amount (Rs. in Crores)* |
|---|---:|
| 1950-51 | 32.00 |
| 1955-56 | 114.00 |
| 1960-61 | 761.00 |
| 1965-66 | 2611.00 |
| 1970-71 | 6485.00 |
| 1974-75 | 6419.00 |
| 1980-81 | 11298.00 |
| 1985-86 | 18153.00 |
| 1990-91 | 31525.00 |
| 1991-92 | 36948.00 |
| 1992-93 | 42269.00 |
| 1993-94 | 47345.00 |
| 1994-95 | 50345.00 |
| 1995-96 | 51249.00 |
| 1996-97 | 54239.00 |
| 1997-98 | 553331.70 |
| 1998-99 | 55960.10 |
| 1999-2000 (B.E.) | 56134.34 |

*Source*: Economic Survey, 1999-2000, Govt. of India, New Delhi.

external public debt from foreign countries so as to meet the rapid development as envisaged in our plans. External debt includes loans taken by the Government of India against the non-negotiable, non-interest bearing securities issued to external financial institutions like International Monetary Fund (IMF), International Bank for Reconstruction and Development (IBRD), International Development Association (IDA), International Fund for Agriculture and Development (IFAD), etc. The Government of India has also raised loans from other friendly countries in addition to the loans taken from the above-noted international institutions. A view of external public debt is evident from the Table 5.

**External Debt**

India's external debt stock stood at US $ 224.59 billion (Rs. 1,142,618 crore) in end-March 2009, that is fractionally higher than its previous year's level of US $ 224.41 billion (Rs. 897,314 crore).

During the first half of 2009-10, total external debt increased by US $ 18.2 billion (8.1 per cent) to US $ 242.8 billion (Rs 1,166,217 crore). Long-term debt posted an increase of US $ 19.2 billion (10.6 per cent) to stand at US $ 200.4 billion, while shortterm debt fell by US $ 985 million (-2.3 per cent) to stand at US $ 42.4 billion. The share of long-term debt was higher at 82.5 per cent in end-September 2009 as against 80.7 per cent in end-March 2009. Concomitantly, the share of short-term debt declined to 17.5 per cent in end-September 2009 from 19.3 per cent in end-March 2009. (Table 6)

The valuation effect arising due to depreciation of the US dollar against major international currencies contributed an increase of US $ 8.3 billion in the total increase of US $ 18.2 billion in external debt as in end-September 2009 over the end-March 2009 level. Excluding the valuation effect, the increase in external debt would have been US $ 9.9 billion.

Commercial borrowings remained the largest component of external debt with a share of 27.5 per cent in end-September 2009 (27.8 per cent in end-March 2009). Reflecting the impact of an increase in NRI deposits attributable to an upward revision in interest rate ceiling on

TABLE 6

## India's External Debt

**Table 6.11 : India's external debt**

| Components | (US$ billion) | | | | | | |
|---|---|---|---|---|---|---|---|
| | End March | | | | | End-June 2009 PR | End-Sept. 2009 QE |
| | 2005 | 2006 | 2007R | 2008 R | 2099 PR | | |
| Long-term Debt | 116.28 | 119.58 | 144.23 | 178.68 | 181.23 | 187.75 | 200.45 |
| Short-term Debt | 17.72 | 19.54 | 28.13 | 45.74 | 43.36 | 42.03 | 42.38 |
| **Total External Debt** | 134.00 | 139.11 | 172.36 | 224.41 | 224.59 | 229.78 | 242.82 |
| **(Rupee crore)** | | | | | | | |
| Long-term Debt | 5,08,777 | 5,33,367 | 6,28,771 | 7,14,433 | 9,21,710 | 9,01,840 | 9,62,640 |
| Short-term Debt | 77,528 | 87,155 | 1,22,631 | 1,82,881 | 2,20,908 | 2,01,234 | 2,03,577 |
| **Total External Debt** | 5,86,305 | 6,20,522 | 7,51,402 | 8,97,314 | 1,142,618 | 1,103,074 | 1,166,217 |

R: Revised; PR: Partially Revised; QE: Quick Estimates.

## Chart: External Public Debt

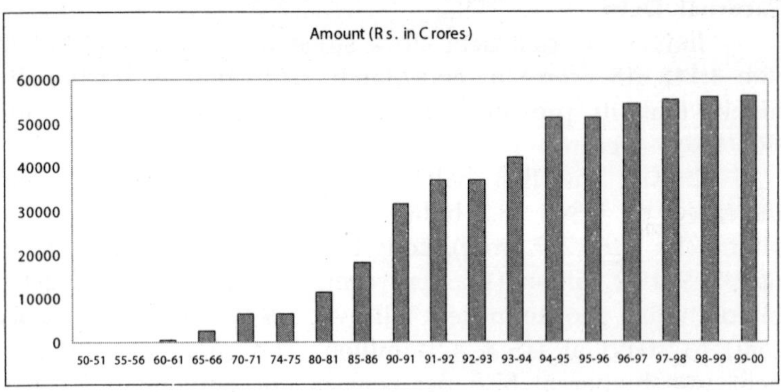


these deposits, there was an improvement in their share from 18.5 per cent in end-March 2009 to 18.9 per cent in end-September 2009. Multilateral debt accounted for 17.4 per cent of total external debt, followed by bilateral debt (9.1 per cent), export credits (6.3 per cent), IMF representing SDR allocations (2.6 per cent) and rupee debt (0.7 per cent) as in end-September 2009. Trade-related credits at US $ 39.3 billion constituted 92.8 per cent of total short-term debt and 16.2 per cent of total external debt at the end of September 2009.

## EXTERNAL COMMERCIAL BORROWING (ECB) POLICY MEASURES DURING 2009-10

The broad ECB policy stance towards liberalization continued during the first half of 2009-10. However, it has been decided to roll back some of the policy measures which were introduced against the backdrop of tightness in financial markets during the period of financial crisis. These policy measures have become effective from January 1, 2010.

Non-banking financial companies (NBFCs), exclusively involved in financing of the infrastructure sector, were allowed to avail of ECBs from multilateral/regional financial institutions and Government-owned development financial institutions for on-lending to borrowers in the infrastructure sector under the approval route, subject *inter alia* to the condition that the direct lending portfolio of these lenders *vis-à-vis* their total ECB lending to NBFCs, at any point of time, should not be less than 3:1 (January 2, 2009). On a review of the policy, it was decided to dispense with this condition with effect from July 1, 2009 (June 30, 2009). Furthermore, it has been decided with immediate effect to allow NBFCs exclusively involved in financing infrastructure projects to avail of ECB from the recognized lender category including international banks under the approval route, subject to complying with the prudential standards prescribed by the Reserve Bank and the borrowing entities fully hedging their currency risk (December 9, 2009).

Payment for obtaining licence/permit for the 3G Spectrum was allowed as an eligible end-use for the purpose of ECB under the automatic route (October 22, 2008). It has been decided to permit eligible borrowers in the telecommunication sector with immediate effect to avail of ECB for the purpose of payment for spectrum allocation (December 9, 2009).

It was decided to extend the permission granted to corporates engaged in the development of integrated township to avail of ECBs under the approval route until December 31, 2009. This has been extended further to December 31, 2010 (December 9, 2009).

Keeping in view the prevailing market conditions, the all-in-cost ceilings applicable to ECBs under the approval route were dispensed with until June 30, 2009 (January 2, 2009). On considering the continuing pressure on credit spreads in the international markets, it was decided in June 2009 to extend the relaxation in all-in-cost ceilings under the approval route until December 31, 2009. However, in view of the improvement in credit market conditions and narrowing credit spreads in the international markets, it has been decided to withdraw the existing relaxation with effect from January 1, 2010. The all-in-cost ceilings under the approval route for ECBs, where loan agreements have been signed on or after January 1, 2010, will be 300 basis points and 500 basis points over six month Libor for an average maturity period of three years and up to five years and more than five years, respectively (December 9, 2009).

Buy-back/pre-payment of foreign currency convertible bonds (FCCBs)

The procedure relating to premature buyback of FCCBs by Indian companies, both under the automatic and approval routes was liberalized on December 6, 2008, by which the Reserve Bank could consider proposals from Indian companies for buyback of FCCBs under the approval route subject to the buyback value of the FCCB being at a minimum discount of 25 per cent on the book value and use of funds out of internal accruals of the company. Total amount of buyback under the approval route is subject to a limit of US $ 50 million of the redemption value per company. The date for completing the entire procedure for buyback of FCCBs was extended from March 31, 2009 to December 31, 2009. Keeping in view the prevailing macroeconomic conditions and global developments, especially the improvement in the stock prices, it has recently been decided to discontinue the facility with effect from January 1, 2010 (December 9, 2009).

Short-term debt by residual maturity, which comprises principal repayments during a one-year reference period under medium- and long-term debt liabilities, and short-term debt with original maturity of one year or less are important indicators of debt sustainability in volatile financial market conditions. Short-term external debt by original maturity stood at US $ 42.4 billion in end-September, while total short-term debt by residual maturity was US $ 93.2 billion, accounting for 38.4 per cent of total external debt outstanding in end-September 2009. NRI deposits maturing within a period of one year at US $ 36.7 billion worked out to 39.4 per cent of total shortterm debt by residual maturity. However, 69.3 per cent of these deposits are denominated and payable in Indian rupees. The observed redemption pattern of NRI deposits indicates that these are generally locally withdrawn and are also renewed by NRIs. Between end-March and end-September 2009, there was an improvement in the ratio of short-term debt by residual maturity to foreign exchange reserves from 37.0 per cent to 33.1 per cent.

Government debt stood at US $ 65.7 billion in end-September 2009 while non-Government debt amounted to US $ 177.1 billion. The share of Government debt in total external debt declined from 40.6 per cent in end-March 2004 to 24.9 per cent in end-March 2009, before rising to 27.1 per cent in end-September 2009. The external assistance component of Government debt at US $ 55.1 billion in end-September 2009 was higher than its end-March 2009 level of US $ 51.8 billion. Other Government external debt also recorded an increase from US $ 4.1 billion in end-March 2009 to US $ 10.6 billion in end-September 2009, attributable mainly to additional SDR allocations of 3,082.51 million under general allocation on August 28, 2009 and 214.57 million under special allocation on September 9, 2009 by the IMF. The ratio of Government debt to GDP remained around 5.0 per cent in the last three years.

US dollar-denominated debt accounted for 51.4 per cent of total external debt in end-September 2009, followed by Indian rupee (16.6 per cent), Japanese yen (13.6 per cent), SDR (12.0 per cent), Euro (3.9 per cent) and pound sterling (2.1 per cent) denominated debt. The currency composition of Government debt indicates predominance of SDR denominated debt, which is attributable to borrowing from the International Development Association (IDA), that is the soft loan window of the World Bank under the multilateral agencies and inclusion of SDR allocations by the IMF as an external debt liability of the Government. The share of the Japanese yen in Government debt is also higher on account of borrowing from Japan, which is denominated in Japanese yen. Table 7.

The debt sustainability indicator, that is ratio of foreign exchange reserves to total external debt showed an

TABLE 7

**Currency Composition of India's External Debt and Sovereign External Debt**

*(as per cent of total external debt)*

| Sl. No. | Currency | Total external debt | | | | Sovereign external debt | | | |
|---|---|---|---|---|---|---|---|---|---|
| | | As at the end of | | | | | | | |
| | | March 2008R | March 2009R | June 2009PR | Sept. 2009QE | March 2008R | March 2009R | June 2009PR | Sept. 2009QE |
| 1. | US Dollar | 55.3 | 54.1 | 52.3 | 51.4 | 26.7 | 29.6 | 29.1 | 25.8 |
| 2. | SDR | 10.5 | 9.8 | 10.0 | 12.0 | 40.8 | 39.5 | 39.2 | 44.2 |
| 3. | Indian Rupee | 16.2 | 15.4 | 16.3 | 16.6 | 7.9 | 5.7 | 6.7 | 6.8 |
| 4. | Japanese Yen | 12.0 | 14.3 | 14.5 | 13.6 | 18.6 | 19.9 | 19.8 | 18.4 |
| 5. | Euro | 3.5 | 4.1 | 4.3 | 3.9 | 5.9 | 5.2 | 5.2 | 4.8 |
| 6. | Pound Sterling | 2.2 | 2.0 | 2.2 | 2.1 | 0.1 | 0.1 | 0 | 0 |
| 7. | Others | 0.3 | 0.3 | 0.4 | 0.4 | 0 | 0 | 0 | 0 |
| | Total | 100.0 | 100.0 | 100.0 | 100.0 | 100.0 | 100.0 | 100.0 | 100.0 |

R: Revised PR: Partially Revised. QE Quick Estimates

improvement from 112.1 per cent in end-March 2009 to 115.4 per cent in end-June 2009 and further to 115.8 per cent in end-September 2009. The ratio of short-term external debt to foreign exchange reserves, which had increased from 14.8 per cent in end-March 2008 to 17.2 per cent in end-March 2009, was also lower at 15.1 per cent in end-September 2009. The concessional debt portion of external debt has declined steadily and worked out to 18.4 per cent in end-September 2009 as against 18.7 per cent in end-March 2009 (Table 8).

## INTERNATIONAL COMPARISON LEVEL

A cross-country comparison of external debt of 20 most indebted developing countries, based on the data given in World Bank's publication titled Global Development Finance, 2009 showed that India was the fifth most indebted country in 2007 in terms of stock of external debt. The ratio of India's external debt stock to gross national income (GNI) as of 2007 at 18.9 per cent was the sixth lowest with China having the lowest ratio at 11.6 per cent. The element of concessionality in India's external debt portfolio was the second highest after that of Indonesia.

### TABLE 8

### India's Key External Debt Indicators

*(per cent)*

| Year | External debt (US$ billion) | Ratio of total external debt to GDP | Debt-service ratio@ | Ratio of foreign exchange reserves to total external debt | Ratio of concessional debt to total external debt | Ratio of short-term debt to foreign exchnage reserves | Ratio of short-term debt to total debt |
|---|---|---|---|---|---|---|---|
| 1990-91 | 83.8 | 28.7 | 35.3 | 7.0 | 45.9 | 146.5 | 10.2 |
| 1995-96 | 93.7 | 27.0 | 26.2 | 23.1 | 44.7 | 23.2 | 5.4 |
| 2001-02 | 98.8 | 21.1 | 13.7 | 54.7 | 35.9 | 5.1 | 2.8 |
| 2003-04 R | 112.7 | 18.0 | 16.1** | 100.3 | 35.8 | 3.9 | 3.9 |
| 2004-05 R | 134.0 | 18.1 | 5.9 ^ | 105.6 | 30.7 | 12.5 | 13.2 |
| 2005-06 R | 139.1 | 16.7 | 10.1# | 109.0 | 28.4 | 12.9 | 14.1 |
| 2006-07 R | 172.4 | 17.5 | 4.7 | 115.6 | 23.0 | 14.1 | 16.3 |
| 2007-08 R | 224.4 | 18.1 | 4.8 | 138.0 | 19.7 | 14.8 | 20.4 |
| 2008-09PR | 224.6 | 20.5 | 4.4 | 112.1 | 18.7 | 17.2 | 19.3 |
| End-June 2009 PR | 229.8 | - | - | 115.4 | 18.9 | 15.9 | 18.3 |
| End-Sept. 2008 PR | 225.1 | - | - | 127.2 | 18.4 | 17.7 | 22.5 |
| End-Sept. 2009 QE | 242.8 | - | - | 115.8 | 18.4 | 15.1 | 17.5 |

R: Revised; PR: Partially Revised; QE: Quick Estimates.
- Not worked out for the broken period.
@ Debt-service ratio is the proportion of gross debt service payments to External Current Receipts (net of official transfers).
^^ Works out to 8.2 per cent, with the exclusion of pre-payment of US$ 3,797 million and redemption of Resurgent India Bonds (RIBs) of US$ 5,549 million.
^ Works out to 5.7 per cent with the exclusion of pre-payment of US$ 381 million.
# Works out to 6.3 per cent, with the exclusion of IMDs repayments of US$ 7.1 billion and pre-payment of US$ 23.5 million.

In terms of the cover of external debt provided by foreign exchange reserves, India's position was the fifth highest at 125.2 per cent after China, Malaysia, Thailand and the Russian Federation. A comparison of the share of short-term debt in total external debt across countries reveals that India's position was the eighth lowest with Mexico having the lowest ratio.

### III. Other Outstanding Liabilities

The government of India is liable to repay its outstanding liabilities against the various small savings schemes, Public Provident Fund, State Provident Fund, Non-government Provident Fund and other reserve funds of government departments like post and telegraph, railways and certain other deposits like income-tax deposits. Super-tax deposits of local funds, and civil deposits. These are known as outstanding liabilities of the government of India. These were earlier termed as unfounded debt.

A view of other outstanding liabilities is evident from the Table 10

## TABLE 9

### International Comparison of Top 20 Debtor Developing Countries, 2007

| Sl No. | Countries | External debt stock (US $ million) | External debt to GNI (per cent) | Short-term debt to external debt (per cent) | Foreign exchange reserves to external debt (per cent) | Concessional debt to total external debt (per cent) |
|---|---|---|---|---|---|---|
| 1 | Argentina | 1,27,758 | 49.7 | 29.8 | 36.1 | 1.3 |
| 2 | Brazil | 2,37,472 | 18.7 | 16.5 | 75.9 | 1.0 |
| 3 | Chile | 58,649 | 40.3 | 22.7 | 28.7 | 0.4 |
| 4 | China | 3,73,635 | 11.6 | 54.5 | 413.9 | 10.1 |
| 5 | Colombia | 44,976 | 22.5 | 11.9 | 46.6 | 2.1 |
| 6 | Croatia | 48,584 | 97.7 | 10.5 | 28.1 | 2.1 |
| 7 | India | 2,20,956 | 18.9 | 19.8 | 125.2 | 21.7 |
| 8 | Indonesia | 1,40,783 | 33.9 | 24.8 | 40.4 | 26.2 |
| 9 | Kazakhstan | 96,133 | 103.7 | 12.2 | 18.4 | 1.0 |
| 10 | Malaysia | 53,717 | 29.4 | 28.4 | 189.9 | 6.1 |
| 11 | Mexico | 1,78,108 | 17.7 | 5.1 | 49.0 | 0.6 |
| 12 | Philippines | 65,845 | 41.9 | 10.8 | 51.2 | 20.0 |
| 13 | Poland | 1,95,374 | 47.7 | 30.9 | 33.6 | 0.4 |
| 14 | Romania | 85,380 | 51.5 | 35.7 | 46.8 | 1.6 |
| 15 | Russian Federation | 3,70,172 | 29.4 | 21.4 | 129.1 | 0.4 |
| 16 | South Africa | 43,380 | 15.8 | 38.2 | 75.9 | - |
| 17 | Thailand | 63,067 | 26.5 | 34.3 | 138.7 | 9.6 |
| 18 | Turkey | 2,51,477 | 38.8 | 16.6 | 30.4 | 2.1 |
| 19 | Ukraine | 73,600 | 52.9 | 31.1 | 44.1 | 2.2 |
| 20 | Venezuela | 43,148 | 18.7 | 27.1 | 78.2 | 0.5 |
| | **All developing countries** | **34,66,045** | | **24.5** | | |

**Source : Global Development Finance 2009, World Bank.**

## TABLE 10

### Total Outstanding Liabilities (Cumulative Picture)

*(Rs. in Crores)*

| *Year* | *Small Savings Plus 5 Year Annuity Deposits* | *Provident Funds (Total of all Kinds)* | *Other Accounts* | *Reserved Funds and Deposits* | *Total* |
|---|---|---|---|---|---|
| 1950-51 | 336.87 | 95.05 | 16.10 | 363.05 | 811.07 |
| 1960-61 | 969.00 | 289.14 | 262.23 | 283.02 | 1803.39 |
| 1990-91 | 50100.18 | 11670.34 | 45336.43 | 21922.17 | 129029.12 |
| 1996-97 | 27961.66 | 118834.30 | 100087.33 | 37919.47 | 284802.76 |
| 1997-98 | 333963.35 | 143277.32 | 12487.33 | 42096.57 | 531824.57 |
| 1998-99 | 172207.32 | 29852.63 | 126243.97 | 32818.43 | 361122.35 |
| 1999-2000 | 25000.00 | 35852.63 | 136625.66 | 27648.86 | 225127.15 |

*Source*: Economic Survey, 1999-2000, Government of India, New Delhi

## OVERALL PICTURE OF PUBLIC DEBT IN INDIA

The combined position (overall) of public debt in India has been given in the table given below (Table 11). The total public debt from different sources like internal, external and others was Rs. 2865.4 crores in 1950-51 which rose to Rs. 9,93,563.28 crores in 1999-2000.

TABLE 11

**Overall Picture of Public Debt of Government of India**

*(Rs. in Crores)*

| *Year* | *Internal Debt* | *External Debt* | *Other Outstanding Liabilities* | *Total* |
|---|---|---|---|---|
| 1950-51 | 2022.30 | 32.03 | 811.06 | 2865.39 |
| 1960-61 | 3978.00 | 760.96 | 1805.28 | 6544.24 |
| 1977-78 | 19025.29 | 8984.74 | 12193.92 | 40203.95 |
| 1980-81 | 29008.49 | 11316.35 | 18393.38 | 58718.22 |
| 1990-91 | 15403.00 | 31524.97 | 129029.12 | 175957.09 |
| 1993-94 | 245712.32 | 47345.35 | 184910.99 | 477968.66 |
| 1994-95 | 266466.96 | 50928.47 | 221215.23 | 538610.66 |
| 1995-96 | 307868.96 | 51248.74 | 247115.01 | 606232.71 |
| 1996-97 | 344475.66 | 54238.56 | 276961.66 | 675675.88 |
| 1997-98 | 388997.78 | 55331.97 | 333963.85 | 778293.60 |
| 1998-99 | 458842.40 | 55960.10 | 361122.35 | 875924.85 |
| 1999-2000 | 712301.79 | 56134.34 | 225127.15 | 993563.28 |

*Source*: Economic Survey, 1999-2000, Government of India, New Delhi

When this happened, certain issues relating to public debt cropped up. As for example, how to raise loans, and at what cost and to what extent it should be raised, how it will affect the economy and how to mitigate its bad effects and finally how to repay the principle and the interest thereon are some of the important issues which necessitated a debt policy.

## DEBT POSITION OF STATES

There is a growing concern over the public debt of the states, which is increasing from year to year. Total debt of States including short-term debt is estimated to have risen

TABLE 12

**Composition of State Governments' Debt as on March 31, 1999**

*(Rs. in lakhs)*

| States | Central Loan | Market Loans and Bonds | Loans from Banks, etc. | W & M Adv. from RBI | Provident Funds and, etc. | Reserve Funds and Deposits | Total Debt | Total |
|---|---|---|---|---|---|---|---|---|
| Andhra Pradesh | 1394127 | 603836 | 118817 | 21984 | 251750 | 439139 | 2829653 | 2368530 |
| Arunachal Pradesh | 34992 | 5170 | 8302 | 555 | 16261 | 1614 | 66894 | 64725 |
| Assam | 429163 | 155793 | 8874 | 8458 | 681836 | 70098 | 740569 | 662013 |
| Bihar | 1337490 | 552236 | -12712 | 0 | 637434 | 168196 | 2682644 | 2514448 |
| Goa | 113032 | 21315 | 7678 | 0 | 29130 | 13804 | 184959 | 171155 |
| Gujarat | 1397564 | 254628 | 55774 | 0 | 210886 | 556884 | 2475736 | 1918852 |
| Haryana | 490898 | 126858 | 46093 | 1841 | 283764 | 70439 | 1019893 | 947613 |
| Himachal Pradesh | 269724 | 48239 | 348136 | 85263 | 146780 | 5708 | 641837 | 499556 |
| Jammu and Kashmir | 342019 | 57658 | 17247 | 110823 | 108008 | 37420 | 673175 | 524932 |
| Karnataka | 90135 | 284094 | 60892 | 0 | 2994414 | 320721 | 1861656 | 1540935 |
| Kerala | 564814 | 341922 | 88133 | 12381 | 562778 | 16685 | 1736213 | 1557647 |
| Madhya Pradesh | 923034 | 340525 | 59541 | 1925 | 584437 | 269072 | 2195863 | 1907537 |
| Maharashtra | 2306223 | 374296 | 65095 | 0 | 371973 | 1167349 | 4284936 | 3117587 |
| Manipur | 33490 | 20203 | 12126 | 41093 | 17966 | 18130 | 143008 | 83785 |
| Meghalaya | 34512 | 23876 | 4213 | 0 | 11798 | 19761 | 91160 | 71399 |
| Mizoram | 32352 | 9419 | 13889 | 8298 | 22066 | 10226 | 96250 | 77726 |
| Nagaland | 32968 | 37767 | 15699 | 19483 | 33807 | 2483 | 141207 | 119241 |

| | | | | | | | | |
|---|---|---|---|---|---|---|---|---|
| Orissa | 676799 | 367452 | 38857 | 30433 | 392130 | 143539 | 1649210 | 1475238 |
| Punjab | 1305698 | 170551 | 143889 | 100591 | 366948 | 82898 | 2170575 | 1987086 |
| Rajasthan | 59337 | 422964 | 66522 | 88499 | 39428 | 606208 | 2416998 | 2022291 |
| Sikkim | 18725 | 13991 | 3075 | 0 | 14576 | 1490 | 51857 | 50367 |
| Tamil Nadu | 1084566 | 417511 | 86079 | 0 | 370033 | 347621 | 2305810 | 1958189 |
| Tripura | 54818 | 27043 | 12476 | 0 | 456285 | 5106 | 144728 | 139622 |
| Uttar Pradesh | 2973512 | 1044884 | 62649 | 57063 | 724302 | 1410013 | 6272423 | 4805347 |
| West Bengal | 2159279 | 437030 | 48038 | 0 | 236371 | 317457 | 3198175 | 2880718 |
| Total | 19900711 | 6159261 | 1066059 | 606019 | 6340508 | 6002871 | 40075429 | 33466539 |

*Notes:* 1. Minus figure of loans from Banks, etc. for Bihar is under consideration.

2. Excluding W & M Advance from RBI (from J & K Bank in respect of J & K State) and Reserve Funds/Deposits. (Total debt minus reserve funds and deposits minus W & M advance from RBI).

*Source*: Report of Eleventh Finance Commission, Govt. of India, New Delhi, p. 282.

TABLE 13

## Composition of State Governments' Debt as on March 31, 2000

*(Rs. in lakhs)*

| *States* | *Central Loan* | *Market Loans and Bonds* | *Loans from Banks, etc.* | *W & M Adv. from RBI* | *Provident Funds and, etc.* | *Reserve Funds and Deposits* | *Total Debt* | *Total Debt** |
|---|---|---|---|---|---|---|---|---|
| Andhra Pradesh | 1605641 | 1703706 | 172113 | 12984 | 285750 | 458740 | 3247934 | 2767210 |
| Arunachal Pradesh | 40919 | 5792 | 21968 | 0 | 19347 | 1614 | 89640 | 88026 |
| Assam | 459044 | 188848 | 22076 | 8458 | 108183 | 68852 | 855461 | 778151 |
| Bihar | 1601754 | 618450 | 16865 | 0 | 790275 | 178241 | 3205585 | 3027344 |
| Goa | 12174 | 25315 | 11877 | 0 | 33920 | 18700 | 213986 | 195286 |
| Gujarat | 1641025 | 300705 | 85319 | 0 | 240379 | 612944 | 2880372 | 2267428 |
| Haryana | 613022 | 146188 | 56112 | 1841 | 328791 | 73839 | 1219793 | 1144113 |
| Himachal Pradesh | 314157 | 61348 | 52967 | 85263 | 179280 | 768147 | 769829 | 607752 |
| Jammu and Kashmir | 362996 | 66519 | 32743 | 110823 | 132907 | 3035 | 709023 | 595165 |
| Karnataka | 1075114 | 364054 | 83212 | 0 | 364414 | 319805 | 2206599 | 1886794 |
| Kerala | 655614 | 392922 | 122078 | 12381 | 658380 | 177793 | 2019168 | 1828994 |
| Madhya Pradesh | 1098965 | 401686 | 77439 | 19254 | 642334 | 259100 | 2498778 | 2220424 |
| Maharashtra | 293340 | 444185 | 115340 | 0 | 456070 | 1406692 | 5155627 | 3748935 |
| Manipur | 40579 | 22444 | 15746 | 41093 | 28016 | 16037 | 163915 | 106785 |
| Meghalaya | 35859 | 30876 | 10761 | 0 | 14798 | 20811 | 113105 | 92294 |
| Mizoram | 35460 | 124169 | 16390 | 8298 | 26923 | 10176 | 109663 | 91189 |
| Nagaland | 35241 | 46402 | 18503 | 16883 | 37987 | 583 | 155599 | 138133 |

| | | | | | | | | |
|---|---|---|---|---|---|---|---|---|
| Orissa | 822411 | 418923 | 54866 | 30433 | 472131 | 15039 | 1949154 | 1768331 |
| Punjab | 148800 | 204924 | 168224 | 100591 | 457426 | 80120 | 2460085 | 2279374 |
| Rajasthan | 1222210 | 501901 | 177646 | 88499 | 651689 | 313927 | 2955872 | 2553446 |
| Sikkim | 22129 | 18581 | 6946 | 0 | 15460 | 949 | 64065 | 63116 |
| Tamil Nadu | 1237732 | 477735 | 118896 | 0 | 426709 | 371773 | 2632845 | 2261072 |
| Tripura | 65717 | 33043 | 17953 | 0 | 54061 | 5106 | 175880 | 170774 |
| Uttar Pradesh | 3522543 | 1187165 | 120521 | 57063 | 863594 | 1442287 | 7193173 | 5693823 |
| West Bengal | 2855202 | 497871 | 132836 | 0 | 297171 | 539456 | 4322536 | 3783080 |
| Total | 23669648 | 7171999 | 1729397 | 602864 | 7585995 | 6607784 | 47367687 | 40157039 |

*Notes*: 1. Excluding W & M advance from RBI (from J & K Bank in respect of J & K State) and Reserve Funds/Deposits. (Total debt minus reserve funds and deposits minus W & M advance from RBI.

*Source*: Report of Eleventh Finance Commission, Govt. of India, New Delhi, p. 283.

from Rs. 4,00,754 crores as on 31st March, 1999 to Rs. 4,73,677 crores as on 31st March, 2000. The stock of debt and its composition at the end of these two years is shown at Tables 12 and 13 respectively.

Loans from the central Government accounted for about 50 percent of the outstanding debt at the end of financial years 1998-99 and 1999-2000. The share of market loans (including loans from banks and ways and means advances) and of provident funds, etc. came to 19.5 and 15.8 percent at the end of 1998-99 and 20.1 and 16.0 percent at the end of 1999-2000 of the total outstanding debt, respectively.

In assessing the overall debt position of the states, the previous finance commission followed the practice of excluding three short-term component of debt. In keeping with this practice and for purposes of comparison, the profile of estimated debt of State Governments excluding ways and means advances, and Reserve Funds and Deposit is shown in Table 14.

TABLE 14

**Total Outstanding Long-term Debt of Sate Governments**

*(Rs. In Crores)*

| *End of March* | *1995* | | *1999* | | *2000* | |
|---|---|---|---|---|---|---|
| | *Amount (Rs.)* | *% of Total Debt* | *Amount (Rs.)* | *% of Total Debt* | *Amount (Rs.)* | *% of Total Debt* |
| 1. Internal Debt | | | | | | |
| (a) Market Loans | 31200 | 17.06 | 61593 | 18.40 | 71720 | 17.86 |
| (b) Loans from Banks, etc. | 3458 | 1.89 | 10661 | 3.19 | 17294 | 4.31 |
| 2. Loans from Centre | 115238 | 63.01 | 199007 | 59.46 | 236696 | 58.94 |
| 3. Provident Funds, etc. | 32991 | 18.04 | 63405 | 18.95 | 75860 | 18.89 |
| Total | 182887 | 100.00 | 334666 | 100.00 | 401570 | 100.00 |

*Source*: Report of Eleventh Finance Commission, 2000-05, Govt. of India, New Delhi.

TABLE 15

**Instalment of Central Loans Due for Repayment by States during 2004-05**

| *Items* | *Rs. in Crores* |
|---|---|
| 1. Plan Loans | 30947 |
| (a) State Plan | 30085 |
| (b) Drought Loans | 13 |
| (c) Others | 15 |
| (d) Central Sector | 177 |
| (e) Centrally Sponsored Schemes | 657 |
| 2. Non-Plan Loans | 20422 |
| (a) Small Saving Loans | 19915 |
| (b) Modernization of Police | 46 |
| (c) Housing for All India Services | 50 |
| (d) Others | 411 |
| Grand Total (1+2) | 51369 |

*Source*: Report of The Eleventh Finance Commission, 02-05, p. 101.

Outstanding long-term debt of the State Governments as on 31st March of different years and clear from Table 16.

Debt as percentage of gross state domestic product of different states in different years is shown in Table 17.

Percentage share, of each state in total debt of all states as on 31st March of the different years is shown in Table 18.

### Challenges

Indian economy has been one of the least affected by the global crisis. In fact, India is one of the growth engines, along with China, in facilitating faster turnaround of the global economy. Risks, however, remain. Firstly, despite recovery, advanced countries continue to face risk of double-dip recession with high unemployment rate, growing fiscal deficit and high public debt-GDP ratios. Such risks can have direct implications for the Indian economy, which is increasingly integrated with the rest of the world.

Secondly, with interest rates at historic low in most advanced economies, capital flows from these countries are finding their way into the fast growing Asian economies

TABLE 16

**Outstanding Long-term Debt of the State Governments**

*(as on March 31)*

| | *1979* | | *1984* | | *1989* | | *1991* | |
|---|---|---|---|---|---|---|---|---|
| | *Amount* | *%* | *Amount* | *%* | *Amount* | *%* | *Amount* | *%* |
| 1. Internal Debt (a+b) | 3348 | 17.82 | 5960 | 15.93 | 12598 | 15.61 | 18157 | 16.55 |
| (a) Market Loans | 2572 | 13.69 | 4236 | 11.32 | 10839 | 13.436 | 15669 | 14.28 |
| (b) Loans from Bank etc. | 776 | 4.13 | 1726 | 4.61 | 1759 | 2.18 | 2488 | 2.27 |
| 2. Loans from Centre | 13463 | 71.67 | 27059 | 72.34 | 55648 | 68.93 | 72938 | 66.46 |
| 3. Provident Funds, etc. | 1974 | 10.51 | 4387 | 11.73 | 12486 | 15.46 | 18647 | 16.99 |
| Total | 18785 | 100.00 | 37406 | 100.00 | 80732 | 100.00 | 109742 | 100.00 |

| | *1995* | | *1998* | | *1999* | | *2000 (B.E.)* | |
|---|---|---|---|---|---|---|---|---|
| | *Amount* | *%* | *Amount* | *%* | *Amount* | *%* | *Amount* | *%* |
| 1. Internal Debt (a+b) | 34658 | 18.95 | 58692 | 21.09 | 72254 | 21.59 | 89014 | 22.17 |
| (a) Market Loans | 31200 | 17.06 | 50944 | 18.30 | 61593 | 18.40 | 71720 | 17.86 |
| (b) Loans from Bank etc. | 3458 | 1.89 | 7748 | 2.78 | 10661 | 3.19 | 17294 | 4.31 |
| 2. Loans from Centre | 115238 | 63.01 | 168653 | 60.60 | 199007 | 59.46 | 236696 | 58.94 |
| 3. Provident Funds, etc. | 32991 | 18.04 | 50979 | 18.32 | 63405 | 18.95 | 75860 | 18.89 |

| | | | | | | | |
|---|---|---|---|---|---|---|---|
| Total | 182887 | 100.00 | 278324 | 100.00 | 234666 | 100.00 | 401570 | 100.00 |

*Notes*: 1. 1978-79 and 1983-84 figures as given in the Second Report of the Ninth Finance Commission and 1988-89 and 1990-91 as given in the report of the Tenth Finance Commission.

2. Outstanding Long-term Debt includes Internal Debt (MH 6003) (excluding W & M advances). Loans form Centre (MH 6004) and Provident Funds. Insurance Funds (MH 8005, 8011, i.e. Total 'I')

*Source*: Report of Eleventh Finance Commission, 2000-05. Govt. of India, New Delhi, p. 284.

TABLE 17

**Debt as Percentage of GDSP**

| *States* | *1993-94* | *1994-95* | *1995-96* | *1996-97* | *1997-98* | *1998-99* | *1999-2000* |
|---|---|---|---|---|---|---|---|
| Andhra Pradesh | 19.08 | 18.46 | 18.70 | 18.54 | 19.18 | 20.29 | 20.95 |
| Arunachal Pradesh | 31.78 | 37.28 | 36.01 | 41.77 | 39.42 | 40.23 | 48.00 |
| Assam | 27.26 | 25.72 | 27.02 | 27.21 | 23.85 | 23.23 | 24.12 |
| Bihar | 32.43 | 32.12 | 34.85 | 32.50 | 32.30 | 33.14 | 34.31 |
| Goa | 42.47 | 39.65 | 35.44 | 31.20 | 32.57 | 34.21 | 34.54 |
| Gujarat | 18.33 | 15.95 | 16.16 | 15.93 | 16.78 | 18.13 | 18.95 |
| Haryana | 18.94 | 17.92 | 19.24 | 17.65 | 19.24 | 21.14 | 22.68 |
| Himachal Pradesh | 38.37 | 38.21 | 45.19 | 42.48 | 44.34 | 55.87 | 58.59 |
| Jammu and Kashmir | 57.38 | 55.19 | 48.83 | 51.31 | 50.04 | 47.98 | 47.15 |
| Karnataka | 16.32 | 16.63 | 16.44 | 16.27 | 16.58 | 17.48 | 18.94 |
| Kerala | 26.32 | 26.66 | 24.87 | 24.10 | 25.18 | 27.13 | 28.16 |
| Madhya Pradesh | 17.70 | 17.57 | 17.46 | 17.27 | 17.66 | 18.63 | 19.17 |
| Maharashtra | 11.99 | 11.79 | 10.83 | 11.56 | 12.29 | 13.08 | 13.92 |
| Manipur | 34.01 | 32.25 | 32.91 | 30.12 | 39.02 | 44.66 | 46.80 |
| Meghalaya | 19.34 | 22.12 | 20.53 | 21.87 | 20.87 | 23.35 | 26.71 |
| Mizoram | 45.49 | 47.75 | 47.04 | 56.31 | 50.46 | 28.39 | 59.76 |
| Nagaland | 39.21 | 39.36 | 44.41 | 45.55 | 48.58 | 50.92 | 50.36 |
| Orissa | 33.16 | 32.25 | 33.28 | 38.75 | 35.24 | 39.79 | 39.95 |
| Punjab | 33.59 | 33.60 | 33.80 | 32.33 | 32.29 | 34.58 | 34.89 |
| Rajasthan | 25.32 | 23.45 | 24.60 | 24.21 | 25.42 | 28.85 | 31.95 |

| | | | | | | | |
|---|---|---|---|---|---|---|---|
| Sikkim | 52.09 | 52.03 | 52.22 | 52.02 | 51.33 | 64.24 | 71.214 |
| Tamil Nadu | 15.82 | 15.72 | 15.15 | 14.88 | 15.45 | 16.41 | 16.77 |
| Tripura | 36.94 | 32.46 | 35.04 | 32.20 | 34.15 | 37.18 | 40.25 |
| Uttar Pradesh | 26.39 | 25.98 | 26.08 | 24.43 | 26.06 | 27.97 | 29.28 |
| West Bengal | 20.15 | 20.43 | 20.50 | 21.47 | 22.88 | 26.19 | 30.44 |
| Total (All States) | 21.54 | 21.01 | 20.89 | 20.71 | 21.39 | 22.98 | 24.33 |

*Notes*: 1. Debt includes Internal Debt, Loans and advances from the Central Government, Provident Funds and Insurance Funds.

2. GSDP figures are on the basis of information received from the CSO. These are for new series from 1993-94 to 1996-97 and thereafter EFC estimates.

*Source*: Report of Eleventh Finance Commission, Govt. of India, New Delhi, p. 286.

TABLE 18

**Percentage Share of each State in Total Debt of All States as on 31st March***

| *States* | *1993* | *1994* | *1995* | *1996* | *1997* | *1998* | *1999* | *2000(B.E.)* | *Growth Rate (1993-2000)* |
|---|---|---|---|---|---|---|---|---|---|
| Andhra Pradesh | 6.59 | 6.98 | 6.99 | 7.11 | 7.03 | 7.04 | 7.06 | 6.86 | 0.42 |
| Arunachal Pradesh | 0.15 | 0.15 | 0.17 | 0.18 | 0.18 | 0.18 | 1.17 | 0.19 | 2.96 |
| Assam | 2.92 | 2.57 | 2.51 | 2.61 | 2.32 | 2.08 | 1.85 | 1.81 | 6.53 |
| Bihar | 8.10 | 8.03 | 7.69 | 7.47 | 7.18 | 7.03 | 6.69 | 6.77 | 2.95 |
| Goa | 0.63 | 0.60 | 0.54 | 0.51 | 0.49 | 0.4 | 0.46 | 0.45 | 4.81 |
| Gujarat | 6.28 | 6.17 | 5.97 | 5.97 | 5.93 | 6.09 | 6.18 | 6.08 | 0.20 |
| Haryana | 2.31 | 2.38 | 2.32 | 2.45 | 2.42 | 2.44 | 2.54 | 2.58 | 1.48 |
| Himachal Pradesh | 1.10 | 1.08 | 1.18 | 1.31 | 1.29 | 1.31 | 1.60 | 1.62 | 6.10 |
| Jammu and Kashmir | 2.53 | 2.42 | 2.10 | 1.92 | 1.91 | 1.897 | 1.68 | 1.50 | 6.71 |
| Karnataka | 4.48 | 4.73 | 4.78 | 4.67 | 4.70 | 4.72 | 4.65 | 4.66 | 0.19 |
| Kerala | 4.00 | 4.10 | 4.25 | 4.28 | 4.30 | 4.37 | 4.33 | 4.26 | 0.96 |
| Madhya Pradesh | 5.84 | 5.83 | 5.60 | 5.57 | 5.55 | 5.43 | 5.48 | 5.27 | 1.33 |
| Maharashtra | 9.97 | 10.13 | 10.00 | 10.08 | 10.42 | 10.60 | 10.69 | 10.88 | 1.30 |
| Manipur | 0.32 | 0.31 | 0.28 | 0.27 | 0.27 | 0.35 | 0.36 | 0.35 | 2.55 |
| Meghalaya | 0.18 | 0.20 | 0.22 | 0.21 | 0.20 | 0.21 | 0.23 | 0.24 | 3.05 |
| Mizoram | 0.18 | 0.21 | 0.21 | 0.22 | 0.26 | 0.24 | 0.24 | 0.23 | 3.58 |
| Nagaland | 0.35 | 0.32 | 0.32 | 0.34 | 0.33 | 0.36 | 0.35 | 0.33 | 0.43 |
| Orissa | 4.04 | 4.14 | 4.08 | 4.15 | 4.17 | 4.14 | 4.12 | 4.11 | 0.17 |

| | | | | | | | | | |
|---|---|---|---|---|---|---|---|---|---|
| Punjab | 5.70 | 5.82 | 5.75 | 5.63 | 5.43 | 5.40 | 5.42 | 5.19 | 1.46 |
| Rajasthan | 5.18 | 5.41 | 5.46 | 5.66 | 5.84 | 2.82 | 6.03 | 6.24 | 2.49 |
| Sikkim | 0.12 | 0.12 | 0.12 | 0.11 | 0.11 | 0.11 | 0.13 | 0.14 | 1.46 |
| Tamil Nadu | 6.02 | 6.18 | 6.16 | 6.00 | 5.96 | 5.85 | 5.75 | 5.56 | 1.28 |
| Tripura | 0.41 | 0.41 | 0.39 | 0.38 | 0.38 | 0.36 | 0.36 | 0.37 | 1.96 |
| Uttar Pradesh | 15.74 | 14.72 | 15.91 | 515.77 | 15.97 | 15.96 | 15.65 | 5.19 | 0.09 |
| West Bengal | 6.872 | 6.99 | 7.00 | 7.13 | 7.36 | 7.57 | 7.98 | 9.12 | 3.59 |
| Total (All States) | 100 | 100 | 100 | 100 | 100 | 100 | 100 | 100 | 1003 |

*Notes*: 1. Absolute Figures of Outstanding Debt Include Internal Debt, Loans from Centre, Provident Funds, Insurance Funds and Reserve Funds and Deposits

*Source*: Report of the Eleventh Finance Commission, Govt. of India, New Delhi.

including India. The issues that arise are whether the inflows are in excess of the domestic absorptive capacity and whether they could lead to overheating of the economy. The related issue is the need to balance the competing objectives of price and exchange stability. This can also be looked at as the "impossible trinity" dilemma of policy choice between price stability, exchange rate stability and capital mobility.

## DEPOSITS OF BIHAR STATE

The case of public Debt is worse. There is a rapid increase since independence. Table 19 reveals that the outstanding debt of the Bihar which stood at Rs. 12 crores by the end of March, 1952 increased to Rs. 15,737 crores by the end of March 1997-98 which further increased to Rs. 18,770 crores in 1998-99.

The outstanding debt of Bihar constituted 27.44 percent of the S.D.P. by the end of 1973-74 and 36.60 percent of the S.D.P. at the end of 1983-84. The per capita outstanding debt has increased also between 1973-74 and 1983-84 from Rs. 165.43 to Rs. 462.09. It is clear from Table 19 that public debt of Bihar has increased during plan period, we have seen composition of public debt of Bihar in Table 20.

## OUTSTANDING LIABILITIES OF GOVERNMENT OF BIHAR

Table 21 shows the outstanding debt liabilities of the state government. The outstanding liability as a percentage of GSDP had decreased consistently from 43.1 percent in 2004-05 to 19.2 percent in 2009-10 and reflects the state government's ability to contain the debt burden effectively. The total outstanding liabilities of the state government, as can be seen from Table 21 has accumulated to Rs. 52,906 crore, as per the revised estimates of 2009-10, which is nearly 29.2 percent of the state's GSDP. This figure is the accumulated effect of past borrowings, growing an annual rate of about 5.5 percent since 2004-05. as can be observed from Table 21 the major part of this debt, about 64 percent, is due to the internal loans raised by the state government from the market, and about 17 percent from the central government.

TABLE 19

**Growth of Public Debt of Bihar (As on March, 31st)**

*(Rs. In Crores)*

| *Year* | *Debt* |
|---|---|
| 1952 | 12 |
| 1957 | 796 |
| 1961 | 187 |
| 1966 | 418 |
| 1974 | 933 |
| 1984 | 3230 |
| 1994-95 | 11063 |
| 1995-96 | 12281 |
| 1996-97 | 13756 |
| 1997-98 | 15737 |
| 1998-99 | 18770 |
| 2004-05 | 30943 |
| 2005-06 | 33733 |
| 2006-07 | 35065 |
| 2007-08 | 35045 |
| 2008-09 | 39291 |
| 2009-10 | 42981 |

*Sources*: 1. Reports of Different Finance Commissions, 1964, p. 212.
3. Figures from 1995-98 have been taken from reports of The Auditor and Comptroller General of India, 1st March, 1996, 31st March, 1998 and 31st March, 1999.
4. Economic Survey (2009-10), Finance Department, Government of Bihar.

**Chart: Growth of Public Debt of Bihar (As on March, 31st)**

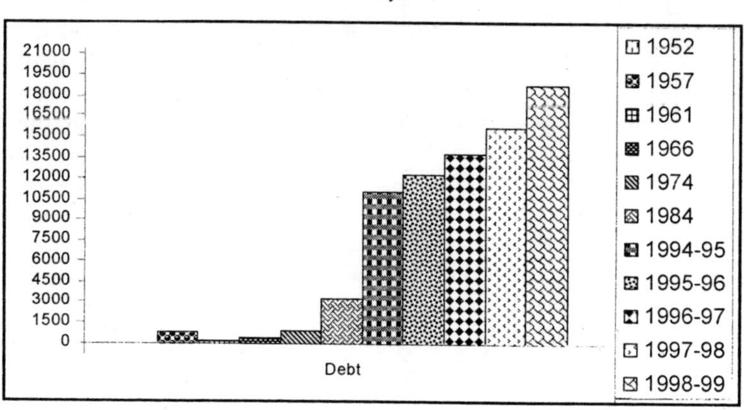

TABLE 20

**Composition of Bihar Government Debt**

*(As on March 31st)*

| *Year* | *Central Loans Market* | *Loans and Bonds* | *Loans from Banks, etc.* | *W & M for RBI* | *Provident Fund, etc.* | *Reserve Funds and Deposits* | *Total Debt* | *Total Debt* |
|---|---|---|---|---|---|---|---|---|
| 1994 | 7126.64 | 2648.01 | 632.83 | 58.03 | 2634.13 | 1433.84 | 15533.52 | 13061.65 |
| 1995 | 7922.64 | 3793.26 | - | - | 3235.16 | 1433.84 | 16384.50 | 14951.06 |
| 1999 | 1337490 | 352226 | 12712 | 0 | 637434 | 168196 | 268264 | 2514448 |
| 2000 | 1601754 | 618450 | 16865 | 0 | 790275 | 178241 | 3205585 | 3027344 |

*Notes*: 1. Figures of 1994 and 1995 are in crores.
2. Figures of 1999 and 2000 are in Lakhs.

*Sources*: 1. 10th Finance Commission 1995 Pp. 143-44.
2. 11h Finance Commission, 2000-20, pp. 282-83.

TABLE 21

**Outstanding Liabilities**

| | 2004-05 | 2005-06 | 2006-07 | 2007-08 | 2008-09 | 2009-10 |
|---|---|---|---|---|---|---|
| Internal debt | 21906 | 25182 | 26829 | 26769 | 31293 | 34052 |
| Central loans | 9037 | 8551 | 8237 | 8277 | 7998 | 8929 |
| Total public debt | 30943 | 33733 | 35065 | 35045 | 39291 | 42981 |
| Public account | 8401 | 8766 | 9161 | 9429 | 9573 | 9924 |
| Total | 39344 | 42498 | 44226 | 44475 | 48865 | 52905 |
| Outstanding liability as % of GSDP | 43.1 | 43.4 | 35.7 | 31.0 | 30.1 | 29.2 |

*Source*: Department of Finance, GoI.

From the above study the composition of Bihar Government Debt becomes clear in the post-independence era. The Government of Bihar has raised market loans for productive purposes. Presently we had seen the pattern of Market borrowing. It shows that the State Government could borrow at increasing rate of interest and at a higher rate of discount. A higher rate of interest had to be paid by the State Government due to the availability of other more remunerative opportunities where the rate of return tended to be higher than what the investor could earn by investing in Government could be successful in its market borrowings only by providing more attractive terms.

There is a misconception that borrowing is inflationary. If the government increases borrowing from the public, it might curtail consumption or business investment or it may absorb idle resources. If the government thus takes the idle money away, there might be some expansionary effect on the economy. If, on the other hand, individuals purchase government securities with the help of the funds, which are used to buy other securities, there occurs a diversion of funds, which will depress the price of the securities, and it will lead to an increase in the rate of interest, which will ultimately lead to concretionary effect on the economy. Likewise, if borrowing from the public reduces their consumption, it will have anti-inflationary effects on the economy. Therefore, public debt need not be inflationary. This is the position of borrowing from the public. But such borrowing is very much limited in an underdeveloped economy, because of the peculiar conditions which obsess such an economy. Under the circumstances, the government has to raise loans from different financial institutions. If borrowing is made from non-bank financial institutions, it will have a very negligible expansionary effect. It is the loans raised from banks that are expansionary. Here also it should be clear to us that if it is self-liquidating then it cannot be of much alarm.

But public borrowing cannot be increased beyond a limit. Government can borrow only to the extent people are saving and saving voluntarily. If the voluntary private saving itself is low, as is the case in India, Government cannot borrow much. Moreover, public borrowing squeezes money from private individuals and consequently, lesser resources are left for the private sector, which may be starved of funds and this may have its adverse effects on the development of the entire economy. But this does not recommend the stoppage of borrowing by the government. Even then, there can be a good case for public borrowing because it may lead to diversion of resources from the private sector to public sector for investment in social capital and the infrastructure of the country.

The public debt, no doubt, has assumed prominence in the fiscal policy of a developing economy and therefore, it has been rising very fast. Here a question arises: Is there any limit to public borrowing? A.P. Lerner holds the view that public debt should go on increasing till there is unemployment in the economy and the moment full employment is achieved, resort to public borrowing should be stopped. According to him, there can be no arbitrarily fixed limit of the public debt; the limit is the achievement of full employment. He observes, "There is no need for an arbitrary limit to the national debt because there is a natural limit which is reached when the ownership of national debt makes people so rich that they spend enough to provide full employment. No deficit is then necessary and no further borrowing is involved". Hansen also has almost the same view when he observes, "much of the discussion about the limits of the public debt is wholly unrealistic. There are no rigid and fixed limits. The problem is manageable one, and can best be taken care of by ensuring that taxation is adequate: (1) to prevent inflation, and (2) to provide a reasonably equitable and workable distribution of wealth and income." As the borrowing depends on savings and income, the limit to debt can be determined by the rate of growth of income. If an increase in public debt is associated with growing income the size of the public debt cannot be considered a burden. It is so because, greater the growth of income, the lower will be the tax-rate to service debt. Here E. Damar's observation is worth quoting: "If all the people and organizations, who work and study, write articles and make speeches, worry and spend sleepless nights could forget about is for a while and spend even half their efforts trying to find wave of achieving a growth with national income their contribution to the benefit and welfare of humanity and to the solution of the debt problem would be far greater." Thus, the fear of the burden of public debt is not so genuine. The only genuine fear is from the "danger that it may redistribute national income in favour of the rich. The real burden of public debt does not, in fact, depend on its size, it depends upon the distribution of the ownership of it."

We may conclude with the following observations. Loans financing occupies a very important place in stimulating economic development. The scope for mobilizing resources through taxation is beset with many difficulties. The scope for inflationary financing is limited. It has already crossed its limits in our country. Therefore, the prospective role and scope of public borrowing is brighter and its urgency and inevitability as a method to mobilize resources becomes unavoidably significant. Public borrowing is more expansionary than taxation, but it is less expansionary than deficit financing.

Borrowing is also a much quicker form of raising funds than taxation. But taxation is the most effective fiscal tool for mobilizing resources. It is the best method to check inflationary pressure and improve the distribution of income more equitably. It is the best method to increase the total volume of savings in our country, where a significant percentage of the people still live below the poverty line and where the propensity to consume is very high. Therefore, an underdeveloped country cannot think of less taxation if it cherishes to develop. But this does not mean, in any way, the minimisation of the importance of public debt. So in a developing economy, there cannot be much scope of choice between loans and taxes to mobilise resources for economic development. Funds should be mobilised from all sources and development should not be allowed to starve due to the scarcity of funds.

## References

The Eleventh Finance Commission Report (2000), Govt. of India, New Delhi.

The Twelfth Finance Commission Report (2004), Govt. of India, New Delhi,

Shandilya, Tapan Kumar (2005), (Emerging Issues in Center State Financial Relations: Approach of Twelfth Finance Commission, Conference Vol. of *Indian Economic Association Journal*, Vishakhapattnam, Andhra Pradesh, p. 903.

Rangrajan, C. (2005), "Twelfth Finance Commission: Approach and Discommendation, Economic and Political Weekly, Vol. XL, No. 31, July 30, 2005.

Economic Survey of India, 2009-10.

Economic Survey of India, 1999.

Economic Survey of India, 2000.

Economic Survey of India, 2005.

Economic Survey of Bihar, 2009-10.

Thirteenth Finance Commission (2010-15), Govt. of India.

A.P. Lerner, Economics of Employment (1951), McGraw-Hill Book Company Inc., New York, Toronto, London.

A.H. Hansen (1941), Fiscal Policy and Business Cycles, W.W. Norton and Company, New York.

E. Damar (1972), "The Burden of the Debt and National Income" in Readings in Fiscal Policy, George Allen and Unwin Ltd., London, 1955, p. 500 as quoted by B.S. Shreekantaradhya in *Public Debt and Economic Development in India*, Sterling Publishers (P) Ltd., Delhi, First Ed.

Mishra, (1966), Fiscal Policy in the Context of Planning-Analysis of Keynesian Economics in Relation to Economic Development, The World Press Private Ltd., Calcutta,

Shandilya, Tapan Kumar (2005), "Emerging Issues in Centre-State Financial Relations: Approach of Twelfth Finance Commission, *Indian Economic Journal* (Conference Vol.), Vishakhapattanam, (Andhra Pradesh), p. 903.

Shandilya, Tapan Kumar (1991), "Central Loans to States Under Five Year Plans., Deep & Deep Publications Pvt. Ltd., New Delhi.

Shandilya, Tapan Kumar (Edt.) (1994), Centre State Financial Relation in India, Deep & Deep Publications Pvt. Ltd., New Delhi.

Agarwal, A.C., Public Finance, Theory and Practice, Laxmi Narayan Agarwal, Agra-3.

Report on Currency and Finance (1999-2000), Reserve Bank of India, Mumbai.

# 4

# Direction of Central Loans to States

The centre provides loans to the states for both plan and non-plan purposes. They are intended for development and non-development purposes. While loans for plan schemes comprise loans for State Plan Schemes, Central Plan Schemes and Centrally Sponsored Schemes, non-plan loans are mainly for purchases of fertilizers and other agricultural inputs, loans against small savings collections, ways and means assistance for tiding over temporary difficulties, etc. The non-development programmes are drought, flood relief, and rehabilitation works. We have seen in the previous chapter that the magnitude of central loans to the states has increased enormously during the planned era under which the states have been assisted by the Central Government largely in the form of loans for plan purposes. Loans are advanced to the states for development activities, which mean economic activities intended to create productive capacity in the economy, which will yield income. The activities are gain classified into plan and non-plan. Plan purpose activities refer to economic activities included in the plans. Plan loans are sanctioned on the recommendations of the Planning Commission. They fall outside the Revenue Budget. The non-plan loans are provided on the recommendation of the Union Ministries, particularly the Ministry of Finance. They are discretionary in nature but they are included in the revenue budget. The plan and non-plan loans may be for development and non-development purposes. But the development and non-development activities do not correspond to plan and non-plan activities, rather they are inter-mingled. The plan and non-plan purpose classification serves only the financial and administrative convenience. They are not useful for economic evaluations. The Sixth Finance Commission classified central loans into development and non-development loans. The development purpose loans include according to it, loans for irrigation, development of agriculture and allied activities, community development and National Extension Schemes, Industrial Housing and such other purposes. Non-development purpose loans include loans for Rehabilitations Schemes and loans for Relief Works. They also include *ad hoc* loans for clearing unauthorized overdrafts, ways and means, advances and loans meant for filling up the gap in the revenue expenditure of the states.

## APPROACH OF EARLIER FINANCE COMMISSIONS

The Second Finance Commission was the first one to handle the issue of state debt and was required to make recommendation on rates of interest and terms of repayment of central loans made to states after independence and up to 31st March 1956. Thereafter, a review of the state debt has been terms of reference from the Sixth Finance Commission. The Terms of Reference of Finance Commissions required them to make an estimation of the non-plan capital gap of the states and to undertake a review of the debt position with particular reference to the central loans to states. These Commissions were asked to suggest debt relief measures having to the overall non-plan capital gap and the purposes for which loans had been utilized and the requirements of the centre. From the Ninth Finance Commissions onwards, the Finance Commissions were mandated to review the debt position of the states as a whole and suggest corrective measures with particular reference to investments made in infrastructure projects and to link them to improvements in financial and managerial efficiency. While the Tenth Finance

Commission had the mandate to suggest corrective measures keeping in view the financial requirements of the centre, the Eleventh Finance Commission (EFC) was required to consider the long-term sustainability of debt for both the centre and the states. The Twelfth Finance Commission's Terms of Reference are at a slight variance with that of the EFC in that, apart from debt sustainability, the measures are to be consistent also with macro-economic stability. In addition, there is a reference to linking the recommendations to performance of the states in the fields of human development and investment climate.

The Twelfth Finance Commission has examined the manner in which the Finance Commissions in the past have approached the problems of states' debt and the fiscal measures necessary for maintaining debt at sustainable levels. The Finance Commissions had commented on the need to consider the cost of debt, the use and the productivity of borrowed funds and the arrangements for amortization of debt while resorting to borrowings. In particular, the Ninth Finance Commission was of the view that public debt lay in borrowed funds: (a) not being used for financing revenue expenditure, and (b) being used efficiently and productively for capital expenditure so as to either earn returns on increase the productivity of the economy resulting in increased governmental revenues. The Tenth Finance Commission had, similarly, commented that the disturbing features of the debt profile of states were the diversion of borrowed funds for meeting revenue expenditure, use of loans in unproductive or non-performing enterprises and non-provision of depreciation or amortization of funds in respect of government owned assets. This led to repayments being made out of fresh borrowings. The EFC observed that the determination of stable and sustainable levels of debt would depend critically upon the rate of growth of (nominal) GDP/ GSDP, the effective interest rate on borrowing by the concerned governments (centre/states), the rate of growth of revenue receipts and the proportion of primary expenditure (expenditure other than interest payments) relative to GDP/ GSDP that may be considered desirable. Given other things, a state, which had a higher growth rate relative to interest rate, would be able to sustain debt at a higher level relative to GSDP. The EFC also identified the steps desirable for reducing the debt burden of states as the following:

(i) Incremental revenue receipts should meet the incremental interest burden and the incremental primary expenditure,
(ii) A surplus should be generated on revenue account to go into a sinking fund to meet future repayment/obligation, and
(iii) State should have and maintain balance in its revenue account.

As required by the Twelfth Finance Commission's TOR the Twelfth Finance Commission has suggested a restructuring plan that would restore budgetary balance and enable the States and the centre to achieve macro-economic stability and debt reduction along with equitable growth. The Twelfth Finance Commission has analyzed the reasons for the mounting debt and the revenue and fiscal deficits of states. The Twelfth Finance Commission has also looked at the various conditions for macro-economic stability. The Twelfth Finance Commission's approach to debt sustainability and the fiscal discipline required for macro-economic stability have been outlined earlier. The suggestions contained therein provide the overall context for the corrective measures in regard to the existing debt to be considered in this chapter.

On debt management, states have protested that they are saddled with high cost debt. It has been pointed out that while states take 80 per cent of the high-cost NSSF loans, the Centre takes 80 per cent of the aggregate open market loans, which are low-cost. Some states have argued that the ratio of the shares of the Centre and states should be similar for all sources of borrowings. It has also been pointed out that the repayment obligation is expected to be higher than ever before during the award period of FC-XIII due to the loans taken for debt swap and increased market borrowings due to reduction in NSSF loans. It has been suggested that this should be taken into account while recommending debt relief schemes and drawing up the revised fiscal consolidation path.

On DCRF, some states have argued that the size of relief recommended was inadequate and have asked for inclusion of NSSF loans under the DCRF scheme. Some states have suggested that the benefit of the debt waiver was not concomitant with its extremely stringent conditionalities. We have received requests for continuation of the scheme during our award period.

The Central Government, in its memorandum, has stated that the Centre has been moving towards fiscal consolidation. It has argued that debt relief schemes tend to give perverse incentives to those who have contracted high debts in the past and thus, need to be carefully designed.

In its comments, the Reserve Bank of India has maintained that the design of the post-FRBM fiscal architecture should ensure long-term sustainability, inter-generational equity and ability to stabilise the fluctuations in employment and output in the economy. Deficits and debt should be contained at tolerable levels so as not to hinder monetary policy objectives. RBI has noted that due to the economic slowdown, the FRBM rules have been relaxed for fiscal years 2008-09 and 2009-10. Therefore, post-FRBM fiscal architecture should exclude these two exceptional years and begin when normalcy returns.

RBI is of the opinion that there is need to maintain a balanced revenue account with a ceiling on deficits and debt. Hence, there is need for a revenue deficit target along with a cap on the fiscal deficit. According to an exercise carried out by RBI, the absorption capacity of the economy for the combined market borrowings of the Centre and the states is in the range of 5 to 6 per cent of GDP during the period 2010-11 to 2014-15. Hence, the combined fiscal deficit of 5 to 6 per cent may be apportioned equally between the Centre and the states. RBI's opinion is that off-budget liabilities must be captured in the calculation of debt. However, in the case of NSSF, the part of the fund utilised by State Governments is to be excluded before setting up any debt targets for the Centre.

The Planning Commission, in its comments, has pointed out that the entire practice of meeting the subsidy requirements through off-budget borrowings and not taking it into account in the revenue and fiscal deficits is a clear violation of the definitions under the FRBM Act. One of the important points raised by the Planning Commission is that the recommendation of elimination of the revenue deficit should be reviewed in the light of the blurring line between revenue and capital spending of governments, at both the central as well as the state level. It has argued that capital expenditure involves a 'sacrifice' of present consumption by the present generation and thus, the future generations have an obligation to repay this sacrifice. The Commission further points out that the current framework provides a straitjacketed approach to the fiscal roadmap and does not prescribe any cyclically adjusted budget balance to build in counter-cyclicality in government spending. It has also pointed out that the conformity of the current classification to the distinction between expenditure on revenue account and other expenditure referred to in the Constitution should be examined. With regard to the fiscal deficit, the Planning Commission has suggested that the approach should be to set a trajectory for the debt stock instead of fixing uniform targets for fiscal deficit. It has also suggested that one aspect of debt sustainability is liquidity of government, which can be assessed as a ratio of debt servicing requirement to the revenues of the government. Putting a cap on this ratio can be an additional measure in the direction of ensuring debt sustainability. The thirteenth finance commission has made an assessment of central loan of states as on 31st March 2010. In this chapter we analyzed the reasons for the mounting debt and the revenue and fiscal deficit of states.

## DEBT POSITION OF THE STATES

The Twelfth Finance Commission has made an assessment of the debt position of the states as on 31st March 2004. The Twelfth Finance Commission has also collected data from the states on their estimates of outstanding debt as on 31st March 2005. The public debt of states comprise internal debt (including market borrowings, loans from banks and financial institutions, special securities issued to the National Small Saving Funds (NSSF), loans from the centre, and small savings and provident funds, etc. The total outstanding debt of states, including short-term borrowings, is estimated at Rs. 865859 crores at the end of March 2004 and is excepted to rise to Rs. 9,63,870 crores by the end of March 2005 as per data collected from states. The share of market borrowings (including loans from banks and ways and means advances) and provident funds and deposits was 35.60 and 14.94 per cent respectively at the end of 2003-04 and is likely to be 37.23 and 14.74 per cent respectively at the end of 2004-05. The state-wise composition of debt at the end of 2003-04 and 2004-05 are given in Tables 1 and 2.

Previous Finance Commissions had followed the practice of excluding the short-term components of debt viz. ways and means advances and reserve funds and deposits, while looking at the debt position of states. Table 3 shows the results of a similar exercise carried out on the basis of information provided to The Twelfth Finance Commission by the states in regard to estimated debt of State Governments, excluding ways and means advances and reserve funds and deposits.

In recent years, market borrowings have emerged as the cheapest source of funds for State Government, with interest rates declining continuously from 14 percent in 1995-96 to around 6 per cent by 2003-04. The states' access to market borrowings is, however, regulated by the central government keeping in view its own requirements and the liquidity in the market. The central loans to states form the largest component of the states' debt. These are often market loans raised by the centre at the prevailing interest rates but on lent to states at rates of interest very different from the market rates. The practice of the central government providing loans to the states, enables the centre to exercise control over the borrowings of states, as under article 293 of the Constitution, a state cannot raise any loan without the consent of Government of India, if any part of a loan, which has been made to a state by the Central Government or a guarantee is still outstanding.

The loans given by the central government to states comprise:

TABLE I

## Composition of State Government Debt as on March 31, 2004

(Rs. In crore)

| Sl. No. | State | Central Loans | National Small Savings Fund Loans | Market Loans and Bonds | Loans from Banks, etc. | W&M Adv. from RBI | Provident Funds and Deposits | Reserve Fund and Deposits | Miscell-aneous (PSUs) | Total Debt | Debt* (Excluding short-term debt) |
|---|---|---|---|---|---|---|---|---|---|---|---|
| 1. | Andhra Pradesh | 18702.17 | 10282.48 | 21283.47 | 1460.35 | | 4601.91 | 4801.93 | | 61132.31 | 56330.38 |
| 2. | Arunachal Pradesh | 594.48 | | 165.85 | 128.42 | | 316.98 | | | 1205.73 | 1205.73 |
| 3. | Assam | 6820.01 | | 4497.17 | 355.99 | 435.31 | 2227.89 | 673.76 | | 15010.13 | 13901.06 |
| 4. | Bihar | 12426.31 | | 7763.52 | 8241.02 | 434.27 | 7213.22 | 3706.20 | | 39784.54 | 35644.07 |
| 5. | Chhattisgarh | 5118.72 | | 2623.25 | 379.57 | | 1209.91 | 454.81 | | 9786.26 | 9331.45 |
| 6. | Goa | 1542.44 | | 797.7 | | | | | | 2340.19 | 2340.19 |
| 7. | Gujarat | 14313.00 | 21375.00 | 12477.00 | 1972.00 | | 3684.00 | 8913.00 | | 62734.00 | 53821.00 |
| 8. | Haryana | 3695.51 | | 5850.95 | 6340.50 | | 4953.95 | 1351.42 | | 22192.34 | 20840.91 |
| 9. | Himachal Pradesh | 1838.07 | | 2909.64 | 6733.13 | 117.91 | 2891.17 | 966.15 | 1090.63 | 16546.70 | 15462.64 |
| 10. | Jammu and Kashmir | 4942.31 | | 3301.69 | 1542.47 | 1381.10 | 2910.49 | 400.56 | | 14478.62 | 12696.96 |
| 11. | Jharkhand | 4327.40 | | 2676.49 | 16.22 | 8.86 | 2823.67 | 1395.03 | | 11247.67 | 9843.78 |
| 12. | Karnataka | 10882.90 | | 9653.36 | 10145.40 | | 5892.02 | 5090.00 | | 41664.68 | 36574.68 |
| 13. | Kerala | 5624.61 | | 13566.09 | 2113.71 | 598.33 | 14403.33 | 1780.33 | | 39186.55 | 36807.74 |
| 14. | Madhya Pradesh | 9632.07 | | 7846.76 | 10468.20 | | 7608.89 | | | 39186.55 | 36807.74 |
| 15. | Maharashtra | 45399.63 | | 14679.95 | 5567.30 | | 9045.09 | 8462.40 | | 83154.37 | 74691.97 |
| 16. | Manipur | 811.37 | | 685.79 | 131.59 | 55.28 | 514.00 | 176.52 | | 2374.55 | 2142.75 |
| 17. | Meghalaya | 406.91 | | 635.12 | 201.36 | | 409.03 | 407.53 | | 2059.95 | 1652.42 |
| 18. | Mizoram | 519.53 | | 467.65 | 386.66 | 112.92 | 601.63 | 98.00 | | 2186.39 | 1975.47 |

| | | | | | | | | | | | |
|---|---|---|---|---|---|---|---|---|---|---|---|
| 19. | Nagaland | 400.53 | | 1202.03 | 400.47 | | 528.80 | 2.93 | | 2534.76 | 2531.83 |
| 20. | Orissa | 12461.68 | | 9907.47 | 1555.48 | | 8386.11 | 2557.58 | | 34868.32 | 32310.74 |
| 21. | Punjab | 9419.13 | | 6059.24 | 18711.91 | 455.27 | 6766.90 | 679.42 | | 42091.87 | 40957.18 |
| 22. | Rajasthan | 24044.58 | | 12290.78 | 2343.48 | | 10520.53 | 4309.75 | | 53509.12 | 49199.37 |
| 23. | Sikkim | 278.48 | | 295.76 | 106.37 | | 256.92 | 38.90 | | 976.43 | 937.53 |
| 24. | Tamil Nadu | 9426.910 | 9773.93 | 14923.37 | 3808.91 | 596.33 | 7129.37 | 4014.85 | | 49673.66 | 45062.48 |
| 25. | Tripura | 1190.22 | | 918.82 | 371.71 | 62.80 | 1083.63 | | | 3626.64 | 3563.84 |
| 26. | Uttar Pradesh | 28302.00 | 21715.00 | 23296.00 | 8156.00 | | 17947.00 | 19806.00 | | 119222.00 | 99416.00 |
| 27. | Uttar Pradesh | 353.33 | 2087.87 | 3236.35 | 776.51 | | 943.38 | | | 7397.44 | 7397.44 |
| 28. | West Bengal | 19335.00 | 31580.67 | 16678.60 | 9017.01 | 830.50 | 4505.02 | 7371.00 | | 89317.80 | 81116.30 |
| | Total | 252809.29 | 96814.95 | 200689.92 | 102531.20 | 5088.88 | 129375.84 | 77458.23 | 1090.63 | 865858.94 | 783311.83 |

**Note*: Excluding W & M advances from RBI and reserve funds and deposit (total debt minus reserve funds and deposits minus W & M advances from RBI), central loans may include NSSF loans.

TABLE 2

## Composition of State Government Debt as on March 31, 2005

(Rs. In crore)

| Sl. No. | State | Central Loans | National Small Savings Fund Loans | Market Loans and Bonds | Loans from Banks, etc. | W&M Adv. from RBI | Provident Funds and Deposits | Reserve Fund and Deposits | Miscell-aneous (PSUs) | Total Debt | Debt* (Excluding short-term debt) |
|---|---|---|---|---|---|---|---|---|---|---|---|
| 1. | Andhra Pradesh | 20133.43 | 13912.18 | 24680.54 | 2621.23 | | 5045.09 | 3499.53 | | 69892.00 | 66392.47 |
| 2. | Arunachal Pradesh | 622.25 | | 196.14 | 158 56 | | 362.26 | | | 1339.21 | 1339.21 |
| 3. | Assam | 7193.66 | | 5271.33 | 542.01 | 435.31 | 2908.24 | 673.76 | | 17024.31 | 15915.24 |
| 4. | Bihar | 12081.51 | | 8363.43 | 11307.03 | 349.94 | 7203.59 | 3706.04 | | 43011.54 | 38955.56 |
| 5. | Chhattisgarh | 5130.97 | | 3129.41 | 612.26 | | 1271.45 | 454.82 | | 10598.91 | 10144.09 |
| 6. | Goa | 1503.35 | 783.25 | | | | | | | 2286.60 | 2286.60 |
| 7. | Gujarat | 15933.00 | 26206.00 | 12786.00 | 2291.00 | | 4099.00 | 8913.00 | | 70228.00 | 61315.00 |
| 8. | Haryana | 2480.91 | | 6795.75 | 8075.35 | | 5431.30 | 1290.03 | | 24073.34 | 22783.31 |
| 9. | Himachal Pradesh | 1851.07 | | 325.12 | 7598.94 | 140.00 | 3304.46 | 966.15 | 871.85 | 17983.59 | 16877.44 |
| 10. | Jammu and Kashmir | 5379.29 | | 3429.54 | 1707.47 | 1381.10 | 3202.16 | 324.04 | | 15423.60 | 13718.46 |
| 11. | Jharkhand | 4806.49 | | 4046.56 | 766.09 | 8.86 | 2978.67 | 1531.48 | | 14156.16 | 12615.81 |
| 12. | Karnataka | 11778.45 | | 10741.32 | 12883.89 | | 6590.07 | 4391.80 | | 46358.43 | 41993.63 |
| 13. | Kerala | 5254.04 | | 15809.97 | 3720.18 | 598.33 | 15806.90 | 2333.59 | | 43523.01 | 40591.07 |
| 14. | Madhya Pradesh | 9322.60 | | 10448.40 | 14481.21 | | 8313.91 | | | 42566.12 | 42566.12 |
| 15. | Maharashtra | 51281.79 | | 15704.84 | 7142.77 | | 9799.94 | 9277.43 | | 93206.77 | 83929.34 |
| 16. | Manipur | 1496.19 | | 749.85 | 129.23 | 55.08 | 514.00 | 176.52 | | 3120.87 | 2889.27 |
| 17. | Meghalaya | 449.89 | | 705.12 | 244.36 | | 485.53 | 449.77 | | 2334.67 | 1884.90 |
| 18. | Mizoram | 459.36 | | 492.62 | 441.93 | | 721.63 | | | 2205.54 | 2205.54 |

| | | | | | | | | | | | |
|---|---|---|---|---|---|---|---|---|---|---|---|
| 19. | Nagaland | 465.57 | | 1378.20 | 431.99 | | 507.36 | 2.93 | | 2786.05 | 2783.12 |
| 20. | Orissa | 13737.44 | | 11822.18 | 1872.61 | | 9183.31 | 1792.48 | | 38408.02 | 36615.54 |
| 21. | Punjab | 8621.92 | | 7604.38 | 22634.23 | 455.27 | 7973.47 | 978.96 | | 48268.23 | 46834.00 |
| 22. | Rajasthan | 26574.04 | | 14997.45 | 2070.35 | | 11869.55 | 4466.36 | | 59977.75 | 55511.39 |
| 23. | Sikkim | 276.18 | | 350.71 | 111.22 | | 268.28 | 38.20 | | 1044.59 | 1006.39 |
| 24. | Tamil Nadu | 8810.78 | 9773.93 | 16522.23 | 3125.32 | | 7592.75 | 4442.18 | | 50267.19 | 45825.01 |
| 25. | Tripura | 1346.83 | | 129.45 | 375.55 | 95.00 | 1190.69 | | | 4299.52 | 4204.52 |
| 26. | Uttar Pradesh | 27860.00 | 27360.00 | 24816.00 | 8365.00 | | 19521.00 | 21670.00 | | 129592.00 | 107922.00 |
| 27. | Uttar Pradesh | 602.43 | 2989.87 | 3546.34 | 1022.50 | | 1243.38 | | | 9404.52 | 9404.52 |
| 28. | West Bengal | 15872.36 | 41405.67 | 21343.46 | 9503.67 | 830.50 | 4715.06 | 6791.40 | | 100462.12 | 92840.22 |
| | Total | 261415.80 | 122430.90 | 230292.34 | 124235.85 | 4349.39 | 142103.05 | 78170.47 | 871.85 | 963869.65 | 881349.79 |

**Note*: Excluding W & M advances from RBI and reserve funds and deposit (total debt minus reserve funds and deposits minus W & M advances from RBI), Central loans may include NSSF loans.

*Source*: State Government.

TABLE 3

**Total Outstanding Debt of State Governments**

*(Rs. In crores)*

| *At the end of Financial Year* | *2003-04* | *2004-05* |
|---|---|---|
| (1) Market Loans | 200690 | 230292 |
| (2) Loans from Banks, etc. | 102531 | 124236 |
| (3) Loans from Centre* | 252809 | 261416 |
| (4) Provident Funds and Deposits, etc. | 129376 | 142103 |
| (5) Others@ | 97906 | 123303 |
| Total | 783312 | 881350 |

*May include NSSF loans also.
@Includes NSSF loans for some states.
*Source*: State Governments.

**Chart: Total Outstanding Debt of State Governments.**

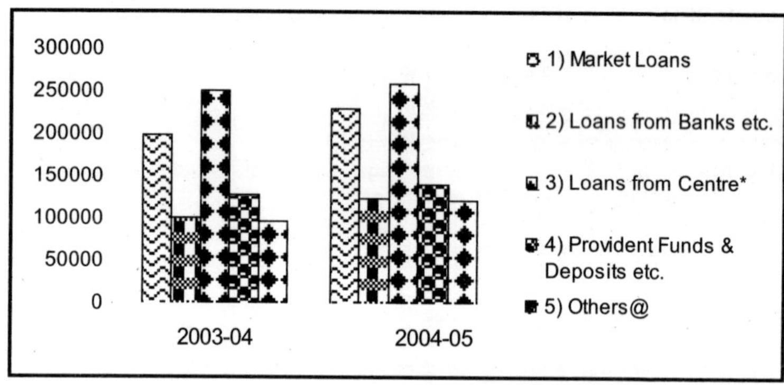


(a) Loans for state plan schemes as a part of normal central assistance, additional central assistance for state projects funded by external agencies and the loan component of the schematic portion of several state plan schemes (state plan loans), which are consolidated as one loan on October I every year, carrying the same rate of interest and other terms of conditions;

(b) Small savings loans comprising of loans given prior to April 1, 1999, when the National Small Savings Fund was created;
(c) Loans for centrally sponsored schemes/central plan schemes and other miscellaneous loans provided through central ministries;
(d) Medium-term loans given by the Ministry of Finance; and
(e) Ways and means advance loans by the Ministry of Finance.

TABLE 4

**Profile of Central Loans to States**

*(Rs. in Crores)*

| *At the end of* | *1999-2000* | *2000-01* | *2001-02* | *2002-03* | *2003-04* | *2004-05* |
|---|---|---|---|---|---|---|
| Central loans outstanding* | 209882 | 218380 | 228902 | 227343 | 193034 | 196346 |
| Total outstanding debt@ | 415142 | 489768 | 576171 | 667891 | 788401 | 885700 |
| | (50.48) | (44.59) | (39.73) | (34.04) | (24.48) | (22.17) |

Figures in parenthesis are percentage share of central loans to total outstanding debt for all states.

*Sources*: *Receipt Budgets, Government of India, 2004-05.
@States' Finance Accounts/State Government Debt (excludes reserve funds and deposits but includes W & M advances).

**Chart: Profile of Central Loans to States**

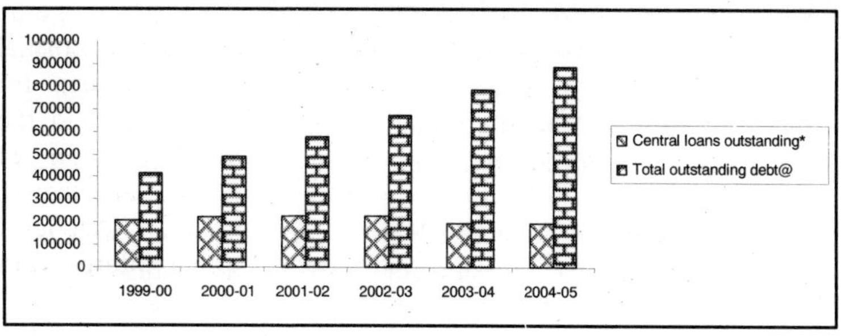

The outstanding central loans to states at the end of each year from 1999-2000 onwards, as indicated in the Receipts Budget 2004-05 of the Government of India, are show in Table 4 above. It would be observed that there has been a gradual reduction in the dependence of the states on the centre for borrowing requirements. While central loans constituted over 50% of outstanding loans of states in 1999-2000, in 2002-03 this figure has declined to 34.03 per cent and expected to come down further to 22.17 percent at the end of 2005. One of the reasons for the decline is that central loans no longer include the borrowings against small savings as the investments made in special securities of states against collections in the NSSF are maintained in the public account with effect from 1.4.99. The other reason for the decline is the 'debt-swap' allowed by the Central Government.

The rates of interest on central loans to states have varied from 7.5 per cent to 13 percent in respect of plan and non-plan loans (other than small savings loans) from the years 1984-2004. In regard to loans against small saving collections given before the NSSF was formed, the rate of interest had varied from 6.25 per cent from 1.8.74 to 31.5.81 to a maximum of 15 percent from 1.6.93 to 1.9.93, after which it was 14.5 percent from 2.9.93 to 31.1298 and 14 per cent from 1.1.99 to 31.3.99. Since central loans formed the largest component of the state debt in the past, increasing interest rates on central loans has contributed, to a large extent, to the growing burden of debt servicing of states. Table 5 indicates details of the rates of interest applicable on central loans from time to time.

The standard criteria for determining the sustainability of debt of states has been to arrive at the acceptable levels of debt-GSDP ratio and the ratio of interest payments to total revenue receipts. An analysis of the relative position of the debt-GSDP ratios of states in the total outstanding debt of states for the year 2002-03, which is the latest year for which the finance accounts are available, shows the result indicated in Table 6.

The aggregate Debt-GSDP ratio for all states works out to 34.21 percent. At the end of 2002-03, all states, except Maharashtra and Jharkhand, have debt-GSDP ratios exceeding

TABLE 5

**Rates of Interest on Central Loans to States (other than small Savings Loans): Plan and Non-Plan**

| *Types of Loans* | *Per cent per annum* |
|---|---|
| (a) Pre-1979 Consolidation State Plan Loans | 4.75 |
| (b) Loans advanced during 1979-84 consolidated for terms ranging from 15 to 30 years | 6.00-6.75 |
| (c) As per Ninth Finance Commission recommendations, State Plan Loans advanced during 1984-89 and outstanding as at the end of 1989-90 consolidated for 15 years | 9.00 |
| *Other Plan and Non-Plan Loans given to State from* | *Percent per annum* |
| (i) 1.6.84 to 31.5.85 | 7.50 |
| (ii) 1.6.85 to 31.5.86 | 8.00 |
| (iii) 1.6.86 to 31.5.87 | 8.75 |
| *Other Plan and Non-Plan Loans given to State from* | *Percent per annum* |
| (iv) 1.6.87 to 31.5.88 | 9.25 |
| (v) 1.6.88 to 31.5.90 | 9.75 |
| (vi) 1.6.90 to 31.5.91 | 10.25 |
| (vii) 1.6.91 to 31.5.92 | 10.75 |
| (viii) 1.6.92 to 31.5.93 | 11.75 |
| (ix) 1.6.93 to 31.5.95 | 12.00 |
| (x) 1.6.95 to 31.5.98 | 13.00 |
| (xi) 1.6.98 to 31.3.2001 | 12.50 |
| (xii) 1.4.2001 to 31.3.2002 | 12.00 |
| (xiii) 1.4.2002 to 31.3.2003 | 11.50 |
| (xiv) 1.5.2003 to 31.3.2004 | 10.50 |
| (xv) 1.4.2004-date | 9.00 |

*Source*: Twelfth Finance Commission Report (2004), Govt. of India, New Delhi.

**Rates of Interest on Loans to State Against Small Savings Collection**

| *Date of Loans* | *Per cent per annum* |
|---|---|
| 1.8.74 to 31.5.81 | 6.25 |
| 1.6.81 to 31.5.82 | 7.25 |
| 1.6.82 to 31.5.83 | 7.25 |
| 1.6.83 to 31.5.84 | 8.75 |
| 1.6.84 to 31.5.85 | 9.75 |
| 1.6.85 to 31.5.86 | 10.25 |
| 1.6.86 to 31.5.89 | 12.00 |
| 1.6.89 to 31.5.91 | 13.00 |
| 1.6.91 to 31.5.92 | 13.50 |
| 1.6.92 to 31.5.93 | 14.50 |
| 1.6.93 to 31.9.93 | 15.00 |
| 2.9.93 to 31.12.98 | 14.50 |
| 1.1.99 to 31.3.99 | 14.00 |

*Source*: Twelfth Finance Commission Report (2004), Govt. of India, New Delhi.

**Chart: Rates of Interest on Loans to State Against Small Savings Collection**

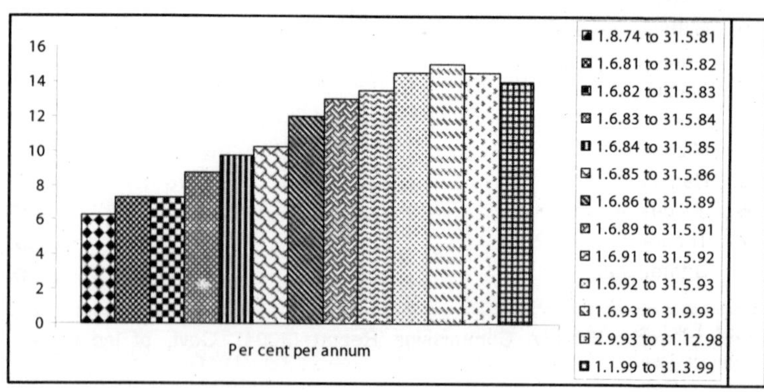

TABLE 6

**Debt-GSDP Ratios and Percentage Share of States in Overall Debt in 2002-03**

| *Sl. No.* | *States* | *Debt GSDP Ratio* | *Share in Total Debt of States* |
|---|---|---|---|
| **General Category States** | | | |
| 1. | Andhra Pradesh | 28.85 | 7.50 |
| 2. | Bihar | 55.33 | 4.79 |
| 3. | Chhatisgarh | 25.46 | 1.20 |
| 4. | Goa | 28.15 | 0.45 |
| 5. | Gujarat | 33.93 | 6.61 |
| 6. | Haryana | 27.85 | 2.70 |
| 7. | Jharkhand | 24.28 | 1.29 |
| 8. | Karnataka | 25.12 | 4.72 |
| 9. | Kerela | 36.34 | 4.65 |
| 10. | Madhya Pradesh | 32.28 | 4.07 |
| 11. | Maharashtra | 21.56 | 9.51 |
| 12. | Orissa | 62.93 | 4.23 |
| 13. | Punjab | 48.51 | 5.52 |
| 14. | Rajasthan | 45.38 | 6.31 |
| 15. | Tamil Nadu | 26.80 | 6.02 |
| 16. | Uttar Pradesh | 39.08 | 11.90 |
| 17. | West Bengal | 41.15 | 10.46 |
| **Special Category States** | | | |
| 18. | Arunachal Pradesh | 55.45 | 0.18 |
| 19. | Assam | 33.91 | 1.94 |
| 20. | Himachal Pradesh | 63.25 | 1.71 |
| 21. | Jammu and Kashmir | 55.80 | 1.65 |
| 22. | Manipur | 43.08 | 0.31 |
| 23. | Meghalaya | 32.17 | 0.22 |
| 24. | Mizoram | 81.56 | 0.27 |
| 25. | Nagaland | 52.10 | 0.38 |
| 26. | Sikkim | 60.27 | 0.13 |
| 27. | Tripura | 37.78 | 0.46 |
| 28. | Uttaranchal | 32.37 | 0.80 |

Debt Excludes reserve funds and deposits.

*Source*: Twelfth Finance Commission Report (2004), Govt. of India, New Delhi.

25 percent. Year-wise figures of debt-GSDP ratios upto 2002-03 are given in Table 7.

In the context of sustainable levels of debt, the EFC had recommended that the proportion of interest payments to revenue receipts, including tax devolution and grants, should be reduced to about 18 percent compared to the then average of 22 percent. The Twelfth Finance Commission, however, finds that from 2000-01 to 2002-03, the average ratio in respect of 17 states has been above 18 percent and in respect of 11 states has been above 22 percent. In terms of this criterion, therefore, 17 out of 28 states have unsustainable levels of debt. The relative position of states is indicated in Table 7

TABLE 7

**Interest Payments as a Percentage of Revenue Receipts**

| *% of Interest Payments to Revenue Receipts (Average of 2000-01 to 2002-03)* | *States* |
|---|---|
| Above 35% | Orissa, Punjab, West Bengal |
| 28-35% | Himachal Pradesh, Rajasthan, Uttar Pradesh |
| 22-28% | Andhra Pradesh, Bihar, Gujarat, Haryana, Kerala |
| 18-22% | Goa, Jharkhand, Karnataka, Madhya Pradesh, Maharashtra, Tamil Nadu |
| 10-18% | Assam, Arunachal Pradesh, Chhattisgarh, Jammu and Kashmir, Manipur, Meghalaya, Mizoram, Nagaland, Sikkim, Tripura, Uttaranchal |

State-wise and year-wise data on the ratio of interest payments to total revenue receipts are given in Table 8. The aggregate position of the ratio of interest payments to revenue receipts for all states for the year 2003-04 (RE) is found to be 26.07 per cent and in the year 2004-05 it is estimated at 25.19 per cent.

The deteriorating debt situation of states is reflected both in terms of the debt-GSDP ratio and the ratio of interest payments to revenue receipts. The position seems particularly grim for the states with high debt-GSDP ratios (i.e. over 35

### TABLE 8

## Interest Payment as a Percentage of Total Revenue Receipts (Incl. Net Lottery)

| Sl. No. | State | 2000-01 | 2001-02 | 2002-03 | 2003-04 | 2004-05 | Average (2000-01 to 2004-05) | Average (2000-01 to 2002-03) |
|---|---|---|---|---|---|---|---|---|
| | 1 | 2 | 3 | 4 | 5 | 6 | 7 | 8 |
| **A.** | **Special Category States** | | | | | | | |
| 1. | Arunachal Pradesh | 12.55 | 10.04 | 11.31 | 10.60 | 11.98 | 11.30 | 11.30 |
| 2. | Assam | 15.35 | 17.80 | 18.32 | 18.37 | 14.55 | 16.88 | 17.16 |
| 3. | Himachal Pradesh | 26.21 | 28.10 | 32.02 | 38.55 | 41.46 | 33.27 | 28.78 |
| 4. | Jammu and Kashmir | 13.58 | 16.15 | 14.51 | 12.93 | 12.09 | 13.85 | 14.74 |
| 5. | Manipur | 16.97 | 16.27 | 19.18 | 18.07 | 21.67 | 18.43 | 17.47 |
| 6. | Meghalaya | 10.04 | 11.46 | 11.74 | 10.78 | 11.50 | 11.10 | 11.08 |
| 7. | Mizoram | 12.23 | 16.86 | 13.03 | 13.23 | 17.53 | 14.58 | 14.04 |
| 8. | Nagaland | 14.13 | 15.14 | 15.94 | 12.28 | 15.40 | 14.58 | 15.07 |
| 9. | Sikkim | 12.31 | 11.22 | 9.86 | 9.88 | 8.97 | 10.45 | 11.13 |
| 10. | Tripura | 13.80 | 13.56 | 15.46 | 14.11 | 13.35 | 14.06 | 14.27 |
| 11. | Uttaranchal | | 18.55 | 17.19 | 21.87 | 17.16 | 18.69 | 17.87 |
| Total-Spl. Cat. (A) | | 15.56 | 17.61 | 17.69 | 18.02 | 16.95 | 17.17 | 16.95 |

(Contd.)

TABLE 8 *(Contd.)*

| *1* | *2* | *3* | *4* | *5* | *6* | *7* | *8* |
|---|---|---|---|---|---|---|---|
| **B. Non.-Special Category States** | | | | | | | |
| 1. Andhra Pradesh | 19.47 | 20.98 | 26.65 | 25.24 | 23.21 | 23.11 | 22.37 |
| 2. Bihar* | 28.11 | 26.72 | 27.55 | 24.57 | 23.63 | 26.12 | 27.46 |
| 3. Chhatisgarh | | 16.71 | 14.95 | 14.35 | 14.49 | 15.13 | 15.83 |
| 4. Goa | 18.90 | 19.86 | 19.75 | 17.53 | 16.78 | 18.56 | 19.50 |
| 5. Gujarat | 19.83 | 26.29 | 27.66 | 27.89 | 28.42 | 26.02 | 24.59 |
| 6. Haryana | 23.82 | 22.56 | 23.66 | 23.74 | 24.72 | 23.70 | 23.35 |
| 7. Jharkhand | | 12.63 | 28.74 | 13.31 | 11.10 | 16.45 | 20.69 |
| 8. Karnataka | 16.14 | 17.56 | 20.53 | 18.83 | 17.22 | 18.05 | 18.07 |
| 9. Kerela | 26.17 | 27.84 | 28.01 | 26.87 | 26.24 | 27.02 | 27.34 |
| 10. Madhya Pradesh* | 18.78 | 20.10 | 18.69 | 23.14 | 21.40 | 20.42 | 19.19 |
| 11. Maharashtra | 17.68 | 21.45 | 23.12 | 23.28 | 25.89 | 22.29 | 20.75 |
| 12. Orissa | 33.13 | 40.22 | 34.198 | 33.94 | 30.20 | 34.34 | 35.85 |
| 13. Punjab | 30.24 | 44.95 | 40.34 | 33.13 | 29.68 | 35.67 | 38.51 |
| 14. Rajasthan | 36.93 | 31.91 | 32.87 | 30.57 | 29.72 | 30.40 | 30.57 |
| 15. Tamil Nadu | 17.12 | 18.75 | 19.95 | 20.46 | 21.09 | 19.47 | 18.61 |
| 16. Uttar Pradesh* | 30.12 | 32.11 | 25.37 | 32.81 | 30.80 | 30.24 | 29.20 |
| 17. West Bengal | 36.20 | 43.92 | 52.86 | 53.47 | 48.11 | 46.91 | 44.33 |
| Total—Non-Special Category (B) | 32.18 | 26.19 | 27.11 | 27.16 | 26.29 | 25.99 | 25.49 |
| Grand Total (A+B) | 22.42 | 25.23 | 26.04 | 26.07 | 25.19 | 24.99 | 24.57 |

*Source*: Twelfth Finance Commission Report (2004), Govt. of India, New Delhi.

percent). These states are: Bihar, Himachal Pradesh, Kerala, Orissa, Punjab, Rajasthan, Uttar Pradesh, and West Bengal.

The Ministry of Finance, Govt. of India, in its review of the Fiscal Reform Facility, has worked out sustainable levels of debt as a percentage of total revenue receipts. In its formulation, debt has been defined as inclusive of guarantees. It considers non-special category states as 'highly stressed' in terms of debt and debt servicing, if this ratio exceeds 300 percent, in the case of special category states, the threshold is 200 percent. The ratio in respect of 20 states considered in the review, in the year 2002-03, ranges from 96.09 percent for Sikkim to 500.93 percent for West Bengal. The corresponding figures are estimated at 98.26 percent to 529.69 percent for the year 2004-05. In 2002-03, out of 20 states, 7 non-special category states and 2 special category states were highly stressed.

An examination of the debt profile of states indicates that the total outstanding debt of states (excluding reserve funds and deposits) has risen steadily from 18.62 percent of GDP in 1993-94 to 27.04 percent of GDP in 2002-03. The corresponding figures for 2003-04 and 2004-05 are 28.43 percent and 28.53 percent respectively. The rising debt of states is a reflection of the deterioration in the fiscal performance of states and signifies a long-term mismatch between the growth of revenues and expenditures of the states. It is the consequence of persistent increases in non-plan revenue expenditure, such as interest payments, subsidies, salaries and pension, together with sluggish growth in tax-GDP ratios; inadequate returns from public investment and insufficient growth in central transfers. Large revenue deficits have led to large fiscal deficits and spiraling debt, resulting in the emergence of vicious cycle of deficit, debt and debt service payments.

**Debt-Swap Scheme**

In the context of the debt of states, a mention needs to be made of the recent initiatives taken by the Government of India to tackle the high level of interest payments. Taking advantage of the falling interest regime, the central government introduced the debt-swap scheme in September

2002, to give relief to the states on the 'high-cost debt' owned by the states to the central government. High-cost debt was defined as the debt, which carried interest rate of 13 percent or above. Only state plan loans and small savings loans given up to 31.3.99 qualified for debt-swap. The Twelfth Finance Commission has been informed that on March 31, 2002, such high-cost debt amounted to Rs. 1,14,325 crores. Two borrowing sources were identified for swapping the 'high-cost' central government loans-additional open market borrowings and State Governments' investment in small savings securities. It was expected that additional market borrowings could be raised at around 7 percent. As the states had over Rs. 65,000 crores of small savings debt, which carried interest in excess of 14.5 percent, this swap was expected to give the State Governments a clear interest savings loan swapped with additional market borrowings. The states' investments in the NSSF securities carried an interest obligation of 9.5 percent. This stream was expected to result in interest saving of 3.5 percent to 5.5 percent. The scheme envisaged that during the year 2002-03, 20 percent of net small savings loans payable to states from September 2002, would be used to pre-pay the past debt. Use of 30 percent of net small savings in the year 2003-04 and 40 percent of net small savings in the year 2004-05 were envisaged for effecting debt-swap. The small savings are supplemented with additional market borrowings by the State Governments depending upon the liquidity position.

The Ministry of Finance has informed the Twelfth Finance Commission that the total debt-swap has so far been Rs. 87,672 crores, the year-wise details of which are indicated in Table 9.

In the year 2004-05, the total debt expected to be swapped is approximately Rs. 46,000 crores. The debt-swap is expected to provide a total interest relief of Rs. 31,000 crores over its lifetime and Rs. 14,500 crores and Rs. 28,000 crores respectively in the first five and ten years. The Twelfth Finance Commission has been informed that these calculations of savings in interest payments are based on the assumption that high cost of loans of Rs. 1.14 lakh crores have equal amortization schedule of 20 years and annual

TABLE 9

**Position of Debt-Swap Already Effected**

*(Rs. in Crores)*

| | *With Small Savings* | *With Additional Open Market Borrowings* | *Total* |
|---|---|---|---|
| 2002-03 | 3766 | 10000 | 13766 |
| 2003-04 | 17943 | 26623 | 44566 |
| 2004-05 up to Sept. 4 | 15559 | 13781 | 29340 |
| Total | 37268 | 50404 | 87672 |

*Source*: The Twelfth Finance Commission Report (2004) Govt. of India, New Delhi.

**Chart: Position of Debt-Swap Already Effected**

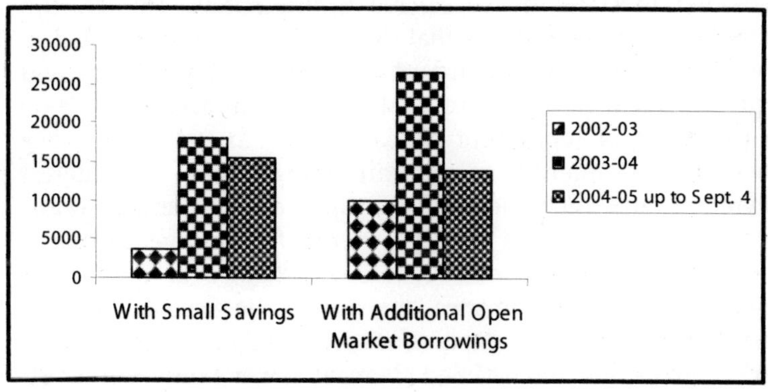


payment of Rs. 6017 crores and that the average interest on swapped loans is 7 percent for additional open market borrowings and 9.5 percent for small savings. The Ministry of Finance has calculated the savings in the revenue expenditure of states as a result of the scheme as 0.75 per cent per annum.

The Central Government has used the proceeds of debt-swap for pre-paying its debt to the NSSF assumed at the time of its creation in 1999. There would, however, be a loss of revenue for the centre as the high cost loans were effectively yielding as average annual interest of 14 percent, whereas even where the centre uses the entire debt-swap proceeds to effect pre-payment of its debt to the NSSF, carrying a rate of interest of 10.5 percent, there would be an interest rate differential of 3.5 percent per annum. For the states, the debt-swap scheme results only in a change in the composition and maturity profile of debt, but not the overall stock of debt. The benefits, however, are that over a period of time, savings by way of lower interest payments would reduce the pressure on the states' revenue account and, consequently, the overall borrowing requirements. Further, the role of the Central Government as an intermediary in respect of loans to State Governments gets reduced.

**Debt Relief by Earlier Finance Commissions**

Before formulating any approach to debt relief, the Twelfth Finance Commission has looked into the debt relief provided to states by successive Commissions. The Twelfth Finance Commission finds that debt relief has been granted in the form of (i) consolidation of loans on common terms and with reduction in the interest rates for the future, (ii) revision in the terms of repayment of loans given to states without a lowering of interest rates, (iii) moratorium on interest payments and repayment of principal due in certain years, (iv) write-off of loans or repayments falling due during a specified period, (v) introduction of schemes of debt relief linked to fiscal performance, etc. While the Second, Seventh and Eighth Finance Commissions consolidated some of the earlier loans and rescheduled them at lower rates of interest, the Sixth Finance Commission revised the terms of repayment of outstanding loans. The Seventh Finance Commission also recommended that small savings loans outstanding at the end of 1978-79 be converted into loans in perpetuity. This recommendation was, however, not accepted by the Central Government. Write-off of specific loans also constituted a part of the recommendations of these commissions. The Twelfth Finance Commission would, however, like to delve in greater detail on the recommendations of the three immediately preceding Commissions in regard to debt relief as these are considered to be more relevant to the Twelfth Finance Commission. The Ninth Finance Commission, in its second report, recommended write-off of loans given to states on account of drought during 1986-89 and outstanding on 31st March, 1989 and those given to Madhya Pradesh during 1984-89 in connection with the Bhopal Gas Leak Tragedy with the stipulation that repayment on account thereof, already made by the State Government by way of principal and interest shall be adjusted against other payments due from the State Government. The Commission also suggested a moratorium of two years on repayment of principal and payment of interest in respect of special loans given to Punjab during 1984-89. Further, the state plan loans advanced during the five-years period of 1984-89 were recommended for consolidation and reschedulement for 15 years in the case of all states. During the first five years, i.e. 1990-95, repayments were to be less than those due on the then existing basis to the extent of 10 per cent in the case of Andhra Pradesh, Karnataka, Madhya Pradesh, Maharashtra, Orissa, Tamil Nadu, Goa and special category states, 7.5 per cent in the case of Gujarat, Rajasthan and Uttar Pradesh and 5 per cent in the case of Bihar, Haryana, Kerala, Punjab and West Bengal.

The Tenth Finance Commission stated that, since many of the relief measures recommended by the previous Commissions continued to operate, any future relief should be viewed only as incremental. The Commission recommended a debt relief scheme in two parts, namely, (i) a scheme for general debt performance, and (ii) specific relief for states with high fiscal stress, special category states and states with debt problems warranting special attention. This was in addition to a scheme for encouraging retirement of debt from proceeds of disinvestments and equity holding of State Governments. The general debt relief scheme of the Tenth Finance Commission measured improvement in fiscal performance by comparing the ratio of revenue receipts (including devolution and grants from the centre) to total revenue expenditure in a given year with the average of the corresponding ratio in the three immediately preceding years.

The performance of each state was measured against its own past performance. Twice the excess of the ratio over the average ratio of fiscal improvement during the preceding three years was recommended for relief on loans contracted during the period 1989-95 and falling due for repayment after 31st March 1995. The relief was admissible only to the extent of ten per cent of the amount due for repayment from these loans in any year. The Twelfth Finance Commission observed that the actual relief sanctioned to states based on the Tenth Finance Commission's recommendations was Rs. 212 crores during the period 1995-2000 compared to the relief of Rs. 565.51 crores (assuring increase in performance by 2.5 percentage points) estimated by the Tenth Finance Commission. A specific relief in the form of write-off of 5 per cent of repayments due in regard to fresh central loans given during 1989-95 and outstanding as on 31.03.95 was also recommended by the Tenth Finance Commission for special category states and three other states (Orissa, Bihar and Uttar Pradesh), considered to have high fiscal stress, as their average ratio of interest payments to revenue expenditure exceeded 17 per cent during 1989-90 to 1993-94. In the case of Punjab, one-third of repayment of principal on special term loans falling due during 1995-2000 was recommended to be waived.

The EFC did not consider any special debt relief scheme for the fiscally stressed states, but continued the general debt relief scheme of the Tenth Finance Commission with the following modifications:

(i) Instead of a factor of 2, a factor of 5 was applied on the ratio of fiscal improvement in terms of revenue receipts to total revenue expenditure.

(ii) The ceiling of stipulated relief was set as 25 percent of repayment due in any one instead of 10 percent.

(iii) In the calculation of revenue receipts, the revenue deficit grants recommended by the EFC under article 275 were to be excluded.

This relief was to be available in respect of fresh loans

granted during 1995-2000 and outstanding on March 2000. Although the estimated debt relief was Rs. 600 to Rs. 700 crores, the Ministry of Finance, Govt. of India that till September 2004, the states qualified for a relief of Rs. 131.77 crores only, has informed the Twelfth Finance Commission. The states, which have benefited under the scheme, are Andhra Pradesh (Rs. 77.52 crores), Arunachal Pradesh (Rs. 1.72 crores), Manipur (Rs. 2.47 crores), Tamil Nadu (Rs. 7.89 crores) and Punjab (Rs. 42.11 crores).

**Views of State Governments**

The Twelfth Finance Commission has considered the suggestions made by the State Governments in their memoranda in regard to debt relief. A large number of states have pleaded that interest rates on central loans to states may be brought down. Suggestions have been made for waiver of interest, consolidation of loans, writing-off of principal, rescheduling and moratorium on repayments. Many states have requested for a consolidation and reschedulement of loans with or without moratorium on interest and repayment. Some states have also suggested that a portion of the consolidated loans may be written-off. The continuation of the debt-swap scheme is another demand of states with some states suggesting that the scheme should be extended to all outstanding high-cost loans including those from financial institutions. Some states have suggested modifications to the scheme of debt relief linked to fiscal performance recommended by the EFC. The other suggestions made by states are summarized below:

(a) External assistance received by the Government of India as grants-in-aid should be passed on to the states as grant and a fee may be collected from the states for covering the transaction cost.

(b) The repayment of the borrowing from external agencies, passed on to states, should be on the same terms and conditions as prescribed by the external agency and the central government should charge only a fee for meeting the transaction cost.

(c) In respect of small savings, central government may recover from the states only the amount, which is to be paid to the investor, plus a nominal cost not exceeding half percent for administration of the schemes.

(d) Debt-swap scheme should be applicable to all high-cost loans and states should be allowed to raise low-cost loans from the market, both internal and external, to repay high-cost loans within certain limits to be imposed by the central government.

(e) Plan assistance given in the form of special term loans for meeting emergencies like insurgency or converted into grant. In future, such assistance should come in the form of grants-in-aid only.

(f) Additional plan assistance given to special category states under Accelerated Irrigation Benefit Programme and Rural Electrification Programme should, like other plan schemes, be converted in to 90 percent grant and 10 percent loan, instead of 100 percent loan as is the case at present.

(g) The Non-Lapsable Central Pool of unspent balance of funds earmarked in various ministries for the northeastern states should be given to the states concerned as 100 percent grant as against the current pattern of 90 percent grant and 10 percent loan.

(h) The rate of interest charged by the Government of India on loans granted to the states should be reviewed every year and should be closely aligned to the prevailing market rate of interest.

(i) The central plan assistance should generally be in the form of grants and the states should have the option to contract the loan component from the open market.

(j) Financial institutions should be advised to extend loans to public sector undertakings on the basis of the viability of a project without insisting on the guarantee.

## Views of the Central Government

The Central Government in its memorandum has stated than an appropriate fiscal management plan for bringing down the ratio of state debt to GDP during the award period is an imperative. It has further been stated that, while the Central Government has been making efforts to reduce burden of states through debt-swap and reduction in interest rates on plan loans and small savings transfers, states' debt to the centre should not be written-off or rescheduled, as the centre is no longer in a position to bear any additional burden on this account. In any case, debt relief to states should not be unconditional and across the board.

The memorandum also states that guarantees given by the State Governments have risen sharply over the years and at the end of March 2002, stood at Rs. 1,66,116 crores, constituting 7.2 percent of GDP for 17 major states. While steps, administrative and legislative, have been initiated by some State Governments to cap the level of guarantees, it may be appropriate if the Commission recommends an appropriate level of guarantees that may be given by an individual State Government is concerned, efforts will be made to limit fresh guarantees to 0.5 percent of GDP each year, as provided in the Fiscal Responsibility and Budget Management Bill (FRBM Bill).

In a subsequent reference, it has been stated that in the case of states, the issue of debt sustainability is being addressed through the medium-term fiscal reform framework. Many states have also been working towards fiscal correction through adoption of Fiscal Responsibility Legislation, ceilings on guarantees, etc. and it is believed that these will favourably impact on their future borrowing requirement and thereby on their overall stock of debt.

On the issue of linking debt relief to progress in Human Development Index, the Twelfth Finance Commission has been urged to balance the considerations of efficiency with equity so that the concerns of states with lower than India's average human development indices, are taken care of. In any case, debt relief should specifically address the issues related to cost of debt rather than write-off, which the centre is not in a position to bear, given the restraints being put into effect by the Fiscal Responsibility and Budget Management Act.

In a further submission on the issue of linkage of debt relief to progress in Human Development Index (HDI), the Ministry of Finance expressed the view that, it may not be appropriate to link HDI to debt relief to states. There is merit in adhering to pure "financial" and "fiscal" indicators in the matter of debt relief.

Since the Central Government stated that the problem of debt sustainability is being addressed through the medium-term fiscal reform framework, the Twelfth Finance Commission specifically studied the features of the Fiscal Reform Facility (FRF) related to debt. The mid-term review of the FRF by the Ministry of Finance has noted that, instead of the conventional definition of sustainable debt based on the Domar principle, the assessment of debt as a percentage of total revenue receipts has been found more appropriate, as there is a methodological problem in using state GSDP as a denominator. Since there is a correspondence between GSDP growth and growth in states' revenues, anchoring of debt as a percentage of total revenue receipts (TRR) was not inappropriate. In the formulation contained in the mid-term review, the definition of debt includes guarantees. Sustainable debt (including guarantees) to TRR ratio has been worked out as 300 percent for non-special category states, keeping in view the need for the gross fiscal deficit to stabilize at 3 percent of GSDP. The review states that general category states can be considered as highly stressed, if the ratio is greater than 300 percent. For special category states, if the ratio is more than 200 per cent, they can be classified as highly stressed. It has been estimated that by 2004-05, the number of highly stressed states is likely to be to eight (special category—Assam and Himachal Pradesh and non-special category—Kerala, Maharashatra, Orissa, Punjab, Rajasthan and West Bengal).

The mid-term review of the FRF by the Ministry of Finance, Govt. of India, further suggests that a practical approach would be to divide states in three categories, viz., (a) severely debt stressed, (b) moderately debt stressed, and (c) non-stressed. For severely debt stressed, modified form of

IMF-World Bank HIPC initiative covering all loans should be conceptualized. Further, the debt-swap scheme must continue and for meeting reform costs, a blend of loans and grants should be adopted where the loan part should not exceed 50 per cent of the mix.

The Twelfth Finance Commission is given to understand that assistance has been available to states for restructuring of debt with financial institutions to take advantage of the lower interest regime. The assistance is for debt reschedulement or refinancing and the Government of India, through the FRF, restructuring by allocation of additional open this assistance till now. Further, under the like voluntary retirement scheme (VRS), etc. borrowings, Jammu and Kashmir, Manipur, Himachal Pradesh, Kerala and Nagaland have benefited.

The Twelfth Finance Commission also notes that the Medium-term Fiscal Policy Strategy of the Government of India placed before Parliament in July 2004 intends to encourage states to approach the market directly rather than routing state debt through central budget and to consider on-lending external loans to states on a back-to-back basis. Further, in the National Common Minimum Programme (NCMP), it has been stated that a structured and transparent approach to be adopted to enable them to increase social sector investments and that the interest rates on loans to states will be reduced.

### Studies Assigned by the Commission

A study was assigned by the Twelfth Finance Commission to the Indian Institute of Management, Ahmedabad to develop a suitable methodology for assessing the fiscal sustainability of debt of the States in India and identifying the major factors that have led to the deterioration of the debt profile in the recent past. Using case studies in respect of six states, the study was required to suggest a model programme of reforms and policy interventions for resolving the debt-related issues. The study has recommended linking of the resource transfers (tax and grants) from the centre to the states. The states' own revenue generation and their own account primary deficit. Once the Finance

Commission determines the level of transfers to a state on whatever basis, its ratio to states' own revenues stands determined and should form the basic of an incentive scheme. It has further been recommended that all high interest loans given for calamity/disaster relief should be considered separately for either writing them off fully or partially or giving a five-year moratorium, apart from reducing interest rates thereon. It has been concluded that four states would need restructuring of about 15 percent of their debt through five-year moratorium on interest payments and for two of the states, this level would be 30 percent and 50 percent respectively. All this should be subject to strict adherence to the achievement of targeted growth in states' own revenues and in primary expenditure of 13.5 percent and 10 percent per annum respectively, failing which, the interest of additional 2 percent. It has been suggested that since loans from the centre have the highest effective interest rate compared to other sources of funds for a state, there should be at least a 200 basis points reduction in the effective interest rate charged by the centre and over a five-year period, it should be brought in line with the market rate of interest. It has further been suggested that the existing cap on market borrowing by states should be reviewed and more freedom should be given to states based on their credit rating and overall economic performance regarding small savings, which carry a higher interest cost, the centre should given an option to states in the matter of availing of these loans. The centre can supply excess of small savings from one state to another in need of such loans. Alternatively, the centre could bear the difference in the interest cost of these loans and the market rate of interest. The study has also suggested that the Central Government should facilitate the pre-payment negotiations of loans by the State Governments to the public sector financial institutions, since they carry a very high effective interest rate due to their loan vintage.

A paper on Debt Sustainability/Debt Relief was also outsourced by the Commission. The paper covered various aspects of debt sustainability, measures of debt relief and the suggested policy for future borrowings. It stresses the importance of the elimination of the revenue deficit with an additional limit on the size of the fiscal deficit. A fiscal deficit target of 3 percent of GSDP for every state and a targeted debt ratio of 25 percent of GSDP has been suggested. The achievement of this would, *inter alia*, require three different forms of debt relief in the case of central loans to states, namely (a) reduction of interest liability by lowering the interest rate on central loans to states to an appropriate level, (b) write-off of debt owed by states to the centre, eliminating future budgetary outflows on amortization and interest payment together with modification of the policy of central lending to states, and (c) reschedulement of debt over a longer period to reduce the annual budgetary outgo for states in terms of amortization. In order to explore the possibility of linking debt relief to performance in human development, the Twelfth Finance Commission examined the reports prepared by the Planning Commission and UNDP. For measuring inter-state differences in investment climate, two indices, namely, index of investment attractiveness and index of investment climate were developed by M/s Indicus Analytics using a number of variables. 20 states were ranked on the basis of percentage change between 1996-2001.

### The Twelfth Finance Commission's Approach

The Twelfth Finance Commission has taken into account the existing levels of debt of states, their fiscal situation, the corrective measures recommended by previous Finance Commissions, the suggestions made by the Central Government and the submissions of the State Governments while formulating their views. The Twelfth Finance Commission has also taken into account the suggestions made by the two studies. Assigned by the Twelfth Finance Commission well other studies. Considering all these factors, the Twelfth Finance Commission is the view that unless concrete and immediate measures are taken to tackle the debt of states, fiscal sustainability of states cannot be achieved. The Twelfth Finance Commission agrees with the approach of the EFC that the incremental revenue receipts should meet incremental interest burden and incremental primary expenditure. The Twelfth Finance Commission however, feels that the pre-requisite to this is the achievement of revenue balance by instituting measures for augmenting revenue receipts and compressing expenditure. As such, debt relief measures will need to be recommended by the Twelfth Finance Commission in the context of debt considered sustainable and with a view to eliminating the revenue deficit of the states. Apart from providing for specific debt relief, qualitative and quantitative measures also need to be prescribed to restrict the future growth of debt stock of states beyond sustainable levels. Specifically, the debt central loans to states need to be substantial performance. The role of the centre *vis-à-vis* the debt of states needs to be re-determined by prescribing a rational lending policy for the future. This should include a rational computation of interest rates for future loans to the states. In addition, the repayments, particularly on open market borrowings, needs to be catered for in a not cause undue fiscal stress.

As debt is the aggregate of borrowing made to finance fiscal deficits over the years, higher revenue and fiscal deficits lead to larger accretions in the stock of debt. The Twelfth Finance Commission feels that states should make efforts to eliminate their revenue deficits so that borrowings are not used to finance revenue expenditure but are utilized for generating capital assets. The Twelfth Finance Commission notes that five states, namely, Karnataka, Kerala, Punjab, Tamil Nadu and Uttar Pradesh have enacted fiscal responsibility legislations to safeguard fiscal discipline and impose a statutory limit on the size of state's debt and/fiscal responsibility bill had also been introduced in the state assembly of Maharashtra. The Twelfth Finance Commission finds that the fiscal responsibility legislations of these six states have specified targets for the fiscal and revenue deficits. In regard to total liabilities, ceilings have been prescribed by Karnataka, Punjab and Uttar Pradesh. Maharashtra proposes to put a restriction on borrowings. Capping of guarantees is provided for the legislation of Karnataka, Tamil Nadu, Punjab, Uttar Pradesh (ceiling to be laid down under the rules or the law) and Maharashtra. The Twelfth Finance Commission has recommended that in the first instance, as a measure of fiscal discipline, all states should enact fiscal responsibility legislations prescribing specific annual targets for reducing their revenue and fiscal deficits and providing for a ceiling along with a path for reduction of borrowings and guarantees. The Twelfth Finance Commission has further recommended that the legislation should provide that the revenue deficit of states be brought down to zero by 2008-09, coinciding with similar targets prescribed for the central government.

The TOR of Twelfth Finance Commission recommended corrective measures giving weightage to performance of states in the fields of human development and investment climate. The Twelfth Finance Commission has considered the matter keeping in view the suggestions of the Central and State Governments and the feasibility of providing such a linkage. While some State Governments have supported the inclusion of these as a criteria for debt relief, other states are not in favour of linking debt relief to progress in human development or performance or the relatively low ranking of states in these fields are largely attributable to fiscal imbalance including unsustainable debt burden. Such a linkage would also widen the gap between the developing and backward states. Further, preparing an index of HDI and judging the performance of a state as on a particular cut-off date may render the assessment subjective. Similarly, defining what constitutes improvement in investment climate could also prove contentious. As far as the Central Government is concerned, their view is that it may not be appropriate to link debt relief to improvements in HDI.

The feasibility of linking debt relief to performance of states in the fields of human development and investment climate has been examined by the Twelfth Finance Commission. The Twelfth Finance Commission notes that their TOR do not clarify whether such performance should be given a positive or negative weight in the scheme of relief. After a careful examination of the issues involved including the methodology and the outcome of the study assigned by them, they are unable to establish any direct link between debt relief and performance in the field of either human development or investment climate. Even the central government has not favoured such a linkage, suggesting that there is merit in adhering to pure financial and fiscal indicators in the matter of debt relief. Besides, given the diverse methodologies, incomplete coverage of state and infrequently availability of data, the linkage of performance in human development with debt relief would not be appropriate. The formulation of an index of investment climate suffers from even greater constraints, as it involves considerable subjective judgement based on perception with no accepted or standard methodology for formulating the index. The Twelfth Finance Commission has; therefore, decide not to link debt relief with performance in human development or investment climate.

The Twelfth Finance Commission has referred earlier to the manner in which previous Commissions have sought to provide debt relief to states. In formulating their scheme of debt relief, they have taken into account the schemes recommended by the Tenth and Eleventh Finance Commissions. The debt-swap scheme of the Central Government has provided substantial relief to the states. The Twelfth Finance Commission's focus, as far as fiscal reforms are concerned, balance is on the states achieving revenue balance by 2008-09. The Twelfth Finance Commission has, therefore, followed a two pronged approach to debt relief, firstly, a general scheme of debt relief applicable to all states and secondly, a write-off scheme linked to fiscal performance with a view to providing as incentive for the achievement of revenue balance by 2008-09. The Twelfth Finance Commission has, however, excluded the loans given to the states from the NSSF from 1.4.99 onwards from the scope of the debt relief as the Fund is maintained in the public account.

As already noted, the debt-swap scheme of the Government of India covers central loans, which have an interest rate of 13 percent and above and is expected to close by 2004-05. States have requested for alignment of interest rates on central loans with interest rates applicable to market borrowings. It is seen from the receipts budget 2004-05 that the weighted average cost of market borrowings of the centre during 2003-04 was 5.74 percent. As per data collected from the Ministry of Finance, Govt. of India, the weighted average cost of the total borrowings in 2003-04 works out to 6.04 percent as indicated in Table 10. The interest rate charged from however, 10.5 percent. The marginal cost of borrowing by the centre is, therefore, much lower than the interest rate charged from states. Large interest payments have been a major factor leading to increase in the outstanding debt of State Governments. In the Twelfth Finance Commission's view, therefore, the reduction of interest payments is integral to attaining debt sustainability. The Twelfth Finance Commission has requested the central and State Governments to provide loan-wise details containing outstanding balances as on 31.3.04 and the quantum of repayments and the interest payments due from the central loans during their award period. Data for each state are being administered by Ministry of Finance and that consolidation of these loans would lend simplicity to the management of these loans. A consolidation exercise in respect of central loans to states outstanding as on 31.3.04, except the loans given by central ministries for which data were not available, has, therefore, been carried out by the Twelfth Finance Commission.

TABLE 10

**Weighted Average Interest Rate of Central Government Borrowings in 2003-04**

| *Net Borrowings* | *Amount* | *Interest Rate (percentage)* |
|---|---|---|
| Market Borrowings | 86797 | 5.74 |
| NSSF | 13765 | 7 |
| NSSF | 32602 | 6 |
| NSSF | 13608 | 5.95 |
| Provident Funds | 5000 | 8 |
| Others (tax-free) | 4520 | 6.5 |
| Other (taxable) | 1588 | 8 |
| Total | 157880 | |
| Weighted Average Interest Rate | | 6.04% |

*Source*: The Twelfth Finance Commission Report (2004), Govt. of India, New Delhi.

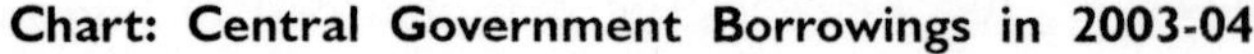

**Chart: Central Government Borrowings in 2003-04**

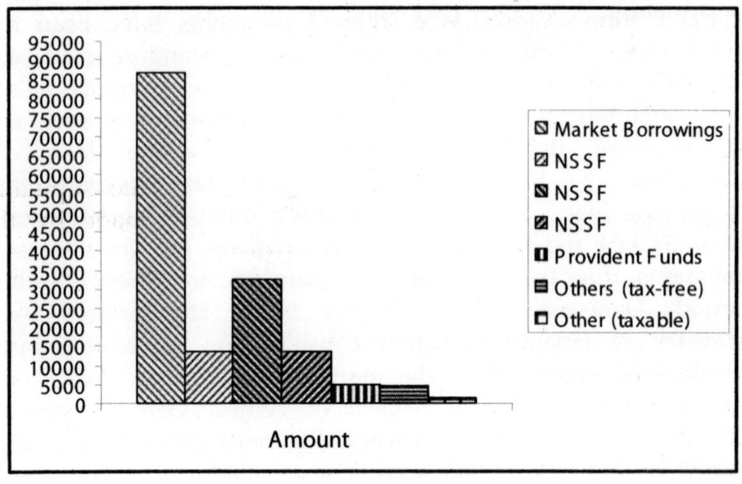


For the purpose of consolidation of outstanding central loans to states as on 31.3.04, the Twelfth Finance Commission has relied on the statement of outstanding central loans supplied to them by the Ministry of Finance for the reason that, (a) the Ministry of Finance data have taken into account the debt-swap expected to take place by the end of 2004-05 and determines the repayments accordingly, and (b) the data of central loans supplied by states in many cases include loans from NSSF. The balance of outstanding central loans to states, as on 31.3.04, consolidated by the Twelfth Finance Commission works out to Rs. 1,84,268 crores. These loans do not include loans given by ministries/departments for central plan/centrally sponsored schemes. The break-up of these outstanding loans is shown in Table 11

A debt-swap of about Rs. 44,000 crores has been indicated as expected to take place in 2004-05 in the data provided. The balance of these consolidated loans, which will remain, as on 31.3.05 after taking into account normal repayments in 2004-05 and the expected debt-swap, is Rs. 1,28,795 crores. The state-wise details of the repayments due on the loans mentioned during their award period shown in Table 12.

TABLE 11

**Break-up of Outstanding Central Loans to States as on 31.3.2004**

| *Balance of Loans on 31.3.04* | *(Rs. in crores)* |
|---|---|
| Block Loans | 146198 |
| Mid-term Loans | 2431 |
| Small Savings Loans granted up to 31.3.99 | 30638 |
| Pre-1979-80 Consolidated Loans (30 years) | 475 |
| Pre-1979-80 Re-Consolidated Loans (30 years) | 1441 |
| 1979-84 Consolidated Loans (20 years) | 27 |
| 1979-84 Consolidated Loans (25 years) | 550 |
| 1979-84 Consolidated Loans (30 years) | 1562 |
| 1979-84 Consolidated Loans (15 years) | 942 |
| Others | 4 |
| Grand Total | 184268 |

*Source*: The Twelfth Finance Commission Report (2004), Govt. of India, New Delhi.

The Twelfth Finance Commission observes that even after the debt-swap scheme close, the effective interest rate on the outstanding loans would be around 11.5 percent. In the Twelfth Finance Commission's view, a relief in interest payments is called for by way of adjustment of the difference between the marginal cost of borrowing of the central government and the effective interest rates charged by the centre on loans. Keeping in view the fact the some premium in the form of transaction costs should be available to the centre, the Twelfth Finance Commission recommended that the central loans to states contracted till 31.03.05 and outstanding on 31.03.04 (amounting to Rs. 1,28,795 crores) may be consolidated and rescheduled for a fresh term of 20 years (resulting in repayment in 20 equal instalments), and an interest rate of 7.5 percent be charged on them. The consolidated loans include some loans, which had been consolidated by the earlier Finance Commissions at interest rates lower than 7.5 percent. The Twelfth Finance Commission has, however, included them in the present

TABLE 12

## Outstanding Balance Central Loans Granted upto 31.03.2004 and Repayment Profile (before Consolidation and Rechedulement) during 2005-06 to 2009-10

(Rs. In crore)

| States | Repayment due from 2005-10 as per existing terms | | | | | | | | | | | |
|---|---|---|---|---|---|---|---|---|---|---|---|---|
| | Out-standing Balance on 31.3.2004 | Out-standing Balance of these Loans as on 31.3.2005 | Block Loans | Small Savings Loans | Mid-term Loans | Pre-79-80 Consoli-dated Loans (30 years) | Pre-79-80 Reconsoli-dated Loans (30 years) | 1979-80 Consoli-dated Loans (30 years) | 1979-84 Consoli-dated Loans (30 years) | 1984-89 Consoli-dated Loans (15 years) | Others | Total Repayment due from 2005 to 2010 |
| Andhra Pradesh | 18545.00 | 15337.14 | 4185.30 | 204.52 | 0 | 0 | 75.44 | 0 | 108.67 | 0 | 0 | 4573.93 |
| Arunachal Pradesh | 409.40 | 389.56 | 116.71 | 0.66 | 0 | 0 | 0 | 0 | 0 | 0 | 0 | 117.37 |
| Assam | 2939.83 | 2099.82 | 347.32 | 92.33 | 465.00 | 0 | 22.12 | 0 | 105.63 | 0 | 0.17 | 1032.57 |
| Bihar | 10181.29 | 7704.08 | 2153.12 | 243.79 | 0 | 0 | 54.32 | 0 | 95.24 | 0 | 0 | 2546.47 |
| Chhattisgarh | 2748.11 | 2281.26 | 618.73 | 50.14 | 0 | 20.30 | 0 | 0 | 27.17 | 0 | 0 | 716.35 |
| Goa | 585.56 | 528.54 | 162.24 | 8.96 | 0 | 0 | 0 | 0 | 0 | 0 | 0 | 171.19 |
| Gujarat | 14037.04 | 10463.92 | 2896.52 | 488.93 | 0 | 52.17 | 0 | 0 | 0 | 27.51 | 0 | 3465.13 |
| Haryana | 3627.74 | 2325.73 | 639.43 | 141.76 | 0 | 23.61 | 0 | 34.92 | 0 | 0 | 0 | 839.73 |
| Himachal Pradesh | 1777.37 | 824.24 | 207.05 | 57.35 | 0 | 0 | 3.92 | 0 | 7.61 | 0 | 0 | 275.94 |
| Jammu and Kashmir | 2697.73 | 1895.35 | 481.47 | 41.23 | 0 | 0 | 27.13 | 0 | 85.38 | 0 | 0 | 635.22 |
| Jharkhand | 3052.48 | 2637.95 | 731.27 | 82.53 | 0 | 0 | 18.39 | 0 | 32.24 | 0 | 0 | 864.43 |
| Karnataka | 10555.40 | 8318.17 | 2229.12 | 258.86 | 0 | 22.88 | 0 | 0 | 0 | 0 | 0 | 2510.86 |

| | | | | | | | | | | | | |
|---|---|---|---|---|---|---|---|---|---|---|---|---|
| Kerala | 5517.28 | 4252.19 | 1223.04 | 101.68 | 0 | 50.35 | 0 | 67.11 | 0 | 0 | 0 | 442.19 |
| Madhya Pradesh | 8977.66 | 7500.42 | 2222.68 | 138.23 | 0 | 55.95 | 0 | 0 | 74.91 | 0 | 0 | 2491.76 |
| Maharashtra | 16166.55 | 7812.88 | 2137.78 | 889.24 | 0 | 59.33 | 0 | 0 | 0 | 0 | 0 | 3086.34 |
| Manipur | 777.11 | 754.16 | 100.70 | 1.49 | 371.00 | 0 | 2.21 | 0 | 5.29 | 0 | 0 | 480.68 |
| Meghalaya | 356.65 | 321.07 | 85.82 | 6.34 | 0 | 0 | 0.36 | 0 | 2.57 | 0 | 0 | 95.08 |
| Mizoram | 290.56 | 271.39 | 74.82 | 0.34 | 0 | 0 | 0 | 0 | 0 | 0 | 0 | 75.16 |
| Nagaland | 341.33 | 320.59 | 95.49 | 1.58 | 0 | 0 | 0 | 0 | 4.43 | 0 | 0 | 101.50 |
| Orissa | 8965.24 | 7005.17 | 1740.60 | 74.36 | 682.00 | 0 | 39.77 | 0 | 77.41 | 0 | 0 | 2624.14 |
| Punjab | 5396.83 | 3053.69 | 885.43 | 227.80 | 1.67 | 0 | 0 | 0 | 0 | 0 | 0 | 1114.90 |
| Rajasthan | 9605.40 | 6833.53 | 1648.98 | 186.35 | 462.50 | 0 | 66.18 | 0 | 81.12 | 0 | 1.02 | 2446.16 |
| Sikkim | 208.45 | 192.28 | 55.45 | 0.85 | 0 | 0 | 0.37 | 0 | 2.10 | 0 | 0 | 58.76 |
| Tamil Nadu | 9180.55 | 6872.68 | 2215.75 | 171.37 | 0 | 19.71 | 0 | 0 | 0 | 0 | 0 | 2406.84 |
| Tripura | 555.96 | 470.10 | 131.42 | 9.32 | 0 | 1.55 | 0 | 0 | 0 | 0 | 0 | 142.29 |
| Uttar Pradesh | 27407.35 | 18340.48 | 5188.90 | 639.18 | 0 | 0 | 85.58 | 224.50 | 0 | 0 | 0 | 6138.16 |
| Uttar Pradesh | 308.17 | 288.09 | 41.83 | 3.63 | 0 | 0 | 4.53 | 11.90 | 0 | 0 | 0 | 64.89 |
| West Bengal | 19056.02 | 9700.29 | 241.67 | 558.97 | 438.00 | 74.06 | 0 | 119.85 | 0 | 0 | 0 | 3612.55 |
| Total | 184268.06 | 128794.75 | 35038.65 | 4681.78 | 2430.17 | 379.92 | 400.31 | 458.28 | 709.78 | 27.51 | 1.19 | 44127.60 |

* *Note*: 1. The above figures do not include loans given by Ministries/Departments for Centrally Sponsored Schemes/Central Plan Schemes

2. These figures do not include fresh loans given in 2004-05.

*Source*: Ministry of Finance, Government of India.

exercise so that management of loans becomes simpler for the central government. States would get benefits in repayment on account of reschedulement of these loans. In terms of these recommendations relating to consolidation, reschedulement and lowering of interest rate, the debt relief during the award period for all states put together, works out to Rs. 21,276 crores in interest payments and Rs. 11,929 crores interest payments. Thus, the proposed scheme provides benefit both in terms of interest rate reduction and a reschedulement of loans, which will ease the liquidity position of states. The state-wise details of debt relief are indicated in Table 13. In the debt consolidation exercise, the Twelfth Finance Commission has not taken into account the fresh loans to be granted by the centre in the year 2004-05, as state-wise details of such loans were not available. The Central Government has, however, lowered the rate of interest on loan to states from 10.5 percent to 9 percent in 2004-05. This general debt relief comprising consolidation, reschedulement and lowering of interest to 7.5 percent shall be available to all states with effect from the year they enact the fiscal responsibility legislation as recommended by the Twelfth Finance Commission.

In addition to providing general debt relief by consolidation and rescheduling at substantially reduced rates of interest the central loans granted to states before 31.3.04 and outstanding as on 31.3.05, the Twelfth Finance Commission has advised a scheme of debt write-off based on fiscal performance. The Twelfth Finance Commission has already stressed the need for each state to enact a fiscal adjustment path for reduction of the revenue deficit to zero by 2008-09. The Twelfth Finance Commission has suggested discontinuation of the states' Fiscal Reform Facility on the ground that the present design of the facility is not conducive to achievement of its objectives. In their opinion, instead of a multiplicity of incentive schemes to reward fiscal performance, incentives for fiscal performance should be built into the debt write-off package. The Twelfth Finance Commission feels that states will be provided a tangible incentive if a reduction of the revenue deficit also entitles them to a write-off of debt. A scheme of this nature would

TABLE 13

**State-wise Debt Relief after Consolidation of Central Loans Contracted Before 31.3.2004 and Outstanding on 31.3.2005**

*(Rs. in crores)*

| *Sl. No.* | *States* | *Total (Debt Servicing During 2005-10)* | | |
|---|---|---|---|---|
| | | *Repayment* | *Interest* | *Total* |
| 1. | Andhra Pradesh | 739.64 | 2683.74 | 3423.38 |
| 2. | Arunachal Pradesh | 19.98 | 71.73 | 91.71 |
| 3. | Assam | 507.62 | 153.87 | 661.49 |
| 4. | Bihar | 620.45 | 1268.27 | 1888.72 |
| 5. | Chhattisgarh | 146.03 | 393.77 | 539.80 |
| 6. | Goa | 39.06 | 94.66 | 133.72 |
| 7. | Gujarat | 849.15 | 1840.02 | 2689.17 |
| 8. | Haryana | 258.30 | 387.67 | 645.96 |
| 9. | Himachal Pradesh | 69.88 | 134.79 | 204.67 |
| 10. | Jammu and Kashmir | 161.38 | 264.02 | 425.40 |
| 11. | Karnataka | 204.94 | 454.49 | 659.43 |
| 12. | Karnataka | 431.32 | 1529.43 | 1960.74 |
| 13. | Kerala | 379.14 | 715.03 | 1094.17 |
| 14. | Madhya Pradesh | 616.66 | 1310.98 | 1927.64 |
| 15. | Maharashtra | 1133.12 | 1217.39 | 2350.51 |
| 16. | Manipur | 292.14 | 27.26 | 319.40 |
| 17. | Meghalaya | 14.82 | 56.49 | 71.30 |
| 18. | Mizoram | 7.31 | 50.54 | 57.85 |
| 19. | Nagaland | 21.35 | 56.06 | 77.41 |
| 20. | Orissa | 872.85 | 1008.43 | 1881.28 |
| 21. | Punjab | 351.48 | 523.18 | 874.66 |
| 22. | Rajasthan | 737.77 | 962.25 | 1700.02 |
| 23. | Sikkim | 10.69 | 33.96 | 44.65 |
| 24. | Tamil Nadu | 688.67 | 1195.47 | 1884.14 |
| 25. | Tripura | 24.77 | 123.97 | 148.73 |
| 26. | Uttar Pradesh | 1553.04 | 3132.68 | 4685.72 |
| 27. | Uttaranchal* | -10.13 | 37.70 | 27.57 |
| 28. | West Bengal | 1187.48 | 1547.81 | 2735.29 |
| | Total | 11928.91 | 21275.65 | 33204.56 |

*The state is not getting benefit in repayments as some loans which would otherwise have got fully repaid during the award period of the Twelfth Finance Commission are getting rescheduled for a fresh period of 20 years and existing repayment profile of Block Loans seems to involve a moratorium on half the repayment during 2005 to 2009.

Source: The Twelfth Finance Commission Report (2004), Govt. of India, New Delhi.

further the efforts at eliminating the revenue deficit of states. The Twelfth Finance Commission, therefore, recommended the introduction of a debt write-off scheme linked to the reduction of revenue deficit of states. Under the scheme, the repayment due on central loans from 2005-06 to 2009-10 after consolidation and reschedulement will be eligible of write-off. The quantum of write-off of repayment will be linked to the absolute amount by which the revenue deficit is reduced in each successive year during the Twelfth Finance Commission's award period. In effect, if the revenue deficit is brought down to zero, the entire repayments during the period will be written-off. The scheme of write-off shall be available for all states from the year they have qualified for the general debt relief by enacting the fiscal responsibility legislation.

The manner in which the scheme will operate is outlined below:

(a) Fiscal performance will be measured with reference to the revenue deficit/revenue surplus, as worked out in absolute numbers by taking an average of three years, viz., 2001-02 (Actuals), 2002-03 (Actuals), and 2003-04 (RE). This average will be taken as the base year figure for 2003-04.

(b) For states which were in revenue surplus, as per the base year figure (Calculated in the manner indicated above), and continue to remain so in the subsequent years till the end of the Twelfth Finance Commission's award period, the instalment of repayment due on the central loans (after consolidation and reschedulement) may be written-off in each of the years from 2005-06 on wards so long as the revenue surplus of the states does not go below the base year level in absolute terms. In the year the revenue surplus is less than that in the base year figure, no write-off will be permitted.

(c) As for the states, which were in revenue deficit as per the base year figure, the revenue deficit is expected to be eliminated by 2008-09, i.e. over a five-year period. Fiscal performance will be measured by the absolute amount by which the revenue deficit is reduced in each year compared to the deficit in the previous year starting from the base year figure. For the purpose of determining the scale at which the relief will be provided, the ratio of the repayment due by a state during the period 2005-10 (of central loans after consolidation and reschedulement) to the base year revenue deficit figure has been worked out. This determines the amount of write-off of repayment that will be allowed to each states for the reduction of each rupee of revenue deficit. Table 14 contains the ratios, which will be applicable to the states for determining the quantum of write-off.

(d) The actual reduction in the revenue deficit in each year over the immediately preceding one would determine the amount of write-off for the state in the repayment due in the immediately succeeding year. This is calculated by multiplying the above-mentioned ratio by the amount of reduction of the revenue deficit. The total amount of write-off in a year will, however, be restricted to the repayments due on the consolidated loans in that year. Further, the write-off will only be admissible if the states reduce the revenue deficit to a level lower than the base year figure.

(e) It may be noted that, other things remaining the same, a reduction of revenue deficit is inherent from 2005-06 onwards as a result of the debt relief due to the lowering of the interest rate recommended. Reduction in revenue deficit, which is at least equal to the interest rate relief, shall be treated as an eligibility requirement. Each state will, therefore, be required to achieve, in each year of the Twelfth Finance Commission's award period, a reduction in the revenue deficit, which, compared to the base year figure, is cumulatively higher than the cumulatively reduction attributable to the interest relief recommended by the Twelfth Finance Commission. Details of the year-wise relief in interest payments and the cumulative reduction in revenue deficit arising out of lowering of interest rate for each state during 2005-10 are at Table 15.

(f) If the reduction in revenue deficit in a year is more than the minimum required for the write-off of the entire repayment due in that year, the excess will be carried forward fully to the next year, provided the revenue deficit continued to follow a downward trend in the next year and is lower than the base year figure. On the other hand, if there is an increase in the revenue deficit in the next year, but the revenue deficit is still lower than the base year figure, the entitlement to write-off shall be determined on the basis of improvement from the minimum revenue deficit figure of the previous year that would have given full relief in the previous year.

(g) To provide an illustration of the Twelfth Finance Commission's scheme, if state A has the base year revenue deficit figure of Rs. 2000 crores and the repayments due from 2005-10 are Rs. 1000 crores (or say Rs. 200 crores in each year), the ratio for determining the quantum of write-off will be 0.50 percent, i.e. the state will be eligible for write-off debt equal to 50 percent of the amount of reduction in revenue deficit. If the states reduce its deficit by Rs. 300 crores in 2004-05, compared to the base year level, it will qualify for a debt write-off of Rs. 150 crores in 2005-06. If, however, the reduction in deficit is of the order of Rs. 600 crores, although the state will be eligible for a write-off of Rs. 300 crores, the debt write-off in that year will be restricted to the instalment of repayment due (i.e. Rs. 200 crores) in the year, the remaining amount (i.e. Rs. 100 crores) qualifying for write-off in the next year subject to the state maintaining or further reducing its revenue deficit

TABLE 14

**Calculation of Incentive for Debt Relief Based on Fiscal Performance**

| Sl. No. | States | 2001-02 (Act.) | 2002-03 (Act.) | 2003-04 (RE) | Average Revenue Surplus/ Deficit (2001-02 to 2003-04) (a) | Repayment due from 2005-10 after consoledtion and reschedulment (b) | Annual Repayment due [(b)/5)] | Ratio of Total Repayment to Average deficit (01-05 to 03-04) [(b)/(a)]*] |
|---|---|---|---|---|---|---|---|---|
| | 1 | 2 | 3 | 4 | 5 | 6 | 7 | 8 |
| | | | | **Revenue Surplus (+)/Deficit (-)** | | | | |
| **General Category States** | | | | | | | | |
| 1. | Andhra Pradesh | -2881 | -3054 | -2904 | -2947 | 3834.29 | 766.86 | 1.30 |
| 2. | Bihar | -1320 | -1287 | -1107 | -1238 | 1926.02 | 385.20 | 1.56 |
| 3. | Chhattisgarh | -569 | -113 | -584 | -422 | 570.31 | 114.06 | 1.35 |
| 4. | Goa | -229 | -167 | -92 | -162 | 132.13 | 26.43 | 0.81 |
| 5. | Gujarat | -6732 | -3565 | -3462 | -4586 | 2615.98 | 523.20 | 0.57 |
| 6. | Haryana | -1055 | -685 | -904 | -881 | 581.43 | 116.29 | 0.66 |
| 7. | Jharkhand | -305 | -573 | 142 | -245 | 659.49 | 131.90 | 2.69 |
| 8. | Karnataka | -3296 | -2646 | -1318 | -2420 | 2079.54 | 415.91 | 0.86 |
| 9. | Kerela | -2606 | -4122 | -3676 | -3468 | 1063.05 | 212.61 | 0.31 |
| 10. | Madhya Pradesh | -3158 | -1169 | -5204 | -3177 | 1875.10 | 375.02 | 5.59 |
| 11. | Maharashtra | -8189 | -9371 | -9037 | -8865 | 1953.22 | 390.64 | 0.22 |
| 12. | Orissa | -2833 | -1576 | -2963 | -2457 | 1751.29 | 350.26 | 0.71 |
| 13. | Punjab | -3781 | -3754 | -3539 | -3692 | 763.42 | 152.68 | 0.21 |

*(Contd.)*

TABLE 14 *(Contd.)*

| 1 | 2 | 3 | 4 | 5 | 6 | 7 | 8 |
|---|---|---|---|---|---|---|---|
| 14. Rajasthan | -3796 | -3934 | -3667 | -3799 | 1708.38 | 341.68 | 0.45 |
| 15. Tamil Nadu | -2739 | -4851 | -3700 | -3763 | 1718.17 | 343.63 | 0.46 |
| 16. Uttar Pradesh | -6195 | -5117 | -19938 | -10417 | 4585.12 | 917.02 | 0.44 |
| 17. West Bengal | -8856 | -8635 | -9376 | -8956 | 2425.07 | 485.01 | 0.27 |
| Total-GC States | -58539 | -54619 | -71329 | -61496 | 30242.03 | 6048.41 | |
| **Special Category States** | | | | | | | |
| 1. Arunachal Pradesh | 56 | 77 | -369 | 31 | 97.39 | 19.48 | |
| 2. Assam | -881 | -319 | -1634 | -945 | 524.95 | 104.99 | 0.56 |
| 3. Himachal Pradesh | -860 | -1482 | -1508 | -1284 | 206.06 | 41.21 | 0.16 |
| 4. Jammu and Kashmir | -336 | 369 | 1910 | 647 | 473.84 | 94.77 | |
| 5. Manipur | -161 | -87 | -280 | -176 | 188.54 | 37.71 | 1.07 |
| 6. Meghalaya | -34 | 84 | 110 | 54 | 80.27 | 16.05 | |
| 7. Mizoram | -260 | -109 | -32 | -134 | 67.85 | 13.57 | 0.51 |
| 8. Nagaland | -103 | -159 | 66 | -54 | 80.15 | 16.03 | 1.47 |
| 9. Sikkim | 143 | 198 | 163 | 168 | 48.07 | 9.61 | |
| 10. Tripura | 54 | -81 | 93 | 22 | 117.53 | 23.51 | |
| 11. Uttaranchal | -205 | -458 | -1463 | -709 | 72.02 | 14.40 | 0.10 |
| Total Spl. Cat. States | -2588 | -1969 | -2582 | -2379 | 1956.66 | 391.33 | |
| Total - All States | -61127 | -56588 | -73911 | -63875 | 32198.69 | 6439.74 | |

This represents the amount by which repayments will be written-off for every Rupee reduction in revenue deficit.

*Source*: The Twelfth Finance Commission Report (2004), Govt. of India, New Delhi.

TABLE 15

**Cumulative Relief on Interest Payments after Consolidation, Reschedulement and Lowering of Interest Rate to 7.5 percent on Central Loans Contracted before 31.03.04 and Outstanding on 31.03.05**

*(Rs. In crore)*

| *Sl. No.* | *State* | *2004-05 Interest Relief* | *2005-06 Interest Relief* | *Cumulative Interest Relief upto 2005-06* | *2006-07 Interest Relief* | *Cumulative Interest Relief upto 2006-07* | *2007-08 Interest Relief* | *Cumulative Interest Relief upto 2007-08* | *2008-09 Interest Relief* | *Cumulative Interest Relief upto 2008-09* | *2009-10 Interest Relief* | *Cumulative Interest Relief upto 2009-10* |
|---|---|---|---|---|---|---|---|---|---|---|---|---|
| | *1* | *2* | *3* | *4* | *5* | *6* | *7* | *8* | *9* | *10* | *11* | *12* |
| 1. | A.P. | 0 | 611.66 | 611.66 | 582.74 | 1194.40 | 548.11 | 1742.51 | 499.42 | 2241.93 | 441.81 | 2683.74 |
| 2. | Arunachal Pradesh | 0 | 16.40 | 16.40 | 15.63 | 32.03 | 14.65 | 46.68 | 13.32 | 60.00 | 1.94 | 153.87 |
| 3. | Assam | 0 | 68.75 | 68.75 | 48.64 | 117.39 | 28.05 | 145.44 | 6.49 | 151.93 | 1.94 | 153.87 |
| 4. | Bihar | 0 | 303.45 | 303.45 | 281.58 | 585.03 | 257.94 | 842.97 | 229.24 | 1072.22 | 196.05 | 1268.27 |
| 5. | Chhattisgarh | 0 | 91.38 | 91.37 | 86.18 | 177.56 | 80.11 | 257.67 | 72.59 | 330.27 | 63.50 | 393.77 |
| 6. | Goa | 0 | 22.26 | 22.26 | 21.10 | 43.27 | 19.32 | 62.60 | 17.20 | 79.80 | 14.85 | 94.66 |
| 7. | Gujarat | 0 | 427.83 | 427.83 | 407.03 | 834.86 | 380.98 | 1215.84 | 347.05 | 1562.89 | 277.13 | 1840.12 |
| 8. | Haryana | 0 | 95.72 | 95.72 | 87.96 | 183.68 | 78.71 | 262.39 | 68.37 | 330.76 | 59.90 | 387.67 |
| 9. | Himachal Pradesh | 0 | 32.46 | 32.46 | 30.11 | 62.57 | 27.63 | 89.92 | 24.23 | 114.15 | 20.64 | 134.79 |
| 10. | Jammu and Kashmir | 0 | 64.00 | 64.00 | 5912 | 123.13 | 53.60 | 176.73 | 47.27 | 224.00 | 40.02 | 246.02 |

*(Contd.)*

TABLE 15 *(Contd.)*

| 1 | 2 | 3 | 4 | 5 | 6 | 7 | 8 | 9 | 10 | 11 | 12 |
|---|---|---|---|---|---|---|---|---|---|---|---|
| 11. Jharkhand | 0 | 103.09 | 103.09 | 118.27 | 221.36 | 87.75 | 309.12 | 78.19 | 387.30 | 67.19 | 454.49 |
| 12. Karnataka | 0 | 348.77 | 348.77 | 332.91 | 681.68 | 312.84 | 994.52 | 284.43 | 1278.95 | 250.48 | 1529.43 |
| 13. Kerala | 0 | 170.47 | 170.47 | 158.90 | 329.37 | 145.43 | 474.80 | 129.81 | 604.61 | 110.42 | 715.03 |
| 14. Madhya Pradesh | 0 | 297.45 | 297.45 | 284.53 | 581.98 | 268.42 | 850.40 | 243.64 | 1094.04 | 216.94 | 1310.98 |
| 15. Maharashtra | 0 | 319.63 | 319.63 | 284.34 | 603.97 | 246.34 | 850.30 | 205.55 | 1055.86 | 161.54 | 1217.39 |
| 16. Manipur | 0 | 29.90 | 29.90 | 16.46 | 46.35 | 2.86 | 49.21 | -11.01 | 38.20 | -10.94 | 27.26 |
| 17. Meghalaya | 0 | 12.84 | 12.84 | 12.25 | 25.08 | 11.49 | 36.57 | 10.55 | 47.12 | 9.37 | 56.49 |
| 18. Mizoram | 0 | 11.22 | 11.22 | 10.83 | 22.05 | 10.29 | 32.34 | 9.56 | 41.90 | 8.64 | 50.54 |
| 19. Nagaland | 0 | 13.12 | 13.12 | 12.35 | 25.47 | 11.41 | 36.87 | 10.26 | 47.13 | 8.93 | 56.06 |
| 20. Orissa | 0 | 277.36 | 277.36 | 240.71 | 518.08 | 200.20 | 718.28 | 155.94 | 874.22 | 134.21 | 1008.43 |
| 21. Punjab | 0 | 129.98 | 129.98 | 118.40 | 248.38 | 105.38 | 353.76 | 90.48 | 444.24 | 78.94 | 523.18 |
| 22. Rajasthan | 0 | 253.98 | 253.98 | 223.94 | 477.92 | 190.97 | 668.89 | 155.39 | 824.28 | 137.97 | 962.25 |
| 23. Sikkim | 0 | 7.82 | 7.82 | 7.42 | 15.24 | 6.91 | 22.15 | 6.27 | 28.42 | 5.54 | 33.96 |
| 24. Tamil Nadu | 0 | 292.30 | 292.30 | 269.44 | 561.74 | 241.98 | 803.72 | 211.20 | 1014.92 | 180.56 | 1195.47 |
| 25. Tripura | 0 | 30.93 | 30.93 | 28.16 | 59.08 | 25.08 | 84.16 | 21.66 | 105.82 | 18.15 | 123.97 |
| 26. Uttar Pradesh | 0 | 743.28 | 743.28 | 695.26 | 1438.53 | 634.65 | 073.78 | 564.15 | 2637.33 | 495.35 | 3132.68 |
| 27. Uttar Pradesh | 0 | 7.21 | 7.21 | 7.0 | 14.61 | 7.53 | 22.15 | 7.69 | 29.83 | 7.87 | 37.70 |
| 28. West Bengal | 0 | 398.77 | 398.77 | 356.52 | 755.29 | 309.18 | 1064.47 | 256.74 | 1321.21 | 226.60 | 1547.81 |
| Total | 0 | 5182.04 | 5182.04 | 4798.09 | 9980.13 | 4307.52 | 14287.65 | 3755.70 | 18043.35 | 3232.30 | 21275.65 |

Source: Ministry of Finance, Government of India.

in the next year. If on the other hand, in the year 2005-06, the revenue deficit increases by say Rs. 100 crores from 2004-05 level, the net improvement over the base year level would only be Rs. 500 crores. In that event, since an amount of Rs 400 crores has already been utilized for debt relief in the previous year, the state will qualify for a relief in repayment amounting to fifty percent of the relief of Rs. 50 crores only in 2006-07.

(h) If the performance of a state deteriorates in a year, with the revenue deficit registering a higher level over the previous year for which relief in repayment has been availed of, any improvement in the not with reference to that year, but the performance level in the previous year up to which relief has been reduction of. If the revenue deficit reduction in the previous year was more than the minimum reduction required to qualify for 100 percent write-off repayment, the revenue determined notionally keeping in view the minimum revenue deficit in that would have qualified the state for 100 percent relief in continuation of sub-Para (g) above, if the revenue deficit of state A goes up to Rs. 1800 crores in 2005-06 after being reduced to Rs. 1400 crores in 2004-05, it will not qualify for relief in repayment in 2006-07. Also, its performance in 2006-08 will be measured from the notional level of 2004-05. The notional level in this case would be Rs. 2000 crores minus Rs. 400 crores, i.e. Rs. 1600 crores. This would ensure that no state will be able to avail of relief more than once for the same level of improvement over the base. Nor would any stand penalized for performing better than the minimum required level in any year.

(i) One criticism against the debt relief scheme of the Tenth and Eleventh Finance Commissions has been the time lag involved in granting the benefit. The Twelfth Finance Commission, therefore, recommend that for the purpose of determining the write-off, the revenue deficit indicated in the revised estimates of the preceding year may be used provisionally, so that the relief in respect of a year is available in the immediately succeeding year. Necessary adjustment may be carried out subsequently and the finance accounts become available.

(j) Looking at the necessity of containing the fiscal deficit, the Twelfth Finance Commission further recommended that the benefit of write-off would be available only if the fiscal deficit of the state is contained to the level of 2004-05. If, in any year, the fiscal deficit exceeds this level, the benefit of write-off, even if eligible otherwise, would not be given.

In terms of the Twelfth Finance Commission's debt write-off package, if a state achieves through a consistent performance, a zero revenue deficit by 2008-09, it will have the facility of having all the repayments due from 2005-10 on central loans contracted up to 31.3.04 and consolidated by us written-off. The total amount which would be written-off if all states achieve revenue balance by 2008-09 is approximately Rs. 32,200 crores in a period of five years.

**Future Lending Policy**

In the context of the debt burden of states, the Twelfth Finance Commission considered the direction in which future-lending policy of the centre should move. While there might have been some justification for the centre to act as a banker to states when market rates of interest were high and in the process of on-lending to states by way of concessional interest, this is no longer valid a low interest rates regime. In some ways, central lending to states, which is done at much higher rates of interest than the marginal cost of borrowing, results in reverse subsidy from the states to the centre. In most federal countries, the federal government's loan intermediation role has been discontinued over the years, subjecting the states to market discipline. Such a dispensation allows the constituent units to borrow on terms that reflect their credit risk. While fiscally prudent states manage to borrow at rates lower than those offered by the federal government, the fiscally imprudent states would find their access to loan finance curtailed. The Twelfth Finance Commission feels that it would be appropriate for states to take advantage of the market rates and avoid the spread charged by the centre. The Twelfth Finance Commission, therefore, recommended that, in future, the central government should not act as an intermediary and allow the states to approach the market directly. If, however, some fiscally weak states are unable to raise funds from the market, the centre could resort to lending, but the interest rates should remain aligned to the marginal cost of borrowing for the centre.

**External Assistance Loans**

A large number of states have suggested the external loans should be passed on to states on the same terms and conditions as granted by the lending agency. External assistance to Indian is project based, except for structural adjustment assistance. The financing terms for externally aided projects and programmes vary according to projects and lending agencies. There are grants, soft loans and non-concessional loans, provided by lending agencies, depending upon the nature, the financial viability of the project and the revenue earning potential of a project. The external assistance received for states' projects is, however, passed on as 70 percent loan and 30 percent grant (10 percent and 90 percent respectively in case of special category states). Interest rates applied are those applicable to block loans.

While the external assistance from some sources and for some projects is highly concessional, in other cases it may be expensive. In the process of pooling and fixing a uniform interest rate in rupee terms, an element of cross-subsidization occurs at two levels: between centre and all states and among the states. In the case of cross-subsidization between the centre and the states, the gain/loss to one side *vis-à-vis* another depends on the rate of depreciation of the Indian rupee case of states, the cross-subsidization takes place, when states having a relatively larger share of grants and soft loans (which may offer relief to social welfare and long gestation, low return type of projects) in their assistance portfolio, are required to pay a higher rate of interest to help sustain the relatively larger share of high cost loans, which may relate to commercial projects, used by some states.

The Twelfth Finance Commission has examined the recommendations of the EFC in this regard and the policy enunciated in the medium-term fiscal policy strategy statement of the government of Indian. Since the transfer of external assistance on back-to-back basis will enable states to participate on an equal footing in concessional external assistance, the Twelfth Finance Commission recommended that external assistance be transferred to states on the same terms and conditions as attached to such assistance by external funding agencies, thereby intermediary without any gain or loss. States would get the same maturity, moratorium and amortization schedule, as the government of India gets from the external lender. As per the Twelfth Finance Commission's information, no loan from the external agency is for less than 20 years, and as such the states would get the benefit of higher maturity (35 years in case of International Development Association (IDA) loans, 25 years in case of Asian Development Bank (ADB) loans and 20 years for International Bank for Reconstruction and Development (IBRD) loans. The states would also get a longer moratorium of 10 years in case of IDA credits. Although the states would gain on interest payments, they would be subject to the risk of foreign exchange fluctuations. The Twelfth Finance Commission further feels that it would be easier to operate the external assistance outside the Consolidated Fund of India and it will result in faster disbursement of external assistance to the states. The Twelfth Finance Commission, therefore, recommended that the external assistance pass through to states should be managed through a separate fund in the public account. The Fund could also be utilized for taking care of the foreign exchange risk.

## Special Term Loans of Punjab

Special term loans amounting to by 5799.92 crores were

given to Punjab by the Government of India during 1984-85 to 1988-89 for combating insurgency and militancy. The Ninth Finance Commission had granted a moratorium of two years (1990-92) on the repayment of principal and payment of interest in respect of these special terms loans. The Tenth Finance Commission had recommended that one-third of the repayment of principal, amounting to Rs. 490.63 crores falling due during the period 1995-2000, be waived in view of the special circumstance prevailing when these loans were advanced, and also keeping view the need for the states to reinvigorate its developmental efforts. The EFC recommended a moratorium on payment of instalments if debt and interest during the period 2000-05 on the outstanding special term loans amounting to Rs. 3772 crores, stating that the expenditure incurred on security be worked out by Ministry of Home Affairs in consultation with the Punjab Government and Ministry of Finance and relief of debt to the extent the state is entitled to reimbursement on account of security-related expenditure be given after the period of moratorium is over and after taking into account waiver already given.

In its submission to the Twelfth Finance Commission, the State Government has requested that the outstanding special term loan of Rs. 3772 crores as on 31st March, 2000 plus the interest thereon may be waived by the government of India. The states has cited article 355 of the Constitution, the assurance by the then Prime Minister of India and the poor finance condition of the state in support of its request. The Twelfth Finance Commission understands that the quantum of the security-related expenditure out of the special term loans and, the consequent debt relief to be given after the moratorium period (2000-05) has not yet been worked out. An account of the security related expenditure has now been submitted by the Government of Punjab to Ministry of Home Affairs. This is still to be examined by the Ministries of Home Affairs and Ministry of Finance. Pending finalization of the amount in respect of which debt relief is to be allowed in terms of the recommendations of the EFC, the Twelfth Finance Commission recommends that the moratorium on repayments and interest payments on these loans may continue for another two years, i.e. up to 2006-07, by which time the central government must finalize the quantum of debt relief to be allowed.

**Relief and Rehabilitation Loan for Gujarat Earthquake**

Government of Gujarat had taken a loan of Rs. 5478 crores from ADB and World Bank through the central government for relief, rehabilitation and reconstruction work in the wake of the earthquake of 2001. This amount was passed on by the central government on the pattern of normal central assistance, namely 30 percent grant and 70 percent loan. The request of the government of Gujarat is that the entire amount may be treated as a grant.

In order to consider the request, the Twelfth Finance Commission called for detailed information from the Ministry of Finance on this loan. The Twelfth Finance Commission has been informed that the IDA credit was passed on to the state on the standard terms applicable to additional central assistance with 1 percent reduction in interest rate on the undisbursed amount of the loan with effect from 27.05.2003. The disbursement under the project till September 2004 was US $ 200 million, while the outstanding loan amount is US $ 242.8 million. As per the amortization schedule, repayment from 15th October, 2012, i.e. no payment needs to be made during the award period of the commission. The interest charges due from 31.3.04 to 15.4.2010 are US $ 6984432.39 and the commitment charges paid till now are US $ 1.779 million.

The Government of Gujarat has informed the Twelfth Finance Commission that the total estimated cost of earthquake rehabilitation and reconstruction was Rs. 8087 crores of which Rs. 2244 crores was to be raised as loan from all sources including external aid from World Bank and ADB. The government of India approved external aid of US $ 699.80 million (Rs. 3219 crores at an exchange rate of Rs. 46 per US dollar) from World Bank and US $ 350 million (Rs. 1610 crores at Rs. 46 per US $) from ADB. Out of this, the Gujarat government has received Rs. 2920.94 crores. These loans have been treated as loan for externally aided projects by government of India. Repayments to the extent of Rs. 621.03 crores and interest payment as Rs. 1158.67 crores are to be made to the central government during the Twelfth Finance Commission's award period.

The Twelfth Finance Commission has examined the request of the Gujarat government keeping in view the terms on which the external agencies have extend the loans and those on which the loans have been passed on to Gujarat. While the Twelfth Finance Commission is unable to recommend a write-off or a conversion of these loans into grants, the Twelfth Finance Commission feels that considerable relief will be available to Gujarat, if the loan is passed on to the state on the same terms and conditions as agreed to between the government of India and the external agencies. The Twelfth Finance Commission, therefore, recommend that if the government of Gujarat so desires, the central government may alter the terms and conditions of these loans so that these are available to Gujarat on a back-to-back basis.

Apart form Punjab and Gujarat; some of the other states have also suggested a write-off or waiver of specific loans. The Twelfth Finance Commission has examined these demands but is unable to recommend further write-off over and above the debt relief package already recommended by the Twelfth Finance Commission.

**Setting up of Sinking Funds**

Some of the states have recommended setting up of sinking funds for amortization of debt. The Twelfth Finance Commission has recommended earlier than in future, the role of the central government as intermediary should be re-defined and the centre should not lend to state. Instead, states should be allowed to access the market directly. In this context, the Twelfth Finance Commission has noted that the Ninth Finance Commission had observed that loans should be repaid out of amortization/sinking funds. The Tenth Finance Commission had recommended the establishment of sinking funds as being EFC has also emphasized the need for setting up of a sinking fund in each state for amortization of debt.

The Twelfth Finance Commission further understands that a consolidated sinking fund has been set-up in 1999-2000 by the Reserve Bank of India to meet redemption of market loans of states. So far, eleven states, viz. Andhra Pradesh, Arunachal Pradesh, Assam, Chhattisgarh, Goa, Maharashtra, Meghalaya, Mizoram, Tripura, Uttaranchal and West Bengal have set-up sinking funds.

In the context of the debt-swap scheme, the Twelfth Finance Commission has been informed that the old debts had a residual life of less than 20 to 25 years (block loans/ small savings loans). The additional open market borrowings used for the purpose of swap are bullet payments, with maturity of ten years/twelve years of some trenches raised in 2003-04. This maturity structure requires the states to make less principal repayments in first ten years and would leave the states with higher cash. As per the Ministry of Finance, there would be bunching of payments in the period 2013-15 when all the additional open market borrowings (expected to be over Rs. 4500 crores) would mature in a short span of three to five years. The states would experience lumps in their servicing profile. This necessitates the constitution of a fund for repayment of debt. This would improve the credit rating of states when they apply for loans. The Twelfth Finance Commission, therefore, recommends that all states should set-up sinking funds for amortization of all loans including loan from banks, liabilities on account of NSSF, etc. The fund should be maintained outside then consolidated fund of the states and the public account and should not be used for any other purpose, except for redemption of loans.

### Guarantee Redemption Fund

The outstanding guarantees of state governments have shown a rising trend during the 1990s. Although contingent liabilities do not directly form a part of the debt burden of the states, the states will be required to meet the debt service obligations in the event of default by the borrowing agency. The outstanding guarantees of State Governments increased from Rs. 1,32,029 crores (6.8 percent of GDP) as at the end of March 2000 to Rs. 1,68,712 crores (8.1 percent of GDP) as the end of March 2001. These are estimated to be lower at Rs. 1,66,116 crores at the end of March 2002 (7.2 percent of GDP). In view of the fiscal implication of rising level of guarantees, many states have taken initiative to place a ceilings on guarantees. While statutory ceilings on guarantee have been imposed by Goa, Gujarat, Karnataka, Sikkim and West Bengal, some other states viz., Assam, Orissa and Rajasthan have taken initiative to place a ceilings on guarantees. While statutory ceiling on guarantees have been imposed a ceiling on guarantees through the mechanism of their fiscal responsibility legislation. In order to provide for sudden discharge of the states' obligations on guarantees, the Twelfth Finance Commission further recommends that states should set-up Guarantee Redemption Funds (GRF) through earmarked guarantee fees. This should be preceded by risk weighting of guarantees. The quantum of contribution to the fund should be decided accordingly.

**Recommendations**

To sum-up, the Twelfth Finance Commission's recommendations are as follows:

(i) Each state must enact a fiscal responsibility legislation prescribing specific annual targets with a view to eliminating the revenue deficit by 2008-09 and reducing fiscal deficit based on a path for reduction of borrowings and guarantees. [Enacting the Fiscal Responsibility Legislation (FRL) on the lines indicated will be a necessary pre-condition for availing of debt relief].

(ii) Debt relief may not be linked with performance in human development or investment climate.

(iii) The central loans to states contracted till 31.3.04 and outstanding on 31.3.05 (amounting to Rs. 1,28,795 crores) may be consolidated and rescheduled for a fresh term of 20 years (resulting in repayment in 20 equal instalments), and an interest rate of 7.5 percent be charged on them. This is, however, subject to the state enacting the fiscal responsibility legislation and will take effect prospectively from the year in which such legislation is enacted.

(iv) A debt write-off scheme linked to the reduction of revenue deficit of states may be introduced. Under the scheme, the repayments due from 2005-06 to 2009-10 on central loans contracted up to 31.3.04 and recommended to be consolidated will be eligible for write-off. The quantum of write-off repayment will be linked to the absolute amount by which the revenue deficit is reduced in each successive year during the Twelfth Finance Commission's award period. In effect, if the revenue deficit is brought down to zero, the entire repayments during the period will be written-off. The enactment of the fiscal responsibility legislation would be a necessary pre-condition for availing the debt relief under this scheme also with the benefit accruing prospectively.

(v) As regards the future lending policy the central government should not act as an intermediary and allow the states approach the market directly. If, however, some fiscally weak states are unable to raise funds from the market, the centre could borrow for the purpose of on lending to such states, but the interest rates should remain aligned to the marginal cost of borrowing for the centre.

(vi) External assistance may be transferred to states on the same terms and conditions as attached to such assistance by external funding agencies, thereby making government of India a financing intermediary without any gain or loss. The external assistance pass through to states should be managed through a separate fund in the public account.

(vii) The moratorium on repayments and interest payments on the outstanding special term loan amounting to Rs. 3772 crores as on 31.3.2000 given to Punjab may continue for another two years, i.e. up to 2006-07, by which time the central government must finalize the quantum of debt relief to be allowed in terms of the recommendations of the EFC.

(viii) In respect of relief and rehabilitation loans given to Gujarat from ADB and World Bank through the central government, if the government of Gujarat so desires, the central government may alter the terms and conditions of these loans so that these are available to Gujarat on the same terms on which the external on which the external agencies have extended these loans.

(ix) All states should set-up sinking funds for amortization of all loans including loans from banks, liabilities on account of NSSF, etc. The fund should be maintained outside the consolidated fund of the states and the public account and should not be used for any other purpose, except for redemption of loans.

(x) States should set-up guarantee redemption funds through earmarked guarantee fees. This should be preceded by risk weighting of guarantees. The quantum of contribution to the fund should be decided accordingly.

**Loans not Consolidated in 2005-10**

As pointed out earlier, FC-XII did not consider central loans given to State Governments for Centrally Sponsored Schemes/Central Plan schemes through ministries other than Ministry of Finance, under DCRF, primarily because they did not have the requisite data. The balance outstanding in this regard stands at Rs. 4506 crore as at the end of 2007-08. The state-wise position for these is shown in following Table 16.

We feel that continuation of these loans is not consistent with the policy of disintermediation recommended by FC-XII, which is being followed today. Therefore, we recommend that these loans, as outstanding at the end of 2009-10, be written-off. It is also recommended that any further lending from Centre to states, under any Centrally Sponsored Scheme, should be completely avoided.

However, as per the recommendations of FC-XII, a window for borrowing from the Central Government should be available for the fiscally weak states that are unable to raise loans from the market.

While 26 states have availed of debt consolidation, two states, viz. West Bengal and Sikkim, have not legislated

TABLE 16

## Central Loans Administered by Ministries other than Ministry of Finance

(*Rs. crore*)

| Sl. No. | States | Balance on 31/3/2008 |
|---|---|---|
| 1 | Andhra Pradesh | 229 |
| 2 | Arunachal Pradesh | 53 |
| 3 | Assam | 502 |
| 4 | Bihar | 107 |
| 5 | Chhattisgarh | 36 |
| 6 | Goa | 158 |
| 7 | Gujarat | 184 |
| 8 | Haryana | 90 |
| 9 | Himachal Pradesh | 64 |
| 10 | Jammu & Kashmir | 117 |
| 11 | Jharkhand | 55 |
| 12 | Karnataka | 309 |
| 13 | Kerala | 106 |
| 14 | Madhya Pradesh | 218 |
| 15 | Maharashtra | 347 |
| 16 | Manipur | 53 |
| 17 | Meghalaya | 35 |
| 18 | Mizoram | 75 |
| 19 | Nagaland | 81 |
| 20 | Orissa | 206 |
| 21 | Punjab | 104 |
| 22 | Rajasthan | 273 |
| 23 | Sikkim | 40 |
| 24 | Tamil Nadu | 242 |
| 25 | Tripura | 78 |
| 26 | Uttar Pradesh | 442 |
| 27 | Uttarakhand | 78 |
| 28 | West Bengal | 224 |
| | **Total** | **4506** |

FRBM Acts and, thus, did not get the benefit of consolidation. We recommend that this facility be extended to these states during our award period, on the condition that they put in place an FRBM Act as stipulated in this chapter. On meeting this condition, the loans contracted by these states till 31 March 2004 and outstanding as at the end of the year preceding the year in which the Act is put in place, shall be consolidated as per the same terms and conditions as recommended by FC-XII. However, the benefit of waiver, as recommended by FC-XII, need not be continued any further to any state.

## IMPLEMENTATION AND COMPLIANCE

The relief measures recommended by us in this chapter are all in the nature of one-step actions leading to relief over the long-term. The above relief should be given to states only if the states with FRBM Acts already in place amend the same as indicated in Para 9.82 and those not having an FRBM Act legislate their FRBM Acts. For interest relief on NSSF loans, the loans contracted till 2006-07 and outstanding till the end of the year preceding the year in which this condition is met should be considered for reset. We have set no conditionalities with regard to compliance with the targets since we believe that the mechanism mentioned in Para 9.85 for setting borrowing limits and allowing open market borrowings to states can act as an effective tool.

The debt waiver, as recommended by FC-XII, was booked in the finance accounts of the states as non-tax revenues under 0075- 'miscellaneous general receipts'. We feel that this is not desirable as it artificially overstates the non-tax revenues of the states. Second, since it is accounted as non-tax revenue, it allows states to spend more within the same fiscal deficit cap, reducing the intended impact on the debt stock of states. Ideally, if it were not treated as notional repayment of debt, it would have ensured that, given a fiscal deficit target, the gross borrowing of states would have to go down, thereby having a dampening impact on debt stock, which was the primary purpose of FC-XII in granting the relief. We recommend that the debt write-off recommended by us is accounted in a manner such that it does not artificially affect the revenue or fiscal deficit of the states.

## STATE FINANCES: ROADMAP AND RECOMMENDATIONS

We specified the medium-term combined debt to GDP ratio target for 2014-15 at 68 per cent. With the target Central Government debt at 45 per cent of GDP in 2014-15, this implies a target debt to GDP ratio of 25 per cent for all states in the same year (the state and central ratios do not add up to the combined ratio because central loans to the states have to be netted out).

This is a feasible target from the perspective of the states. In the 2005-09 period, the states have undertaken considerable fiscal correction and their aggregate debt to GDP ratio is not expected to be higher than 30 per cent in 2009-10. Given that the ratio was 27 per cent in 2008-09, we consider any increase from this ratio to be temporary, in the sense that it reflects the allowance for debt financed counter-recessionary expenditures by State Governments. Recognising the need for such expenditures, the Government of India has relaxed the borrowing limits for the states to 3.5 per cent and 4 per cent of GSDP for all the states for the years 2008-09 and 2009-10 respectively, as opposed to the 3 per cent target set out in the roadmap of the Government of India for states, following the action taken on the recommendation of FC-XII.

It should, therefore, be feasible to undertake a small reduction in the aggregate debt to GDP ratio of the states from about 27 per cent of GDP in 2007-08 to 25 per cent by 2014-15, especially if, as we recommend above, the Central Government assumes responsibility for all borrowings due to unanticipated shocks and/or parameter changes of a global or national dimension. However, the adjustment path will have to allow for temporary increases in revenue and fiscal deficits in 2008-09 and 2009-10, given the need for counter-recessionary expenditure.

A long-term and permanent target for the states should be to maintain a zero revenue deficit. The arguments advanced in favour of the application of the 'golden rule' to the Centre also apply in the case of the states. It is encouraging that most states in the Union are already following this rule. In essence, all that the future fiscal roadmap requires is that they continue to do so and the few states that have not yet reduced revenue deficits to zero, endeavour to do so, by 2014-15.

We recognise that the exceptional circumstances of 2009-10 may increase the fiscal pressure on all states. We are unable to provide a quantified assessment of the extent to which this is likely to be the case in individual states in 2009-10 on account of data lags. However, given our growth assumptions, we are of the view that all states that incurred zero revenue deficit or achieved a revenue surplus in 2007-08 should be able to undertake fiscal corrections to return to a zero revenue deficit by 2011-12. Thus, we recommend that the zero revenue deficit target be attained by all such states from 2011-12 onwards.

**General Category States**

Three of the general category states incurred a revenue deficit in 2007-08. For these we recommend an adjustment path commencing 2011-12, to eliminate the revenue deficit by 2014-15. This is shown in Table 17.

TABLE 17

**RD Path for General Category States with RD in 2007-08**

*(per cent of GSDP)*

| State | 2007-08 | 2011-12 | 2012-13 | 2013-14 | 2014-15 |
|---|---|---|---|---|---|
| 1 Kerala | 2.3 | 1.4 | 0.9 | 0.5 | 0.0 |
| 2 Punjab | 2.9 | 1.8 | 1.2 | 0.6 | 0.0 |
| 3 West Bengal | 2.7 | 1.6 | 1.1 | 0.5 | 0.0 |

An aggregate indicator does not take into account the individual circumstances of states. For the purpose of striking a balance between the virtues of customisation and the need to adopt the same procedure for determining targets for all states in similar circumstances, we recommend the differentiated adjustment paths detailed in the subsequent paras.

All states having a revenue surplus in 2007-08 had fiscal deficits of less than 3 per cent of GSDP, except Uttar Pradesh, which had a fiscal deficit of 3.9 per cent. A state should have adequate room for capital expenditure by using its revenue surplus and a deficit not exceeding 3 per cent of GSDP. Any state that has a revenue surplus along with a higher fiscal deficit should compress its capital expenditure, or alternately, increase its surplus on the revenue account. We, therefore, expect that Uttar Pradesh too will be able to come back to the 3 per cent level of fiscal deficit by 2011-12.

We recommend that in the case of all states that attained a zero revenue deficit or a revenue surplus in 2007-08, a fiscal deficit of 3 per cent of GSDP be achieved by 2011-12 and maintained thereafter. We expect that the maximum fiscal deficit that these states would incur in 2009-10 is 4 per cent of GSDP, which corresponds to the maximum allowable net borrowing ceiling for that year. The reform path sets targets from the year 2011-12 onwards. The methodology to be adopted for 2010-11 is given in Para 9.86.

In the case of states having revenue deficit in 2007-08, we recognise that the process of adjustment in the revenue deficit would have a concomitant virtuous impact on the fiscal deficit. Since we have recommended an achievable correction path for revenue deficit, an abrupt reduction in fiscal deficit would lead to compression of capital expenditure, which is not desirable. Thus, it is required that a fiscal deficit higher than 3 per cent is allowed till the revenue deficit comes down to a certain level, so as to prevent any undesirable compression of capital expenditure. We have noted in these states' memoranda their willingness to attempt a fiscal correction exercise that would allow them to maintain and even increase their fiscal space for capital expenditure. Thus, in the case of these states, the fiscal adjustment path requires them to have capital expenditure less than the states that have already carried out fiscal correction, but with a slightly relaxed fiscal deficit target in the years 2011-12 and 2012-13, so that capital expenditure is not compressed to undesirable levels.

Moreover, additional reduction in the revenue deficit

TABLE 18

**FD Path for General Category States with RD in 2007-08**

*(per cent of GSDP)*

| State | 2007-08 | 2011-12 | 2012-13 | 2013-14 | 2014-15 |
|---|---|---|---|---|---|
| 1 Kerala | 3.6 | 3.5 | 3.5 | 3.0 | 3.0 |
| 2 Punjab | 3.5 | 3.5 | 3.5 | 3.0 | 3.0 |
| 3 West Bengal | 3.8 | 3.5 | 3.5 | 3.0 | 3.0 |

will allow these states greater fiscal space on the capital account. The fiscal adjustment path is indicated in Table 18.

**Special Category States**

Unlike in general category states where the fiscal adjustment path has been fixed on the basis of 2007-08, in the case of special category states the deficit parameters are highly volatile and, thus, the fiscal adjustment path cannot be fixed depending only on 2007-08 levels. For this purpose we have taken the average of three years, viz. 2005-06, 2006-07 and 2007-08 to determine the base fiscal parameters on which the future adjustment path can be decided.

While the revenue deficit is the primary driver of the fiscal deficit amongst the general category states, this is not the case with special category states. All the special category states have had an average revenue surplus over the 2005-08 period, while six states have an average fiscal deficit higher than 3 per cent of GSDP over the same period. The reason is that these states are highly dependent on central grants and although all grants from the Central Government are classified as revenue receipts, capital expenditure incurred out of these grants is not accounted in the revenue deficit. Thus, for special category states, the revenue balance is not of much significance for purposes of fiscal adjustment.

Depending upon the base figure for the fiscal deficit, special category states can be divided into three groups. Four states viz. Manipur, Nagaland, Sikkim and Uttarakhand have a base level fiscal deficit of more than 3 per cent but less than 6 per cent. These states will need to make a relatively higher effort in terms of achieving a 3 per cent fiscal deficit and thus, we require that they achieve this level by 2013-14, following the same path prescribed for the three general category states.

Jammu and Kashmir and Mizoram have even higher levels of base fiscal deficits, at 7.8 per cent and 10.3 per cent of GSDP respectively. We recognize that these states require more customised fiscal correction paths, which require reforms at their end, but are achievable, nevertheless. Jammu and Kashmir had a fiscal deficit of 7.8 per cent in 2007-08 that included Rs. 606 crore interest payment on NSSF loans of past years due in the previous year. Thus, the fiscal deficit of Jammu and Kashmir for 2007-08 is overstated by this amount. Correcting for this onetime expenditure, the fiscal deficit adjustment path of Jammu and Kashmir can start from 5.9 per cent to reach 3 per cent in 2014-15, with equi-proportional adjustments each year (for J&K please also refer to Para 12.177). Mizoram had a fiscal deficit of 6 per cent in 2006-07 and 11 per cent in 2007-08. The primary reason for this has been the grant received in 2006-07, a considerable portion of which got spent only by 2007-08. Thus, a better point to start the fiscal adjustment path of Mizoram would be the average of the two, i.e., 8.5 per cent, to be reduced to 3 per cent by 2014-15, with equi-proportional annual adjustments. The fiscal adjustment path of the six states with a base level fiscal deficit of more than 3 per cent is as shown in Table 19.

TABLE 19

**FD Path for Special Category States with High Base FD**

*(per cent of GSDP)*

| State | Base | 2011-12 | 2012-13 | 2013-14 | 2014-15 |
|---|---|---|---|---|---|
| 1 Jammu & Kashmir | 5.9 | 4.7 | 4.2 | 3.6 | 3.0 |
| 2 Manipur | 4.1 | 3.5 | 3.5 | 3.0 | 3.0 |
| 3 Mizoram | 8.5 | 6.4 | 5.2 | 4.1 | 3.0 |
| 4 Nagaland | 4.8 | 3.5 | 3.5 | 3.0 | 3.0 |
| 5 Sikkim | 5.2 | 3.5 | 3.5 | 3.0 | 3.0 |
| 6 Uttarakhand | 5.2 | 3.5 | 3.5 | 3.0 | 3.0 |

*Note: The base in the case of each state is explained in paras 9.77 and 9.80.*

The remaining five states, viz. Arunachal Pradesh, Assam, Himachal Pradesh, Meghalaya and Tripura, have a base level fiscal deficit of less than 3 per cent and thus, we require that these states attain a fiscal deficit of 3 per cent of GSDP or less by 2011-12 while maintaining their revenue balance in the same way as general category states with revenue surplus in 2007-08. All special category states are

TABLE 20

## Outstanding Debt (Base year and feature projection)

*(as per cent of GSDP)*

| Sl. No. | State | 2009-10 | 2010-11 | 2011-12 | 2012-13 | 2013-14 | 2014-15 |
|---|---|---|---|---|---|---|---|
| 1 | Andhra Pradesh | 30.9 | 30.3 | 29.6 | 28.9 | 28.2 | 27.6 |
| 2 | Arunachal Pradesh | 64.0 | 61.3 | 58.2 | 55.2 | 52.5 | 50.1 |
| 3 | Assam | 28.1 | 28.2 | 28.3 | 28.4 | 28.4 | 28.5 |
| 4 | Bihar | 49.4 | 48.2 | 46.4 | 44.6 | 43.0 | 41.6 |
| 5 | Chhattisgarh | 21.3 | 22.0 | 22.5 | 23.0 | 23.5 | 23.0 |
| 6 | Goa | 33.7 | 33.0 | 31.9 | 30.8 | 29.9 | 29.1 |
| 7 | Gujarat | 30.1 | 29.4 | 28.8 | 28.1 | 27.6 | 27.1 |
| 8 | Haryana | 22.0 | 22.4 | 22.6 | 22.7 | 22.8 | 22.9 |
| 9 | Himachal Pradesh | 52.1 | 49.7 | 47.0 | 44.4 | 42.1 | 40.1 |
| 10 | Jammu & Kashmir | 56.4 | 56.1 | 55.1 | 53.6 | 51.6 | 49.3 |
| 11 | Jharkhand | 29.0 | 29.0 | 28.5 | 27.8 | 27.3 | 26.9 |
| 12 | Karnataka | 25.9 | 26.2 | 26.0 | 25.7 | 25.4 | 25.2 |
| 13 | Kerala | 33.2 | 32.8 | 32.3 | 31.7 | 30.7 | 29.8 |
| 14 | Madhya Pradesh | 38.8 | 38.4 | 37.6 | 36.8 | 36.0 | 35.3 |
| 15 | Maharashtra | 26.4 | 26.3 | 26.1 | 25.8 | 25.5 | 25.3 |
| 16 | Manipur | 68.9 | 65.8 | 62.9 | 60.1 | 57.0 | 54.3 |
| 17 | Meghalaya | 33.5 | 33.1 | 32.7 | 32.3 | 32.0 | 31.7 |
| 18 | Mizoram | 87.5 | 87.3 | 85.7 | 82.9 | 79.2 | 74.8 |
| 19 | Nagaland | 57.7 | 56.8 | 55.8 | 54.9 | 53.5 | 52.3 |
| 20 | Orissa | 31.5 | 31.0 | 30.6 | 30.2 | 29.8 | 29.5 |
| 21 | Punjab | 43.0 | 42.5 | 41.8 | 41.0 | 39.8 | 38.7 |
| 22 | Rajasthan | 41.5 | 40.4 | 39.3 | 38.3 | 37.3 | 36.5 |
| 23 | Sikkim | 71.8 | 68.4 | 65.2 | 62.1 | 58.8 | 55.9 |
| 24 | Tamil Nadu | 23.6 | 24.1 | 24.5 | 24.8 | 25.0 | 25.2 |
| 25 | Tripura | 44.9 | 45.2 | 44.9 | 44.6 | 44.2 | 43.8 |
| 26 | Uttar Pradesh | 49.9 | 48.7 | 46.9 | 45.1 | 43.4 | 41.9 |
| 27 | Uttarakhand | 43.3 | 42.2 | 41.1 | 40.0 | 38.5 | 37.2 |
| 28 | West Bengal | 42.0 | 40.6 | 39.1 | 37.7 | 35.9 | 34.3 |
| **Total General Category** | | **33.1** | **32.6** | **31.9** | **31.2** | **30.5** | **29.8** |
| **Total Special Category** | | **43.5** | **42.7** | **41.7** | **40.7** | **39.5** | **38.3** |
| **Grand Total** | | **33.7** | **33.2** | **32.5** | **31.7** | **31.0** | **30.3** |
| **As per cent of GDP** | | **27.1** | **26.7** | **26.1** | **25.5** | **24.9** | **24.3** |

**Note:**

1. The outstanding debt for the base year has been estimated using the outstanding debt for 2007-08 as reported in Finance Accounts and estimated fiscal deficits for 2008-09 and 2009-10.
2. The fiscal deficit for 2008-09 is assumed to be the lower of the revised estimate for 2008-09 and 3.5 per cent of GSDP. The fiscal deficit for 2009-10 is assumed to be 4 per cent of GSDP.
3. For projecting the outstanding debt for 2010-11, the fiscal deficit for 2010-11 is normatively fixed at 3 per cent of GSDP or that assumed for 2008-09, whichever is higher.
4. For the remaining years of the award period, outstanding debt has been projected on the basis of fiscal deficits prescribed in Annex 9.2

TABLE 21

**Fiscal Deficit (Past trends and Future targets)**

*(as per cent of GSDP)*

| Sl. No. | State | 2005-06 | 2006-07 | 2007-08 | 2011-12 | 2012-13 | 2013-14 | 2014-15 |
|---|---|---|---|---|---|---|---|---|
| 1 | Andhra Pradesh | 3.4 | 2.0 | 2.7 | 3.0 | 3.0 | 3.0 | 3.0 |
| 2 | Arunachal Pradesh | 8.6 | -3.0 | 0.2 | 3.0 | 3.0 | 3.0 | 3.0 |
| 3 | Assam | -0.6 | -1.1 | -1.0 | 3.0 | 3.0 | 3.0 | 3.0 |
| 4 | Bihar | 4.4 | 3.4 | 1.7 | 3.0 | 3.0 | 3.0 | 3.0 |
| 5 | Chhattisgarh | 0.8 | -0.1 | 0.2 | 3.0 | 3.0 | 3.0 | 3.0 |
| 6 | Goa | 4.5 | 3.2 | 3.0 | 3.0 | 3.0 | 3.0 | 3.0 |
| 7 | Gujarat | 2.9 | 2.2 | 1.6 | 3.0 | 3.0 | 3.0 | 3.0 |
| 8 | Haryana | 0.3 | -1.0 | 0.9 | 3.0 | 3.0 | 3.0 | 3.0 |
| 9 | Himachal Pradesh | 2.6 | 3.0 | 1.6 | 3.0 | 3.0 | 3.0 | 3.0 |
| 10 | Jammu & Kashmir | 9.5 | 6.3 | 7.6 | 4.7 | 4.2 | 3.6 | 3.0 |
| 11 | Jharkhand | 8.3 | 1.4 | 2.5 | 3.0 | 3.0 | 3.0 | 3.0 |
| 12 | Karnataka | 2.0 | 2.2 | 2.2 | 3.0 | 3.0 | 3.0 | 3.0 |
| 13 | Kerala | 3.3 | 2.6 | 3.6 | 3.5 | 3.5 | 3.0 | 3.0 |
| 14 | Madhya Pradesh | 3.8 | 2.1 | 1.9 | 3.0 | 3.0 | 3.0 | 3.0 |
| 15 | Maharashtra | 3.9 | 2.2 | -0.5 | 3.0 | 3.0 | 3.0 | 3.0 |
| 16 | Manipur | 5.4 | 8.7 | -1.7 | 3.5 | 3.5 | 3.0 | 3.0 |
| 17 | Meghalaya | 2.8 | 1.0 | 2.4 | 3.0 | 3.0 | 3.0 | 3.0 |
| 18 | Mizoram | 13.8 | 6.0 | 11.2 | 6.4 | 5.2 | 4.1 | 3.0 |
| 19 | Nagaland | 5.6 | 2.7 | 6.2 | 3.5 | 3.5 | 3.0 | 3.0 |
| 20 | Orissa | 0.3 | -0.9 | -1.2 | 3.0 | 3.0 | 3.0 | 3.0 |
| 21 | Punjab | 2.4 | 0.5 | 3.5 | 3.5 | 3.5 | 3.0 | 3.0 |
| 22 | Rajasthan | 3.8 | 2.5 | 1.9 | 3.0 | 3.0 | 3.0 | 3.0 |
| 23 | Sikkim | 7.9 | 4.8 | 2.8 | 3.5 | 3.5 | 3.0 | 3.0 |
| 24 | Tamil Nadu | 1.0 | 1.4 | 1.2 | 3.0 | 3.0 | 3.0 | 3.0 |
| 25 | Tripura | 1.2 | -1.3 | 0.1 | 3.0 | 3.0 | 3.0 | 3.0 |
| 26 | Uttar Pradesh | 3.5 | 3.0 | 3.9 | 3.0 | 3.0 | 3.0 | 3.0 |
| 27 | Uttarakhand | 7.5 | 3.0 | 5.1 | 3.5 | 3.5 | 3.0 | 3.0 |
| 28 | West Bengal | 4.1 | 4.3 | 3.7 | 3.5 | 3.5 | 3.0 | 3.0 |
| **Total General Category** | | **3.1** | **2.1** | **1.8** | **3.1** | **3.1** | **3.0** | **3.0** |
| **Total Special Category** | | **3.8** | **1.9** | **2.3** | **3.4** | **3.3** | **3.1** | **3.0** |
| **Grand Total** | | **3.1** | **2.1** | **1.9** | **3.1** | **3.1** | **3.0** | **3.0** |

required to remain in surplus on revenue account during the period. The path for debt, fiscal deficit and revenue deficit is given at Tables 20, 21 and Table 22 respectively.

TABLE 22

**Revenue Deficit (Past trends and Future targets)**

*(as per cent of GSDP)*

| Sl. No. | State | 2005-06 | 2006-07 | 2007-08 | 2011-12 | 2012-13 | 2013-14 | 2014-15 |
|---|---|---|---|---|---|---|---|---|
| 1 | Andhra Pradesh | 0.0 | -1.0 | 0.0 | 0.0 | 0.0 | 0.0 | 0.0 |
| 2 | Arunachal Pradesh | -6.1 | -19.4 | -18.5 | 0.0 | 0.0 | 0.0 | 0.0 |
| 3 | Assam | -2.5 | -3.4 | -3.4 | 0.0 | 0.0 | 0.0 | 0.0 |
| 4 | Bihar | -0.1 | -2.8 | -4.7 | 0.0 | 0.0 | 0.0 | 0.0 |
| 5 | Chhattisgarh | -2.5 | -4.4 | -4.3 | 0.0 | 0.0 | 0.0 | 0.0 |
| 6 | Goa | 0.2 | -0.9 | -0.9 | 0.0 | 0.0 | 0.0 | 0.0 |
| 7 | Gujarat | 0.2 | -0.7 | -0.7 | 0.0 | 0.0 | 0.0 | 0.0 |
| 8 | Haryana | -1.2 | -1.3 | -1.6 | 0.0 | 0.0 | 0.0 | 0.0 |
| 9 | Himachal Pradesh | -0.3 | -0.6 | -2.4 | 0.0 | 0.0 | 0.0 | 0.0 |
| 10 | Jammu & Kashmir | -1.4 | -1.0 | -3.1 | 0.0 | 0.0 | 0.0 | 0.0 |
| 11 | Jharkhand | 0.0 | -1.4 | -1.5 | 0.0 | 0.0 | 0.0 | 0.0 |
| 12 | Karnataka | -1.2 | -1.0 | -1.5 | 0.0 | 0.0 | 0.0 | 0.0 |
| 13 | Kerala | 2.5 | 1.8 | 2.3 | 1.4 | 0.9 | 0.5 | 0.0 |
| 14 | Madhya Pradesh | 0.0 | -2.5 | -3.4 | 0.0 | 0.0 | 0.0 | 0.0 |
| 15 | Maharashtra | 0.9 | -0.2 | -2.5 | 0.0 | 0.0 | 0.0 | 0.0 |
| 16 | Manipur | -8.1 | -8.2 | -10.9 | 0.0 | 0.0 | 0.0 | 0.0 |
| 17 | Meghalaya | -1.1 | -3.1 | -2.1 | 0.0 | 0.0 | 0.0 | 0.0 |
| 18 | Mizoram | -2.3 | -8.0 | -3.7 | 0.0 | 0.0 | 0.0 | 0.0 |
| 19 | Nagaland | -3.8 | -9.4 | -6.6 | 0.0 | 0.0 | 0.0 | 0.0 |
| 20 | Orissa | -0.6 | -2.4 | -3.8 | 0.0 | 0.0 | 0.0 | 0.0 |
| 21 | Punjab | 1.1 | -1.7 | 2.9 | 1.8 | 1.2 | 0.6 | 0.0 |
| 22 | Rajasthan | 0.5 | -0.4 | -0.9 | 0.0 | 0.0 | 0.0 | 0.0 |
| 23 | Sikkim | -10.4 | -11.3 | -15.3 | 0.0 | 0.0 | 0.0 | 0.0 |
| 24 | Tamil Nadu | -0.8 | -1.0 | -1.4 | 0.0 | 0.0 | 0.0 | 0.0 |
| 25 | Tripura | -6.6 | -8.3 | -8.2 | 0.0 | 0.0 | 0.0 | 0.0 |
| 26 | Uttar Pradesh | 0.4 | -1.5 | -1.0 | 0.0 | 0.0 | 0.0 | 0.0 |
| 27 | Uttarakhand | 0.3 | -3.0 | -1.9 | 0.0 | 0.0 | 0.0 | 0.0 |
| 28 | West Bengal | 3.1 | 3.1 | 2.7 | 1.6 | 1.1 | 0.5 | 0.0 |
| **Total General Category** | | **0.4** | **-0.7** | **-1.0** | **0.3** | **0.2** | **0.1** | **0.0** |
| **Total Special Category** | | **-2.1** | **-3.7** | **-4.1** | **0.0** | **0.0** | **0.0** | **0.0** |
| **Grand Total** | | **0.2** | **-0.9** | **-1.2** | **0.2** | **0.2** | **0.1** | **0.0** |

## LOANS FROM NATIONAL SMALL SAVINGS FUND

NSSF was created in the public account of India with effect from 1 April 1999 with the objective of de-linking small savings transactions from the Consolidated Fund of India and ensuring their operation in a transparent and self-sustaining manner. Since NSSF operates in the public account, its transactions do not impact the fiscal deficit of the Centre.

The National Small Savings Funds (NSSF) was created in the Public Account of India with effect from April 1999 with the Central Government taking on the responsibility of servicing the small savings deposits outstanding as on the date of creation of NSSF. The modality was that the Central Government issued special securities to NSSF for Rs. 1,76,221 crore equal to the face value of the outstanding deposits as on April 1999. These special securities against outstanding deposits carried interest rate of 11.5 per cent per annum on the date of issue and did not have any specific term. Since loans against the deposits outstanding on April 1999 had been extended to State Governments from the Consolidated Fund of India (CFI) prior to creation of NSSF, interest from states on these loans was also credited to CFI and accounted as a non-tax receipt of GoI. These loans were included in the corpus of high-coupon loans pre-paid by the states under the Debt Swap Scheme as well as in the subsequent debt relief awarded by the Twelfth Finance Commission.

Till 2001-02, the net small savings collections in a state (gross collections minus repayments to depositors) were being shared between the Central and State Governments, with the share of the State Government being progressively increased from 66.66 per cent to 75 per cent from 1 April 1987 and to 80 per cent from April 2000. From 1 April 2002 to 31 March 2007, the entire net collections in a state were being invested in special securities issued by the concerned State Governments. However, with effect from 2007-08, the mandatory share of State Governments has been reduced to 80 per cent with the option to go upto 100 per cent.

The sums received in NSSF on redemption of special securities are re-invested in special Central Government securities. The special securities issued by the Central Government against such redemption amounts carry a tenure of 20 years with bullet repayment on maturity and coupon rates benchmarked to average secondary market yields on Central Government securities (G-sec) of comparable maturity.

With effect from 2007-08, an enabling provision has been made through amendment to the NSSF (Custody and Investment) Rules, 2001 to allow for investment in other instruments. A sum of Rs. 1500 crore has been given as loan @ 9 per cent per annum (payable annually), to India Infrastructure Finance Company Limited (IIFCL) in 2007-08 for financing infrastructure development. The loan carries a bullet repayment after a period of 15 years.

The interest paid to depositors plus the management cost is expenditure of the Fund while the interest received from the Central Government and State/UT Governments with legislature on investment of the collections in their long-term securities is income of the Fund. The management cost comprises remuneration to post-offices/banks for operating the schemes, commission to agents for mobilising deposits and cost of printing of certificates.

All deposits under small savings schemes are credited to NSSF and all withdrawals by the depositors are made out of accumulations in the Fund. The balance is invested in special securities issued by Central and State/UT Governments as per their respective shares. These securities are issued for a period of 25 years, including a moratorium of five years on the principal amount. The special securities carry a rate of interest as fixed by the Government of India from time to time. The current rate of interest is 9.5 per cent per annum.

During the period 1999-00 to 2008-09, the states had issued special securities to NSSF amounting to Rs. 4,48,857 crore, of which an amount of Rs. 16,919 crore has been redeemed, leaving a balance of Rs. 4,31,938 crore outstanding as on 31 March 2009. Four states, viz. Maharashtra, West Bengal, Gujarat and Uttar Pradesh, account for 52 per cent of the total outstanding NSSF debt of states as on 31 March 2009.

Even though the interest rates have come down over this period, the states have had various issues with the overall scheme regarding the inflexibility of having to borrow based on availability rather than requirement, asymmetry between effective interest rates to the states and the Centre and the difference between cost to the NSSF and interest rates.

In 2005, a sub-committee of the National Development Council was set-up to examine the various issues raised by the states. Based on its recommendations, the following changes were made in the scheme:

(I) The states were not compelled to take 100 per cent of the net collections under small savings and were permitted to go down to 80 per cent, with the remainder being taken by the Centre.

(II) The rate of interest payable on NSSF securities issued during the years 1999-2000 to 2001-02 was reduced from 13.5 per cent, 12.5 per cent and 11 per cent per annum respectively, to 10.5 per cent per annum with effect from 1 April 2007 as shown in Table 23

TABLE -23

**Interest Rates Applicable on Loans From NSSF**

*(per cent)*

| Year | Original Interest Rates | Interest Rates post NDC sub-committee recommendations |
|---|---|---|
| 1999-2000 | 13.5 | 10.5 |
| 2000-01 | 12.5 | 10.5 |
| 2001-02 | 11.0 | 10.5 |
| 2002-03 | 10.5 | 10.5 |
| 2003-04 onwards | 9.5 | 9.5 |

Source: Thirteenth Finance Commission, Vol. 1 (2010-15), Govt. of India.

(III) The states were allowed to pre-pay a part of their liabilities to NSSF (this was availed of only by Tamil Nadu and Orissa with pre-paid sums of Rs. 1126 crore and Rs. 200 crore respectively during 2007-08).

Despite this relief, there is a difference between the effective rate of interest payable by the Centre and that by the states shows the effective interest rates on NSSF loans to the Centre and states and their difference since inception of the Fund.

Both the Centre and the states have seen the interest cost of their respective NSSF debts decline over the years. However, the average interest rate paid by the states has

**Effective Rate of Interest of NSSF Loans to Centre and States**

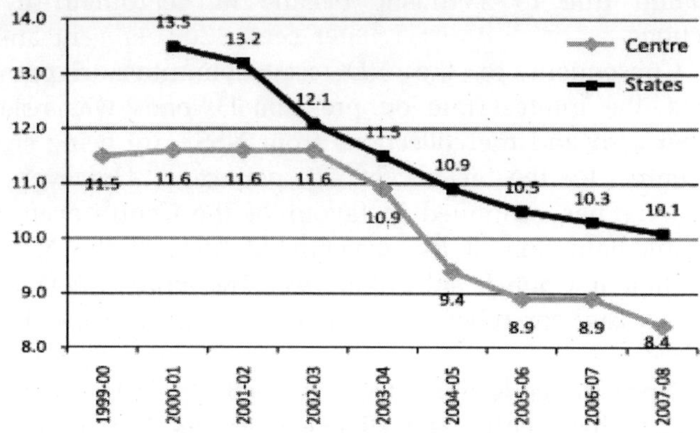


been higher than that of the Centre from the commencement of NSSF in 1999-2000. This is primarily because the states have been paying interest only on securities issued against collections on current small savings from 1 April 1999, whereas the Centre is also paying interest on securities against the deposits outstanding on that date, which, at 11.5 per cent, was lower than the rate of interest on transfers during 1999-2000 and 2000-01. The gap between the average interest paid by the states and the Centre on their respective NSSF debt had narrowed from 1.9 percentage points in 2000-01 to 0.5 percentage points in 2002-03, but thereafter, increased to 1.7 percentage points in 2007-08.

This widening after 2002-03 has arisen due to the following decisions taken by the Centre: (i) Reduction in interest rate on central special securities issued against outstanding balances on central liabilities from 11.5 per cent to 10.5 per cent with effect from 1 March 2003, in line with general softening of market interest rates. (ii) Use of debt swap receipts from states to partly redeem the central special securities issued against the initial outstanding balances and to replace them with fresh securities at lower market rates of interest. The total amount redeemed between 2002-03 and 2004-05 was Rs. 92,652 crore. (iii) Further redemption of high-interest central special securities against outstanding balances for a sum of Rs. 10,000 crore in 2007-08 in order to infuse cash into the NSSF consequent upon negative cash balance in the Fund due to a drastic decline in net small savings collections.

Consequent to the NDC sub-committee recommendations, the interest rate on pre-2002-03 loans was reset to 10.5 per cent and the collections from NSSF are being shared by Centre to the extent of 20 per cent. However, the asymmetry has continued in favour of the Centre even after the implementation of the recommendations of the National Development Council sub-committee. Therefore, we feel that there is a case for relief to the states on loans advanced from the NSSF.

Since the collections, from 2007-08 onwards, have been flowing to the Centre as well, we have decided to consider relief on loans contracted till 2006-07. The state-wise position of loans contracted till 2006-07 and outstanding estimated as at the end of 2009-10. Keeping in view the existing effective rate of interest for the Centre, the fact that now the Centre too is using 20 per cent of the collections and the recent trends in flows to NSSF, we recommend that the loans contracted till 2006-07 and outstanding at the end of 2009-10 be reset at a common interest rate of 9 per cent per annum in place of 10.5 per cent or 9.5 per cent. The repayment schedule, however, should remain unchanged.

The total benefit that would accrue to states, estimated on the basis of outstanding at the end of 2009-10, is Rs. 13,517 crore during our award period. State-wise details of estimates of the benefit are given in Table 24 The benefit shall continue to accrue even beyond the award period and is estimated to reach Rs. 28,360 crore by the maturity of the last loan coming under purview.

While the relief recommended above only addresses the interest asymmetry between the Centre and states, the structural problems in the existing arrangement need to be reviewed. The issue of high interest rate on these instruments arises because of the administrative mechanism presently in place.

A rise in the difference between the interest rates paid on small savings instruments and the market rate causes an

## TABLE 24

# Interest Relief on NSSF Loan

(Rs. crore)

| Sl. No. | State | NSSF Loans Outstanding on 31/3/2010 | Interest to be Paid with Reset Rates | | | | | | Interest Relief | | | | | |
|---|---|---|---|---|---|---|---|---|---|---|---|---|---|---|
| | | | 2010-11 | 2011-12 | 2012-13 | 2013-14 | 2014-15 | 2010-15 | 2010-11 | 2011-12 | 2012-13 | 2013-14 | 2014-15 | 2010-15 |
| 1 | Andhra Pradesh | 22223.26 | 2000.09 | 1909.65 | 1800.56 | 1691.47 | 1582.39 | **8984.17** | 164.29 | 155.90 | 146.47 | 137.04 | 127.61 | **731.31** |
| 2 | Arunachal Pradesh | 480.45 | 43.24 | 41.58 | 39.34 | 37.10 | 34.86 | **196.12** | 2.82 | 2.70 | 2.55 | 2.40 | 2.25 | **12.71** |
| 3 | Assam | 4172.40 | 375.52 | 354.74 | 333.39 | 312.04 | 290.69 | **1666.36** | 36.33 | 34.20 | 32.04 | 29.87 | 27.71 | **160.15** |
| 4 | Bihar | 13269.46 | 1194.25 | 1136.58 | 1069.39 | 1002.20 | 935.02 | **5337.44** | 112.50 | 106.32 | 99.61 | 92.90 | 86.19 | **497.53** |
| 5 | Chhattisgarh | 4013.99 | 361.26 | 345.35 | 325.99 | 306.63 | 287.28 | **1626.51** | 28.16 | 26.78 | 25.21 | 23.65 | 22.08 | **125.88** |
| 6 | Goa | 2419.36 | 217.74 | 208.48 | 196.80 | 185.12 | 173.44 | **981.58** | 16.18 | 15.40 | 14.50 | 13.59 | 12.69 | **72.36** |
| 7 | Gujarat | 40152.60 | 3613.73 | 3439.94 | 3240.15 | 3040.37 | 2840.59 | **16174.79** | 318.18 | 301.07 | 282.53 | 263.98 | 245.43 | **1411.19** |
| 8 | Haryana | 9528.10 | 857.53 | 815.12 | 767.43 | 719.73 | 672.04 | **3831.85** | 76.96 | 72.74 | 68.23 | 63.72 | 59.20 | **340.85** |
| 9 | Himachal Pradesh | 3445.95 | 310.14 | 296.51 | 279.83 | 263.14 | 246.46 | **1396.08** | 24.08 | 22.90 | 21.54 | 20.19 | 18.84 | **107.55** |
| 10 | Jammu & Kashmir | 2869.34 | 258.24 | 245.99 | 231.70 | 217.41 | 203.11 | **1156.45** | 22.69 | 21.48 | 20.15 | 18.83 | 17.50 | **100.65** |
| 11 | Jharkhand | 7204.90 | 648.37 | 619.53 | 584.71 | 549.88 | 515.06 | **2917.55** | 50.89 | 48.39 | 45.55 | 42.72 | 39.88 | **227.43** |
| 12 | Karnataka | 17866.26 | 1602.56 | 1526.59 | 1438.95 | 1351.31 | 1263.67 | **7183.08** | 132.77 | 125.77 | 118.12 | 110.47 | 102.83 | **589.96** |
| 13 | Kerala | 11121.17 | 1000.91 | 957.14 | 903.34 | 849.55 | 795.75 | **4506.68** | 73.68 | 70.10 | 65.96 | 61.81 | 57.67 | **329.22** |
| 14 | Madhya Pradesh | 13402.34 | 1206.18 | 1149.45 | 1083.17 | 1016.90 | 950.62 | **5406.32** | 101.34 | 96.00 | 90.12 | 84.25 | 78.38 | **450.09** |
| 15 | Maharashtra | 65640.28 | 5907.63 | 5625.28 | 5301.19 | 4977.09 | 4653.00 | **26464.18** | 503.29 | 476.51 | 447.40 | 418.30 | 389.20 | **2234.70** |
| 16 | Manipur | 462.42 | 41.62 | 40.46 | 38.28 | 36.11 | 33.93 | **190.40** | 2.90 | 2.80 | 2.64 | 2.48 | 2.32 | **13.13** |
| 17 | Meghalaya | 253.71 | 22.83 | 21.68 | 20.41 | 19.14 | 17.88 | **101.94** | 2.02 | 1.91 | 1.79 | 1.67 | 1.55 | **8.94** |
| 18 | Mizoram | 127.93 | 11.51 | 10.61 | 10.27 | 9.63 | 8.99 | **51.31** | 1.02 | 0.96 | 0.90 | 0.84 | 0.78 | **4.51** |
| 19 | Nagaland | 102.95 | 9.27 | 8.82 | 8.30 | 7.79 | 7.28 | **41.45** | 0.83 | 0.79 | 0.74 | 0.69 | 0.64 | **3.69** |
| 20 | Orissa | 6303.82 | 567.34 | 541.04 | 509.86 | 478.68 | 447.49 | **2544.42** | 47.93 | 45.42 | 42.63 | 39.85 | 37.07 | **212.90** |
| 21 | Punjab | 19184.40 | 1726.57 | 1643.40 | 1546.77 | 1450.14 | 1353.51 | **7720.38** | 158.87 | 150.22 | 140.82 | 131.42 | 122.02 | **703.34** |
| 22 | Rajasthan | 21941.72 | 1974.75 | 1872.31 | 1761.13 | 1649.95 | 1538.77 | **8796.91** | 188.16 | 177.50 | 166.35 | 155.20 | 144.05 | **831.27** |
| 23 | Sikkim | 105.08 | 9.46 | 8.95 | 8.42 | 7.89 | 7.36 | **42.09** | 0.84 | 0.80 | 0.75 | 0.70 | 0.65 | **3.73** |
| 24 | Tamil Nadu | 23868.04 | 2148.12 | 2050.10 | 1934.02 | 1817.94 | 1701.86 | **9652.05** | 166.69 | 158.25 | 148.81 | 139.36 | 129.92 | **743.04** |
| 25 | Tripura | 1010.36 | 90.93 | 86.56 | 81.51 | 76.47 | 71.42 | **406.89** | 8.44 | 7.99 | 7.49 | 7.00 | 6.51 | **37.44** |
| 26 | Uttar Pradesh | 38734.72 | 3486.12 | 3319.65 | 3125.40 | 2931.16 | 2736.91 | **15599.25** | 319.36 | 302.09 | 283.28 | 264.47 | 245.65 | **1414.85** |
| 27 | Uttarakhand | 4075.46 | 366.79 | 349.78 | 330.09 | 310.39 | 290.69 | **1647.74** | 28.62 | 27.18 | 25.58 | 23.99 | 22.40 | **127.77** |
| 28 | West Bengal | 55430.60 | 4988.75 | 4750.48 | 4473.05 | 4195.63 | 3918.20 | **22326.12** | 455.85 | 431.28 | 404.53 | 377.77 | 351.02 | **2020.46** |
| | **Total** | **389349.63** | **35041.47** | **33376.06** | **31443.46** | **29510.86** | **27578.26** | **156950.11** | **3045.70** | **2883.42** | **2706.29** | **2529.17** | **2352.04** | **13516.62** |

**Note:** 1. These figures are estimates and have to be reconciled before actual interest relief is given.
2. The figures above pertain to loans only contracted till 2006–07.
3. The actual interest payment and outstanding would be higher and would include loans contracted post 2006–07.

increase in subscription to these instruments, thereby increasing flows of NSSF loans to states. With overall borrowings capped by FRBM targets, the states cannot take recourse to open market borrowings. This has already been witnessed during 2003-04 and 2004-05. Thus, states may not be able to benefit from the lower interest rates, even when market rates go down, as they are saddled with high inflows from high-cost NSSF loans. Conversely, when market interest rates increase, the subscriptions to small savings instruments dip and flows from NSSF dry up. This has been witnessed in 2006-07 and 2007-08 when net flows for many states even became negative.

States have also raised issues about the tenor of this loan, extending to 25 years, which has been used to justify the high interest rate and has led to a situation where states are locked with fixed interest debt for a long time with no option of reset and pre-payment. There is a significant mismatch between the maturity period of five to seven years for most small savings instruments and the term of the loan extended from NSSF.

These issues highlight the need for more comprehensive reforms in the overall administration of the National Small Savings Fund. Various committees constituted in the past to look into these issues have made far-reaching recommendations. One of the important recommendations has been linking of interest rate on small savings instruments to the prevailing G-sec rates, which we endorse. We recommend, against this background, that all aspects of the design and administration of the scheme be examined with the aim of bringing transparency, market linked rates and other much needed reforms to the scheme.

Some reforms are also required at the state level. In the past there has been a practice of giving various incentives such as cash awards to officials and other similar measures to promote subscription to small savings instruments. These measures also interfere with normal market dynamics. While most of these incentives, like awards to officials, have outlived their utility, all such incentives that either add to the cost of administration or affect normal market linked subscription, should be proactively withdrawn by the states.

## RECOMMENDATION OF THIRTEENTH FINANCE COMMISSION (2010-15) FOR MINIMIZE THE CENTRAL LOANS TO STATES

(i) Revenue deficit of the Centre needs to be progressively reduced and eliminated, followed by emergence of a revenue surplus by 2014-15.

(ii) Target of 68 per cent of GDP for combined debt of Centre and states to be achieved by 2014-15. Fiscal consolidation path embodies the steady reduction in augmented debt stock of Centre to 45 per cent of GDP by 2014-15 and for the states to less than 25 per cent of GDP by 2014-15.

(iii) MTFP to be reformed and made a statement of commitment rather than a statement of intent. Tighter integration between the multi-year framework provided by MTFP and annual budget exercise.

(iv) The following disclosures to be made along with the annual Central budget/MTFP:

- (a) Detailed breakup of grants to states under the overall category of non-plan and plan grants.
- (b) Statement on tax expenditure to be systematised and the methodology to be made explicit.
- (c) Compliance costs of major tax proposal to be reported.
- (d) Revenue Consequences of Capital Expenditure to be projected in MTFP.
- (e) Fiscal impact of major policy changes to be incorporated in MTFP.
- (f) PPP liabilities to be reported along with MTFP.
- (g) MTFP to make explicit the values of parameters underlying projections for receipts and expenditure and the band within which they can vary while remaining consistent with targets.

(v) Transfer of disinvestment receipts to the public account to be discontinued and all disinvestment receipts be maintained in the consolidated fund.

(vi) GoI should list all public sector enterprises that yield a lower rate of return on assets than a norm to be decided by an expert committee.

(vii) The FRBM Act specify the nature of shocks that would require a relaxation of FRBM targets.

(viii) In case of macroeconomic shocks, instead of relaxing states' borrowing limits and letting states borrow more, the Centre to borrow and devolve the resources using the Finance Commission tax devolution formula for *inter-se* distribution among states.

(ix) Structural shocks such as arrears arising out of Pay Commission awards to be avoided by, in the case of arrears, by making the pay award commence from the date on which it is accepted.

(x) Independent review mechanism to be set-up by the Centre to evaluate its fiscal reform process. The independent review mechanism to evolve into a Fiscal Council with legislative backing over time.

(xi) Given the exceptional circumstances of 2008-09 and 2009-10, the fiscal consolidation process of the states was disrupted. It is expected that states would be able to get back to their fiscal correction path by 2011-12, allowing for a year of adjustment in 2010-11:

(a) States that incurred zero revenue deficit or achieved revenue surplus in 2007-08 should eliminate revenue deficit by 2011-12 and maintain revenue balance or attain a surplus thereafter. Other states to eliminate revenue deficit by 2014-15.

(b) The general category states that attained a zero revenue deficit or a revenue surplus in 2007-08 should achieve a fiscal deficit of 3 per cent of GSDP by 2011-12 and maintain such thereafter. Other general category states to achieve 3 per cent fiscal deficit by 2013-14.

(c) All special category states with base fiscal deficit of less than 3 per cent of GSDP in 2007-08 could incur a fiscal deficit of 3 per cent in 2011-12 and maintain thereafter, Manipur, Nagaland, Sikkim and Uttarakhand to reduce their fiscal deficit to 3 per cent of GSDP by 2013-14.

(d) Jammu and Kashmir and Mizoram should limit their fiscal deficit to 3 per cent of GSDP by 2014-15.

(xii) States to amend/enact FRBM Acts to build in the fiscal reform path worked out. State specific grants recommended for a state to be released upon compliance.

(xiii) Independent review/monitoring mechanism under the FRBM Acts to be set-up by all states.

(xiv) Borrowing limits for states to be worked out by MoF using the fiscal reform path, thus acting as an enforcement mechanism for the fiscal correction by states.

(xv) Loans to states from National Small Savings Fund contracted till 2006-07 and outstanding at the end of 2009-10 to be reset at 9 per cent rate of interest subject to conditions prescribed.

(xvi) National Small Savings Scheme to be reformed into a market-aligned scheme. State Governments also required to undertake relvant reforms at their level.

(xvii) Loans from GoI to states and administered by ministries/departments other than MoF, outstanding as at the end of 2009-10, to be written-off subject to conditions prescribed.

(xviii) A window for borrowing from the Central Government to be available for the fiscally weak states that are unable to raise loans from market.

(xix) For states that have not availed the benefit of consolidation under DCRF, the facility, limited to consolidation and interest rate reduction, to be extended subject to enactment of FRBM Act.

(xx) Benefit of interest relief on NSSF and write-off available to states only if they bring about the necessary amendments/enactments of FRBM

**Public Debt Management of Bihar**

Public debt is a useful of income generation if it is utilized for the creation of productive assets. As can be seen from Table-25 the accrual to the state exchequer on this account was negative except in 2004-05 and 2008-09. it would indeed be very difficulty to come out of this situation without adequate help from the central government. The state government is looking at the Thirteenth Finance Commission with much hope to ease its debt burden.

TABLE 25

| | *2004-05* | *2005-06* | *2006-07* | *2007-08* | *2008-09* | *2009-10* |
|---|---|---|---|---|---|---|
| Gross Central Loans received | 1654 | 2 | 3 | 468 | 150 | 1401 |
| Internal Debt received | 5972 | 3769 | 2355 | 1144 | 5778 | 4173 |
| PF Small Savings | 1198 | 1088 | 1012 | 1084 | 1153 | 1223 |
| Total Debt received | 8824 | 4858 | 3370 | 2696 | 7081 | 6797 |
| Recoveries of Loans and Advances | 15 | 51 | 7 | 26 | 11 | 29 |
| Interest payments | 3474 | 3649 | 3416 | 3707 | 3796 | 4171 |
| Interest received | 75 | 216 | 176 | 171 | 305 | 54 |
| Repayment of debt | 3882 | 1703 | 1642 | 2447 | 2691 | 2756 |
| Net debt received | 1558 | -227 | -1505 | -3262 | 910 | -48 |
| Net debt received as % of total borrowing | 18 | -5 | -45 | -121 | 13 | -1 |

*Source*: Department of Finance, GoB.

TABLE 26

**Outstanding Liabilities of Bihar**

| | *2004-05* | *2005-06* | *2006-07* | *2007-08* | *2008-09* | *2009-10* |
|---|---|---|---|---|---|---|
| Internal debt | 21906 | 25182 | 26829 | 26769 | 31293 | 34052 |
| Central loans | 9037 | 8551 | 8237 | 8277 | 7998 | 8929 |
| Total public debt | 30943 | 33733 | 35065 | 35045 | 39291 | 42981 |
| Public account | 8401 | 8766 | 9161 | 9429 | 9573 | 9924 |
| Total | 39344 | 42498 | 44226 | 44475 | 48865 | 52905 |
| Outstanding liability as % of GSDP | 43.1 | 43.4 | 35-7 | 31.0 | 30.1 | 29.2 |

Source: Department of Finance, GoB.

It is clear from the above study that the outstanding debt liability had decreased consistently from 2004-05 to 2009-10 and reflects the state govt. ability to contain the debt burden effectively. We can see Table 26.

The Sarkaria Commission Report (1988) observed, "Some State Governments as well as experts have complained that the borrowing powers of the State have been unduly restricted by the Constitution does not permit States to borrow outside India. ... Even internally the States are not free to borrow, i.e., if the Union Government has guaranteed an outstanding loan of the State, without the consent of the Union Government. ... It is argued that restrictions do not obtain in a federation like USA. If it is felt that in a planned economy like India there is need for some such restrictions should apply only to long, and medium-term borrowing from the open market and not to the borrowing from financial institutions or to short-term loans for less than one year. In fact, the State Governments or state enterprises should be encouraged to access markets on the basis of their financial strengths and viability rather through tax incentives which distort the allocation of resources.

It may be mentioned that the 13th Finance Commission has suggested a fundamental change in the borrowing pattern, which absolve the Union Government from any such responsibility and expose the poor States to higher interest cost. The practice of centre giving loans, (including plan loans) to the States has been stopped, which requires that all plan assistance now onwards will flow as grants. Thus, under the new scheme of market borrowings, States will have to compete with the Centre and other corporate bodies to raise resource from the market. This may make the financing of plan difficult and enforce the State Government to cut the size of their Plans.

Then, of course, in order to give some relief to the States, the 13th Finance Commission has suggested consolidating the State public debt, rescheduling the repayment for 20 years at 7.5 per cent rate of interest. The second part consists of a debt write-off, which is linked to reduction in revenue deficit. But to get these reliefs the State will have to enact Fiscal Responsibility and Budget Management legislation, which further entails many preconditions like phasing out the revenue deficit by 2010-11, keeping the fiscal deficit at 3 per cent, etc. then States will have to create sinking funds outside their Consolidated Funds to ensure a smooth redemption of public debt.

It must be mentioned that in view of the precarious resource positions of the States these are only temporary aberrations, which do not go deep into the problem of States indebtedness. Loans are not always bad if used productively and lead to a fall in debt-income ratio. Therefore, in order to monitor the related issues there is a need to create Union-State Loan Council and have its regular sittings.

Then there is a chronic problem of imbalance in the resource position of the Centre *vis-à-vis* the States. Another chronic controversy deals with the working of the Finance Commission and the Planning Commission. Since the grant component in the transfer of resources through the planning Commission has surpassed that of the Finance Commission, which is a constitutional body, the issue has to be looked into and needs a serious debate.

To conclude we can say that because of certain developments in the post-reform period, there is an urgent need to examine afresh the working of Union-State Financial relations. The various committees and commissions, which have so far been appointed, appear to expect too much from the State Government. Finance Commission is always bound by their terms of reference. Therefore, too much cannot be excepted from them insofar as the working of federal financial relations is concerned. Since in a developing federation like India some dynamism in the working of financial relations between different tiers of the government is an ongoing process, therefore, there is an urgent need to keep a constant vigil. The meeting of the inter-State Council and other similar bodies should be regular and more frequent and some new such institutions as Loan Council can be created to deal with the chronic problem of indebtedness.

## References

The Eleventh Finance Commission Report (2000), Govt. of India, New Delhi.

The Twelfth Finance Commission Report (2004), Govt. of India, New Delhi.

Shandilya, Tapan Kumar (1991), Central Loans to States Under Five Year Plans, Deep & Deep Publications, New Delhi.

Shandilya, Tapan Kumar (2005), (Emerging Issues in Center State Financial Relations: Approach of Twelfth Finance Commission, Conference Vol. of Indian Economic Association Journal, Vishakhapattnam, Andhra Pradesh, p. 903.

Shandilya, Tapan Kumar (1994), Centre-State Financial Relation in India (Edt.), Deep & Deep Publications, New Delhi.

Rangrajan, C. (2005), "Twelfth Finance Commission: Approach and Discommendation, *Economic and Political Weekly*, Vol. XL, No. 31, July 30, 2005.

Economic Survey of India, 1999.

Economic Survey of India, 2000.

Economic Survey of India, 2005

Economic Survey of India 2009-10

Economic Survey Bihar, 2009-10.

Economic and Political Different Volumes.

The Eight Finance Commission Report (1984), Govt. of India, New Delhi.

The Ninth Finance Commissions Report (1989), Govt. of India, New Delhi.

The Tenth Finance Commissions Report (1994), Govt. of India, New Delhi.

The Thirteenth Finance Commissions Report (2010-15), Govt. of India, New Delhi.

# 5

# The Impact on Central Loans to States

The method of loan financing is a fiscal tool in the hands of the Government and it works through the revenue and capital accounts of the budget. Public debt of a State affects the economy in numerous ways. In itself, it is neither good nor bad. The nature and extent of the impact depend upon many factors, such as the purposes for which loans have been advanced, their terms and conditions, their structures and the maturity mix, their types and interest rates, the debt management policy and the general economic and social conditions of the State. Broadly speaking, the impact of loans depends on how the debt is managed. The way in which the debt is managed and the success achieved will directly affect source of security, banking legislations. The conservation programmes and many other matters of public policy that the country has been accustomed to determine with little reference to their effects upon their federal finance.

In this context it would be useful to build up a theoretical base for analyzing the impact of Central loans on the economy of the State. A brief discussion of the theories will also be used to study the impact of inter-government loans. There are classical and modern approaches to the theory of public debt. According to Prof. R.A. Musgrave, there are two main classical theories 'Pay-as-you-go' theory and 'Inter-generation equity' theory. The former, i.e. "Pay-as-you-go" is also called the 'self-liquidating' theory which maintains that any loan which is not self-liquidating has a bad impact on the economy, because it has to be repaid out of the proceeds of tax revenues and the tax-proceeds becomes additional burden on the economy. The 'inter-generation equity' theory maintains that if a loan is raised, it may impose a burden on the present generation in form of additional taxation for debt servicing, whereas the beneficiaries of public expenditure undertaken with loans may be future generation. The modern approach towards public debt rejects the classical views. It maintains that loan financing is an important instrument in the hands of the government for the regulation of the stabilization and economic growth and its effects should be examined in the context of overall objectives of economic growth and stability whether it promotes economic growth-oriented policies with social justice.

No doubt, the burden controversy is one of the oldest subjects of academic discussions, but the controversy reached its logical conclusion following the Keynesian revolution in 1930s. However, the publication of the book of J.M. Buchanan, 'Public Principles of Public Debt', in 1958 set the ball rolling, being aware of limitations and the drafty receptions of the thesis of Prof. Buchanan, three economists of Priston University, William G. Bomen, Richard G.D. Davis and David H. Koph (B.D.K.) also challenged the Pigou-thesis (No Burden Theory). The modern school approaches the problem of public debt in the same way as Prof. S.E. Harris maintains, "How great a burden the debt will be, depends upon the rate of interest, the tax system, the weight of other expenditures of the government and above all upon the level of national income." Lesser will be the subjective burden borne by the society, smaller the amount of interest charges and more equal distribution of ownership of public debt. The impact would be measured with reference to the growth of national income and the growing loans do not cause any concern so long as the national income rise adequately, E. Domer maintains a case for growing national debt provided it leads to increasing productivity and ever rising national income. He writes, "If all the people and organizations who work, study, write articles and make speeches, worry and spend sleepless night—all because of fear of debt that could forget about it for a while and spend even their efforts trying to find ways of achieving a growing national income. Their contribution to the benefit and welfare of humanity and to the solution of the debt problem would be far greater. Thus, what emerges from the foregoing discussion is that the existence of a large debt is neither an evil nor a blessing in itself. It is an instrument of fiscal policy, but it is one, which should be used with care. The loan should be managed in such a way that it does the least harm and the maximum good to be the community as a whole.

We have built up the theoretical base to evaluate the impact of public debt in general. Now, it is pertinent to examine its relevance in the context of the impact of Central loans on the State. The theories can be adopted in this field with certain modifications tasking into view the nature of the debtor and creditor, here both being governments, Central Government and State Governments. Both Governments serve the same purpose because the development of the country as a whole is the collective responsibility of the Central and the State Governments. In this peculiar circumstance we shall try to analyse the impact of Central loans on the economy of the State by analyzing the impact of debt servicing charges on revenue and capital budgets of the State. In this context, the ratio of interest charges on central loans and repayment of central loans to state tax revenue, revenue expenditure, capital receipts, capital disbursements, gross loans, total debts, additional resource mobilization, net domestic product, etc. will be examined.

The impact of public debt and loans may be analyzed under two heads: firstly, those which are related with the raising of the loans and their spending, and secondly, those effects which are due to the existence of the debt. The first may be called the "process or preliminary effects" and the second may be termed as 'asset effects' and 'transfer effect.' The preliminary effects of central loans are the effects upon the investment and production of the state, which are generated in the very process of Government borrowing and the spending of the resources available through borrowing. Thus, preliminary effects are related with the raising and spending the central loans. They depend chiefly upon the nature and the purpose of the loan. The impact may be financial and economic, they may be primarily and secondary and accordingly the burden of union loans may be financial and economic. When the Government obtains a debt, the level of taxation in the economy has to be increased in order to meet the debt servicing charges as David M.C. Wright observes, "The financial burden of the debt is to be measured by the effects of the interest charges and the taxes levied to meet them. The relation, which the taxes bear to the national money income, is the question of primary importance. The higher level of taxation caused by the rising public debt may have some repercussion on the economy, in the form of adverse effects on the capacity and willingness to mobilize necessary resources by the State. These effects may be called the 'real burden' and 'secondary burden' of the loan.

Thus, it is clear that the financial impact of central loans on state refers to the amount of debt servicing charges, i.e., interest charges and repayment of the loans. Such type of financial burden falls both on the revenue and the capital accounts of the budgets. The interest charges are non-development expenditure of the revenue account and repayments are capital disbursements of the capital account. In view of this discussion, the financial effects can be classified as: (i) Income effects, and (ii) Substitution effects. The former relate to the financial transfer from the state budget to the central budget in shape of debt servicing charges, i.e. interest charges and repayments. Therefore, the income effects of the financial impacts of central loans on the state may be measured, as referred above, in form of: (a) the percentage of interest charges to the total revenue, total tax revenue and total revenue expenditure; (b) the percentage of repayments to total capital receipts and capital disbursements, (c) the percentage of interest and repayment charges to total revenue expenditure, total debt, total gross loans and total net domestic product. The substitution effects relate to the impact of union loans on the revenue mobilizing efforts of the State.

Coming to the economic impact of central loans of the

State, we know that it relates to long-term economic effects of the loans on the economy of the State. In this context, the impact relates to locational aspect of the loans, whether they are used for productive or unproductive purposes, whether capital formation and income generation are not adversely affected. In this context, we may examine the proportion of interest charges and repayments to net domestic product and capital formation.

Let us examine, first of all, the preliminary of financial impact of central loans on the State. As discussed earlier, it refers to the amount of interest charges and repayments which are paid annually and which are imposed on the budget of the state. We have also seen that the financial impact has been classified into income effects and substitution effects. The former refers to the annual flow of resources from the State to the Central Government on account of debt repayments and interest charges. The latter refers to the state's failure to mobilize financial resources in adequate amount because financial assistance is readily available from the Central Government. The income effects of the financial burden/impact may be measured, as pointed out earlier, in terms of the percent of interest charges to state's total revenue, total tax revenue, state's revenue expenditure, the percentage of repayments to gross loans, total capital receipts, total capital disbursements and the percentage of interest charges and repayments to state's total revenue, total tax revenue and total revenue expenditure.

## FISCAL IMBALANCES IN BIHAR

The most alarming and harmful feature of Bihar Finance is its increasing fiscal deficit. Fiscal deficit as measured officially by the government of India is difference between aggregate disbursements excluding debt repayments, and aggregate receipts. Besides this over all or conventional deficit there are four other concepts of deficit. (Bhatia, 2003).

### Revenue Deficit

Revenue deficit (RD) is excess of expenditure on revenue account over receipts on revenue account.

### Gross Fiscal Deficit

Gross Fiscal Deficit (GFD) for a state is measured as aggregate disbursements, ignoring debt repayments and recovery of loan, minus revenue receipts and other non-debt receipts. In other words in GFO net leading is excluded.

### Net Fiscal Deficit

Net Fiscal Deficit (NFD) = (GFD) – NL (Net leading). It is gross fiscal deficit minus net leading (NL). Net leading is minus loans and advances to third parties plus recovery of outstanding loans and advance.

### Primary Deficit

Primary Deficit (PD) is measured as GFD minus interest payments. A better measure of PD is GFD less interest payments plus interest receipts.

Fiscal deficit is an indicator of the borrowings by the government. Overall fiscal deficit, including the revenue deficit, gross fiscal deficit, net gross fiscal deficit, net fiscal deficit as well as primary deficit have been increasing during the last decade pushing Bihar into the trap of increasing indebtedness (EPWRF, 2004). The following Table 1 presents the revenue deficits of Bihar Government along with Revenue Receipts (RR) and expenditure.

The Table 1 reveals that the expenditure of the government of Bihar has been continuously increasing during the last decade. The expenditure of the Bihar Government was Rs. 6569.6 crores accounting 19.5 percent of SGDP in 1992-93, which rose to Rs. 16128.3 crores (23.1 percent of the SGDP) in 1999-2000. It touched to the highest point of Rs. 13533.1 crores in 2002-03. There has been rising trend also in revenue receipts but its pace is slower than that of the expenditure. The result is increasing revenue deficit from Rs. 606.0 crores in 1992-93 to Rs. 1517.6 crores in 2002-03 budget estimate. To understand the problem more clearly let us see Gross Fiscal Deficit of Bihar.

It is clear from the table that the Gross Fiscal Deficit of Bihar increases from Rs. 1330.9 crores in 1992-93 to Rs. 3576.7 crores in 2002-03. We see in the Table 2 that the Revenue Receipts of the state are nearly constant fluctuating between

TABLE I

**Revenue Deficits of Bihar Government**

| *Year* | *Receipts* | | *Expenditure* | | *Deficit/Surplus* | |
|---|---|---|---|---|---|---|
| 2002-03BE | 12015.5 | (-) | 135331 | (-) | -1517.6 | (-) |
| 2001-02 RE | 10218.5 | (-) | 12560.4 | (-) | -2341.9 | (-) |
| 2000-01 | 11384.7 | (-) | 14345.4 | (-) | -2960.7 | (-) |
| 1999-00 | 12578.6 | (18.0) | 16128.3 | (23.1) | -3549.7 | (-5.1) |
| 1998-99 | 9272.1 | (14.1) | 10622.5 | (16.2) | -1350.5 | (-2.1) |
| 1997-98 | 8692.6 | (14.2) | 8956.5 | (14.6) | -263.9 | (-0.4) |
| 1996-97 | 8037.9 | (15.0) | 8253.9 | (15.4) | -216.0 | (-0.4) |
| 1995-96 | 7377.4 | (16.7) | 8456.2 | (19.1) | -1078.8 | (-2.4) |
| 1994-95 | 6797.8 | (15.4) | 7731.2 | (17.6) | -933.4 | (-2.1) |
| 1993-94 | 6629.1 | (17.0) | 7318.6 | (18.8) | -689.5 | (-1.8) |
| 1992-93 | 5963.6 | (17.7) | 6569.6 | (19.5) | -606.0 | (-1.8) |

*Notes*: (i) BE = Budget Estimates, (ii) RE = Revised Estimates
(iii) figures in brackets are percentage to state Gross Domestic Products. (-) = NA.

*Source*: *Economic and Political Weekly*, May 8, 2004.

15 and 18 percent of the SDGP, but the total expenditure of the State grows rapidly between 15 percent and more than 26 percent of SGDP. In absolute term the expenditure of the states has just doubled from Rs. 7294.5 Crores in 1992-93 to Rs. 15592.2 Crores in 2002-03. This gap between the aggregate expenditure and revenue receipts has compelled the state to adopt deficit financing. This widening Gross Fiscal Deficit is financed by Net Loans from Centre, net market, and borrowing and by other loans increasing the indebtedness of the state (Prasad, Goyal and Praksh 2004). Primary Deficit of Bihar has also been increasing in recent years. See the following Table 2.

Fiscal imbalances in the state of Bihar are structural. Expenditures have grown faster than revenues in recent years. Growth of revenues has been constant around 20 percent of the SGDP while aggregate expenditure has gone up to about 28 percent of the SGDP. Given the difference between levels of expenditure and revenues growth rate, differences are changed into revenue deficit. The question arises, what are the causes of declining revenues and

TABLE 2

**Gross Fiscal Deficit of Bihar Government**

*(In Rs. Crores)*

| *Year* | *Receipts* | | *Expenditure* | | *Deficit/Surplus* | |
|---|---|---|---|---|---|---|
| 2002-03BE | 12015.5 | (-) | 15592.2 | (-) | 3576.7 | (-) |
| 2001-02RE | 10218.5 | (-) | 14228.8 | (-) | 4010.3 | (-) |
| 2000-01 | 11384.7 | (-) | 16269.1 | (-) | 4884.4 | (-) |
| 1999-00 | 12578.6 | (18.0) | 18686.3 | (26.8) | 6107.7 | (8.8) |
| 1998-99 | 9272.1 | (14.1) | 11651.01 | (17.8) | 2378.9 | (3.6) |
| 1997-98 | 8692.6 | (14.2) | 9674.0 | (15.8) | 981.4 | (1.6) |
| 1996-97 | 8037.9 | (15.0) | 8928.5 | (16.6) | 890.6 | (1.7) |
| 1995-96 | 7377.4 | (16.7) | 8948.0 | (20.2) | 1570.6 | (3.6) |
| 1994-95 | 6797.8 | (15.4) | 8139.9 | (18.5) | 1342.1 | (3.0) |
| 1993-94 | 6629.1 | (17.0) | 7968.4 | (20.4) | 1339.3 | (3.4) |
| 1992-93 | 5963.6 | (17.7) | 7294.5 | (21.6) | 1330.9 | (3.9) |

*Notes*: Figures in brackets are percentage to state Gross Domestic Product at Factor Cost. (-) indicates N.A.

*Source*: EPW Research Foundation, *Economic and Political Weekly*, May 8, 2004.

TABLE 3

**Primary Deficit of Bihar**

*(in Rs. Crores)*

| *Year* | *Primary deficit* |
|---|---|
| 2000-01 | 2,510 |
| 1999-00 | 3,246 |
| 1998-99 | 507 |
| 1997-98 | -555 |
| 1996-97 | -526 |
| 1995-96 | -97 |

*Note*: This table too, shows the worsening deficit position of Bihar state.

*Source*: Articles on State Finance: Various Issues, Reserve Bank of India.

expanding expenditures of the state? Let us consider the declining trends of revenues and rising trends of expenditures one by one in brief.

Chart: Primary Deficit of Bihar (in Rs. Crores)

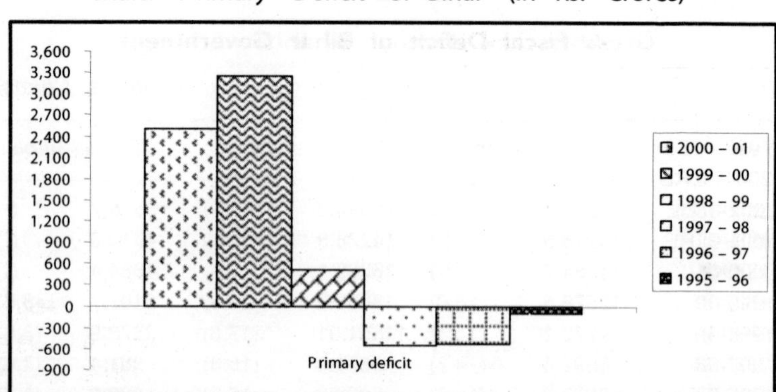


**Sources of Fiscal Imbalance in Bihar: Declining Revenues, Expanding Expenditures**

Declining Revenues of the State are the result of slow growth of Tax-Revenues and decreasing Non-tax Revenues. Bihar got only Rs. 575.7 Crores in 1995-96, 3.8 percent of the state gross Domestic Product, which rose to Rs. 2813.7 Crores, about 5.5 percent of the SGDP. So, the growth rate of Bihar's own tax revenue is very low. Let us see the slow growth of Bihar's own tax revenue in the table given on next page.

## Reasons for Slow Growth of Tax Revenues

Several studies show that the growths of each of the major states taxes have shown deceleration in recent years. This deceleration has been particularly marked in the case of taxes on land and agriculture, stamps and registration, state excises and sales taxes. The taxes on land and agriculture generate negligible amount in Bihar. Low-level of agricultural productivity caused by continual famine and flood in Bihar has lowered the collection of land tax. Due to poverty of the farmers government in Bihar as well as in other states has not been able to levy agricultural income tax.

There has been seen deceleration in the growth rate of sales taxes also in Bihar. The main reason for the declaration in the growth rate of sales taxes has to be found in the inability to extend the base to the service sector as well as in the corruption of the officer responsible for the collection of the sale-tax. The base of taxes in Bihar is rendered narrow

TABLE 4

**Own Tax Revenue of Bihar State**

| Year | Bihar State Own Tax Revenue (in Rs. Crores) | % |
|---|---|---|
| 2002-03BE | 2813.7 | - |
| 2001-02RE | 244.24 | - |
| 2000-01 | 2934.8 | - |
| 1999-00 | 3637.6 | (5.2) |
| 1998-99 | 2671.6 | (4.1) |
| 1997-98 | 2390.4 | (3.9) |
| 1996-97 | 2250.8 | (4.2) |
| 1995-96 | 1973.3 | (4.5) |
| 1994-95 | 1836.0 | (4.2) |
| 1993-94 | 1748.4 | (4.5) |
| 1992-93 | 1563.9 | (4.6) |
| 1991-92 | 1309.6 | (4.2) |
| 1990-91 | 1141.5 | (4.1) |
| 1989-90 | 924.8 | (3.9) |
| 1988-89 | 830.8 | (3.7) |
| 1987-88 | 760.7 | (4.1) |
| 1986-87 | 658.7 | (3.6) |
| 1985-86 | 575.5 | (3.8) |

*Notes*: (i) Figures before 2002 include those of Jharkhand also.
(iii) Figures in the brackets are percentages of State Gross Domestic Product at Factor cost current price.

*Source*: EPW Research Foundation, *Economic and Political Weekly*, May 8, 2004.

because of large-scale exemptions, evasions and avoidance of taxes. In the case of sales tax for example, besides wide ranging exemptions, there are generous schemes of incentives in terms of tax exemptions and deferment. The result is slow growth of tax-revenues.

In Bihar the major source of tax revenues is its share in central taxes. This can be seen in the following Table 5.

This Table 5 shows that the share of Bihar in Central taxes has been increasing day by day. So much so it has rose to the extent of more than 253 percents of its own tax revenues in 2002-03. Except Manipur, Mizoram, Meghalaya, Nagaland, Sikkim and Tripura (All Small States), not any Major state in India has got as much amount as Bihar has

TABLE 5

**Share of Bihar in Central Taxes**

| *Year* | *Share in Central Taxes* | *Percentage of State's own tax revenue* |
|---|---|---|
| 2002-03BE | 7139.9 | 253.8 |
| 2001-02 RE | 6158.0 | 252.5 |
| 2000-01 | 6574.0 | 224.0 |
| 1999-00 | 5099.0 | 140.2 |
| 1998-99 | 4441.2 | 166.2 |
| 1997-98 | 4074.4 | 170.4 |
| 1996-97 | 4078.2 | 181.2 |
| 1995-96 | 3485.5 | 176.6 |
| 1994-95 | 2788.1 | 151.9 |
| 1993-94 | 2496.5 | 142.8 |
| 1992-93 | 2288.0 | 146.3 |
| 1991-92 | 1916.2 | 146.3 |
| 1990-91 | 1615.9 | 141.6 |
| 1989-90 | 1544.2 | 167.0 |
| 1988-89 | 1195.8 | 143.0 |
| 1987-88 | 1010.7 | 132.9 |
| 1986-87 | 990.4 | 150.4 |
| 1985-86 | 855.2 | 148.6 |

*Sources*: (i) Economic and Political Weekly, Research Foundation, May 8, 2004.
(ii) Special Statistics-37.

shared in Central taxes. In spite of this the level of Tax Revenues in Bihar is very low.

**Declining Non-tax Revenues in Bihar**

The share of Non-tax Revenues of Bihar in its total revenues is very small. Not only that it has been continuously decreasing in recent years. This can be noted in the Table 6.

We see that the amount of Non-tax Revenue in Bihar was Rs. 977.7 Crores about 4.1 percent of the states. Gross Domestic Production in 1989-90, which decreased to Rs. 331.9 Crores in 2002-03. It is only about 2 percent of the SGDP. Inability to recover reasonable returns from the large investment made in state's undertakings has been a major

TABLE 6

**Bihar State's Own Non-tax Revenue**

| *Year* | *Non-tax Revenue of the State* | *%* |
|---|---|---|
| 2002-03BE | 331.9 | - |
| 2001-02RE | 360.9 | - |
| 2000-01 | 805.9 | - |
| 1999-00 | 1758.9 | (2.5) |
| 1998-99 | 1146.0 | (1.7) |
| 1997-98 | 389.9 | (0.6) |
| 1996-97 | 1061.3 | (2.0) |
| 1995-96 | 914.5 | (2.1) |
| 1994-95 | 974.8 | (2.2) |
| 1993-94 | 886.8 | (2.3) |
| 1992-93 | 777.7 | (2.3) |
| 1991-92 | 542.3 | (1.7) |
| 1990-91 | 765.2 | (2.7) |
| 1989-90 | 977.7 | (4.1) |

*Note*: Figures in brackets are percentage of Gross Domestic, Product of Bihar in respective years.

*Source*: Special Statistics-37, *EPW* Research Foundation, May 8, 2004..

cause of declining growth in non-tax revenues of Bihar. We may take the example of Bihar State Road Transport Corporation (BSRTC) and Bihar State Electricity Board. (BSEB). BSRTC has proved to be a white elephant of Bihar Government. Not to speak of BSEB. A major portion of total investment in the state level public enterprises invested in electricity utilities. The poor performance of Bihar State Electricity Board has been a major cause of drain in state's non-tax revenues. The cost of supply of electricity paise/ KWH was 318.5 in 2001 while average price per unit paise/ KWH was only 200.1, in 2001. So the rate of return on capital of the board was 47.9 percent causing huge commercial losses of Rs. 679.8 Crores. Bad infrastructure and bad governance also are responsible for declining Non-tax Revenues in Bihar.

**Expanding Expenditure**

We have seen that expanding expenditures of Bihar Government has been responsible for increasing deficit. Here we shall analyse this problem in some more details. The expenditure of a government is divided into two groups: namely, Developmental Expenditure and Non-developmental Expenditure. Developmental Expenditure itself is divided in to (i) Expenditures on Social and Community services which include education, art and culture, medical and public health and natural calamities like famine and flood, and (ii) Expenditure an Economic Services which include agriculture, industry, forest, soil conservation roads and bridges, dairy development, irrigation, etc.

Non-developmental expenditure covers debt servicing and interest payments, administrative services including police and pensions.

Studies have shown that despite attempts to contain the expenditures during the last decade, state's revenues, expenditure-GDP ratio has increased. A major proportion of increase in revenue expenditure is due to interest payment, pay and pension revision. In Bihar the main cause of increasing public expenditure is huge political expenditure on numerous ministers as well as misuse of developmental resources by M.L.A.s and Ministers. The following Table 7 shows the developmental expenditure of Bihar.

The Table 7 shows that the developmental expenditure of Bihar State has increased to Rs. 8582.6 Crores in 2002-03 from only Rs. 2115.9 Crores in 1985-86. But it is a matter of paradox that ironically the percentage of development expenditure has lowered to the level of only 52.4 percent of the total expenditure in 2002-03 from about 71 percent of the total expenditure in 1985-86. It is a bitter comment on the performance of Bihar Government Non-developmental expenditure of the Government is raising causing economic backwardness of the state. Let us see the Non-developmental expenditure of Bihar Government in Table 8.

The Table 8 reveals that the Non-developmental expenditure of Government of Bihar has been increasing. It has risen to 43 percent of the total state expenditure in 2002-03, while it was only 20.5 percent of the state total expenditure in 1986-86. This growing trend of non-developmental expenditure is detrimental to economic development of the state causing the problems of poverty and unemployment.

TABLE 7

**Development Expenditure of Bihar State**

*(in Rs. Crores)*

| *Year* | *Developmental Expenditure* | *Percentage of State's total Expenditure* |
|---|---|---|
| 2002-03BE | 8582.6 | 52.4 |
| 2001-02RE | 7898.8 | 53.1 |
| 2000-01 | 10089.3 | 59.5 |
| 1999-00 | 12052.4 | 61.7 |
| 1998-99 | 7037.5 | 57.8 |
| 1997-98 | 5874.4 | 57.8 |
| 1996-97 | 5463.4 | 58.1 |
| 1995-96 | 5514.4 | 58.6 |
| 1994-95 | 5075.9 | 59.3 |
| 1993-94 | 5267.4 | 62.5 |
| 1992-93 | 4893.7 | 63.2 |
| 1991-92 | 4390.5 | 64.5 |
| 1990-91 | 4173.2 | 67.1 |
| 1989-90 | 3439.0 | 65.6 |
| 1988-89 | 2957.3 | 66.3 |
| 1987-88 | 2700.9 | 69.0 |
| 1986-87 | 2381.6 | 70.9 |
| 1985-86 | 2115.9 | 70.8 |

*Notes*: (i) Development Expenditure here includes expenditure on revenue and capital account of Bihar State.

(ii) Data of Jharkhand are included in the data of Bihar before 2000.

*Source*: Compiled from Special Statistics, *EPW*, May 8, 2004.

**Increasing Indebtedness of Bihar**

The public debt of a state comprises market borrowings, loans from bank and other financial institutions, special securities issued to the National Small Saving Fund (NSSF), loans from the Centre and small savings and provident funds, etc. (Prasad, Goyal and Prakash, 2004). The debt/GSDP rations of all states of India have increased during the last decade. Let us see the following Table 9 to understand this problem of all states in general and that of Bihar in particular.

TABLE 8

**Non-development Expenditure of Bihar State**

*(in Rs. Crores)*

| *Year* | *Non-developmental Expenditure* | *Percentage of State's Total Expenditure* |
|---|---|---|
| 2002-03BE | 7042.4 | 43.0 |
| 2001-02RE | 6366.1 | 42.8 |
| 2000-01 | 6244.1 | 36.8 |
| 1999-00 | 6875.6 | 35.2 |
| 1998-99 | 4624.1 | 38.0 |
| 1997-98 | 3812.2 | 37.3 |
| 1996-97 | 3468.4 | 38.8 |
| 1995-96 | 3440.2 | 36.5 |
| 1994-95 | 3106.0 | 36.3 |
| 1993-94 | 2730.8 | 32.4 |
| 1992-93 | 2426.5 | 31.3 |
| 1991-92 | 2094.0 | 30.8 |
| 1990-91 | 1772.0 | 28.5 |
| 1989-90 | 1486.5 | 28.3 |
| 1988-89 | 1075.5 | 24.1 |
| 1987-88 | 955.5 | 24.4 |
| 1986-87 | 728.7 | 21.7 |
| 1985-86 | 611.2 | 20.5 |

*Sources*: (i) Compiled from Special Statistics, *EPW*, May 8, 2004
(ii) *The Economic Times*, Kolkata, July 26, 2004.

The Table 9 shows that Debt/GSDP ratios are the highest in Bihar about 68 percent in 1995-96 and 73.1 percent in 2000-01.

**Central Loan to Bihar**

It is clear from the study that total debt of the government of Bihar has also increased in recent years. The result of this growing debt is that Bihar has to spend much on interest payment every year.

Table 10 marks the recent central loan position of Government of Bihar quite clear. In 1991 the total central loan of Government of Bihar was Rs. 5792.35 Crores which increased to Rs. 15,691.20 Crores by 2006. Thus the Central loan almost tripled in between 1991 to 2006.

TABLE 9

**Debt GSDP Ratios of Some Major States of India**

*(Percent)*

| States | Years | | | |
|---|---|---|---|---|
| | *1995-96* | *1998-99* | *1999-00* | *2000-01* |
| Andhra Pradesh | 19.0 | 20.8 | 23.5 | 25.9 |
| Arunachal Pradesh | 53.5 | 56.7 | 56.7 | 54.6 |
| Assam | 28.1 | 26.7 | 29.3 | 33.2 |
| Bihar | 67.7 | 59.7 | 66.9 | 73.1 |
| Goa | 35.2 | 27.7 | 28.5 | 32.7 |
| Gujarat | 15.5 | 17.8 | 21.6 | 26.6 |
| Haryana | 19.4 | 21.8 | 23.9 | 24.5 |
| Himachal Pradesh | 45.4 | 53.4 | 54.0 | 60.8 |
| Jammu and Kashmir | 56.5 | 50.4 | 55.5 | 61.5 |
| Karnataka | 17.6 | 17.6 | 19.5 | 21.0 |
| Kerala | 26.1 | 27.9 | 32.3 | 34.6 |
| Madhya Pradesh | 26.7 | 28.0 | 30.4 | 36.2 |
| Maharashtra | 11.6 | 14.6 | 15.9 | 17.3 |
| Manipur | 34.9 | 44.0 | 44.6 | 51.2 |
| Meghalaya | 21.7 | 24.2 | 26.5 | 28.9 |
| Orissa | 35.3 | 44.2 | 50.5 | 60.5 |
| Punjab | 35.5 | 37.4 | 37.9 | 40.7 |
| Rajasthan | 25.8 | 28.9 | 33.3 | 40.1 |
| Tamilnadu | 16.0 | 16.4 | 18.7 | 20.9 |
| Uttar Pradesh | 28.2 | 31.5 | 35.2 | 36.7 |
| West Bengal | 20.8 | 24.8 | 28.9 | 33.7 |
| Total | 17.9 | 19.6 | 21.7 | 23.7 |

*Note*: Figures of Bihar, Madhya Pradesh and Uttar Pradesh include those of newly created states, viz. Jharkhand, Chhattisgarh and Uttaranchal respectively.

*Source*: R.B.I., Report on Currency and Finance, Volume II and State Finances, Various Issues.

Table 11 below presents a picture of outstanding debt of Government of Bihar from 1993-94 to 2003. Table 11 shows that outstanding debt of the government of Bihar has although rising very rapidly. In 1993-94 the debt was 32.43 percent only, which increased very rapidly by the end of 2003 the debt, was 55.33 percent. This was stupendous increase in

TABLE 10

**Central Loan to Bihar**

*(Rs. in Crores)*

| *Year* | *Loans* |
|---|---|
| 1991 | 5,792.35 |
| 1992 | 6401.30 |
| 1993 | 6858.82 |
| 1994 | 7368.00 |
| 1995 | 7957.25 |
| 1996 | 8772.32 |
| 1997 | 9739.72 |
| 1998 | 11,061.48 |
| 1999 | 13,374.90 |
| 2000 | 15862.02 |
| 2001 | 13009.59 |
| 2002 | 13,759.73 |
| 2003 | 14,217.66 |
| 2004 | 15,091.78 |
| 2005 (RE) | 16263.60 |
| 2006 (BE) | 15691.20 |

*Source*: State Finances: A Study of Budgets of 2005, R.B.I., Mumbai.

**Chart: Central Loan to Bihar (Rs. in Crores)**

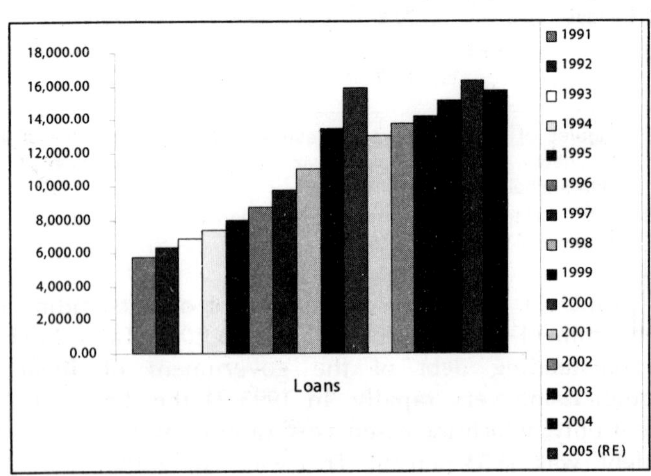

outstanding debt of the Government of Bihar. But, in 2009-10 the outstanding debt in Bihar was 49.4 percent only, which decreased by the end of 2014-15, the debt was only 41.6 percent. It is feature projections of standing debt of Bihar (13th Finance Commission).

TABLE 11

**Outstanding Debt of Bihar as a Percentage of GSDP as on 31st March**

| *Year* | *Loans* |
|---|---|
| 1993-94 | 32.43 |
| 1994-95 | 32.12 |
| 1995-96 | 34.85 |
| 1996-97 | 33.46 |
| 1997-98 | 33.62 |
| 1998-99 | 33.16 |
| 1999-2000 | 35.46 |
| 2000-2001 | 44.83 |
| 2001-2002 | 53.32 |
| 2002-2003 | 55.33 |
| 2009-10 | 49.4 |
| 2010-11 | 48.2 |
| 2011-12 | 46.4 |
| 2012-13 | 44.6 |
| 2013-14 | 43.0 |
| 2014-15 | 41.6 |

*Source*: Twelfth Finance Commission Report, 2004, Govt. of India, New Delhi.
Thirteenth Finance Commission Report (2010-15).

**Outstanding Liabilities**

The Government of India is liable to repay its outstanding liabilities against the various small serving schemes, Public Provident Fund, State Provident Fund, Non-Government Provident Fund and other reserve Funds of Government departments like post and telegraph, railways and certain other deposits like income-tax deposits, super tax deposits of local funds and civil deposits. These are known as outstanding liabilities of Government of India. These were

**Chart: Outstanding Debt of Bihar as a Percentage of GSDP as on 31st March**

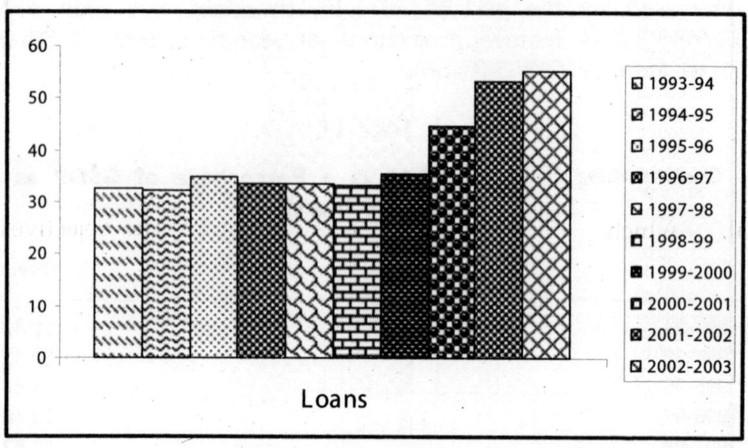


TABLE 12

**Total Outstanding Liabilities of Bihar State**

| *Year* | *Loans* |
|---|---|
| 1991 | 10,581.65 |
| 1992 | 11,720.79 |
| 1993 | 13,484.71 |
| 1994 | 14,686.81 |
| 1995 | 16,637.34 |
| 1996 | 18,631.48 |
| 1997 | 20,689.97 |
| 1998 | 23,521.89 |
| 1999 | 27,152.59 |
| 2000 | 32,971.88 |
| 2001 | 30,033.71 |
| 2002 | 34,226.69 |
| 2003 | 38.345.62 |
| 2004 | 43,154.74 |
| 2005 (RE) | 48,539.27 |
| 2006(BE) | 53,087.81 |

*Source*: State Finances: A Study of Budgets of 2005-06, R.B.I., Mumbai.

**Chart: Total Outstanding Liabilities of Bihar State**

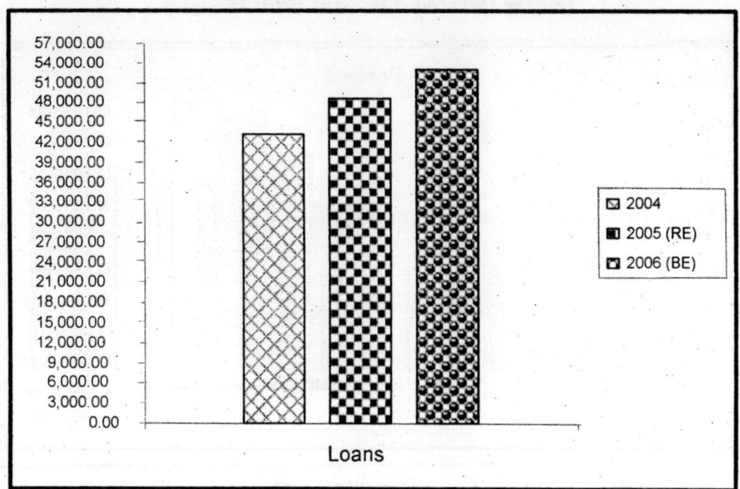


TABLE 13

**Total Outstanding Liabilities Percentage of GSDP (Bihar State) (As on End March)**

| *Year* | *Percent* |
|---|---|
| 1991 | 37.9 |
| 1992 | 37.6 |
| 1993 | 40.6 |
| 1994 | 37.7 |
| 1995 | 37.8 |
| 1996 | 42.1 |
| 1997 | 38.5 |
| 1998 | 38.3 |
| 1999 | 39.0 |
| 2000 | 45.3 |
| 2001 | 64.0 |
| 2002 | 72.6 |
| 2003 | 70.9 |
| 2004 | 76.5 |
| 2005 (RE) | 77.3 |
| 2006(BE) | 66.2 |

*Source*: State Finances: A Study of Budgets of 2005-06, R.B.I., Mumbai.

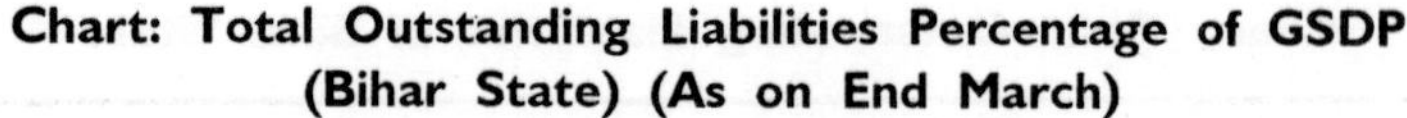

**Chart: Total Outstanding Liabilities Percentage of GSDP (Bihar State) (As on End March)**

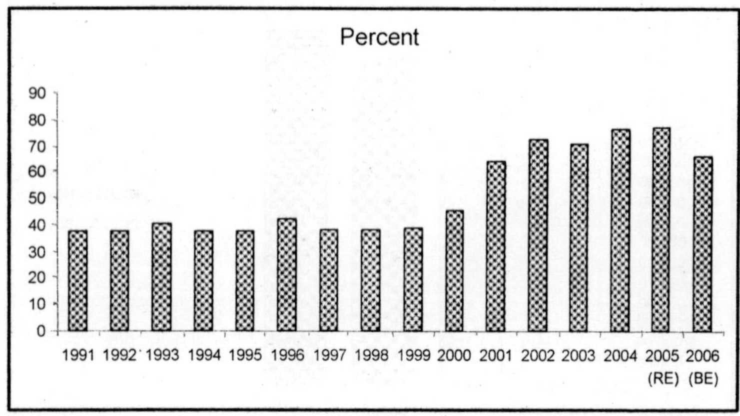


earlier termed as unfounded debt. The overall outstanding liabilities of the Government of Bihar have been given in the Table 12. The total outstanding liabilities was Rs. 10,581.65 Crores in 1991 which rose to Rs. 53,087.87 Crores in 2005-06. See Table 12.

Above Table 13 has reveled the percentage outstanding liability of Bihar Government. The outstanding liability of Bihar has increased from 37.9 percent in 1991 to 66.2 percent in 2005-06. Situation of Bihar, in the context of outstanding liabilities is increasing from year to year. The composition of outstanding liabilities is evident from the Table 14. It is clear from this table that the share of market loans was 1,487,27 Crores at the end of 1991 which rose to 10,462.99 Crores at the end of 2005-06. In assessing the overall loan position of Bihar, the previous Finance Commissions followed the practice of excluding their short-term component of loans. In keeping with this practice and for purposes of comparison, the profile of estimated loan of Bihar Government is shown in this study. We know that central loans still continue to be the single component of the total debt of Bihar.

### Interest Payment of Government of Bihar

Let the interest rate policy of the State be analysed from the point of view its effects on the government

TABLE 14

**Composition of Outstanding Liabilities to State of Bihar (Rs. Crores)**

| Year | Total Internal Debt | Market Loans | NSSF | WWA from RB9 | Loans from Banks and F9s | Loans from LIC | Loans from GIC | Loans from NABARD | Loans from SB9 and other Banks | Loans from NCDC |
|---|---|---|---|---|---|---|---|---|---|---|
| *1* | *2 = sum (3-6) + 4* | *3* | *4* | *5* | *6=sum (7-13)* | *7* | *8* | *9* | *10* | *11* |
| 1991 | 1603.57 | 1487.27 | - | 53.20 | 63.10 | 21.81 | 9.36 | 0.43 | 0.09 | 17.61 |
| 1992 | 1969.16 | 1826.26 | - | 32.29 | 60.61 | 21.70 | 9.36 | - | 0.09 | 16.12 |
| 1993 | 2,259.63 | 2262.51 | - | - | -2.88 | 21.52 | 9.21 | - | 0.01 | 14.27 |
| 1994 | 2626.35 | 2647.67 | - | - | -21.32 | 21.31 | 8.58 | -4.70 | -16.68 | 18.85 |
| 1995 | 3041.66 | 3086.93 | - | - | -45.27 | 21.03 | 8.21 | -9.33 | -35.88 | 20.69 |
| 1996 | 3444.66 | 3595.01 | - | - | -150.35 | 19.15 | 8.21 | -55.47 | -35.88 | 22.37 |
| 1997 | 4012.00 | 41453.51 | - | - | -141.93 | 19.1 | - | -101.13 | -35.88 | 20.33 |
| 1998 | 4671.21 | 4793.14 | - | - | -121.92 | 15.93 | - | -101.13 | -16.68 | -29.21 |
| 1999 | 5459.08 | 5522.36 | - | 52.72 | -116.00 | 17.79 | - | -105.62 | 2.52 | -31.75 |
| 2000 | 7681.52 | 5693.05 | 1700.00 | 52.72 | 195.27 | 17.65 | - | 113.85 | 22.52 | -31.74 |
| 2001 | 8695.75 | 4937.23 | 3170.07 | 39.39 | 506.97 | 13.04 | - | 414.69 | 36.83 | -1.96 |
| 2002 | 11152.59 | 5932.23 | 4610.07 | 39.39 | 527.52 | 12.93 | - | 446.69 | 36.83 | -1083 |
| 2003 | 14624.59 | 7086.23 | 6607.57 | 59.39 | 848.76 | 12.83 | - | 768.03 | 36.83 | -1083 |
| 2004 | 18565.58 | 8803.23 | 8476.78 | 39.39 | 1204.1 | 12.72 | - | 1101.52 | 36.70 | 1.37 |
| 2005 | 22818.29 | 10462.99 | 6397.10 | 1960.61 | 787714 | 12.61 | - | 1088.74 | 36.70 | -4.88 |
| 2006 | 28341.00 | 28341.00 | 11159.05 | 6235.79 | 3960.61 | 14866.21 | 1250 | - | 1075.55 | 36.70 |

*(Contd.)*

TABLE 14 *(Contd.)*

| *Year* | *Loans from other Institutions* | *Other Loans* | *Competition and other Bands* | *Loans and Awareness from Center* | *Provident Funds, etc.* | *Reserve Finance* | *Deposits and Advance* | *Contingency* | *Out-standing Liabilities* |
|---|---|---|---|---|---|---|---|---|---|
| *1* | *12* | *13* | *14* | *15* | *16* | *17* | *18* | *19* | *20=2+sum (15-19)* |
| 1991 | 13.54 | 0.27 | 51.58 | 5,792.35 | 1959.58 | 0.16 | 1,036.34 | 189.64 | 10,581.65 |
| 1992 | 13.08 | 0.27 | 56.70 | 6401.30 | 2313.59 | 0.16 | 898.35 | 138.23 | 11,720.79 |
| 1993 | -48.15 | 0.27 | 0.27 | 6858.82 | 2795.99 | -28.31 | 1540.62 | 57.96 | 13484.71 |
| 1994 | -48.95 | 0.27 | 66.53 | 7368.00 | 3263.85 | 16.97 | 1452.23 | -40-59 | 14,686.81 |
| 1995 | -50.23 | 0.27 | 65.11 | 7957.25 | 3856.55 | 17.59 | 1662.45 | 101.84 | 16,637.34 |
| 1996 | -109.00 | 0.27 | 64.06 | 8772.32 | 4615.14 | 13.04 | 1,609.46 | 176.86 | 18,631.48 |
| 1997 | - | -44.24 | 64.00 | 9739.72 | 5321.44 | 14.42 | 1,461.78 | 140.61 | 20,689.97 |
| 1998 | - | 7.17 | 62.51 | 11061.48 | 5909.40 | 14.92 | 1517.49 | 347.40 | 23521.89 |
| 1999 | - | 1.6 | 62.38 | 13374.90 | 6374.34 | 16.82 | 1580.06 | 347.40 | 2752.59 |
| 2000 | - | 52.95 | 61.76 | 15862.02 | 7310.57 | 25.57 | 1742.21 | 350.00 | 32971.88 |
| 2001 | - | 42.44 | 60.49 | 13009.59 | 6655.73 | -46.45 | 1457.61 | 261.49 | 30,033.71 |
| 2002 | - | 41.90 | 44.12 | 13759.73 | 7501.73 | -46.45 | 1597.61 | 261.49 | 34226.69 |
| 2003 | - | 41.90 | 43.38 | 1421.66 | 7694.73 | -46.45 | 1593.61 | 261.49 | 38,345.62 |
| 2004 | - | 51.30 | 42.64 | 15091.78 | 7435.09 | -46.45 | 1847.26 | 261.49 | 43154.74 |
| 2005 | - | 6743.97 | 42.17 | 16263.60 | 7425.45 | -46.45 | 1816.90 | 261.49 | 48,539.27 |
| 2006 | 12.55 | - | 41.671 | 1569.20 | 7358.58 | 46.45 | 1481.99 | 261.49 | 53087.81 |

Funds and deposits.

*Source*: State Finance Accounts and Central Statistical Organistion. Government of India.

borrowing programmes. The Table 15 gives the picture of the interest payments of the public debt of government of Bihar. That the rate of interest maintained raising trend throughout the period. The rising trend of the rate of interest is justified in view of the inflationary trend in the economy and for encouraging saving of the people. The rising trend is also justified in view of the rise in the bank rate, which started to rise in 1951 in pursuance of a dear money policy. Table 16 shows the repayment liabilities of the Bihar State Government.

TABLE 15

**Interest Payments of Government of Bihar**

*(in Crores)*

| *Year* | *Gross Interest* | *Net Interest* |
|---|---|---|
| 1992-93 | 1240.6 | 1233.4 |
| 1993-94 | 1350.9 | 1318.3 |
| 1994-95 | 1561.1 | 1532.2 |
| 1995-96 | 1667.6 | 1647.5 |
| 1996-97 | 1417.1 | 1360.6 |
| 1997-98 | 1536.0 | 1448.2 |
| 1998-99 | 1872.3 | 1736.3 |
| 1999-00 | 2861.4 | 2532.8 |
| 2000-01 | 2374.1 | 2241.3 |
| 2001-02 (RE) | 2752.3 | 2663.2 |
| 2002-03 (BE) | 2863.9 | 2834.9 |

*Source*: *EPW*, 8th May, 2004.

TABLE 16

**Repayment Liabilities**

| | *2004-05* | *2005-06* | *2006-07* | *2007-08* | *2008-09* | *2009-10* |
|---|---|---|---|---|---|---|
| Discharge of internal debt | 365 | 493 | 708 | 1203 | 1254 | 1414 |
| Repayment of loans to centre | 2723 | 488 | 317 | 429 | 429 | 471 |
| Discharge of other liabilities | 795 | 723 | 617 | 815 | 1009 | 872 |
| Total repayment | 3882 | 1703 | 1642 | 2447 | 2692 | 2757 |
| Total interest payment | 3474 | 3649 | 3416 | 3707 | 3753 | 4171 |
| Total debt service burden | 7356 | 5352 | 5058 | 6154 | 6445 | 6928 |

*Source*: Department of Finance, GoB.

Although the government took loans from the market at increasing rate of interest, but the rate cannot be considered to be adequate in view of the inflationary situation in the economy and the peculiar problems of an under-developed state. It has been pointed out above that the government-borrowing rate should be increased to make investment in government securities more attractive and profitable. If the rate is not increased, the public savings will continue to be invested in the purchase of land, ornaments and construction of buildings. If they yields from government securities are comparatively low, the savings of the people will continue to flow into other lines of investment, which offer higher return. If the genuine savings of the people are not attached, the government will have to depend under compulsion, more on the Reserve Bank of India and other banks for loans, which will further aggravate the problem of inflationary rise in prices and monetary instability.

Thus there is a strong case for increasing the rate of interest on public borrowing. The case of central loans to the states stands on a different footing. Bihar is heavily indebted to the centre because nearly 90% of the outstanding debt of the state comprises the central loans. This has led to the centralization of the debt and it has made debt-management easier for the state, no doubt, but it has created a disquieting situation. As has been brought out previously in this chapter that right from 1967-68 the state has been paying to the centre in the form of principal and interest substantially more than what it has been receiving in the form of central plan assistance. Thus a substantial sum of money has flown from the state to the centre since the beginning of the Fourth Plan Period. This queer situation has developed because of the policy and pattern adopted by the centre for extending financial assistance to state. Apart from the fact during successive plan periods, nearly 70% of the central assistance has been given in the shape of loan, even assistance given for undertaking measures for relief in years of natural calamities has had a substantial loan component. Something has to be done to life the state out of the morass. Here it is sufficient to say something about the rate of the interest charged by the centre. The rate charged by the Government of India is according to the Second Finance Commission 1957, exorbitant. In their opinion the Government of India should not deal with the States as if it were a commercial banker. "The Union and the States are partners in big enterprise of national development."

There is no justification for charging the states more than the cost of borrowing. The Central Government takes recourse to deficit financing also and the loans given out of it costs them nothing. The Third Finance Commission, 1961, also observed that the position is far from satisfactory and requires analysis and review. There is scope for reduction in the rate of interest charged by the Government of India. The grant component of the central assistance should also be increased at least the assistance given for unproductive expenditure should be in the nature of grant.

No doubt, the rising central loans have certainly contributed to the increase in the State income because the volume of investment in the Five Year Plans would not have been what it is without central loans. Therefore, at least the part of rise in states' income may be attributed to the rise in central loans which provided funds for public investment under the plans. Tax revenue is mostly utilized for the normal expenditure of the Government and therefore, for financing economic development of the state, there is heavy reliance on finances borrowed from the centre.

The assets of poor state like Bihar have exceeded the liabilities but a very important proportion of the assets is in the form of loans advanced to the Bihar State Electricity Board, Co-operatives Institutions, Local Bodies, Social Security Schemes, Natural Calamities, Bihar State Housing Board, Bihar State Road Transport Corporation, etc. They are yielding either no returns or inadequate returns. The utilization part is certainly more significant because it is neither the volume of the central loans nor the magnitude of debt servicing charges that determines the burden. If the Central loans and the debt servicing charges are increasing rapidly and simultaneously the assets are also increasing in the economy, the impact of the loans. But unfortunately, as discussed above, the State Government is not utilizing central loans properly. So, what is important is not the magnitude of the loans in relation with their effects on the productive capacity of the State is not favourable. Ordinarily third parties should have enabled the State to repay its loans easily but all the capital outlay does not go to commercially viable investments. The State provides major portion of infrastructural facilities for social and economic development. The developmental outlay on this account is not income yielding. Unfortunately, even those projects, which are expected to be income yielding are showing either no return or insufficient returns.

A part from the swelling volume of union loans, a serious financial problem, which has been causing constant worry emanates from the increasing debt servicing liability. The problem, however, was not so acute during the first three plan periods, but from 1967-68, the trend was reversed and almost during the whole Fourth Plan Period, the total repayment liability (including interest) exceeded the total plan assistance.

The result has been that the financial equilibrium of a backward state like Bihar with a weak resource base has remained continuously upset due to heavy repayment liability resulting in frequent overdrafts on the Reserve Bank. In fact, resources were following out to the centre from the state instead of the flow in reverse direction, are a disquieting phenomenon which is impoverishing this backward State and is undermining its capability for investment to boost up its own economy. Each year larger proportion of central assistance is eaten up by the liability of debt and interest repayment. The size of the plan assistance is, therefore, becoming illusory.

The net central assistance for the plan has been dwindling. It is no surprise that the State had to end up with a negative closing balance.

Consequently, the financial position of the State is completely upset. The present pattern of plan assistance is mainly responsible for this state of affairs.

According to the prevailing practice, the central assistance is composed of 70 percent loans and 30 percent grants so that major portion of the state's debt consist of plan loans from the centre. The present arrangement of providing central assistance loses sight of the capacity of the borrower to repay, which in other words, refers to the overall financial working the viability of the scheme for which the loans are utilized. It is not unknown that the bulk of the plan-outlay has been spent on Roads, Health and Education, Water supply, Power generation and transmission and such infrastructures, which do not create new resources to enable the state to discharge repayment obligations of the loan components of the plan assistance. Moreover, the scheme of central assistance tends to accord equal treatment to unequal states as regards the loans and grant components of the assistance so that it results in placing unequal burdens on the state related to their capacity of repayment. Consequently, the backward state unlike the developed states are not in a position to fruitfully utilize the loan portion of assistance for further economic development and instead, are forced to deploy the amount on making the critical minimum efforts for creation of take-off conditions. Thus, the scheme of assistance fails to serve the objectives of rapid economic development, balanced regional growth and raising the effort to equalization of living standards of the people and in effect result in perpetuating the widening gap between the developed states and the states, which have lagged behind the more fortunate states in the matter of development.

There is yet another way in which the larger component of loans in central assistance has accentuated the financial imbalance of less developed states like Bihar. For one thing as shown earlier in this chapter, because of larger outflow from the State budget to the central budget on account of repayment of loan and interest there on, the net inflow of central assistance has shown a declining trend in the last few years. For example, a fixed ratio for all states respective of their financial strength cost unequal burden on the poorer states and worsen their position of overall deficit, hence, the Finance Commission will have to give a serious thought in the implications, as analyzed above, of all the policy behind union loans and the scheme of treating a major part of central assistance to the States as loan and give a new re-orientation to the policies in this regard so as to provide for adequate relief to the states against the damage caused to the interest of the states by the policy followed so far.

We have discussed the impact of central loans to the states from different points of views. We have examined the financial and economic impact of loans, the economic effects and the substitution effect of the financial impact and the distribution and economic development impact also. In course of the discussion, it has been seen that the pattern of plan assistance has led to a reverse flow of resource from the States to the Centre, leaving insignificant resource from the State, thus undermining its capability for investment to boost up its economy. The present arrangement for providing plan assistance has made the size of the plan assistance illusory because the net central assistance for the plan remains very small.

The problem of central loans to the state has given rise to one more serious situation. It has given rise to a sort of financial imperialism of Central Government. The State Government has lost its autonomy. The state is completely dependent upon the centre. The provisions of the constitution are such that the State cannot borrow from the open market unless it is free from central loans. The State can never be free from central loans. Therefore, it cannot be free to borrow from the market independently. The state will remain the beggar at the door of the centre. The development policy and the plan assistance have been devised in such a way that the State is and will remain indebted to the centre. Thus, it can be concluded that increasing volume of union loans has eroded the financial autonomy of the state. The process has now reached a stage when it threatens to reduce the State to the status of a subordinate department of the centre under the aegis of the Central Home Ministry. It is partly due to the constitutional provisions and pattern of plan assistance from the centre. The State Government is not less responsible in this connection. There are huge lack of financial discipline on part of the State have also resulted its financial position weak. Consequently, the alarm bell for debt-trap and its ominous consequences have started ringing, more to the discomfiture of the common man than the Government. It is the people of Bihar, not the Governments who have virtually trapped.

**Debt Management**

Management of large government borrowing programme in a manner supporting the expansionary counter-cyclical fiscal policy stance of the Government without creating any disruptive pressures on the government securities market was a key challenge for the Reserve Bank in 2008-09. To deal with the growth dampening moderation in private consumption and investment demand, some deviation from the fiscal consolidation path and introduction of adequate fiscal stimulus became essential, which concomitantly escalated the size of the borrowing programme significantly. In 2008-09, larger recourse to market borrowing and flight to safety were the common trends across countries around the world; while the cost of borrowings declined in general, reflecting the low policy interest rates and quantitative easing stance of the central banks, significant increase in risk aversion and resultant preference for government securities led to a larger demand for these securities.

Recognising the challenge, the Reserve Bank had to continuously review and adapt its debt management strategy, in consultation with the Central Government, in response to the evolving economic conditions, while striving to ensure that the sharp and abrupt increase in the Government's market borrowing programme was conducted in a non-disruptive manner, without any conflict with its monetary management function. Higher government borrowings could potentially raise the interest rates in the system by pushing up yields on government securities, which entail the risk of conflicting with the low interest rate stance that may be pursued by the monetary authority in the face of an economic slowdown. During the second half of 2008-09, the Reserve Bank's policy stance aimed at increasing bank credit to the commercial sector at lower cost, reflecting the trends in policy rates to support the revival of economic growth; this objective had to be attained while managing a large Government borrowing programme. The Reserve Bank, therefore, employed a combination of measures involving easing of monetary conditions and use of innovative tools for debt management such as synchronising the Market Stabilisation

Scheme (MSS) buyback auctions and open market purchases with Government's normal market borrowings and de-sequestering of MSS balances. The release of liquidity to the financial system by the Reserve Bank was timed appropriately to coincide with the auctions of government securities, ensuring the smooth conduct of the large market borrowing programme of the Government.

The debt management operations of the Reserve Bank during 2008-09 are presented in this chapter in the context of specific policy issues. The fiscal year 2008-09 saw a sharp increase in the market borrowings of Central and State Governments on account of the fiscal stimulus measures undertaken by the Governments in the wake of the global economic slowdown and other additional expenditures such as the Agricultural Debt Waiver and Debt Relief Scheme, various rural development schemes and the revision in Central Government pay scales following the recommendations of the Sixth Pay Commission.

Despite the sharp increase in the quantum of market borrowings, the debt management strategy continued to be guided by the prime objectives of minimization of cost over time and determination of maturity profiles consistent with rollover risk. In the first half of the year, the debt management operations were undertaken in an environment of pre-emptive monetary tightening measures that aimed at containing the inflationary impulses in the economy. During the second half, however, while the monetary conditions eased significantly, in response to the softening of inflationary pressures coupled with economic slowdown, the frequency and amount of issuance by the Central and State Governments increased significantly.

The gross market borrowing programme of the Central Government (dated securities and 364-day Treasury Bills) was about 181 per cent of the budget estimate for 2008-09 and the net borrowing, about 210 per cent of the budget estimates. During the first half of the year, the auctions for dated securities were broadly in accordance with the relevant issuance calendar. For the second half, though, three additional calendars were issued in supersession of the scheduled issuance calendar, which became necessary to meet the additional expenditure approved under supplementary demands for grants. The weighted average cost of market borrowings moved upwards up to August 2008 but decelerated subsequently, up to January 2009, largely reflecting the pattern in monetary policy rates. Due to higher than expected borrowing programme by both the Central and the State Governments, however, the weighted average cost of borrowings moderately increased thereafter. For the year as a whole, the weighted average yield was lower than in 2007-08.

Public debt management has been recognized as an important instrument of state policy and an essential complement to the monetary policy of the central bank in all the countries developed, developing and under developed as well. But the objectives and nature of debt-management policy differ according to the nature of the economies. The techniques of borrowing adopted in different under-developed countries have not been uniform. This is because of the differences in the development of money and capital markets in the various under-developed countries and the structure of their economic and financial organizations.

The policy of the management of public debt is a great weapon in the hands of the government. It "involves control by the fiscal and monetary authorities of the size and composition of the debt (volume of different types of debt), distribution of ownership of debt between the banks, non-banks institutions and individuals, maturity pattern of the debt and the level and structure of interest rates and retirement of debt". "Thus in every borrowing government must face the same set of questions: first, how to borrow the money from whom, for how long, and at what interest rate and second, what effects each borrowing choice will have upon the economy as a whole and upon particular section within it". C.C. Abbott has expressed similar ideas about the meaning of the public debt management. He defines it as "the choice of debt forms and the proportionate amounts of the different types used, the selection of the pattern of debt maturities, the amount obligations, the refunding terms offered, the treatment given to different classes of debt and different types of bond holders, determination of the provisions attached to new bond issues, adaptation of new issues to the needs of the prospective holders, policies pursued in the retirement or creation of new debt and the relative weights given to all these matters in the government's general fiscal policy". Thus the public Debt Management policy is wide term, which includes every aspect of the public debt problem.

**Objectives of Debt Management**

The objectives of the management of the public debt in any country are three-fold. In the first place, it must subserve the economic policy of the government. For example, it should help to raise the purchasing power and demand in the economy during a period of depression and to reduce it during the period of inflation, or, again, it should provide adequate funds for the needs of the government as for example, for war finance or economic development. In the second place, the borrowings must be undertaken in such a way as to be most advantageous to the government. This is largely a matter of timing, placing and rates of interest, etc. Borrowing should be undertaken at such times and in such a way that the cost is the least; conversion, refunding and repayment should be undertaken from this point of view. In the third place, government borrowing should be undertaken in such a way as to have no adverse effects on the money market. It should, on the other hand, be managed in such a way as to strengthen the money market.

The objectives and techniques of the public debt management depend on the nature of the economic system and the level of the economic development. The manager of the public debt is confronted with some peculiar problems in a backward state like ours, which has further adopted a policy of planned development. These problems arise because of the less developed and unorganized money market of the State. Though there are well developed banking institutions in the state, they operate in a limited sphere of the economy and they have very negligible relation with non-organized indigenous banking sector. Consequently. The interest rates structure is not scientifically integrated. There is no uniformity in the rates of interest. Different rates prevail in the different money markets and different sectors of the same market. As a result of these, the debt policies have a limited role to play, firstly, in relation to the overall trends in supply, demand and the flow of funds on the market and secondly, with respect to the working of the various institutions on the market. Planning has also created some problems of the debt management policy. It has led to the astronomical growth of the public debt and so it becomes necessary for the debt management policy to guard against the inflationary rise in prices. But in the developed country, the objective of debt-management is quite different. There it aims at minimizing the debt-burden. This is possible with the help of a low rate of interest policy, which besides making the debt burden minimum facilitates the attraction of sufficient funds into government bonds to maintain level of employment and economic stability. Here it would not be out of place to quote R.N. Tripathy when he says that "in advance countries the objective of debt-management have been the maintenance of a suitable structure of interest rates, the minimization of the cost of servicing the national debt, the attraction of sufficient funds into government bonds, the maintenance of effective demand in the economy consistent with a high level of employment and a reasonable condition of monetary stability".

## CENTRAL GOVERNMENT

### Market Borrowings

*Dated Securities*

In line with global trends of increased Government spending as a response to counter-economic slowdown, the Government of India announced three stimulus packages in 2008-09. Accordingly, the net market borrowing through dated securities was nearly twice the amount raised in 2007-08 and more than twice the budget estimate for 2008-09 (Table 17). The gross market borrowing through dated securities was 75 percent higher than during 2007-08 (6.8 per cent higher in 2007-08).

TABLE 17

**Gross and Net Market Borrowings of the Central Governments**

(Rupees crore)

| Item | 2007-08 | 2008-09 | | | 2009-10 | |
|---|---|---|---|---|---|---|
| | Actual | Budget Estimates | Revised Estimates | Actual | Budget Estimates | Actual* |
| 1 | 2 | 3 | 4 | 5 | 6 | 7 |
| Gross borrowing | 1,88,205 | 1,76,453 | 3,42,769 | 3,18,550 ^ | 4,91,044 ^ | 2,63,302 ^ |
| Net Borrowing | 1,09,504 | 1,15,571 | 2,66,539 | 2,42,317 ^ | 3,97,957 ^ | 2,16,368 ^ |
| i. Dated Securities | 1,10,671 | 1,00,571 | 2,61,972 | 2,28,972 ^ | 3,97,957 ^ | 2,19,911 ^ |
| ii. 364-day Treasury Bills | -1,167 | 15,000 | 4,567 | 13,345 | - | -3,543 |
| *Memo* | | | | | | |
| i. Additional 182-day Treasury Bills | -76 | -1,000 | 19,390 | 10,995 | - | 200 |
| ii. Additional 91-day Treasury Bills | -431 | -1,571 | 43,720 | 45,224 | - | 951 |
| iii. MSS de-sequestering | - | - | - | 12,000 | 33,000 | 28,000 |

# : Dated securities and 364-day Treasury Bills. ^ : Includes MSS de-sequestering * : Up to August 17, 2009.

The Reserve Bank continued with the policy of passive consolidation of dated securities during 2008-09. Barring four new securities, of which two were 10-year benchmark securities, the remaining securities issued during the year were reissuances. In 2007-08, out of the securities issued during the year, only one was a new security. Over one quarter of the outstanding securities, each with a minimum outstanding amount of Rs. 25,000 crore, accounted for 61 per cent of the total outstanding amount as at end-March 2009 as against 54 per cent at end-March 2008. In a year that encountered pressures on market liquidity, this trend provides an indication of potential liquidity in these securities.

The aggregate amount raised during the first half of 2008-09 was Rs. 1,06,000 crore, which was Rs.10,000 crore more than the amount indicated in the issuance calendar. The issuances were in accordance with the calendar for the first half of the year, except on two occasions. In the auction of July 24, 2008, a 10-year benchmark security was issued in place of a security with higher maturity in view of the uncertain market conditions.

An auction of dated securities amounting to Rs. 10,000 crore was advanced to September 26, 2008 from the second half of the year, keeping in view the emerging requirements of the Government, market conditions and other relevant factors. The auction schedule for the second half of 2008-09 (October-March) was revised due to the unprecedented developments in the global financial market and their impact on India in terms of the increased demand for liquidity as well as the substantial increase in Government borrowings.

There were two cancellations of auctions scheduled for October 2008. While the auction scheduled for October 10, 2008 for dated securities amounting to Rs. 10,000 crore was cancelled in view of the then prevailing tight liquidity conditions that emerged from the financial turmoil in the global markets, the auction scheduled for October 20, 2008 was cancelled in view of the cut in the repo rate that was announced on the same day. The proposed market borrowing of Rs. 39,000 crore in the second half of the year was completed by end-November 2008 with the advancement of an auction scheduled for December 5-12, 2008. Due to the sharp increase in government spending and deceleration in tax revenues, the Reserve Bank, in consultation with the Central Government, issued three additional indicative calendars on December 5, 2008, January 6, 2009 and February 10, 2009 and accordingly, Rs. 1,16,000 crore was raised between December 2008 and March 2009.

The challenge posed to the debt management function needs to be viewed in the context of global developments whereby many countries, including advanced economies, announced fiscal stimulus packages to compensate for the fall in consumption and investment demand (Box VII.1). In India, specific strategic measures

**Debt Management and the Global Financial Crisis**

The global financial crisis created large and unanticipated pressures on the fiscal position of many countries. While some countries had to support the financial sector directly or through operations giving rise to higher contingent liabilities, most countries had to expand fiscal expenditure to contain recessionary impulses.

While fiscal balances have been affected by the crisis in the short-run, the impact on government debt ratios will be felt over the medium-term. The deterioration of the fiscal outlook raises issues of fiscal solvency and has the potential to trigger adverse market reactions. In turn, higher interest rates (and exchange rate depreciations in countries with significant borrowing in foreign currency, like most emerging economies) could further add to government debts which in some cases, result in 'snowballing' debt dynamics.

Market confidence in gilts issued by various Governments has been a source of stability and has, so far, helped to avoid a complete meltdown of financial markets, notwithstanding the hardening of credit default swap (CDS) premia for many Government issues, implying higher cost of insurance against default. Thus far, government debt market reaction to the weaker fiscal outlook has been relatively muted. Nevertheless, some of the Government bond auctions since January 2009 have witnessed pressures. UK, Germany and Netherlands could not mobilise the notified amount on some occasion/s whereas France, Italy, Austria and Portugal were forced to pay higher interest rates. On May 25, 2009, the UK DMO failed for the first time since 1995 to sell conventional government bonds in an auction, attracting bids of 1.63 billion pounds against the notified amount of 1.75 billion pounds of 2049 gilts. The Ministry of Finance, China also failed to sell, for the first time since 2003, one-year government bonds of yuan 28 bn in an auction held on July 7, 2009. On May 7, 2009, US Treasury yields soared by 20 basis points to 4.30 per cent after the 30-year bond auction saw poor demand.

The rating outlook of sovereign borrowings for countries, such as Portugal, Spain, Greece and the UK was downgraded by credit rating agencies. An abrupt market reaction to weakening fundamentals remains a concern. Towards boosting nominal demand by increasing broad money, lowering gilt yields and improving corporate credit markets, the Bank of England has undertaken open market purchase of government bonds while the US Federal Reserve and the Bank of Japan have also carried out such open market purchases towards 'quantitative' easing. In the context of the on-going global financial crisis, Iceland has recently shifted debt management from the DMO to the central bank. For smooth conduct of large borrowing programme of the Governments, with minimal impact on the financial markets, closer co-ordination between the Treasury and the central bank, as is being practised in large countries like the US,

Canada and India has assumed greater importance. Deterioration in the fiscal position and increased government borrowings have raised the level of roll-over risk even for advanced economies. Many sovereign defaults have originated in the past, from situations of excessive shcrt-term debt. It is, therefore, imperative for the debt management authorities to set an acceptable level of roll-over risk. If there is a high default risk premium built into longer term rates, shorter-term debt may be cheaper but could increase risk by increasing the volatility of debt-servicing costs. Building up liquidity in longer benchmark maturities could help in reducing refinancing risk and also decrease risk premia over time, even if there are higher debt-servicing costs when this strategy is initially adopted.

In some countries, Government support to weak financial institutions has been extended as implicit or explicit guarantees or similar forms of contingent liability. A sharp increase in contingent liabilities introduces greater uncertainty to the fiscal position as it could complicate accurate estimation of the probability of devolvement. Debt managers need to not only reckon such contingent liabilities but also estimate probability of devolvement and consequent addition to public debt.

As the frequency and volume of public debt increases significantly, debt managers need to ensure transparency so that investors are not taken by surprise. Clarity in communication and adherence to the indicative borrowing programme would add credibility and thereby cushion volatility in market yields, which ultimately may help in contributing to lower cost of borrowing were initiated to conduct the increased market borrowings in a non-disruptive manner. The Memorandum of Understanding (MoU) signed between the Government of India and the Reserve Bank in March 2004 on the Market Stabilisation Scheme (MSS) was amended on February 26, 2009, to enable the Reserve Bank to de-sequester MSS cash balance for financing the Government's approved expenditure in lieu of the approved market borrowings. Accordingly, it was decided to transfer an amount of Rs. 45,000 crore in instalments, as and when necessitated, from the MSS cash account to the regular cash account of the Government of India by March 31, 2009. An equivalent amount of government securities was to form part of the normal borrowing of the Central Government. An amount of Rs. 12,000 crore was, accordingly, transferred from the MSS cash account to the regular cash account of the Central Government on March 4, 2009. In view of its comfortable cash position, the Government of India, in consultation with the Reserve Bank, decided not to transfer the balance amount of Rs. 33,000 crore in 2008-09.

Based on the emerging funding requirements of the Government, an amount of Rs. 28,000 crore was de-sequestered from the MSS cash account on May 2, 2009 against the approved market borrowing programme for 2009-10.

During the first half of 2008-09, the weighted average yield increased from 8.14 per cent in April 2008 and peaked at 8.81 per cent in September 2008. The yields softened thereafter, reflecting the availability of liquidity in the system. The weighted average yield on dated securities issued during the year, therefore, decreased for the first time in the last five years in 2008-09. The weighted average coupon on the outstanding stock of dated securities as on March 31, 2009 also declined over the previous year. The weighted average maturity of the dated securities issued during the year was the lowest since 2003-04. As a result, the weighted average maturity of the outstanding stock as on March 31, 2009 decreased over the previous year (Table 18).

The yield movement in the primary market was, in general, marginally higher than the secondary market yield (10-year bench-mark securities) (Table 19). As opposed to the variable price auctions normally used, during 2008-09, uniform price-based auctions for dated securities were held on July 24, August 8 and 22, 2008 and March 26, 2009, in view of the uncertain market conditions. Overall, the weak market sentiments subsequent to the announcement of additional market borrowings, were reflected in higher devolvement on primary dealers (PDs) during the year (Rs. 10,773 crore) than in 2007-08 (Rs. 957 crore).

The maturity pattern of outstanding Government of India securities (excluding MSS) shows that two-thirds of the

Table 18

## Central Governments Market Loans—A Profile

(Yield in per cent / Maturity in years)

| Year | Range of YTMs at Primary Issues | | | Issues during the year | | | Outstanding Stock | |
|---|---|---|---|---|---|---|---|---|
| | under 5 years | 5-10 years | Over 10 years | Weighted Average Yield | Range of Maturities | Weighted Average Maturity | Weighted Average Maturity | Weighted Average Coupon |
| 1 | 2 | 3 | 4 | 5 | 6 | 7 | 8 | 9 |
| 2003-04 | 4.69 | 4.62-5.73 | 5.18-6.35 | 5.71 | 4-30 | 14.94 | 9.78 | 9.30 |
| 2004-05 | 5.90 | 5.53-7.20 | 4.49-8.24 | 6.11 | 5.30 | 14.13 | 9.63 | 8.79 |
| 2005-06 | - | 6.70-7.06 | 6.91-7.79 | 7.34 | 5-30 | 16.90 | 9.92 | 8.75 |
| 2006-07 | 7.69-7.94 | 7.06-8.29 | 7.43-8.75 | 7.89 | 4-30 | 14.72 | 9.97 | 8.55 |
| 2007-08 | - | 7.55-8.44 | 7.62-8.64 | 8.12 | 6-29 | 14.90 | 10.59 | 8.50 |
| 2008-09 | 6.24-6.77 | 5.44-9.14 | 6.53-10.03 | 7.69 | 4-30 | 13.81 | 10.45 | 8.23 |

*: Excludes issuances under MSS; YTM: Yield to Maturity; -: No Issues

## Chart : Weighted Average Yield of Primary Issues of Dated Securities

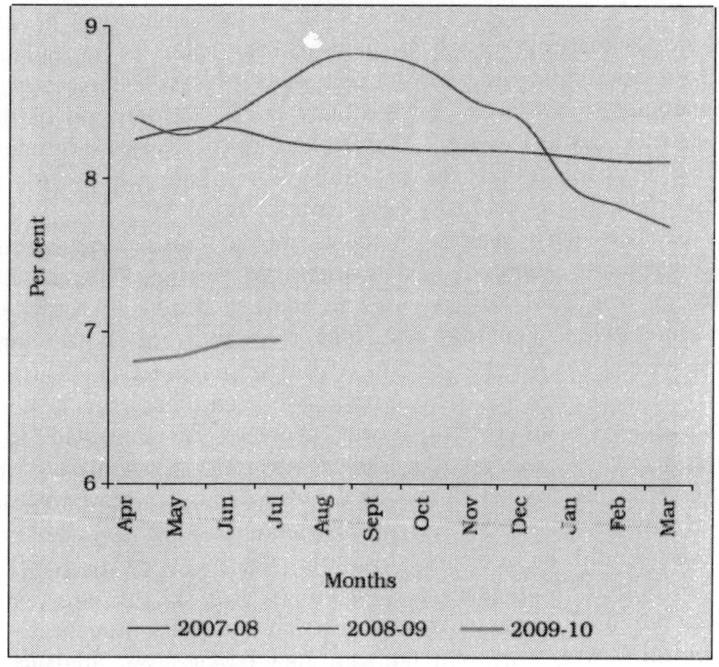


securities (face value) had residual maturity of less than 10 years, while 15.6 per cent of the securities had a residual maturity of more than 20 years as at end-March 2009.

TABLE 19

**Primary Cut-off Yield and Prevailing Secondary Market Yield**

| Date of Auction | Residual Maturity (Years) | Gross Amount Raised (Rs. Crore) | Cut-off Yield (%) | Prevailing Secondary Market Yield (%) | Spread (basis points) (4-5) | Bid- Cover Ratio |
|---|---|---|---|---|---|---|
| 1 | 2 | 3 | 4 | 5 | 6 | 7 |
| April 21, 08 | 10.00 | 6,000 | 8.24 | 8.23 | 1 | 3.49 |
| May 23, 08 | 9.91 | 6,000 | 8.07 | 8.13 | -6 | 3.16 |
| June 6, 08 | 9.87 | 6,000 | 8.26 | 8.26 | 0 | 3.13 |
| July 4, 08 | 9.79 | 6,000 | 9.13 | 8.92 | 21 | 2.03 |
| August 8, 08 | 9.70 | 6,000 | 9.14 | 9.10 | 4 | 2.50 |
| September 12, 08 | 9.60 | 5,000 | 8.30 | 8.27 | 3 | 2.11 |
| November 7, 08 | 9.45 | 6,000 | 7.73 | 7.71 | 2 | 2.62 |
| January 16, 09 | 9.26 | 3,000 | 5.44 | 5.71 | -27 | 2.30 |
| January 30, 09 | 10.00 | 4,000 | 6.05 | 6.18 | -13 | 4.51 |
| February 13, 09 | 9.96 | 6,000 | 5.94 | 5.89 | 5 | 3.48 |
| March 6, 09 | 9.90 | 8,000 | 6.50 | 6.30 | 20 | 1.72 |
| March 20, 09 | 9.86 | 6,000 | 6.59 | 6.51 | 8 | 2.36 |
| March 26, 09 | 9.84 | 7,000 | 6.97 | 6.97 | 0 | 1.79 |

During 2008-09, 61 per cent of the market borrowings was raised through issuances of dated securities having residual maturity of up to 10 years, the same as in 2007-08. However, while the predominant share of market borrowings belonged to the 5-10 year maturity bucket, 6 per cent of the securities issued during 2008-09 had residual maturities less than 5 years, unlike the previous year when no security of less than 5-year maturity was issued (Table 20).

The sharp increase in the financing requirements of the Government, some of which were not provided for in the Budget for 2008-09, gave rise to market strains in terms of rising yields. As the size and frequency of borrowings increased, the Reserve Bank's efforts were aimed at ensuring that the borrowing programme was completed in a non-disruptive manner. The sharp increase in the size and frequency of borrowings raised apprehensions about the ability of the market to absorb the borrowing programme and whether the issue of private placements with the Reserve Bank should be revisited. In India, the Fiscal Responsibility and Budget Management (FRBM) Act, 2003, precludes the Reserve Bank from subscribing to the primary issuances of Central Government, barring under exceptional circumstances. Cross-country practices indicate that while in some countries the constraint on Central Government's access to central bank credit is binding, in some others it is weak.

TABLE 20

Maturity Profile of Central Government Dated Securities*

(per cent)

| Year | Issued during the year | | | Outstanding Stock # | | |
|---|---|---|---|---|---|---|
| | Under 5 Years | 5-10 Years | Over 10 Years | Under 5 Years | 5-10 Years | Over 10 Years |
| 1 | 2 | 3 | 4 | 5 | 6 | 7 |
| 2004-05 | 11 | 11 | 78 | 25 | 31 | 44 |
| 2005-06 | 0 | 26 | 74 | 25 | 32 | 43 |
| 2006-07 | 7 | 47 | 46 | 26 | 35 | 39 |
| 2007-08 | 0 | 61 | 39 | 26 | 38 | 36 |
| 2008-09 | 6 | 55 | 39 | 26 | 40 | 34 |

* : Excludes issuances under MSS. #: As at end-March.

## Market Borrowings during 2009-10

The gross and net market borrowings of the Central Government through dated securities for 2009-10 are budgeted higher, at Rs. 4,51,093 crore and Rs. 3,97,957 crore, respectively, than the actual amount raised in 2008-09. On March 26, 2009, the issuance calendar for dated securities for the first half of 2009-10 (April-September) was released in consultation with the Central Government.

Accordingly, an amount of Rs. 2,41,000 crore was scheduled to be raised as compared with Rs. 1,06,000 crore raised during the corresponding period of the previous year. Following the revision in the market borrowing requirement as per the Union Budget, 2009-10, a new issuance calendar for dated securities was released on July 16, 2009 for mobilization of Rs. 1,10,000 crore during July 18, 2009 through September 30, 2009 (as against Rs. 79,000 crore as per the earlier calendar issued on March 26, 2009).

During 2009-10 so far (up to August 17, 2009), the Central Government raised Rs. 2,25,000 crore on gross basis (excluding MSS desequestering of Rs. 28,000 crore) and the net market borrowings amounted to Rs 1,91,911 crore, through dated securities under the market borrowing programme. Market borrowing through dated securities was higher than that indicated in the calendar on account of increased requirement of the Government. The monthly amount raised increased from Rs.48,000 crore in April 2009 to Rs.60,000 crore in June 2009 before declining to Rs. 39,000 crore in July 2009. The weighted average yield of dated securities issued during 2009-10 (up to August 17, 2009) declined to 6.96 per cent from 8.72 per cent in the corresponding quarter of the previous year. The weighted average maturity of securities issued was lower at 10.92 years as compared with 15.21 years in the corresponding period of the previous year.

**Treasury Bills**

The notified amounts of 91-day, 182-day and 364-day Treasury Bills under the normal market borrowing programme as per the annual issuance calendar released on March 24, 2008, were kept unchanged at Rs.500 crore (weekly auction), Rs. 500 crore (fortnightly auction) and Rs. 1,000 crore (fortnightly auction), respectively, for 2008-09. Additional Treasury Bills over and above the notified amounts were, however, raised during 2008-09, which were nearly seven times those raised during 2007-08. The additional Treasury Bills issuances were spread throughout the year unlike in 2007-08 when they were concentrated in the month of June to enable the Government to acquire the Reserve Bank's stake in State Bank of India in 2007. During 2008- 09, while initially the additional resources raised through Treasury Bills were meant to partly meet the expenditure on agricultural debt waiver scheme,

*Private Placement of Sovereign Debt with the Central Banks—Cross-country Practices*

The extent of accommodation of fiscal deficit by the central bank is often seen as an indicator of the nature of coordination between monetary and fiscal authorities. The monetisation of fiscal deficit through devolvement in auctions or private placement entails the risk of subordinating monetary policy to the fiscal policy, which, in turn, could engender inflationary expectations. Since inflation expectations play a key role in determining actual inflation, central banks aim at entrenching their credibility so that inflation expectations could be stabilised at lower levels. Prohibition of central bank credit to the Government is one of the instruments for achieving this credibility. The sanctity of prohibition on central bank credit to the Government usually stems from frameworks based on clear mandate/fiscal rule as enshrined in fiscal responsibility legislation or central bank Act. Countries with binding constraints on Government's access to central bank credit include the US, the UK, the Euro zone, Mexico, Peru and Argentina. Countries with weak constraints or flexible legislation include Canada, Chile, Japan, Korea, Malaysia and South Africa permitting central bank purchases of Government securities from the primary market as detailed below.

Canada: The Bank of Canada Act, 1934 permits the central bank to make loans to the Government of Canada or the Government of a province, within stipulated limits. Chile: The Basic Constitutional Act of the Central Bank of Chile prohibits the Central Bank from directly purchasing securities from the Government. However, in the event of foreign war or threat of foreign war, to be qualified by the Council on National Security by means of a secret resolution, the Bank may obtain, confer or finance credits to the state and to public or private entities.

Japan: The Public Finance Law, 1947 explicitly prohibits the Bank of Japan from directly participating in the primary issuance of public bonds and from underwriting the issue. However, the prohibition is relaxed for some special reasons and the DIET (the Japanese Parliament) may allow private placement within the approved limits.

Korea: Korean Central Bank is permitted by the Bank of Korea Act, 1950 to subscribe to the Government Bond issues and also to the bonds guaranteed by the Government.

Malaysia: Bank Negara Malaysia is permitted by the Central Bank of Malaysia Act, 1958 to invest in Central Government securities and also to underwrite the same.

South Africa: South African Central Bank is prohibited from holding government securities directly purchased from the Treasury, beyond certain limits stipulated by the South African Reserve Bank Act of 1989.

In the Indian context, the Reserve Bank of India Act, 1934 authorises the Bank to grant advances repayable not later than three months from the date of advance, thereby enabling the Government to bridge the temporary mismatches in its receipts and expenditures. These provisions are, however, enabling and are not mandatory. In practice, this became a permanent source of financing the Government budget deficit through automatic creation of adhoc Treasury Bills (with a tenor of 91 days) whenever overnment's balances with the Reserve Bank fell below he minimum stipulations. Monetisation of deficit was not restricted to the amount issued through the ad hoc Treasury Bills but also by way of subscription to primary issuances of Government securities. In September 1994, the Reserve Bank and the Central Government signed a landmark agreement to phase out automatic monetisation through *ad hoc* Treasury Bills. Effective April 1997, with the phasing out of ad hoc Treasury Bills, the scheme of Ways and Means Advances (WMA) was introduced which provides temporary accommodation to the Government (up to 90 days) and is subject to limits. The Fiscal Responsibility and Budget Management (FRBM) Act, 2003 which was subsequently enacted has since prohibited direct borrowings by the Centre from the Reserve Bank with effect from April 2006 except by way of WMA or under exceptional circumstances. Till date, the proviso in the FRBM Act, 2003 permitting borrowings from the central bank under exceptional circumstances has not been invoked subsequently, in view of the large increase in the gross fiscal deficit (GFD) which could not be entirely funded by issuances of dated securities, Treasury Bills also served as an instrument of financing GFD. Reflecting the disinvestment by States in the non-competitive segment of the auction treasury bills, the net issuances of Treasury Bills during 2008-09 amounted to Rs. 69,564 crore, contributing to financing 21.3 per cent of GFD (as per the revised estimates) as against a negative contribution of 1.8 per cent to GFD financing in 2007-08.

The primary market yields of Treasury Bills across all maturities hardened up to August 2008 and softened, thereafter, reflecting the interest rate cycle coupled with improvement in liquidity conditions from October 2008 (Table 21 and Chart). During March 2009, however, the yields hardened from their levels in January and February 2009 due to increased market borrowings by both the Central and the State Governments and quarterly advance tax outflows.

The calendar for the regular auction of Treasury Bills for 2009-10 was announced on March 31, 2009. It was

TABLE 21

## Treasury Bills in the Primary Market

| Year / Month | Notified Amount * (Rs. Crore) | Average Implicit Yield at Minimum Cut-off Price (Per cent) | | | Average Bid-Cover Ratio | | |
|---|---|---|---|---|---|---|---|
| | | 91-day | 182-day | 364-day | 91-day | 182-day | 364-day |
| 1 | 2 | 3 | 4 | 5 | 6 | 7 | 8 |
| **2008-09** | 2,99,000@ | 7.10 | 7.22 | 7.15 | 3.43 | 2.91 | 3.47 |
| April | 26,000 | 7.28 | 7.41 | 7.53 | 2.64 | 3.17 | 2.36 |
| May | 17,000 | 7.41 | 7.55 | 7.61 | 2.92 | 2.73 | 3.43 |
| June | 11,500 | 8.01 | 8.42 | 7.93 | 2.45 | 2.76 | 2.80 |
| July | 21,000 | 9.07 | 9.33 | 9.39 | 2.84 | 2.72 | 3.52 |
| August | 18,500 | 9.15 | 9.31 | 9.24 | 2.99 | 2.86 | 4.24 |
| September | 25,000 | 8.74 | 8.92 | 8.83 | 3.06 | 3.04 | 3.57 |
| October | 35,000 | 8.13 | 8.36 | 7.92 | 1.95 | 2.42 | 4.00 |
| Novemher | 28,000 | 7.30 | 7.13 | 7.23 | 2.40 | 2.97 | 3.51 |
| December | 18,000 | 5.49 | 5.35 | 5.47 | 7.01 | 4.67 | 5.59 |
| January | 37,000 | 4.89 | 4.60 | 4.55 | 2.30 | 3.22 | 3.54 |
| February | 32,000 | 4.78 | 4.71 | 4.62 | 2.81 | 1.86 | 2.62 |
| March | 30,000 | 4.77 | 4.86 | 5.25 | 2.60 | 2.67 | 1.44 |
| **2009-10** | | | | | | | |
| April | 39,000 | 3.81 | 4.11 | 4.07 | 3.22 | 2.79 | 5.07 |
| May | 29,000 | 3.26 | 3.54 | 3.58 | 3.18 | 2.25 | 3.14 |
| June | 22,500 | 3.35 | 3.56 | 3.99 | 3.37 | 5.65 | 2.86 |
| July | 40,000 | 3.23 | 3.45 | 3.76 | 3.92 | 2.86 | 3.90 |

@ : Total for the financial year.
* : Excludes issuances under MSS.

## Chart: Primary Market Yields of Treasury Bills

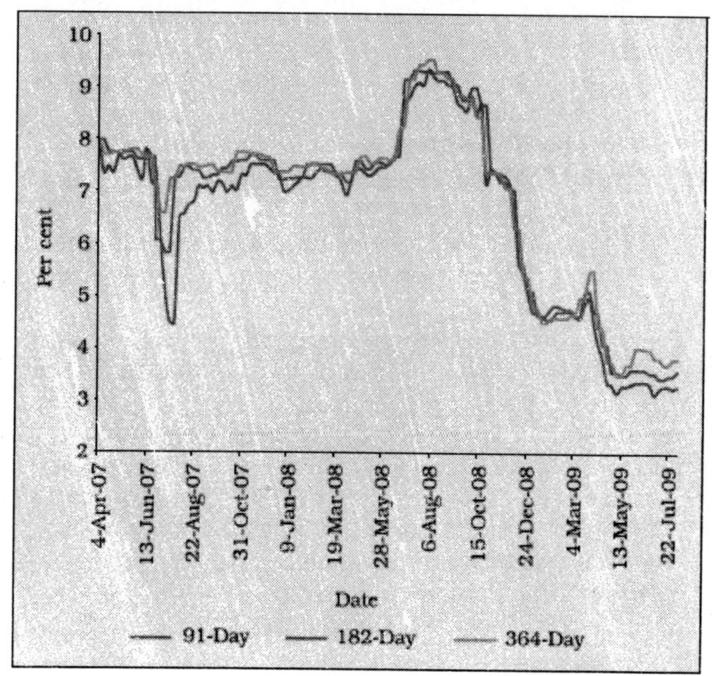

decided to rollover the Treasury Bills which were issued for enhanced amounts in the fiscal year 2008-09 and were due for redemption in the first quarter of 2009-10. Accordingly, the issuance of 91-day Treasury Bills for the first quarter was raised to Rs. 8,000 crore for five weekly auctions since April 10, 2009, which was revised downward to Rs. 5,000 crore for the remaining weekly auctions during the first quarter except for June 5, 2009 where the notified amount was fixed at Rs. 4,500 crore. On July 16, 2009, it was decided to rollover the maturing amount of Treasury Bills till September 30, 2009.

Accordingly, Treasury Bills amounting to Rs. 1,27,000 crore, Rs. 14,375 crore and Rs. 10,302 crore were issued in respect of 91-day, 182-day and 364-day Treasury Bills up to August 17, 2009.

**Cash Management**

The limits for Ways and Means Advances (WMA) for 2008-09 were initially fixed at Rs.20,000 crore for the first half of the year (April to September) and Rs.6,000 crore for the second half (October to March) in consultation with the Government of India. In view of the unanticipated mismatches between Government receipts and payments arising from the cancellation of two auctions scheduled for October 2008 due to the then prevailing liquidity conditions, and the bunching of the expenditure following the approval of supplementary demand for grants, the limit for the third quarter (October-December) was retained at the first half limit of Rs. 20,000 crore, while that for the fourth quarter was kept at the original limit of Rs. 6,000 crore.

As the Central Government started the year 2008-09 with a large surplus cash balance of Rs. 76,686 crore, which was built up primarily from the State Governments' surplus balances invested in Treasury Bills, its recourse to WMA was limited to brief spells during the first half of 2008-09, viz., during August 4-6, 2008 and again during September 2-14, 2008. During the third quarter of 2008-09, following the unfolding ramifications of the global financial crisis, the Central Government announced fiscal stimulus packages even as revenue receipts, as estimated in the Budget did not materialise due to the sluggishness in tax revenues.

**Chart: Cash Balances of the Central Government**

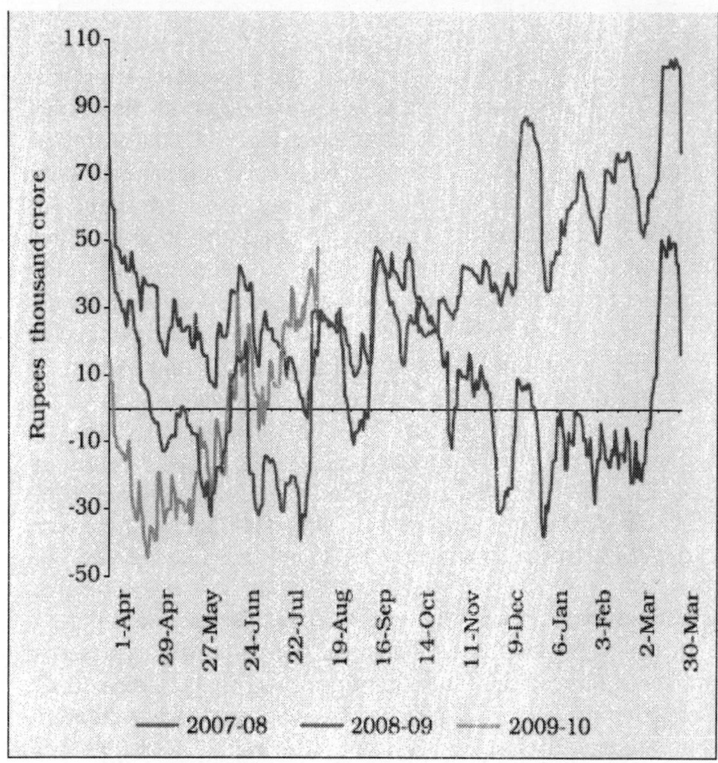


Consequently, the Central Government had to resort to WMA for 23 days and was in overdraft (OD) for 10 days during the third quarter. With the cash flow mismatches persisting during the fourth quarter, the Central Government resorted to WMA for 70 days and was in OD for 55 days. Thus, for the year as a whole, the Central Government was in cash deficit for 109 days (65 days in OD) as against 91 days (37 days in OD) during 2007-08. The daily average utilization of WMA and OD by the Central Government during 2008-09 were at Rs. 2,077 crore and Rs. 1,823 crore, respectively, as compared with Rs.3,605 crore and Rs. 647 crore, respectively, during 2007-08. Unlike the previous years, the Government was in cash deficit mostly during the second half of the year. Consequently, the cash surplus, which generally remained high in recent years, was at a lower level of Rs. 16,319 crore as on March 31, 2009.

The WMA limit for the first half of 2009-10 was kept unchanged at Rs. 20,000 crore, as in the previous year while the limit for the second half was fixed higher at Rs. 10,000 crore. The Central Government started the year 2009-10 with a modest surplus cash balance of Rs. 16,319 crore, and soon took recourse to WMA on April 4, 2009 due to its expenditure commitments. Having reached the WMA ceiling of Rs. 20,000 crore on April 15, 2009, it went into OD. The Central Government continued to be in WMA up to June 15, 2009 and was also on OD on three occasions during the year so far. The cash balances turned positive thereafter on account of the quarterly advance tax inflows and stood at Rs. 33,918 crore as on August 11, 2009. The surplus transfer from the Reserve Bank amounting to Rs. 25,009 crore on August 13, 2009 boosted the Government's cash balance to Rs. 48,071 crore as on August 13, 2009. The Centre, however, availed WMA during July 6-9, 2009.

**Special Securities issued by the Central Government**

In addition to dated securities, the Central Government issued special securities aggregating to Rs. 95,942 crore to oil marketing companies and fertiliser companies during 2008-09, as compared with Rs. 38,050 crore during 2007-08. With a view to compensating oil marketing companies towards estimated under-recoveries on account of sale of petroleum products at administered prices, the Central Government issued four special securities to three oil marketing companies for an aggregate amount of Rs. 75,942 crore: Rs. 22,000 crore (15-year maturity) on November 10, 2008, Rs. 22,000 crore (16-year maturity) on December 23, 2008, Rs. 21,942 crore (17-year maturity) on February 4, 2009 and Rs. 10,000 crore (17-year maturity) on March 23, 2009. During 2008-09, the Central Government issued three special securities of 14-year maturity, each, aggregating to Rs. 20,000 crore to fertiliser companies as compensation towards fertiliser subsidy during 2008-09: Rs. 10,000 crore on December 10, 2008, Rs. 4,000 crore on December 24, 2008 and Rs. 6,000 crore on January 29, 2009.

## STATE GOVERNMENTS

### Market Borrowings

The net allocation under the market borrowing programme of State Governments inclusive of additional allocations for shortfall in National Small Savings Fund (NSSF) collections and towards the second stimulus package for 2008-09 was about two-thirds higher than that in 2007-08. Taking into account the repayments, the gross allocation amounted to Rs. 1,29,081 crore during 2008-09, of which 91.5 per cent was actually raised by the State Governments during the year Table 22. The entire amount was raised through the auction route during 2008-09. as in the previous year. Two States (viz., Chhattisgarh and Orissa) did not participate in

TABLE 22

**Annual Market Borrowings of State Governments**

(Rupees crore)

| Item | 2007-08 | 2008-09 |
|---|---|---|
| 1 | 2 | 3 |
| 1. Net Allocation | 28,781 | 51,719 |
| 2. Additional Allocation | 4,454 | 14,326 |
| 3. Additional Allocation on account of NSSF shortfall | 35,780 | 19,768 |
| 4. Additional Allocation towards second stimulus package | - | 28,896 |
| 5. Total Net Allocation (1+2+3+4) | 69,015 | 1,14,709 |
| 6. Repayments | 11,555* | 14,371 |
| 7. Gross Allocation (5+6) | 80,570 | 1,29,081 |
| 8. Total Amount Raised | 67,779 | 1,18,138 |
| 9. Net Amount Raised (8-6) | 56,224 | 1,03,766 |
| 10. Outstanding State Development Loans (end-period) | 2,98,845 | 4,02,611 |

# : Includes the Union Territory of Puducherry.

* : Excludes Rs.156 crore of buy-back of securities by the Government of Orissa.

the market borrowing programme during 2008-09 as against four States (viz., Chhattisgarh, Haryana, Orissa and Tripura) during 2007-08. Besides, 13 States did not raise their full allocations as against 11 States during 2007-08.

During 2008-09, 27 State Governments/UT (i.e., except Chhattisgarh and Orissa) accessed the market in 23 tranches as compared with 25 States/UT through 18 tranches during 2007-08. Almost all the States accessed the market during the second half of the year raising 86.6 per cent of the total borrowings during the year, the bulk of which was in the fourth quarter. In March 2009 alone, more than a quarter of the total borrowings was raised, which exerted pressure on the market. As a result, the net supply of State Development Loan (SDL) securities in the market increased from Rs. 8,472 crore during the first half of 2008-09 to Rs. 95,294 crore during the second half. The bunching of SDLs of the States/ UT during the last quarter was mainly due to the Government of India's sanctions under Article 293(3) towards NSSF shortfalls and the second stimulus package sanctioned during the quarter. All the issues during 2008-09 were of 10-year maturity.

Reflecting the softer interest rate environment since the second half of the year, the weighted average yield of State Government securities issued during 2008-09 was lower than the previous year despite the significantly larger market borrowings (Table 23). The average range of cut-off yield during 2008-09, however, was considerably wide due to large intra-year variations.

The cut-off yield increased gradually and peaked in July 2008 before declining till January 2009 due to easy liquidity conditions in the market. The cutoff yield moved up, thereafter, in February and March 2009 (Table 24). The spread in the auction of the SDLs over the corresponding Central Government securities of 10-year tenor was widely dispersed, reflecting the investor response to the sheer size of the borrowings and the concentration of the issuances of securities in the second half of the year. The spread between the weighted average yield of SDLs and that of the Central Government 10-year security narrowed in the auction held on September 25, 2008 but widened significantly thereafter, upto

TABLE 23

**Yield on State Government Securities**

(Per cent)

| Year | Range | Weighted Average |
|---|---|---|
| 1 | 2 | 3 |
| 1997-98 | 12.30-13.05 | 12.82 |
| 1998-99 | 12.15-12.50 | 12.35 |
| 1999-00 | 11.00-12.25 | 11.89 |
| 2000-01 | 10.50-12.00 | 10.99 |
| 2001-02 | 7.80-10.53 | 9.2 |
| 2002-03 | 6.60-8.00 | 7.49 |
| 2003-04 | 5.78-6.40 | 6.13 |
| 2004-05 | 5.60-7.36 | 6.45 |
| 2005-06 | 7.32-7.85 | 7.63 |
| 2006-07 | 7.65-8.66 | 8.10 |
| 2007-08 | 7.84-8.90 | 8.25 |
| 2008-09 | 5.80-9.90 | 7.87 |

December 2008. The spread declined briefly in January 2009 but reached its maximum in the auction held on March 9, 2009 (Chart VII.4). Following the monetary easing, the yield curve shifted downwards and the spread over Central Government yield declined in the last auction held on March 24, 2009. The weighted average spread was lower at below 50 basis points for Sikkim and over 200 basis points for Assam. The spread was between 100-150 basis points in respect of 14 States during the year (Table 25). The differential in spread is observed to be a function, among others, of the liquidity conditions in the market, supply of securities, the timing of the borrowing and the market perceptions of fiscal conditions.

Some State Governments accessed the market very frequently during the year. West Bengal accessed the market as many as eleven times, followed by Andhra Pradesh, Kerala and Tamil Nadu, on ten occasions. Arunachal Pradesh,

TABLE 24

## Month-wise Market Borrowings of State Governments

| Month/ Date | No. of States /U.T. | No. of Tranches | Amount (Rupees crore) | Cut-off Yield (Percent) | Spread over Central Government Dated Security (Basis points) |
|---|---|---|---|---|---|
| 1 | 2 | 3 | 4 | 5 | 6 |
| **2008-09** | | | | | |
| 1. April | 4 | 1 | 2,648 | 8.50-8.60 | 35-45 |
| 2. May | 5 | 1 | 3,264 | 8.39-8.68 | 30-59 |
| 3. June | 3 | 1 | 2,300 | 9.38-9.59 | 77-98 |
| 4. July | 4 | 2 | 2,600 | 9.81-9.90 | 48-52 |
| 5. August | 3 | 1 | 2,060 | 9.30-9.44 | 34-48 |
| 6. September | 5 | 2 | 3,012 | 8.90-8.88 | 21-34 |
| 7. October | 8 | 2 | 6,312 | 7.97-8.89 | 41-85 |
| 8. November | 12 | 2 | 8,445 | 7.77-8.54 | 51-84 |
| 9. December | 13 | 2 | 10,705 | 6.34-7.10 | 43-80 |
| 10. January | 15 | 3 | 18,498 | 5.80-7.13 | 58-120 |
| 11. February | 19 | 3 | 26,935 | 7.24-7.98 | 132-196 |
| 12. March | 24 | 3 | 31,358 | 8.08-8.89 | 136-236 |
| **Total** | | **23** | **1,18,138** | **5.80- 9.90** | **21-236** |
| **2009-10** | | | | | |
| 1. April | 7 | 3 | 7,316 | 7.04-7.77 | 83-115 |
| 2. May | 5 | 2 | 7,000 | 7.10-7.53 | 77-100 |
| 3. June | 10 | 1 | 5,950 | 7.80-7.89 | 81-90 |
| 4. July | 9 | 3 | 12,300 | 7.76-7.97 | 85-96 |
| 5. August* | 6 | 1 | 7,474 | 7.95-8.03 | 95-103 |

*: Up to August 17, 2009. U T: Union Territory of Puducherry.

## Weighted Average Spreads during 2008-09

| Weighted Average Spread (Basis Points) | General Category States/UTs | Special Category States |
|---|---|---|
| 1 | 2 | 3 |
| up to 50 | – | Sikkim |
| 51-100 | Kerala, Punjab and West Bengal | Manipur and Uttarakhand |
| 101-150 | Andhra Pradesh, Goa, Gujarat, Madhya Pradesh, Maharashtra, Rajasthan, Tamil Nadu, Uttar Pradesh and Puducherry | Himachal Pradesh, Jammu & Kashmir, Meghalaya, Mizoram and Nagaland |
| 151-200 | Bihar, Haryana, Jharkhand, Karnataka | Arunachal Pradesh and Tripura |
| above 200 | – | Assam |

## Chart: Weighted Average Yield on SDLs and Yield to Maturity (YTM) on 10 years' Central Government Security

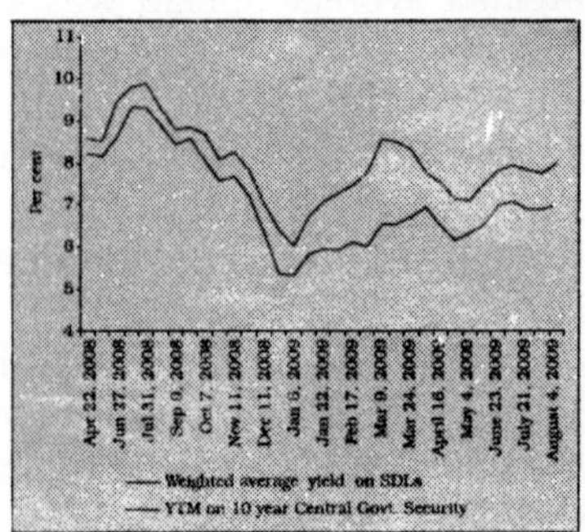

Sikkim and Tripura raised their loans on one occasion only Table 26. In all, 141 new securities were issued by all the States taken together during 2008-09 for a gross amount of Rs. 1,18,138 crore averaging Rs. 838 crore per issue. The corresponding average issue size stood at Rs. 565 crore during the previous year. The increase in the average issue size of State Governments securities during 2008-09 was mainly on account of the additional allocation compensating for the NSSF shortfall and for meeting the fiscal stimulus package.

At end-March 2009, about 71 per cent of the total outstanding debt of State Governments was in the maturity bucket of 6-10 years as compared with 68.1 per cent at end-March 2008. The share of loans in the maturity bucket of 6-10 years ranged between 39.7 per cent (Orissa) and 100.0 per cent (Puducherry). It may be noted that Orissa did not raise resources through market borrowings since 2006-07 and Puducherry started participation in market borrowing

TABLE 26

**Frequency Distribution of Trenches of Auctions during 2008-09**

| No. of times States accessed the market | No. of States* | No. of Securities Issued |
|---|---|---|
| 1 | 2 | 3 |
| 1 | 3 | 3 |
| 2 | 4 | 8 |
| 3 | 3 | 9 |
| 4 | 3 | 12 |
| 5 | 3 | 15 |
| 6 | 3 | 18 |
| 8 | 1 | 8 |
| 9 | 3 | 27 |
| 10 | 3 | 30 |
| 11 | 1 | 11 |
| Total | 27 | 141 |

* : including Union Territory of Puducherry.

programme only since 2007-08. The maturity profile of market borrowings shows large repayment obligations in the years 2017-18 and 2018-19 reflecting the sharp increase in market borrowings in the past two years. The outstanding SDLs and power bonds of all the State Governments increased by 31.2 per cent in 2008-09 over the previous year (Table 27). Market Borrowings of State Governments during 2009-10

TABLE 27

**Maturity Profile of Outstanding State Development Loans and Power Bonds**

(Rupees crore)

| Year of Maturity | State Development Loans | Power Bonds | Total Outstanding |
|---|---|---|---|
| 1 | 2 | 3 | 4 |
| 2009-10 | 16,238 | 2,907 | 19,145 |
| 2010-11 | 15,660 | 2,907 | 18,567 |
| 2011-12 | 21,993 | 2,907 | 24,900 |
| 2012-13 | 30,628 | 2,870 | 33,498 |
| 2013-14 | 32,079 | 2,870 | 34,949 |
| 2014-15 | 33,384 | 2,870 | 36,254 |
| 2015-16 | 35,191 | 2,907 | 38,098 |
| 2016-17 | 31,522 | 1,453 | 32,975 |
| 2017-18 | 67,779 | 0 | 67,779 |
| 2018-19 | 1,18,138 | 0 | 1,18,138 |
| **Total** | **4,02,611** | **21,691** | **4,24,302** |

During 2009-10 (up to August 17, 2009), ten tranches of auctions have been conducted under the market borrowing programme of the State Governments. Seventeen State Governments raised an aggregate amount of Rs.40,041 crore as compared to Rs.10,812 crore by eight State Governments during the corresponding period of the previous year. The cut-off yield ranged between 7.04-8.03 per cent as compared to 8.39-9.90 per cent during the corresponding period of the previous year. The spread arrived in the auctions of the SDLs over the corresponding Central Government securities of 10-year tenure ranged between 77-115 basis points compared to 30-98 basis points during the corresponding period of 2008-09. The weighted average yield of gross borrowings of the States was 7.72 per cent as compared with 9.07 per cent during the corresponding period of 2008-09.

**Cash Management**

Keeping in view the cash position of the State Governments, the WMA limits of State Governments have been left unchanged since 2006-07. Accordingly, the extant State-wise Normal WMA limits was fixed at Rs. 9,925 crore for 2008-09 (inclusive of Rs. 50 crore for the Union Territory of Puducherry) and the limit has been retained for the year 2009-10. The rate of interest on Normal and Special WMA and OD continued to be linked to the repo rate. The net incremental annual investment in the revised Consolidated Sinking Fund (CSF) and the revised Guarantee Redemption Fund (GRF) continued to be eligible for fixing Special WMA limit, up to a ceiling equivalent to the Normal WMA limit. The monthly average utilisation of Normal WMA by the State Governments showed a fluctuating trend. During 2008-09, six States, viz., Kerala, Madhya Pradesh, Nagaland, Punjab, West Bengal and Uttarakhand resorted to WMA as against eight States, viz., Kerala, Nagaland, Punjab, West Bengal, Himachal Pradesh, Manipur, Mizoram and Uttarakhand in the previous year. The monthly average utilisation of ODs by the States in 2008-09 was significantly lower than the previous year (Table 28). Three States, viz., Nagaland, West Bengal and Uttarakhand resorted to ODs during 2008-09 while Kerala, West Bengal and Nagaland were the three states that resorted to overdraft in 2007-08. During 2008-09, West Bengal availed of WMA for a maximum 39 days whereas Uttarakhand availed of OD for 15 days during the year (Table 29).

Despite some deterioration in their finances during the second half of 2008-09 on account of the fiscal stimulus measures undertaken by them, most of the State Governments accumulated sizeable cash surpluses, reflecting the sharp

## TABLE 28

## WMA/Overdrafts of the State Governments*

(Rupees crore)

| Month | Special WMA | | | Normal WMA | | | Overdraft | | | Total | | |
|---|---|---|---|---|---|---|---|---|---|---|---|---|
| | 2007-08 | 2008-09 | 2009-10 | 2007-08 | 2008-09 | 2009-10 | 2007-08 | 2008-09 | 2009-10 | 2007-08 | 2008-09 | 2009-10 |
| 1 | 2 | 3 | 4 | 5 | 6 | 7 | 8 | 9 | 10 | 11 | 12 | 13 |
| April | 235 | 489 | 619 | 114 | 287 | 294 | 15 | 139 | 111 | 364 | 916 | 1024 |
| May | 437 | 310 | 126 | 654 | 3 | 50 | 461 | 0 | 2 | 1552 | 313 | 178 |
| June | 204 | 9 | 5 | 222 | 0 | 67 | 10 | 0 | 0 | 436 | 9 | 72 |
| July | 389 | 25 | 76 | 310 | 0 | 7 | 3 | 0 | 0 | 702 | 25 | 83 |
| August | 307 | 2 | | 476 | 47 | | 281 | 0 | | 1064 | 49 | |
| September | 961 | 139 | | 601 | 18 | | 225 | 0 | | 1787 | 158 | |
| October | 254 | 653 | | 184 | 83 | | 128 | 0 | | 566 | 736 | |
| November | 279 | 754 | | 351 | 152 | | 127 | 0 | | 757 | 906 | |
| December | 161 | 223 | | 103 | 0 | | 13 | 0 | | 277 | 223 | |
| January | 72 | 370 | | 81 | 0 | | 34 | 0 | | 187 | 370 | |
| February | 72 | 86 | | 8 | 0 | | 0 | 0 | | 80 | 86 | |
| March | 5 | 320 | | 1 | 62 | | 0 | 11 | | 6 | 392 | |
| **Average** | **281** | **282** | **206** | **259** | **54** | **105** | **108** | **13** | **28** | **648** | **349** | **339** |

*: Average of daily outstanding.

## TABLE 29

## State-wise Availment of WMA/Overdraft

| States | WMA | | Overdraft | | | |
|---|---|---|---|---|---|---|
| | 2007-08 | 2008-09 | 2007-08 | | 2008-09 | |
| | Number of days | Number of days | Number of Occasions* | Number of days | Number of Occasions* | Number of days |
| 1 | 2 | 3 | 4 | 5 | 6 | 7 |
| **Non-Special Category States / U.T.** | | | | | | |
| 1. Kerala | 184 | 18 | 9 | 51 | 0 | 0 |
| 2. Madhya Pradesh | 0 | 2 | 0 | 0 | 0 | 0 |
| 3. Punjab | 19 | 21 | 0 | 0 | 0 | 0 |
| 4. West Bengal | 142 | 39 | 6 | 65 | 1 | 4 |
| **Special Category States** | | | | | | |
| 1. Himachal Pradesh | 1 | 0 | 0 | 0 | 0 | 0 |
| 2. Manipur | 3 | 0 | 0 | 0 | 0 | 0 |
| 3. Mizoram | 4 | 0 | 0 | 0 | 0 | 0 |
| 4. Nagaland | 30 | 18 | 1 | 3 | 1 | 4 |
| 5. Uttarakhand | 5 | 28 | 0 | 0 | 2 | 15 |

*: Refers to fresh occurrences of overdrafts during the year.

increase in their market borrowings during 2008-09. The surplus cash balances of State Governments are automatically invested in 14-day Intermediate Treasury Bills, the discount rate of which is fixed at 5 per cent. While the monthly average outstanding investment in the 14-day Intermediate Treasury Bills by the State Governments during 2008-09 increased by around 35 per cent, that in auction Treasury Bills decreased by around 15 per cent over the previous year. Total investment in Treasury Bills was, however, higher on an average in 2008-09 than in 2007-08 (Table 30).

TABLE 30

### Investments of the State Governments/UT

(Rupees crore)

| Month | Investment in 14-day Treasury Bills | | | Investment in Auction Treasury Bills | | | Total | | |
|---|---|---|---|---|---|---|---|---|---|
| | 2007-08 | 2008-09 | 2009-10 | 2007-08 | 2008-09 | 2009-10 | 2007-08 | 2008-09 | 2009-10 |
| 1 | 2 | 3 | 4 | 5 | 6 | 7 | 8 | 9 | 10 |
| April | 31,160 | 48,192 | 74,607 | 34,496 | 31,780 | 8,875 | 65,656 | 79,972 | 83,482 |
| May | 31,359 | 48,280 | 66,585 | 32,612 | 32,244 | 8,664 | 63,971 | 80,525 | 75,249 |
| June | 44,430 | 42,865 | 69,482 | 32,500 | 40,285 | 6,125 | 76,930 | 83,150 | 75,607 |
| July | 35,938 | 46,742 | 75,403 | 39,557 | 38,802 | 2,125 | 75,495 | 85,543 | 77,528 |
| August | 36,458 | 44,110 | | 42,477 | 43,069 | | 78,935 | 87,179 | |
| September | 34,282 | 40,112 | | 39,201 | 40,927 | | 73,483 | 81,038 | |
| October | 32,052 | 39,328 | | 35,195 | 32,705 | | 67,247 | 72,033 | |
| November | 30,556 | 41,878 | | 33,872 | 26,988 | | 64,428 | 68,866 | |
| December | 38,042 | 51,551 | | 31,565 | 24,055 | | 69,607 | 75,606 | |
| January | 45,029 | 63,420 | | 29,661 | 20,084 | | 74,690 | 83,504 | |
| February | 50,633 | 75,193 | | 32,403 | 14,150 | | 83,036 | 89,342 | |
| March | 65,910 | 1,01,557 | | 29,181 | 6,893 | | 95,091 | 1,08,450 | |
| **Average** | **39,654** | **53,602** | **71,519** | **34,393** | **29,332** | **6,447** | **74,047** | **82,934** | **77,966** |

*: Average of Friday outstanding.

## Consolidated Sinking Fund (CSF) and Guarantee Redemption Fund (GRF)

The Reserve Bank maintains the consolidated sinking fund (CSF) and the guarantee redemption fund (GRF) on behalf of the State Governments from contributions made by them. While the CSF provides a cushion for amortization of market borrowing/liabilities, the GRF provides a cushion for the servicing of contingent liability arising from invocation of guarantees issued by the State Governments in respect of bonds issued and other borrowings by state level undertakings or other bodies. The aggregate outstanding investments in CSF by the 18 State Governments increased to Rs. 24,032 crore at end-March 2009 from Rs. 18,946 crore in respect of 17 States at end-March 2008. As on March 31, 2009, nine States notified their GRF scheme and the aggregate outstanding investments in GRF by these States increased to Rs.3,082 crore as on March 31, 2009 from Rs. 2,805 crore in respect of 8 States as on March 31, 2008.

## Conference of State Finance Secretaries

The 21st Conference of State Finance Secretaries was held on May 15, 2008. Apart from operational issues pertaining to Government transactions, the discussions primarily focused on issues relating to the fiscal transparency at the State level, financing of local (urban) bodies, management of investment portfolio of the States, estimation of the States' market borrowings and budget management of the States. Following discussions in the Conference, three Working Groups, viz., Working Groups on 'Fiscal Management beyond FRBM', 'Local (urban) Finances' and 'Fiscal Transparency at State Level' have been set-up to examine the related issues. The major issues focused in the 22nd Conference of the State Finance Secretaries held on May 29, 2009, related to surplus cash balances of the State Governments; projections on market borrowings of the States; advance planning for borrowing by the States; imparting of liquidity to the State Development Loans by reissuance and consolidation; electronic benefit transfer to the beneficiaries of the social security assistance of the Governments and impact of counter-cyclical fiscal measures taken by the States.

The Reserve Bank has responded to the challenge of managing the large market borrowing programme with an appropriate assessment of the liquidity conditions and market disruptions have been avoided by synchronising liquidity enhancing operations, such as unwinding balances under the MSS and conducting open market purchases of government securities, with the timing of borrowing programmes, while also seeking feedback from market participants on a regular basis. Hence, despite the sharp increase in the size of borrowings, the market borrowing programme of the Central and State Governments during 2008-09 could be completed in a non-disruptive manner.

Apart from the Reserve Bank's active and dynamic debt management strategy which was well coordinated with monetary management in terms of ensuring ample liquidity in the system and cut in monetary policy rates, other factors which facilitated the relatively smooth conduct of the market borrowing programme included decline in inflation, weak private sector demand for credit and greater appetite for government securities by commercial banks due to higher risk aversion.

The size of combined net market borrowing requirements of the Central and State Governments for 2009-10 (dated securities and 364-day Treasury Bills), at Rs. 5,37,957 crore, is estimated to be higher than the 2008-09 actual borrowings by 55.4 per cent, which was on top of an increase of 108.8 per cent over 2007-08. Accordingly, the smooth conduct of debt management would assume even greater importance during the current fiscal year. Hardening of yields witnessed in recent months could militate against the low interest rate regime required to stimulate and revive the economy. The Reserve Bank would continue with its active liquidity management policy to ensure that the large government borrowing does not crowd out present and potential credit demand from the private sector. As the private sector demand picks up with the revival of the economy, and the need for fiscal stimulus also declines correspondingly, the Government could phase out its large borrowings, thereby allowing the private sector demand to propel and sustain the growth momentum, without being constrained by concerns on the availability of liquidity in the system.

## INTEREST PAYMENTS

Interest payments have been projected on the basis of the debt stock indicated in the fiscal reform path shown in this study. For the years 2008-09 and 2009-10 the lower of Revised Estimates (RE) or 3.5 per cent of GSDP and Budget Estimates (BE) or 4 per cent of GSDP respectively, has been taken as the fiscal deficit for projection of debt stock.

The debt stock has been divided into three components. The breakup of the outsanding debt stock at the end 2009-10 for each state is given in Table 31 The first component, non-interest bearing loan, has been pegged at the 2007-08 levels in nominal terms on the assumption that the fiscal deficit will be financed only through borrowings.

Any increase in non-interest bearing debt would not be due to the fiscal deficit. This component has been deducted from the debt stock for purposes of projecting interest payments.

Out of the interest bearing debt, the borrowings with the highest cost are the loans from the National Small Savings Fund (NSSF). Within the outstanding debt stock of NSSF loans of Rs. 4.3 lakh crore, Rs. 4.1 lakh crore pertains to loans contracted till 2006-07, for which we have recommended an interest rate of 9 per cent. The remaining stock of Rs. 20,000 crore carries an interest rate of 9.5 per cent, implying an effective rate of 9.02 per cent on the entire stock of NSSF loans. We have used this rate to estimate interest payments on the NSSF loans. Gross collection under NSSF has dropped in recent years and net collection for 2008-09 has been negative. In line with the institutional reforms recommended by us in this study, we have assumed that there would be no net addition to the debt stock of NSSF for the base year and the projection period.

The remainder of the debt stock comprises open market loans, loans from the Centre, and loans from financial institutions such as National Bank for Agriculture and Rural Development (NABARD), Life Insurance Corporations (LIC)/ General Insurance Corporations (GIC). Central loans have been consolidated at 7.5 per cent by FC-XII, which is also the interest rate for most of the market loans. Rural Infrastructure Development Fund (RIDF) loans are cheaper, while some of the negotiated loans may carry an interest rate marginally higher than 7.5 per cent. Thus, for this component of the stock, we have assumed an interest rate of 7.5 per cent. Based on the projected debt stock and the interest rates assumed, the interest payments have been calculated for each state for each year in the projection period.

### Debt Management Policy

Thus the debt-management policy aims at the stabilisation of total effective demand at a high level of employment in an advanced and developed economy, and at accelerated economic growth with stability in a developing economy. In India and therefore, in Bihar, the field of public debt-management is wide enough to include "those measures of the government and the Reserve Bank of India which change the size, the composition and the ownership distribution of pubic debt, affect the level and structure of interest rates, determine the timings and the mode of borrowing, refunding and conversion operations and also those policies which influence the volume and the extend of trading in the securities market".

## Table 31

### Debt Book

(Rs. crore)

| | State | Outstanding Debt as on 31 March 2010 | Outstanding Non Interest Bearing Debt as on 31 March 2008 | Outstanding NSSF Loans as on 31 March 2009 |
|---|---|---|---|---|
| 1 | Andhra Pradesh | 124039.22 | 10818.01 | 24208.71 |
| 2 | Arunachal Pradesh | 3335.78 | 112.16 | 542.68 |
| 3 | Assam | 25935.67 | 1362.39 | 4716.62 |
| 4 | Bihar | 58307.05 | 6515.07 | 15260.20 |
| 5 | Chhattisgarh | 18846.13 | 2313.78 | 4736.25 |
| 6 | Goa | 7448.15 | 108.60 | 2703.73 |
| 7 | Gujarat | 115648.80 | 6556.89 | 44315.07 |
| 8 | Haryana | 40089.85 | 2112.40 | 10455.93 |
| 9 | Himachal Pradesh | 22470.28 | 1171.91 | 3869.22 |
| 10 | Jammu & Kashmir | 25692.05 | 2834.26 | 3158.90 |
| 11 | Jharkhand | 25006.90 | 2334.07 | 8566.41 |
| 12 | Karnataka | 80796.86 | 8427.65 | 19350.51 |
| 13 | Kerala | 70103.12 | 2656.51 | 11879.09 |
| 14 | Madhya Pradesh | 67176.45 | 4950.67 | 14174.43 |
| 15 | Maharashtra | 198084.21 | 17259.51 | 73279.22 |
| 16 | Manipur | 5068.01 | 849.02 | 880.26 |
| 17 | Meghalaya | 3789.30 | 608.46 | 293.49 |
| 18 | Mizoram | 3897.55 | 313.03 | 137.42 |
| 19 | Nagaland | 4030.45 | 290.83 | 112.67 |
| 20 | Orissa | 45730.15 | 2206.82 | 6822.27 |
| 21 | Punjab | 66165.89 | 1013.31 | 21428.87 |
| 22 | Rajasthan | 91120.60 | 5625.97 | 23708.00 |
| 23 | Sikkim | 2494.51 | 236.02 | 112.94 |
| 24 | Tamil Nadu | 92000.35 | 4128.80 | 24075.74 |
| 25 | Tripura | 5228.67 | 237.80 | 1096.14 |
| 26 | Uttar Pradesh | 213349.24 | 39318.84 | 44214.61 |
| 27 | Uttarakhand | 35403.16 | 1508.81 | 4972.48 |
| 28 | West Bengal | 162740.77 | 4931.74 | 62234.52 |
| | **All States** | **1615073.15** | **130894.32** | **431937.78** |

*Source*: Thirteenth Finance Commission, 2010-15.

Thus the debt-management has mainly two important objectives in the context of economic planning. They are: (a) to promote saving and provide more funds for investment in the public sector without impinging on the private sector, and (b) to ensure large borrowing and debt retirement without frustrating the objective of maintaining price stability in the economy or in other words, to promote development within the frame-work of overall monetary stability". Firstly, the debt policy should encourage saving, which is so essential for capital formation and economic development. The debt policy should be capable of attracting funds from all possible sources. Debts of different maturities at attractive rates of interest should be floated at a time when the atmosphere is favourable. Here caution should be taken so that the private sector is not adversely affected. Care should be taken of the private sector because it occupies significant place in the economy, which is mixed in character. Secondly, the debt-management policy should encourage accelerated rate of economic growth with stability. The public debt policy should support and not disturb the objective of maintaining price stability in the economy. Debt policy should have the aim of minimizing the risk of inflation. Fiscal policy, monetary policy and direct controls play a significant role in controlling inflation. But these measures, to be affective, should be supplemented by debt-management. If the debt-management policy is growth-oriented, it should restrict the increase in money supply so that prices may not rise out of control. The borrowing programmes of the government would draw the excess money from the people through the saving bonds. Inflation can be controlled by a suitable management policy, i.e., by increasing the volume of saving bonds and by retiring the government securities held by the banking system. A growth-oriented debt-management has its objective to promote economic development within the framework of monetary stability. Here is seems that debt-management is similar to fiscal policy and monetary policy. In practice, the objectives of debt-management, fiscal policy and monetary policy are so similar and interrelated that it is difficult to distinguish.

**Debt Swap Scheme**

The Central Government introduced the debt swap scheme in September 2002 to give relief to the states in the "high-cost debt" owed by the states to the central government. High cost debt was defined as the debt which carried interest rate of 13 percent or above. Only state plan loans and small savings loans given up to 31.3.99 qualified for debt swap. States have requested for alignment of interest rates on central loans with interest rates applicable to market borrowings. As per data collected from the Ministry of

Finance, the weighted average cost of the total borrowings in 2003-04 works out to 6.04 percent. The interest rate charged from the states by the centre in 2003-04 was 10.5 percent. The marginal cost of borrowing by the centre is, therefore, much lower than the interest rate charged from states. Large interest payments have been a major factor leading to increase in outstanding debt of State Government. In our view, therefore, the reduction of interest payments is integral to attaining debt sustainability. Data provided reveal that a large number of loans for each state are being administered by Ministry of Finance and that consolidation of these loans would lend simplicity to the management of these loans. The outstanding loans of Bihar had adjusted under debt swap scheme during 2002-03 to 2004-05. It is shown in Table 32.

**Public Debt: Some Considerable Facts**

The first is that over the years the debt of all states of India has grown. Bihar is not an exception.

Secondly, the major portion of debt of the State Government including that of Bihar comes from the centre meaning thereby that State Governments have heavily depended of the centre. The centre has becomes a sort of 'Captive market' for all states so far as borrowings are concerned.

Thirdly, lethargy has been noticed on the part of the State Government is mobilizing their own resources to their full capacity.

Fourthly, sometimes-borrowed amount is not rationally utilized which weakens the capacity of the State Government to pay-off the principal and interest thereon.

Fifthly, finance mismanagement on the part of the State Government has also contributed to the rising debt and for the emergence of a debt trap like situation in the state. The government of Bihar borrowed excessively during 1998-99 for plan expenditure, but did not spend the amount even as the plan scheme languished. As a result, Rs. 2388 Crores was accumulated. The government is, thus, slack enough to utilize the borrowed amount for the development purpose.

Sixthly, there are many impediments in the way of debt creation and until and unless those are removed, government may not be able to get sufficient amount from the public by way of borrowing. Some of the impediments may briefly be summarized here as follows:

(a) Income of the people in under-developed economies is low and the propensity to consume in high, saving is less and this sets a limit to public borrowing.
(b) Estimates of propensity to save in the various sectors and income groups are not available on an accurate basis and this poses a problem before public authorities when effecting borrowing.
(c) There are no organized money and capital markets in many of the under-developed countries and even where such markets exist, there is lack of relationship between the organized and unorganized markets.
(d) The demand for fund by the private sector for investment also reduces the part of the savings that would be lent to the government. Private sector in many cases offers lucrative rate of interest. This also works as an impediment of public borrowing programme.
(e) The developing countries are marked by deficiency of well-developed financial institutions and it becomes difficult to mobiles the saving potential of the individual for productive purposes.
(f) People prefer to hold a large portion of their savings in the form of real estate or in the form of gold and silver jewelry and even the higher rate of interest fails to attract such funds for investments by the government.
(g) Rising prices are usual phenomenon in under-developed economics. Prices rise reduces the capacity of the people to save.
(h) There maybe problem of co-ordination in debt operation between different layers of government such as the central government and the State Government. There may be sometimes a

TABLE 32

**Outstanding Loans from Center Adjusted under Debt Swap Scheme (DSS) During 2002-03 to 2004-05**

*Bihar State (As on End March 2005)*

*(Rs. In crore)*

| | 2002-C3 | | | 2003-05 | | | 2004-05 | | | 2002-03 to 2004-05 | | | | |
|---|---|---|---|---|---|---|---|---|---|---|---|---|---|---|
| Outstanding High Cost Loan as on March 31, | Small Savings | Market Borrowings | Total | Small Borrowings of | Market Borrowings | Amount of High Cost Debt Relief | Total | Small Borrowings of | Market Borrowings | Total | Small Borrowings of | Market Borrowings | Amount of High Cost Debt Relief | Total Swapper till March 31, 2005 |
| 4,983 | 191 | 597 | 788 | 621 | 1,329 | - | 1,839 | 920 | 910 | 18,30 | 1,732 | 2,726 | - | 4,458 |

*Source*: State Finance, A Study of Budgets of 2005-06, RBI, Bombay.

competition between different layers of governments for rising loans.

(i) Lastly, dependence of the governments for raising loans on 'Captive Market' such as Reserve Bank of India and other financial institution like LIC of India, etc. poses another problem before public authorities while effecting borrowing programmes. Such loans are generally inflationary and in economies where prices are already high, this will add fuel to the fire. There is least public participation and loans are not coming directly from public which would have been less inflationary.

## SUGGESTIONS OR POLICY RECOMMENDATIONS

1. Financial institutions be developed and extend into the rural sector of the economy in order to inculcate the habit of thrift in the population and to mobilizes the amount of savings originating in this sector for productive purposes. This will give a boost to public participation in the borrowing programmes and the proportion of non-market borrowing will gradually increase.
2. It is also essential to regulate and check the direction of savings into unproductive investments like silver and gold ornaments and in creating real estate.
3. Suitable techniques of borrowing have to be developed. The bonds issued by the government may be adjusted to the preferences of the public and of the financial institutions. Bonds of large denominations may be offered to the institutional investors whereas those of small denominations may be meant for the public. Short-term and medium-term loans may be offered by the banks and insurance companies because of their preferences for liquidity. Thus by a judicious combination of the short-term, medium-term and long-term loans and maintaining a proper balance

them; the government may attempt to achieve the objectives of growth with stability.

4. In spite of these limitations of the rate of interest in mobilizing a large volume of resources through public borrowings, there may exist in a developing economy, some scope of offering attractive terms on government bonds and securities without disrupting the structure of its monetary policy. The National Council of Applied Economic Research (NCAER) has recommended an increase in the interest rates of government securities and reduction in the redemption period with a view to lessening the present dependence on institutional support for the success of government's borrowing programmes.
5. The technique of borrowing may be reoriented by giving sufficient publicity to the issue of government bonds and by linking up their issue with financing of specific projects the awareness of the advantages of which may arouse sufficient response from the potential lenders.
6. Mobilization of hoards gold and silver through public borrowing programme constitutes a highly desirable source of development finance and the developing country will have to evolve a suitable technique of public borrowings for the mobilization of these in idle resource.
7. Transfer of resources from the centre to the states should be mainly in the form of tax sharing and grants rather than loans. In fact, loans have had a dominating position in resource transfers.
8. Loan amount should not be used for non-productive expenditure or for serving the repayment of older debt.
9. States are not tapping their resources to their full capacity. They should try to mobilize their own resources to their maximum.
10. There is financial laxity on the part of the State Government. There is need to put a check on available expenditure and plunge revenue leakages.

11. Increasing importance should be placed on small savings and the role of market borrowing and subscriptions to treasury bills should be gradually limited.
12. There should be reduction in government ownership of securities to control the money supply and ease inflationary pressure.
13. The government should try to borrow from general public rather than from the 'captive market' so that more genuine savings may be tapped.

## References

Abbt, C.C. (1946), "Management of the Federal Debt', New York.

Harrs, S.E, (1947), "The National Debt and the New Economics".

Domar, E., (1955), "The Burden of the Debt and National Income", in "Readings in Fiscal Policy", George Allen and Unwin Ltd., London.

Wright, David, M.C. (1940), "The Economic Limit and Economic Burden of an Internally held National Debt", *Quarterly Journal of Economics*, LV, Nov., p. 119.

Whittlesey (1963), "Money and Banking; Analysis and Policy", Chates R., The Macmillan Company, New York.

Sarkaria Commission (1988), "Report on Centre-State Relations", Part I, Government of India.

Shandilya, Tapan Kumar (2005), "Emerging Issues in Centre-State Financial Relations: Approach of Twelfth Finance Commission, Indian Economic Journal (Conference Vol.), Vishakhapattanam (Andhra Pradesh).

Shandilya, Tapan Kumar (1991), Central loans to states under Five Year Plans, Deep & Deep Publications Pvt. Ltd., New Delhi.

Shandilya, Tapan Kumar (1991), Centre States Financial Relations in India, Deep & Deep Publications Pvt. Ltd., New Delhi.

R.B.I. Report on Currency and Finance, Vol. 2, and State Finance, Various Issues.

Rao. M. Govind (2002), State Finance in India; Issues and Challenges, *Economic and Political Weekly*, August 3.

Ahluwalia, Montek S. (2002), Economic Performance of States in Post-Reform Period, *Economic and Political Weekly*, May 6.

Panwar, Deshpal Singh (2004), The Bitter Truth, *The Hindustan*, Patna, August 18.

Bhatia, Dr. H.L. (2003), Public Finance 24th ed., Vikash Pub. House Pvt. Ltd.

EPW Research Foundation (2004), Finances of State Governments, *EPW*, May.

Bahal, Roy W. (2002), Implementation Rules for Fiscal Decentralization in Govind Rao (ed.), Poverty, Development and Fiscal Policy, Oxford University Press New Delhi.

Government of India, Planning Commission (2001), Annual Report on the Working of State Electricity Boards.

Kannan K.P., Mohan Rajan (2004), Twelfth Finance Commission, View from Kerala, *EPW*, June, 5.

Prasad, Abha, Goyal Rajan, Prakash Anupam (2004), State Debt and Debt Relief, *EPW*, June 26, 2004.

*Dainik Jagran*, Patna, 20, 2004.

Gurumirthi, S. (2002), Twelfth Finance Commission and States' Debt Burden, *EPW*, October 5, 2002.

Mohan, R. (2000), Fiscal Correction for Economic Growth, *EPW*, June 10-16.

Chakraborty, P. (1999), Recent Trends in State Government Finances: A Comment, *EPW*, October 30-Nov. 5.

Acharya Shankar (2002), India's Macro Economic Management, *EPW*, April 20-27.

Roy, Piyali, Mahanti, Tushar, K. (2004), *The Economic Times*, Kolkata, July 26.

Shreekantaradhya, B.S. (1972), Public Debt and Economic Development in India, Sterling Publishers (P) Ltd., New Delhi.

Jonathan Levin (1972), "The Management of Public Debt in Developing Countries" in *Finance and Development*, Quarterly, No. 2, A Publication of the International Monetary Fund and the World Bank Group.

Dr. R.N. Tripathy (1964), Public Finance in Under-Developed Countries; The World Press Private Ltd., Calcutta.

National Council of Applied Economic Research, New Delhi (1965), "Management of Public Debt in India".

Melvin, D. Brockie (1954), "Debt Management and Economic Stabilisation", *Quarterly Journal of Economic*, LXIX (Nov.).

*Reserve Bank of India Bulletin*, July 1961.

H.G. Molition (1960), Can Inflation be Controlled?, George Allen and Unwin, Ltd.

Chief Minister's Address before the Sixth Finance Commission (1973), Government of Bihar, February 24.

Mobilisation of Domestic Capital through Financial Institutions for the E.C.A.F.E. Region., (1951).

George Rosen (1958), "Capital Market and the Industrialization of Under-Developed Economics", *Indian Economic Journal*.

James M. Buchanan (1960), The Public Finance, An Introductory Text Book, Richard D. Irvin, Inc., Homewood, Illinois.

Chandra Dalaya, The Internal Debt of the Government of India, Vora & Co. Publishers Pvt. Ltd., 3 Round Building, Bombay.

R.N. Bhargava (1967), Theory and Working of Union Finance, Chaitanya Publishing House, 5-A, University Road, Allahabad-2.

Patnik, K.M., Monetary Police and Economic Development in India, S. Chand & Co., New Delhi.

Report of the Second Finance Commission (1957), Government of India, New Delhi.

Report of the Third Finance Commission (1961), Government of India, New Delhi.

Report of the Eleventh Finance Commission (2000), Government of India, New Delhi.

Report of the Twelfth Finance Commission (2004), Government of India, New Delhi.

Sharma, S.D. (1971), Public Debt in Bihar, Unpublished Thesis, Patna University, Patna, Bihar.

Thirteenth Finance Commission (2010-15), Govt. of India.

R.B.I. Annual Report, 2009-10.

BIS Quarterly Review (2009), Government Debt Management at Low Interest Rates, June 2.

The IMF (2009), The State of Public Finances: Outlook and Medium-Term Policies After the 2008 Crisis, March 6.

Standard and Poors (2009), United Kingdom Outlook Revised To Negative On Deteriorating Public Finances; 'AAA/A-1+' Ratings Affirmed, May 21. *Source*: Websites of respective central banks.

# 6

# Central Loans to States: Some Policies

It is no secret public debt has become a very important method of resource mobilization to finance economic development. Even the Eighth Finance Commission took the view that "there is nothing basically wrong in the growth of public debt. With the expanding public functions, no Government particularly in a developing economy, can undertake large scale programmes of development without recourse to borrowing." The Sarkaria Commission in its "Report on Centre-State Relation" has agreed with the above observation of the Commission. The Eighth Finance Commission took the stand, "the Centre has to view States' requirements in perspective of total national needs." "The development of the country as a whole is a collective responsibility of the Centre and State Governments. For the purpose of development, the Central Government territory includes all the States." The Eighth Finance Commission also views, "The growing volume of central assistance for the plan is an indication of the partnership between the union and states in the common endeavour for future economic development. Thus, loan financing has become 'an important instrument in the hands of the Government for regulating the economy'. Loans are "raised by the Governments in order to pursue their economic growth-oriented policy and also to promote the social welfare of the society." No doubt, till the recent times it was not conceived of as playing a significant role. The classical economists believed in the policy of balanced budgets. So they viewed loan with high eyebrows and uneasiness, loan had a place of contempt in their analysis.

The depression of 1930's was an eye-opener and it exposed the hallowness of the classical principles and practices. The Keynesian revolution challenged the classical doctrines and gave public debt a place of pride the gamut of the fiscal of the Government. No doubt, the Keynesian theory was applicable in the short period and his main concern was the problem of depression in a developed economy. He supported the increase in public debt even for unproductive purposes. Harris observes, "Once the economists, in more realistic mood, allowed for unemployment, assumed elasticity in money supplies, and agreed that government expenditure could be productive and need not necessarily be wasteful, the case for public borrowing was strengthened. The post-Keynesians economists had assigned the government a more positive role to play in the development of an underdeveloped economy. It is so because, as Kurihara observes, in the underdeveloped economy "private initiative and risk-taking are obviously too deficient to bring about productive investment in sufficient quantities." He observes further, "the Harrod-Domar-Robinson models of *laissez-faire* growth have the negative virtue of demonstrating how precarious and unfruitful it is to leave the secular growth of an economy to the vagaries of private saving and investment to the accident of profit, motivated inventions and innovations, and to the working of unguided market forces. All these growth models have this positive lesson for underdeveloped economies that the state should be allowed to play not only a stabilizing role but also a developmental role.

Basically, it is because of the limited availability of financial resources on the one hand, the need for increasing state investment for development of welfare expenditure, on the other that the volume of public debt has been rising and thus the debt policies have come to occupy a significant role in the fiscal policy of the state.

In our country the case for public debt was strengthened after 1951 when planning was adopted. The State of Bihar, like other states of the country, has relied increasingly on loan during all her plans. The Central loans to the State Governments constitute a overwhelming part of the states' total public debts. The trends in the pattern of indebtedness of Bihar. The position of the state of Bihar is not different.

The States receive central assistance in three forms-share in taxes and duties, grants and loans; and there are three institutional processes through which states are receiving funds from the centre, namely, (1) on the basis of recommendations of the Finance commission, (2) on the basis of suggestions of Planning Commission, and (3) at the discretion of the Central Ministries. It is plan as well as discretionary transfer by which central loans are given conditional grants and conditional loans. It is significant to note that grant-loan proportion of the plan assistance was not uniform before 1969 and also the loan component varied from programme to programme and from state to state.

The fiscal situation of states has deteriorated drastically since 1997-98, and state finances held in total disarray. The combined revenue deficit of all states zoomed from Rs. 5309 crores in 1991-91 to Rs. 5,00,000 crores in 2003-04. Their fiscal deficit increased from Rs. 18787 crores to Rs. 1,16,000 crores during the same period. The outstanding liabilities of states increased relatively from Rs. 1,60,077 crores in 1993-94 to Rs. 8,00,000 crores in 2003-04. The debt GSDP ratio increased from 18.6 percent to 29.1 percent over the same period. The growth of debt and deficit of states has been a matter of concern. The persistence of states fiscal deficit in the past two decades and the sharp rise in the deficits after 1998 requires careful analysis.

The outstanding debts of the states increased from about 16 per cent of the GSDP in the mid-1970s to 27.7 percent in 2002-03 as discuss in Chapter 1. In several outstanding debts accounted 30 per cent of their respective Gross States Domestic Product. For many states debt liabilities as a proportion of revenue receipts exceed 200 per cent. With growing debt stock, interest burden on state budgets increased sharply, the interest payments preempted 21.6 per cent of the revenue receipts of state in 2000-01 as against 13 per cent in 1990-91.

States have been resorting to issuing larger amounts of guarantees on behalf of the public sector entities, undertaking infrastructure investment and other development activities. Guarantees represent a direct liability on state budgets. The rising guarantees and assured payment arrangements at the state level pose issues of sustainability of state finances. Government's off-budget liabilities could be a potential threat to the fiscal and financial stability of the states.

This study explains the procedure of setting up of Finance Commission as well as Planning Commission. The two separate bodies having separate identity working on the same objective, i.e. financial equalization between centre and state. We have studied also about the role of Finance Commission and Planning Commission for smooth financial relation between centre and states.

The allocation of financial resources between the centre and the state in any federal set-up is the most vital and at the same time the most difficult problem. Perhaps no federation in the world has fully solved this problem. Every federation has tried to reduce the intensity of the problem in its own way. In this sphere, the Indian Constitution provides for a financially strong Centre. Following the precedent set in the Government of India Act, 1935; the Constitution has sought to make a more or less clear division of the financial resources between the Centre and the States.

The Finance Commission, a statutory body, was excepted to develop set of sound principles on the basis of which the states would get resources from the Centre according to their needs. Removal of regional economic disparities was to be attained through the scheme of resource transfer as recommended by the Finance Commissions. Equally it is true that the successive Finance Commissions have asserted frequently pertaining to realization of the said objectives. On the other hand, a careful analysis of the recommendations of the successive Finance Commissions reveals that the statutory approach has not been much conducive in this context. For example, the successive Finance

Commissions, by and large, have endorsed population factor in their scheme of resource transfer to the states. Further, resource has been given to the state on the basis of recommendation of successive Finance Commissions in order to cover the budgetary deficits of the State Governments. Almost, the Finance Commissions have estimated the gap between revenue resources and expenditure of the states and this gap has been attempted to be covered through the tax-share and grants-in-aid. In fact, in comparison to population factor, there is much substance in the other factors like inverse of per capita income, Tax-efforts as well as economy in expenditure performance of the states, which have been ignored by the successive Finance Commissions in their scheme of resource transfer. Moreover, the accent on budgetary need of the states has not been much congenial in realizing the well-desired objective of reduction in the regional economic disparities.

The Planning Commission has emerged as an important channel of resource transfer to the states. Since, inception of planned economic development in India, realization of economic growth with social justice has been the supreme target. Reckoning of the facts indicate that Plan transfers were not much conducive towards realization of the said been designed in such a manner that it has resulted in reverse flow of resources from the states to the Centre in form of repayment of interest as well as principal. Such a trend has created major financial problems before the State Governments, especially the economically backward states and thus the gap between backward states and economically developed states has widened over the period. Here, it should be noted that while assigning Plan grants to the states, the Planning Commission has assigned higher weight age to the population, which is rather less satisfactory in the Indian context. At the same time, the factors like 'Tax-efforts of the states,' 'Inverse of per capita income of the states,', etc. have not been given due weight age and relatively backward states have been assigned smaller quantum of resources in per capita terms. It is, therefore, the entire approach of the Planning Commission towards Central resource regarding realization of reduction in the regional economic disparities not it has established a healthy Centre-State fiscal relationship in India.

Thus, the Finance Commission as well as the Planning Commission has failed to evolve a set of sound principles for central resource transfer to the states and, therefore, they have not succeeded in order to establish an amicable relationship between the Centre and the States in the field of finance. It is virtually the policies of the Finance Commission and the Planning Commission due to which several anomalies have emerged like mounting Central loan to the states, problem of state's overdrafts, the questions of fiscal autonomy of the states.

The central loans to the States have been increasing by leaps and bounds. The poorer States are experiencing heavier burden of central loans than the economically well-off States of the country. The States' indebtedness in India, particularly Central loans to States have been growing rapidly since the advent of planning. Therefore, the mounting debt-burden of the States *vis-à-vis* the Centre is the most abrasive and irrigating element in the Centre-state financial relations. In Federal type of Government the States Governments burdened with expensive social and development functions whereas the sources of tax revenues assigned to them are rigid. The problem is more difficult in India where the State Governments have not fully exploited their tax resources due to the fear of losing votes. On the other hand, their fiscal needs have increased on account of expansion of social and development services.

The states have had very little surpluses after meeting their non-development expenditure as discussed in this study. The surplus over non-development expenditure has not grown. Markedly, in spite of the buoyancy of states revenues whatsoever and the efforts of additional taxation, the increase in revenues having been absorbed particularly by the mounting interest charged on debts. This is a very strange situation indeed. This shows how much the growing predominance of the capital account has affected the state finances adversely leading to deficit budgets and borrowing. Added to these things, the capital outlay of the states does not go to commercially viable investments. The states provide major portion of infrastructural facilities for social and economic development but the irony of the situation is this that the developmental outlay on this account is not income yielding. Unfortunately, even those projects, which are expected to be income yielding are not showing sufficient returns. Loans and advances given to the Electricity Board, Road Transport Corporation, Irrigation Projects, etc., are not giving sufficient returns. Moreover, the pattern of plan assistance according to Gadgil formula is also responsible to a great extent, for the prevailing debt burden. Even the assistance for relief against natural calamities is often in the form of loans. Curiously enough the phenomenon of inadequacy starts with the policy of the Finance Commission. The budgetary projections of the states are scrutinized with utmost care, as if states are financially imprudent. In this process, many legitimate parts of projections are cancelled. The expenditure of states is also under-estimated. The net result is that many states appear to have surplus or non-plan revenue account for the projected period while in reality they may face even heavy deficits. We may also add the policy of the central government to the total picture of inadequacy. There are examples when central government has ignored the interests of the states and taken measures to irritate them. Firstly, the centre has not taken adequate steps to levy all the taxes under article 269 of the constitution, the proceeds of which go to States. Secondly, in case additional Excise Duties the central government has not cared to impose the duties on those items whose proceeds would go to the States. Thirdly, change in tax-laws to convert a part of income tax into corporation tax has also reduced states' share in the proceeds of income tax. Moreover, it is Central Government's responsibility to keep prices stable because currency and mint, money and Banking and many other relevant financial powers are with it. But its failure to check the price rise has made the situation of states even worse. It may be emphasized that the blames for the existing difficulties of the states do not lie entirely with the Centre, states should exploit their tax and revenue and partly because of the growing fiscal needs of the State Governments, there has been an enormous growth in their public debt.

Loans have been advanced to the State for Plan and non-Plan purposes. They are for development and non-development programmes. Plan loans are further classified into State Plan Schemes, Central Plan Schemes and centrally sponsored schemes. The centre provides loans to the states for both plan and non-plan purposes. They are intended for development and non-development purposes. While loans for plan schemes comprise loans for State Plan Schemes, Central Plan Schemes and Centrally Sponsored Schemes, non-plan loans are mainly for purchases of fertilizers and other agricultural inputs, loans against small savings collections, ways and means assistance for tiding over temporary difficulties, etc. The non-development programmes are drought, flood relief, and rehabilitation works. We have seen in the previous chapter that the magnitude of central loans to the states has increased enormously during the planned era under which the states have been assisted by the Central Government largely in the form of loans for plan purposes. Loans are advanced to the states for development activities, which mean economic activities intended to create productive capacity in the economy, which will yield income. The activities are gain classified into plan and non-plan. Plan purpose activities refer to economic activities included in the plans. Plan loans are sanctioned on the recommendations of the Planning Commission. They fall outside the Revenue Budget. The non-plan loans are provided on the recommendation of the Union Ministries, particularly the Ministry of Finance. They are discretionary in nature but they are included in the revenue budget. The plan and non-plan loans may be for development and non-development purposes. But the development and non-development activities do not correspond to plan and non-plan activities, rather they are inter-mingled. The plan and non-plan purpose classification serves only the financial and administrative convenience. They are not useful for economic evaluations. The Sixth Finance Commission classified central loans into development and non-development loans. The development purpose loans include according to it, loans for irrigation, development of agriculture and allied activities, community development and National Extension Schemes, Industrial

Housing and such other purposes. Non-development purpose loans include loans for Rehabilitations Schemes and loans for Relief Works. They also include *ad hoc* loans for clearing unauthorized overdrafts, ways and means advances and loans meant for filling up the gap in the revenue expenditure of the states.

The mounting burden of central loans with their increasing liability of repayment has produced adverse financial and economic impact on the economy of the state leading to serious erosion of the financial position of a poor state like Bihar with weak resource base.

In this context it would be useful to build up a theoretical base for analyzing the impact of Central loans on the economy of the State. A brief discussion of the theories will also be used to study the impact of inter-government loans. There are classical and modern approaches to the theory of public debt. According to Prof. R.A. Musgrave, there are two main classical theories 'Pay-as-you-go' theory and 'Inter-generation equity' theory. The former, i.e. "Pay-as-you-go" is also called the 'self-liquidating' theory which maintains that any loan which is not self-liquidating has a bad impact on the economy, because it has to be repaid out of the proceeds of tax revenues and the tax-proceeds becomes additional burden on the economy. The 'inter-generation equity' theory maintains that if a loan is raised, it may impose a burden on the present generation in form of additional taxation for debt servicing, whereas the beneficiaries of public expenditure undertaken with loans may be future generation. The modern approach towards public debt rejects the classical views. It maintains that loan financing is an important instrument in the hands of the government for the regulation of the stabilization and economic growth and its effects should be examined in the context of overall objectives of economic growth and stability whether it promotes economic growth-oriented policies with social justice.

The impact of public debt and loans may be analyzed under two heads: firstly, whose which are related with the raising of the loans and their spending and secondly, those effects which are due to the existence of the debt. The first may be called the "process or preliminary effects" and the second may be termed as 'asset effects' and 'transfer effect.' The preliminary effects of central loans are the effects upon the investment and production of the state, which are generated, in the very process of Government borrowing and the spending of the resources available through borrowing. Thus, preliminary effects are related with the raising and spending the central loans. They depend chiefly upon the nature and the purpose of the loan. The impact may be financial and economic, they may be primarily and secondary and accordingly the burden of union loans may be financial and economic. When the Government obtains a debt, the level of taxation in the economy has to be increased in order to meet the debt servicing charges as David M.C. Wright observes, "The financial burden of the debt is to be measured by the effects of the interest charges and the taxes levied to meet them. The relation, which the taxes bear to the national money income, is the question of primary importance. The higher level of taxation caused by the rising public debt may have some repercussion on the economy, in the form of adverse effects on the capacity and willingness to mobilize necessary resources by the State. These effects may be called the 'real burden' and 'secondary burden' of the loan.

The assets of poor state like Bihar have exceeded the liabilities but a very important proportion of the assets is in the form of loans advanced to the Bihar State Electricity Board, Co-operatives Institutions, Local Bodies, Social Security Schemes, Natural Calamities, Bihar State Housing Board, Bihar State Road Transport Corporation, etc. They are yielding either no returns or inadequate returns as discussed in Chapter V. The utilization part is certainly more significant because it is neither the volume of the central loans nor the magnitude of debt servicing charges that determines the burden. If the Central loans and the debt servicing charges are increasing rapidly and simultaneously the assets are also increasing in the economy, the impact of the loans. But unfortunately, as discussed above, the State Government is not utilizing central loans properly.

The problem of central loans is a macro-economic problem; therefore, it requires multi-pronged strategy. The strategy should have short-term and long-term perspectives. The short-term measures are required for the reduction of the immediate financial burden of the Union loans. The long-term measures will reduce the economic as well as financial strains. The short-term measures will be chiefly concerned with debt-adjustment in the form of writing-off certain loans and interest payments. They will also be concerned with rescheduling of certain loans. The long-term measures will approach the problem from different angles, e.g., efforts of resource mobilisation by the states, greater devolution from the centre, rationalization of expenditure policy and cautious loan policy.

The Twelfth Finance Commission has recommended a Debt Relief Facility (DRF) in place of Fiscal Reform Facility (FRF). There are two components of the scheme. One relates to consolidation and rescheduling of the loan and passage of FRBM Act. The second relates to reduction of revenue deficit and maintaining GFD at 2000-05 level.

The Twelfth Finance Commission has recommended that the central loans to the State contracted till 31.03.2004 and outstanding on 31.03.2005 may be consolidated and re-scheduled for fresh term of twenty years; and interest rate of 7.5 percent be charged on this amount with certain conditionality. The first condition to be fulfilled to attain eligibility for relief is that each State should enact the Fiscal Responsibility Legislation. The total relief, which can be availed of by all the States, can go upto Rs. 33,000 crores in five years of the award period. The interest saving will be about Rs. 21,300 crores and principal repayment saving of Rs. 11,900 crores.

A special scheme of debt write-off linked to reduction of revenue deficit of the State has also been introduced. The salient features of this scheme are:

(a) The three years average (2001-02, 2002-03 and 2003-04) amount of Revenue Surplus/Deficit will be taken as the base year figure for 2003-04.

(b) For Revenue Surplus States, which continue to remain in revenue surplus during the award period, the repayment of loans will be written-off if they do not go below base year figure. If the surplus figure goes below the base year figure, no write-off will be given.

(c) In case of revenue deficit States, the write-off will be given if the revenue deficit goes below the base year figure. For the purpose of determining the scale at which the relief will be provided, the repayment due by the State during the period 2005-10 to the base year figure of revenue deficit has been worked out. This determines the amount of write-off of repayment that will be allowed to each State for the reduction of each rupee of revenue deficit. In case of U.P. this ratio is 0.44.

(d) The write-off amount will be restricted to the repayment due on the consolidated loan for the year.

(e) Further, each State will be required to achieve in each year of award period a reduction in the revenue deficit, which compared to base year figure is cumulatively higher than the cumulative reduction attributable to interest relief.

(f) If the revenue deficit level deteriorates, then the performance in the subsequent year will be measured for not that particular year figure is cumulatively higher than the cumulative reduction attributable to interest relief.

(g) The benefit of write-off would be available only if the fiscal deficit of the State is contained to the level of 2004-05.

(h) The enactment of FRBM act is a necessary pre-condition.

The savings, which the State will have if the conditions are fulfilled, have not been quantified. However, these can be up to the principal repayment amount subject to a ceiling fixed for each State in terms of formula.

The Twelfth Finance Commission has recommended a new policy of Central Loans to States. According to this scheme, the Centre should release only the grant portion (30%) of Central Assistance for State plan and leave it to the

State to raise loan portion (70%) from other sources. The Central Government should not act as an intermediary for future lending and allow the States to approach the market directly. If some fiscally weak States are unable to raise funds from the market, the Centre could borrow for the purpose of on lending to such States, but the interest rates should remain aligned to marginal cost of borrowing for the Centre. Govt. of India, has accepted this new approach in principle, to be implemented in phases, in consultation with RBI. The ATR further states that from 2005-06 the States would be allowed at their discretion not to draw the loan portion of CPA.

The new loan policy and ceiling on borrowings suggested by The Twelfth Finance Commission and implemented by the Govt. of India in full and not gradually as given ATR clearly favours the Central Government and not the States. With no provision of block loans, the Centre has reduced its capital disbursement and thereby its gross fiscal deficit. This is the second device of notionally reducing the GFD. Earlier, the Govt. of India had taken out the loans against small savings from the consolidated account and had created a separate National Small Saving Funds (NSSF) and thereby reduced the GFD. This fiscal engineering not fiscal restructuring has been done by Govt. of India to fulfil the FRBM Act targets.

Further the Finance Minister in his budget speech for 2005-06 said that because of TFC recommendations "I was left with no option but to press the pause button *vis-à-vis* the FRBM Act". But the close examination of the impact of the Twelfth Finance Commission recommendations on budget (*EPW*, April 23, 2005, pp. 1675-79) shows the Govt. of India will have a saving or Rs. 12,248 crores because of non-disbursement of plan Rs. 29,003 crores even with an incremental burden of Rs. 19,755 crores in the shape of high tax shares and grants-in-aid. Thus as a result of Twelfth Finance Commission recommendations the Govt. of India has gained without affecting any fiscal restructuring.

For the first time, the Twelfth Finance Commission has recommended annual borrowing limits for the State Government. While discussing dimensions of restructuring, the Twelfth Finance Commission has suggested the need to specify annual ceiling of borrowing for each State and implement a hard budget constraint. This is one of the most important and far reaching recommendations of the Twelfth Finance Commission. The Commission has recommended both the limit and its institutionalization. For this purpose the 2004-05 has been taken as a base year and this has been made a pre-condition for debt relief also.

For institutionalizing this limit the Twelfth Finance Commission talks of loans council. The Government of India will try to enforce this condition while giving permission to States for borrowing under Article 293(3) of the Constitution of India. But there are certain borrowings where permission of Central Government is not required like Provided Fund and Small Savings. Sometime the State may overshoot the limit of borrowings and it is not clear how the Government of India will then enforce the ceiling.

External assistance may be transferred to States on the same term and conditions as attached to such assistance by external funding agencies, thereby making Government of India a financial intermediary without any gain or loss. The external assistance passed on to the State should be managed through a separate fund in the public account. Though Govt. of India has accepted the recommendation but has put a condition that the service cost and exchange rate fluctuations would also be passed on to the states.

In the earlier regime, the EAP Central Assistance used to come as part of block loan and block grant and the repayment clearly laid down. Now with many donor agencies funding the project with different conditions of loans, it will be very difficult for the States to project the receipt and the liability of payment hence difficult to make adequate provisions in the budget. There is a need to discuss this issue in greater detail and the Ministry of Finance has to come out with a detailed procedure of release of the amount and its repayment and accounting.

All State should set-up Sinking Fund (SF) for amortization of all loans including loans from banks, liabilities on account of NSSF, etc. The Fund should be maintained outside the Consolidated Fund of the State and the Public Account and should not be used for any other purpose, except for redemption of loans.

State should set-up Guarantee Redemption Fund (GRF) through earmarked guarantee fees. This should be preceded by risk weighing of guarantees. The quantum of contribution to the fund should be decided accordingly. On the above line a Sinking Fund and Guarantee Redemption Fund will have to be set-up in the State.

Though the creation of these funds is a welcome step and recommended earlier by RBI also but it has not been made mandatory for the States. With the condition of reduction of revenue deficit already there for restructuring and debt relief, will it be prudent for a revenue deficit State to set apart a substantial part of revenue outside public account and thereby raise its revenue deficit further and thus loose the chance getting some debt relief under the special relief scheme.

As per ATR the Govt. of India has accepted this recommendation in principle. The Government Accounting Standard Board (GASB) in the office of C&A.G. of India would be asked to draw a detailed road map and operational framework for its implementation.

In chapter six, the main findings of the study have been interwoven in summary form and suggestions have been made to check this pernicious and regressive trend and release the State from the "debt-trap".

The following measures are suggested within the framework of the above strategy:

(1) No Federal Government can, hardly have a short or long-term practical relevance unless it begins with measures to chop-off the extravagant and populist expenditure of the state. The state should rationalize its expenditure policy. The state's expenditure policy is defective insofar as the non-development expenditure has risen rapidly. The non-development revenue expenditure is dominated by outlays on servicing the State's debt, particularly central loans. The non-development capital expenditure is dominated by the amortization charges of the state's debt. Such tendency should be checked. There are pockets of

extravagances where economy is feasible. In doing so, the large amount of precious resources will be freed for really worthwhile schemes of development and to that extent; the state's dependence on central loans will be reduced. No doubt, improvement is not possible unless it begins with measures of economy in non-development expenditure.

(2) The State, on its part, will have to take stricter steps to generate more resources for investment. The State Government does not exhibit enough political courage in the levy of new taxes and raising the rates of existing taxes. There is no doubt that the State has not been able to mobilize financial resources commensurate with the rising expenditure, mainly because of its inability to tax adequately the agricultural sector. It is a fact beyond doubt that there are some rich islands in agriculture, which need to be brought within the tax net. During the plan period, a very substantial volume of expenditure has been allocated to irrigation, power, industry and road transport. Such investments may not yield returns in the short-run. But in the long-run, they must be able to pay their way and also contribute some surplus to the public ex-checker. Public investments in certain sectors may not yield direct returns but they must, in the long-run, increase the tax paying capacity of the state, which may be exploited by the Government to fuel the economic development. There is enough scope for improving the performance of two big enterprises e.g., the Bihar State Electricity Board (BSEB) and the Bihar State Road Transport Corporation (BSRTC). Besides these efforts to boost the revenue potential of the States, the Government should take stringent steps to collect tax arrears and loans advanced to different parties. It should check tax evasion also. Perhaps, it would be worthwhile for the Government to devote more attention to these

aspects of raising more revenues instead of taking to easy course of taking loans.

(3) The Centre should increase the devolution of taxes, duties and grants to the State. Thus, on the one hand, amounts to the recognition of the right of the State on national resources and, on the other hand, reduce their dependence on the Central loans. Therefore, a dynamic pattern of fiscal transfers from the Centre to the State should be evolved so that not only the gap in the non-plan revenue and capital accounts of the State is fully bridged but also the State is enabled to emerge as a financial viable unit of the Union. In evolving a pattern of devolution, the Finance Commission should necessarily aim at giving the State a measure of independence in the command of resources so that the State is not only in a position to meet adequately its non-plan commitments but it should also have sufficient surplus to invest in developmental activities and to finance any new or unforeseen items of expenditure without having to hang on the Centre. The total transfers of resources from the Centre to the State must increase so that the resource-base of the State is strengthened.

The three steps outlined above may wipe out not only the revenue deficit but also balance or create surpluses in the revenue budget. This is the basic objective of the normative approach adopted by the Ninth Finance Commission, which has, on its own, suggested phasing out the deficit in such a manner as to reach zero level by 1994-95, if not achieving a surplus.

(4) Now comes the loan policy of the State. The problem can be divided into two categories: (i) that which relates to past debts, and (ii) that which relates to future debts. It is suggested that the problem of existing central loans may not be tackled merely through rescheduling of repayment. The existing loans may be classified into

> productive and unproductive ones. The latter should be outright written-off and the former should be rescheduled and made softer. Within the framework of this policy guidance, the following suggestions are worth considering.

Rescheduling of the terms of the repayment and writing of certain loans made for socially and financially unproductive purposes are short-term measures. It is relevant to mention here that there are certain loans given in the past by the Central Government for such purposes as meeting a part of the expenditure on natural calamities, relief and rehabilitation, clearance of over-drafts, meeting gaps in resources, schemes for modernization of police and police housing which should also have been written-off, because none of these loans was such as would yield any return, which could have covered the repayment of loans or interest thereon. In view of inherent deficient resources-position of the state, it is suggested that such loans should either be written-off or converted into grants with retrospective effects.

It may be noted that major part of the plan assistance it invested in infrastructure projects and in social services like Health, Education, Roads, Welfare, etc. These investments do not yield direct tangible monetary returns to the State and, therefore, the plan expenditure on these items should be in shape of grants. It is suggested to write-off the interest payment due on such loans and convert the principal amount into grants. The central Government should provide grants to the State for such works in future. It will reduce the allocational burden of Union loans on the State.

There has to be a time lag between plan investment and flow of benefits from such investments. This time lag has to be reflected in the terms of repayment. Therefore, in the case of such loans, there should be an initial period of moratorium both on capital and interest payment and the period should correspond with the expected time taken for the fructification of such schemes. The repayment schedule should coincide with the maturity of such schemes. Besides these loans may carry interest rates equivalent to the estimated internal rate on each project.

As regards financing of relief expenditure, the amount of central assistance should consist entirely of grants and there should be no loan component whatsoever. These relief works are in the form of social security schemes, which are expected by the suffering people from the society. They happen cyclical in all the states over a period of time. Hence, they become a national problem, which should be looked after by the Central Government by assisting the States financially in the form of grants. The present Finance Commission should recommended that all outstanding loans and interest payments due from the states for undertaking such relief works should be written-off... Central Government should provide grants to the States for undertaking such works in the future. This policy measure will reduce the allocational burden of Central loan of the state.

A substantial amount of Central loans have been utilized for building flood protection embankments, etc. They are essential for the protection of crops, human life and property but they do not yield any direct monetary returns. They are, no doubt, unproductive but are in the nature of expenditure to avoid national (Natural) calamities. It is suggested that the past loans given to the State for flood protection works should be converted into grants and future assistance for this purpose should also be in the shape of grants rather than loans.

The State Government has advanced a substantial amount of loans to the Bihar Electricity Board and Bihar State Road Transport Corporation. But the Government have not received any amount from them either by way of repayments of loan or direct payment of interest there on. Nor there seems to be any possibility of any receipt in the near feature. They are running in loss. But the state has to make regular payments of the capital and interest to the Centre. The previous Commission adopted the same norms for the assumed rate of return from Electricity Board and State Transport Undertakings for both the rich and the poor States. This was a wrong approach. The returns in the power sector will be higher where there are larger percentages of industrial or urban consumers. Losses in transmission will be less, the rate of return will be higher and realization will be better. In predominantly rural economies, the transmission lines are stretched for longer distances, carry fewer loads and therefore, transmission limes are not cost effective. Because of predominantly origin economy, long transmission lines and old power plants, the losses of the State Electricity Board are likely to continue In this situation all such outstanding loans and inters thereon should be written-off and the Electricity Act for not paying interest to the State Government and the low priority accorded to repayment to Government, should be amended to delete the special provisions. The case with Road Transport Corporation is similar. It has to run uneconomic services in the rural areas and so there is loss. Consequently, it is not in a position to repay even the interest. Therefore, a part of central loans equal to the loans advanced to this Corporation also should be written-off and in future, they should be made financially viable so that they contribute something to the public exchequer.

Share in small savings collection constitutes an important source of financing the plan. Under present arrangement (effective from 1987-88), the loans given to the States are three-fourths of the net collection within the States. These loans carry an initial moratorium of 5 years and are repayable in 25 years. The Seventh Financial Commission has recommended that small savings loans be converted into 'loans in perpetuity'. But the Eighth Finance Commission did not agree because it felt that this would confer disproportionately larger benefits on some advanced states and would defeat the purpose of any rational system of debt-relief which is to take into account the need for relief as well as the purposes for which the loans have been utilized. The Eighth Finance Commission felt that such steps would also affect the resources of the Central Government and its capacity to help the backward states.

It is suggested that the Ninth Finance Commission should reconsider the decision. The entire outstanding on the small savings of the states, which are below the national average in per capita income terms, should be converted into 'loans in perpetuity.' The States, which are above the national average, should have only 50 percent of the loans outstanding converted into 'loans in perpetuity'.

The present pattern of plan assistance (70 percent loan and 30 percent grants) had led in effect to a reverse flow of resources from the state to the centre, making the size of plan assistance illusory. The necessity to change the Gadgil formula has been felt in cross-sections of the society. There is no logic also of these proportions. The Sarkaria Commission also holds the view that the pattern of central plan assistance "needs to be reviewed by the Planning Commission in view of the latest developments". Dr. A.K. Gaur writes that "the current division of plan transfers into grant (30 percent) and loan (70 percent) is totally arbitrary". He suggests, "There is an urgent need to reshuffles the grant-loan proportion". Mr. Sastry and Reddy also suggest "the present pattern of central assistance to states may warrant a review. Any upward revision in the grant component will go a long way in reducing the debt burden of the states".

It is suggested in this connection that the states having per capita income below the all states' average per capita income should be given central assistance in the ratio of 70 percent grants and 30 percent loans and the reverse may be the case for the states whose per capita income is higher than the all states' average per capita income. This will serve two objectives, viz., (i) reducing the burden of states' indebtedness, and (ii) really adding to the resources of the states, which can be spent on achieving marked progress in development so as to enable this backward state to catch up with the developed states.

The recommendation of the Sarkaria Commission may also be considered favourably. The Commission observes that '....a time has come to review the two-fold loan-grant pattern of central assistance, 70: 30 and 10: 90 and replace it by suitable three or four-fold patterns, such as 70: 30, 50: 50 and 20: 80 or 90: 10, 60: 40 and 10: 90 respectively taking into account loan servicing capacity of the states and their per capita state Domestic Product. A decision may be taken by the NEDC on this after expert examination by the Planning Commission and consideration of various options. The Planning Commission further observes that, "The revision of the pattern of Central assistance favouring a higher grant component will reduce the need for extensive debt rescheduling by the Finance Commission."

The future loans should be on softer terms both in respect of scheduling of repayment of the principal amount and interest thereon. The states argued before the Sixth Finance Commission (as they argued before the Second Finance Commission) that the Centre enjoys the right of deficit financing and external assistance, which the Centre gets either free or at concessional rate of interest. Therefore, they should get cheap loans from the Centre.

The states' borrowing power are restricted unduly by the constitution under Article 293 (1 and 3). The Sarkaria Commission has taken the view that "It should apply only to long and medium-term borrowing from the open market and not to borrowing from financial institutions or short-term loan for less than one year. It can be done under Article 293(4) of the Constitution and no amendment of the Constitution shall be needed for this. This will give more elbowroom to the State.

What emerges from the above study boils down to what Professor Thimmaiah writes, "The only solution to this problem is to reduce the size of the loan assistance to the states. If the Central Government is interested in assisting the states in development activity, as far as possible, all non-self-liquidating projects should be assisted by grants... The loan assistance should be categorically confined to self-liquidating (revenue yielding) projects. This should exclude irrigation projects which are presently classified as self-liquidating".

Having regard to the considerations in the preceding paragraphs, it is suggested that the Ninth Finance Commission should give a purposive reorientation to the future loan policy of the Central Government because after all, the centre and the states are co-partner in the common endeavour for future economic development and the spirit behind this relationship has to be preserved while evolving a wholesome creditor-debtor relationship between the two. The whole problem needs to be approached in the way the Eighth Finance Commission has viewed when it observed: "The centre has to view states' requirements in the perspective of total national needs and provide for them." "The loan funds constitute a pool of resources recycled between the union and the states." The real question is how best the total resources of the whole country can be allocated because the present arrangement for allocation of savings are unsatisfactory and hence the problem.

The Ninth Finance Commission is requested to take into account the implications of increasing financial burden of this poor state (discussed previously) and aim at steps to reduce the economic development burden resulting from union loans not leading to increased capital formation as well as the distributional economic burden resulting from the less developed states' dependence more on union loans than on grants.

The suggestions for reforms outlined above are worth trying. They can take the state out of the rut into which it has fallen and the State can look for a prosperous future, which can usher in a milieu of progress and financial discipline. Unless these steps are taken, and taken expeditiously, the legacy that the Seventh Plan will leave for the future generation will not be a pleasant one. The warnings of the Fourth Finance Commission are still resounding in our ears that the entire question of indebtedness of state should be reviewed "as much in the interest of the states at that of the Government of India", and that "in the interest of financial soundness, such an enquiry ought not be delayed any further". The Ninth Finance Commission, no doubt, will have to perform a tight ropewalk. It may be repeated once more that the vice-like debt-trap is fast closing in on the state and unless multipronged strategy is not adopted to stem it, the State is likely to reach the points on any return before the turn of the country.

But the terms of reference of the Ninth Finance Commission mark a significant departure from the past. There is a pointed reference to the need for providing incentives for entire resource mobilization and financial discipline. There is stipulation of the objective of balancing the receipts and expenditure on revenue account of both the States and the Centre and also generating surpluses for capital investment. Serious misgivings have been expressed over the above departures in the terms of reference of the Ninth Finance Commission. They have been expressed in the following words:

> "Removal of the distinction between Plan and non-Plan together with the direction to ensure generation of surpluses of investment indicates that the Finance Commission would have to assess the dimension of the revenue component of the next Plan. Practical difficulties apart, it is apprehended that this would result in an overlap of the function of the Planning Commission and the Finance Commission and undermining of the Gadgil formula, by passing the NDC."

We must note that the Planning Commission itself is a body, which continues to be entirely subordinate to the Central Government, while Plans grants and loans form a large part of the total resources transferred from the centre to the states. During the Sixth Plan, plan grants and loans, on a average annual basis at Rs. 5277.6 crores constituted 42.2 percent of the gross transfers from the centre to the States. During the Seventh Plan period, the corresponding figure was 40 percent, while in the budget estimates of 1993-94; it increased to 44.3 percent. Such large transfer by a body which is not genuinely federal are seen by the states as a handicap in the smooth functioning of the Centre-State relations in the matter of development planning and financing. Even a well meaning Finance Commission is not likely to do much at present in the matter of ensuring better financial justice to states. Hence there is a suggestion to create a body like the inter-state council as envisaged by the constitution. Pending the creation of this body, the National Development Council in which all the states are represented should be consulted before the terms of reference of the Finance Commission and its composition are decided. After all, the states increasingly look to a statutory body like the Finance Commission to do them justice rather than to the Planning Commission

Keeping in view this controversy, the terms of reference of the Tenth Finance Commission (TFC) go back to the traditional guidelines. However, there is one important difference. In making its recommendation the Commission shall have regard, among other considerations, to the objective of not only balancing the receipts and expenditure on revenue account of both the states and the central government, but also generating surplus for capital investment and reducing fiscal deficit. Chelliah says that the reference to fiscal deficit is an innovation. It shows that the terms of reference are conscious towards seriousness of fiscal imbalance prevailing in the country.

Another important aspect of the term of reference of Tenth Finance Commission is that its recommendation for transfer should not encourage fiscal laxity or excessive expenditure. It follows from the fact that the Tenth Finance Commission is to consider the "potential for raising additional taxes, efforts made by the states, the scope for better fiscal management and the need to ensure reasonable returns on departmental and non-departmental enterprises".

The Eleventh Finance Commission, in its report had given stress and the calamity Relief Funds and debt relief of scheme, as advocated by earlier Finance Commissions. It gives relief to the states facing fiscal deficit the recommend as are as follows:

1. Continuance of the existing scheme of Calamity Relief Funds, with an aggregate size of Rs. 11007.29 crores (with centre's share of Rs. 8225.69 crores) to be distributed only for natural calamities of National Calamity Relief Fund for calamities of rare severity, establishment of national centre for calamity management.
2. Continuance of existing scheme of debt relief, linked to improvement in the ratio of revenue receipts of states to its total revenue expenditure, with enhanced inventive and moratorium on payment of instalment of debt and interest on loan given to Punjab.

As per the recommendation of the Twelfth Finance Commission during the period between 2005 and 2010 the centre as share in the Central taxes and the grants-in-aid would transfer a total of Rs. 7,55,751 crore to the States. Out of this, share of Central taxes and duties would be Rs. 6,13,112 crores, while the grants-in-aid would amount to Rs. 1,42,639 crores. This devolution of taxes comes to 30.5 percent of the total divisible pool, while earlier it was 29.5 percent. The recommendations would entail an annual outgo of Rs. 26,000 crore from the Central kitty to the States during 2005-06, which is almost one percent of the GDP.

In addition to the above, main recommendations of the Twelfth Finance Commissions are as under:

(a) The Twelfth Finance Commission has recommended increasing the weighted of total population of the States to 25 per cent, as against the weight of 10 recommended the Eleventh Finance Commission (EFC). In addition, weight given to per capita income by the Eleventh Finance Commission to the distance from per capita income has been reduced from 62.5 per cent to 50 per cent. The weight to the geographical area of the State has been recommended to be increased from 7.5 per cent to 10 per cent. The weight for additional tax effort has also been raised from 5 to 7.5 per cent. In other words, has tried to consider the requirements of the States based on their geographical size and population. Moreover, it has also been decided to reward the efficiency and resource mobilization effort, rather than inefficiency and complacency.

(b) The Twelfth Finance Commission has opened a new source of income for the oil and gas producing States, by recommending that the profit earned by the centre on petroleum should be shared by it with the States concerned. The government of India has accepted these recommendations for 2005-10, but not as general principle of sharing of centre's non-tax revenues. Petroleum profit is the Government of India's share in the crude oil or the natural gas explored within the country, after adjusting the exploration and other costs. This amount is about Rs. 4,000 crore per annum and half of it is to be shared by the centre with the States producing the mineral oil and natural gas.

(c) The Twelfth Finance Commission's recommendations may turn out to be a boon for the local bodies, as it has recommended the augmentation of their financial resources through grants-in-aid of Rs. 25,000 crore, from the consolidated funds of the States. This sum would be around 1.24 per cent of the sharable tax revenues and 0.9 per cent of the gross revenues of the centre, as estimated by the Commission. 80 per cent of this amount would go to the Panchayats and the remaining 20 per cent to the Municipalities.

(d) The recommendations of the TFC also provide for debt relief to the States. This includes a debt write-off scheme linked to the reduction of revenue deficit of the States in place of the Fiscal Reform Facility (FRF). The Commission said the aggregate fiscal deficit of the States taken together has gone from 4.64 per cent of the GDP in 1999-2000, to 4.9 per in the year 2003-04, as against the target of 2.9 per cent of the GDP set by the EFC. The Twelfth Finance Commission, thus, recommended rescheduling of all the State loans from the centre outstanding as on March 31, 2005 to 20 years' repayment plan, after their consolidation. These loans would be to the tune of Rs. 1,28,795 crors and would be rescheduled at the rate of 7.5 per cent per annum. This measure would immensely help the States in continuing their current debt service and would improve their finances. The Commission has also recommended that all the States should also enact their physical responsibility laws.

(e) The Twelfth Finance Commission has also recommended that the States should move towards the accrual-based accounting and that the definition of revenue and fiscal deficit should be standardized across the country. It has also been recommended that the Finance Commission Division of the Finance Ministry should be converted into a full-fledged Department. With a view improve the accounting in the government, the Twelfth Finance Commission has recommended setting up of a National Institute of the Public Financial Accountants, in consultations with the Comptroller and Auditor General of India.

(f) Realizing the growing need to equip the States with the capacity to successfully manage natural disasters every now and then, the Twelfth Finance Commission has recommended the continuation of the scheme of Calamity Relief Fund (CRF) in its present form. The size of the CRF for the five-year period (2005-10) has been kept at Rs. 21,333 crores with the centre contributing. Rs. 16,000 crores and the States Rs. 5,333 crores. The commission has recommended that the definition of disaster should be expanded to cover the disasters like landslides, avalanches, cloudbursts and pest attacks on the crops.

Most of the recommendations, while providing the States with some relief, also provide able suggestions to them, as well as to the centre, for improvements in future. There is a significant increase in the funds to be transferred as grants to the States. EFC had recommended 13.5 per cent of the total transfers in the form of grants but this figure has been increased to 18.9 per cent by the recommendations of Twelfth Finance Commission. This measure would go a long way in providing cushion to the States from the volatilities in the growth of central tax Revenues over five-year period.

In addition, the Commission has made an important departure from the past by allowing States to borrow from any source. The erstwhile compulsion to borrow from the Centre at rate of interest to be fixed by it has been undone. Further, significant debt relief has been recommended for the

States and the States doing well in reducing their revenue deficit would get the benefit of debt write-off. This measure, in particular, would help in inculcating self-discipline among the States.

One good measure that would have long lasting impact on the finances of the States is the recommendation that the States must also enact fiscal responsibility legislations on the lines of one passed by the Union. This would not only bring relief to the States in terms of loans write-off, but would assist them in warding-off the political pressure to take populist measures.

## RECOMMENDATIONS OF THE THIRTEENTH FINANCE COMMISSION (2010-15)

The main recommendations of the Thirteenth Finance Commission are as under:

(xxi) Target of 68 per cent of GDP for combined debt of Centre and states to be achieved by 2014-15. Fiscal consolidation path embodies the steady reduction in augmented debt stock of Centre to 45 per cent of GDP by 2014-15 and for the states to less than 25 per cent of GDP by 2014-15.

(xxii) Loans to states from National Small Savings Fund contracted till 2006-07 and outstanding at the end of 2009-10 to be reset at 9 per cent rate of interest subject to conditions prescribed.

(xxiii) National Small Savings Scheme to be reformed into a market-aligned scheme. State Governments also required to undertake relevant reforms at their level.

(xxiv) Loans from GoI to states and administered by ministries/departments other than MoF, outstanding as at the end of 2009-10, to be written-off subject to conditions prescribed.

(xxv) A window for borrowing from the Central Government to be available for the fiscally weak states that are unable to raise loans from market.

(xxvi) For states that have not availed the benefit of consolidation under DCRF, the facility, limited to consolidation and interest rate reduction, to be extended subject to enactment of FRBM Act.

(xxvii) Benefit of interest relief on NSSF and write-off available to states only if they bring about the necessary amendments/enactments of FRBM

The problem of central loans is a macro-economic problem and therefore, it requires multi-pronged strategy. The strategy should have short-term and long-term perspectives. The short-term measures are required for the reduction of the immediate financial burden of the Union loans. The long-term measures will reduce the economic as well as financial strains. The short-term measures will be chiefly concerned with debt-adjustment in the form of writing-off certain loans and interest payments. They will also be concerned with rescheduling of certain loans. The long-term measures will approach the problem from different angles, e.g., efforts of resource mobilisation by the State, greater devolution from the centre, rationalisation of expenditure policy and cautious loan policy. The following measures are suggested within the framework of the above strategy:

(1) No federal Government can hardly have a short or long-term practical relevance unless it begins with measures to chop-off the extravagant and populist expenditure of the State. The state should rationalise its expenditure policy. The state's expenditure policy is defective insofar as the non-development expenditure has risen rapidly. The non-development revenue expenditure is dominated by outlays on servicing the State's debt, particularly central loans. The non-development capital expenditure is dominated by the amortisation charges of the state's debt. Such tendency should be checked. There are pockets of extravagances where economy is feasible. In doing so, the large amount of precious resources will be

freed for really worthwhile schemes of development and to that extent, the state's dependence on central loans will be reduced. No doubt, improvement is not possible unless it begins with measures of economy in non-development expenditure.

(2) The State, on its part, will have to take stricter steps to generate more resources for investment. The State Government does not exhibit enough political courage in the levy of new taxes and raising the rates of existing taxes. There is no doubt that the State has not been able to mobilise financial resources commensurate with the rising expenditure, mainly because of its inability to tax adequately the agricultural sector. It is a fact beyond doubt that there are some rich islands in agriculture which need to be brought within the tax-net. During the plan period, a very substantial volume of expenditure has been allocated to irrigation, power, industry and road transport. Such investments may not yield returns in the short-run. But in the long-run, they must be able to pay their way and also contribute some surplus to the public ex-checker. Public investments in certain sectors may not yield direct returns but they must, in the long-run, increase the tax paying capacity of the state which may be exploited by the Government to fuel the economic development. There is enough scope for improving the performance of two big enterprises e.g., the Bihar State Electricity Board and the Rajya Transport Corporation. Besides these efforts to boost the revenue potential of the State, the Government should take stringent steps to collect tax arrears and loans advanced to different parties. It should check tax evasion also. Perhaps, it would be worthwhile for the Government to devote more attention to these aspects of raising more revenues instead of taking to easy course of taking loans.

(3) The Centre should increase the devolution of taxes, duties and grants to the State. Thus, on the one hand, amounts to the recognition of the rigbt of the State on national resources and, on the other hand, reduces their dependence on the Centre for resources in the form of loans. Reduced dependence on plan finance means reduced dependence of Central loans. Therefore, a dynamic pattern of fiscal transfers from the Centre to the State should be evolved so that not only the gap in the non-plan revenue and capital accounts of the State is fully bridged but also the State is enabled to emerge as a financially viable unit of the Union. In evolving a pattern of devolution, the Finance Commission should necessarily aim at giving the State a measure of independence in the command of resources so that the State is not only in a position to meet adequately its non-plan commitments but it should also have sufficient surplus to invest in developmental activities and to finance any new or unforeseen items of expenditure without having to hang on the Centre. The total transfers of resources from the Centre to the State must increase so that the resource base of the State is strengthened.

The three steps outlined above may wipe out not only the revenue deficit but also balance or create surpluses in the revenue budget. This is the basic objective of the normative approach adopted by the Ninth Finance Commission which has, on its own, suggested phasing out the deficit in such a manner as to reach zero level by 1994-95, if not achieving a surplus.

(4) Now comes the loan policy of the State. The problem can be divided into two categories: (i) that which relates to past debts, and (ii) that which relates to future debts. It is suggested that the problem of existing central loans may not be tackled merely through rescheduling of repayment. The existing loans may be classified into

productive and unproductive ones. The latter should be outright written-off and the former should be rescheduled and made softer. Within the framework of this policy guidance, the following suggestions are worth-considering.

Rescheduling of the terms of the repayment and writing-off certain loans made for socially and financially unproductive purposes are short-term measures. It is relevant to mention here that there are certain loans given in the past by the Central Government for such purposes as meeting a part of the expenditure on natural calamities, relief and rehabilitation, clearance of overdrafts, meeting gaps in resources, schemes for modernisation of police and police housing which should also have been written-off, because none of these loans was such as would yield any return, which could have covered, the repayment of loans or interest thereon. In view of inherent deficient resource-position of the State, it is suggested that such loans should either be written-off or converted into grants with retrospective effects.

It may be noted that major part of the plan assistance is invested in infrastructure projects and in social services like Health, Education, Roads, Welfare, etc. These investments do not yield direct tangible monetary returns to the State and, therefore, the plan expenditure on these items should be in the shape of grants. It is suggested to write-off the interest payments due on such loans and concert the principal amount into grants. The Central Government should provide grants to the State for such works in future. It will reduce the allocational burden of Union loans on the State.

There has to be a time-lag between plan investments and flow of benefits from such investments. This time-lag has to be reflected in the terms of repayment. Therefore, in the case of such loans, there should be an initial period of moratorium both on capital and interest payment and the period should correspond with the expected time taken for the fructification of such schemes. The repayment schedule should coincide with the maturity of such schemes. Besides these loans may carry interest rates equivalent to the estimated internal rate on each project.

As regards financing of relief expenditure, the amount of central assistance should consist entirely of grants and there should be no loan component whatsoever. These relief works are in the form of social security schemes which are expected by the suffering people from the society. They happen cyclically in all the states over a period of time. Hence they become a national problem which should be looked after by the Central Government by assisting the State financially in the form of grants. For the present, the Finance Commission should recommended that all outstanding loans and interest payments due from the States for undertaking such relief works should be written-off. Central Government should provide grants to the State for undertaking such works in the future. This policy measure will reduce the allocational burden of Central loan to the State.

A substantial amount of Central loans have been utilized for building flood protection embankments, etc. They are essential for the protection of crops, human life and property but they do not yield any direct monetary returns. They are, no doubt, unproductive but are in the nature of expenditure to avoid national calamities. It is suggested that the past loans given to the State for flood protection works should be converted into grants and future assistance for this purpose should also be in the shape of grants rather than loans.

The State Government has advanced a substantial amount of loans to the Bihar Elecricity Board and Bihar Rajya Transport Corporation. But the Government have not received any amount from them either by way of repayments of loan or direct payment of interest thereon. Nor there seems to be any possibility of any receipt in the near future. They are running in loss. But the State has to make regular payments of the capital and interest to the Centre. The previous Commissions adopted the same norms for the assumed rate of return from Electricity Board and State Transport Undertakings for both the rich and the poor States. This was a wrong approach. The returns in the power sector will be higher where there are larger percentage of industrial or urban consumers. Losses in transmission will be less, the rates of return will be higher and realisation will be better. In predominantly rural economies, the transmission lines are stretched for longer distances, carry less load and therefore, transmission lines are not cost effective. Because of predominantly original economy, long transmission lines and old power plants, the losses of the State Electricity Board are likely to continue. In this situation all such outstanding loans and interest thereon should be written-off and the Electricity Act for not paying interest to the State Government and the low priority accorded to repayment to Government, should be ammended to delete the special provisions. The case with Rajya Transport Corporation is similar. It has to run uneconomic services in the rural areas and so there is loss. Consequently, it is not in a position to repay even the interest. Therefore, a part of central loans equal to the loans advanced to this Corporation also should be written-off and in future. they should be made financially viable so that they contribute something to the public exchecker.

Share in small savings collection constitutes an important source of financing the plan. Under present arrangement (effective from 1987-88), the loans given to the States are three-fourths of the net collection within the States. These loans carry an initial moratorium of 5 years and are repayable in 25 years. The Seventh Finance Commission has recommended that small savings loans be converted into 'loans in perpetuity'. But the Eighth Finance Commission did not agree because it felt that this would confer disproportionately larger benefits on some advanced states and would defeat the purpose of any rational system of debt-relief which is to take into account the need for relief as well as the purposes for which the loans have been utilized. The Eighth Finance Commission felt that such steps would also effect the resources of the Central Government and its capacity to help the backward states.

It is suggested that the Thirteenth Finance Commission (2010-15) should reconsider the decision. The entire outstanding on the small savings of the states which are below the national average in per capita income terms should be converted into 'loans in perpetuity.' The States which are above the national average should have only 50 per cent of the loans outstanding converted into 'loans in perpetuity'.

The present pattern of plan assistance (70 per cent loan and 30 per cent grants) has led in effect to a reverse flow of resources from the state to the centre. making the size of plan assistance illusory. The necessity to change the Gadgil formula has been felt in cross-sections of the society. There is no logic also of these proportions. The Sarkaria Commission also holds the view that the pattern of central plan assistance "needs to be reviewed by the Planning Commission in view of the latest developments". Dr. A.K. Gaur writes that "the current division of plan transfers into grant (30 per cent) and loan (70 per cent) is totally arbitrary." He suggests that "there is on urgent need to reshuffle the grant-loan proportion." Mr. Sastry and Reddy also suggest that "the present pattern of central assistance to states may warrant a review. Any upward revision in the grant component will go a long way in reducing the debt burden of the states".

It is suggested in this connection that the states having per capita income below the all states' average per capita income should be given central assistance in the ratio of 0 per cent grants and 30 per cent loans and the reverse may be the case for the states whose per capita income is higher than the all states' average per capita income. This will serve two objectives, viz., (i) reducing the burden of states' indebtedness, and (ii) really adding to the resources of the states which can be spent on achieving marked progress in development so as to enable this backward state to catch up with the developed states.

## References

Alllresh Bagchi, Tapas Sen and V.B. Tulasidhas (1988), "Issues Before Ninth Finance Commission, *Economic and Political Weekly*, May 7.

Amresh Bagchi (1988), "First Award of the Ninth Finance Commission—An Appraisal", Economic and Political Weekly Dec. 3.

Gaur, Achal Kumar, 1986, Federal Finance in India, Deep and Deep Publications, F-159, Rajouri Garden, New Delhi, 110027.

H.K. Paranjape (1988), "Task of the Ninth Finance Commission: The Planning Commission Tanglc", *Economic and Political Weekly*, September 17.

Hansen and Perloff, "Local Debt and National Fiscal Policy", in Harold M. Groves (ed.), "View Points Oil Public Financc".

K.K. George (1989), "Ninth Finance commission's First Award—An Evaluation", *Economic and Political Weekly*, April 1.

K.K. Simla (1968), "Local Txation in a Developing Economy", Vora & Co, Bombay.

R.J. Chelliah, *et. al.*, (1992), "Issues Before Tenth Finance Commission", *Economic and Political Weekly*, November 21.

References AT Eapcn (1983). "Inter-Governmental Financial Relations in India". in J.S. Uppal (Ed), India's Economic Problems, Tata McGraw Hill.

Report of Eight Finance Commission, 1984, Govt. of India, New Delhi.

Report of Third Finance Commission, 1965, Govt. of India, New Delhi.

Reports of the Finance Commissions, I to XI, Govt. of India, New Delhi.

Sastry, M.L. and Reddy., G.R., 1988, Centre-State Financial Relations, Centre for Economic and Social Studies, Hyderabad.

Shandilya, Tapan Kumar (1991), "Central Loans to States Under Five Year Plans., Deep and Deep Publications Pvt. Ltd., New Delhi.

Shandilya, Tapan Kumar (1994), Centre State Financial Relation in India. Deep and Deep Publications Pvt. Ltd., New Delhi.

Shandilya, Tapan Kumar (2005), "Emerging Issues in Centre-State Financial Relations: Approach of Twelfth Finance Commission, *Indian Economic Journal* (Conference Vol.). Vishakhapattanam (Andhra Pradesh).

Sinha, R.K. (Ed.), 1986, Centre-State Financial Relations in India, Deep & Deep Publications Pvt. Ltd., F-159, Rajouri Garden, New Delhi-110027.

The Sarkaria Commission Report, Part I, 1988.

The Sarkaria Commission Report, Part I, 1988..

Thimmaiah, G., 1985, Burning Issues in Centre-State Financial Relations, Ashish Publishing House, 8/81 Punjabi Bagh, New Delhi, 110026.

Thimmaish, G. and Rao, Hemlata, Financial Commission and Centre-State Financial Relations, Ashish Publishing House, 8/81, Punjabi Bagh, New Delhi, 110926

U.K. Hicks (1961), "Development from below", Garendon Press.

# Bibliography

## A. BOOK

Abbott, C.C., 1946, Management of Federal Debt., McGraw Hill Book Company, New York.

Agarwal A.C., Public Finance, Theory and Practice, Laxmi Narayan Agarwal, Agra-3.

Bhargava, P.K., 1969, Uttar Pradesh's Finances Since Independence, Vora & Co., Publishers, Pvt. Ltd., Bombay-Allahabad.

———, 1982, Centre State Resources Transfers in India, Academic Press, Gurgaon.

———, 1986, Eassy on Indian Public Finance, Chug Publications, Allahabad.

Bhargava, R.N., 1967, The Theory and Working of Union Finance in India, Chaitanya Publishing House, 5-A, University Road, Allahabad.

Buchanan, James M., 1960, The Public Finance: An Introductory Text-Book, Richard D. Irwin, Inc., Home Wood, Illinois.

Bhatnagar, Sudha, 1979, Union State Financial Relations and Finance Commission, Chug Publications, Allahabad.

Bomball, K.R., 1967, The Foundations of India Federalism, Asia Publishing House, Bombay.

———, 1970, Federal Financial Relations in India, Meenakshi Prakashan, Meerut.

Bajaj, J.L. and others, 1985, Finance Commission and Backward States, Print House, Lucknow.

Chelliah, Raja J., 1962, Fiscal Policy in Under Developed Countries, George Allen & Unwin Ltd., London.

Chandra, Ashok, 1965, Federalism in India, A Study of Union-State Relations, George Allen and Unwin Ltd., London.

Chellia, Raja J. and Associates, 1981, Trends and Issues in Indian Federal Finance, Allied Publishers, New Delhi.

Dalya, Chandra, 1966, The Internal Debt of the Government of India Vora & Co. Publishers, Private Ltd., 3, Round Building, Bombay.

Diwan, Paras, 1981, Union-State Fiscal Relations: An Overview, Light and Life, New Delhi.

Gulati, I.S., 1979, Centre-States Financial Relations, University of Baroda, Baroda.

Harris, S.E., 1947, National Debt and New Economics, McGraw Hill Book Company, New York.

———, 1970, Federal Financial Relations in India, Meenakshi Prakashan, Meerut.

Hicks, U.K., 1965, Development Finance, Planning and Control, Clarendon Press, Oxford.

———, 1961, Federalism and Economic Growth in Underdeveloped Countries, Allen and Unwin Ltd.

———, 1978, Federalism, Failure and Success, Mcmillan.

Indian Institute of Public Administration, April 21, 1969: Problems of Resources Mobilization in the States, Conference Proceedings, Indian Institute of Public Administration, Indraprastha Estate, Ring Road, New Delhi.

Jha, Dibakar, 1962, Bihar Finance, Grantha Mala Karyalaya, Patna.

Jha, Dibakar and Ganguly, Bireshwar (ed.), 1969, Bihar Finances during the Three Periods, University Department of Economics, Patna University, Patna.

Joshi, M.D. (ed.), 1967, Mobilisation of State Resources, Impex India, New Delhi.

Jha, P.K., 1983, Federal Finance in Developing India, Capital Publishing House, Delhi.

Kurihara, K.K., 1959, The Keynesian Theory of Economic Development, George Allen and Unwin Ltd., 40, Museum Street, London, W.C.I.

Kurian, K. and Others, Centre-State Relations, Macmillan, Delhi 1981.

Lakdwala, D.R., 1967, Union-State Financial Relations, Lalwani Publisher, Bombay.

Maxwell, J.A., Commonwealth, 1967, State Finance Relations in Australia, Melbourne University Press, Carlton.

Maxwell, J.A., 1967, Theory of Public Finance, McGraw Hill, New York.

Musgrave, R.A. (ed.), 1965, Eassy in Fiscal Federalism, The Brookings Institution, Washington, D.C.

Mugrave, R.A. and Musgrave, P.B., 1973, Public Finance in Theory and Practice, McGraw Hill.

Nanjudappa, D.M., 1974, Inter-Government Financial Relations in India, Sterling Publishers, New Delhi.

Pal, Chandra, 1983, Centre-State Relations and Co-operative Federation, Deep and Deep Publications, New Delhi.

———, 1984, State Autonomy in Indian Federation, Deep and Deep Publications, New Delhi.

Prasad, Anirudh, 1985, Centre-State Relations in India, Deep and Deep Publications, New Delhi.

Paranje, H.K., 1971, Centre-State Relations and Planning, I.I.P.A., New Delhi.

Rao, Hemlata, 1981, Centre-State Finance Relations, Allied Publishers, New Delhi.

Rao, N.R., 1972, Union-State Finance Relations in India, Karnataka University, Dharwar.

Ray, Amal, 1970, Tension Areas in India's Federal System, World Press.

Sastri, K.V.S., 1966, Federal State Fiscal Relations in India, Oxford University Press, Bombay.

Shreekantaradhy, B.S., 1972, Public Debt and Economic Development in India, Sterling Publishers (P) Ltd., New Delhi.

Santhanam, K., 1960, Union-State Relations in India, Asia Publishing House, Bombay.

———, 1966, Federal Financial Relations in India, Forum of Free Enterprise, Bombay.

Setalvad, M.C., 1974, Union-State Relations under the Indian Constitution.

Singh, Shailendra, 1980, (ed.), Union-State Financial Relations in India: With Special Reference to the Underdeveloped States, Sterling Publications, New Delhi.

Sharma, J.N., 1974, Union and the States—A Study in Fiscal Federalism, Sterling Publications, New Delhi.

Sinha, R.K., 1986 (ed), Centre-State Financial Relations in India, Deep and Deep Publication, New Delhi.

Shandilya, Tapan Kumar, 1991, "Central Loans to States Under Five Year Plans., Deep and Deep Publications, New Delhi.

Shandilya, Tapan Kumar, 1994 (ed.), "Central-State Financial Relations in India, Deep and Deep Publications, New Delhi.

———, 1956, Fiscal Federation in India, Sterling Publihers, New Delhi,.

———, 1981, Evolution of Fiscal Federalism in India, South Asian Publishers, New Delhi.

———, 1985, Regional Imbalances and Fiscal Equalisation in India, South Asian Publishers, Delhi.

Thimmaiah, G., 1977, Burden of Union Loans on the States, Sterling Publishers Pvt. Ltd., New Delhi.

———, 1981, A Critique of the Finance Commission, Wheeler Publications, Allahabad.

———, 1974, Union-State Financial Relations in India.

———, Burning Issues in Centre-State Financial Relations, Ashish Publishing House, New Delhi, 1985.

———, 1973, Studies in Federal Finance, Padma Prakashan, Bangalore.

Thimmaiah, G. and Rao, Hemlata, 1986, Finance Commission and Centre-State Financial Relations, Ashish Publishing House, New Delhi.

Triphthi, R.N., 1980, Federal Finance in Developing Economy.

Veer Raghavachart, S.M., 1969, Union-State Financial Relations in India, Sterling Publication (P) Ltd., New Delhi.

Venkataraman, K., 1968, States' Finances in India, George Allen and Unwin Ltd., Ruskin House, Muslim Street, London.

Venu, S., The Finance Commissions of India, Institute for Financial Management and Research.

## B. REPORTS AND JOURNALS

The Sarkaria Commission's "Report on Centre-State Relations", Part I, Part II, Government of India 1988.

Report of the First Finance Commission, 1952, Govt. of India, New Delhi.

Report of the Second Finance Commission, 1957, Govt. of India, New Delhi.

Report of the Third Finance Commission 1961, Govt. of India, New Delhi.

Report of the Fourth Finance Commission, 1965, Govt. of India, New Delhi.

Report of the Fifth Finance Commission, 1969, Govt. of India, New Delhi.

Report of the Sixth Finance Commission, 1973, Govt. of India, New Delhi.

Report of the Seventh Finance Commission, 1978, Govt. of India, New Delhi.

Report of the Eight Finance Commission, 1984, Govt. of India, New Delhi,

Report of the Ninth Finance Commission, 1989, Govt. of India, New Delhi,

Report of the Tenth Finance Commission, 1994, Govt. of India, New Delhi,

Report of the Eleventh Finance Commission, 2000, Govt. of India, New Delhi.

Report of the Twelfth Finance Commission, 2004, Govt. of India, New Delhi.

Report on Currency and Finance, 1968-69 to 2004-05, Reserve Bank of India, Mumbai.

*Reserve Bank of India Bulletins* (Monthly), Various Issues Relating to State's Finance.

Indian Economic Association Conference, Number, 1972.

Memoranda Presented to the Sixth, Seventh, Eighth and Ninth Finance Commissions, Government of Bihar, Patna.

Financial Accounts, 1969-70 to 1988-89, Government of Bihar, Patna.

Chief Ministers' Addresses before the Seventh and Eighth Finance Commissions, Government of Bihar, Patna, 7-6-1978 and 28-9-1983.

Budget Speeches of Finance Minister, Government of Bihar, Patna.

State Income of Bihar (1970-71 to 1986-87), Directorate of Statistics and Evaluation, Planning Department, Government of Bihar, Patna, 1988.

Selected Plan Statistics, Bihar State Planning Board, Government of Bihar, Patna, 1982 and 1986.

Report of the Study Team of Centre-State Relationship, Administrative Reforms commission, Government of India, New Delhi, 1967.

*Southern Economist*, 106-108, Infantry Road, Bangalore-56000, Various Issues.

Government of Tamil Nadu, Report of the Centre-State Relations Inquiry Committee, 1971.

Different Planning Commissions' Report, Govt. of India, New Delhi.

# Index